Praise for **net guide** W9-CNO-635

"Thanks to Wolff and friends, the cyberswamp may just have become a little less murky."—*Entertainment Weekly*

"*Net Guide* is the computer world's online *TV Guide*."—*Good Morning America*

"*Net Guide* will keep you from wandering around aimlessly on the Internet, and is full of good ideas for where to pull over."—*Forbes FYI*

"*Net Guide* is the liveliest, most readable online guide yet."—*USA Today*

"What you need to connect."—*Worth Magazine*

"*Net Guide* is the *TV Guide* to Cyberspace!"— Louis Rossetto, publisher/editor, *Wired*

"One of the more complete, well-organized guides to online topics. From photography to the Church of Elvis, you'll find it here."—*PC Magazine*

"The best attempt yet at categorizing and organizing all the great stuff you can find out there. It's the book people keep stealing off my desk."—Joshua Quittner, *New York Newsday*

"It's changed my online life. Get this book!"— Mike Madson, "Computer Bits," Business Radio Network

"My favorite for finding the cool stuff."—*The Louisville Courier-Journal*

"*Net Guide* focuses on the most important aspect of online information—its content. You name it, it's there—from erotica to religion to politics."
—Lawrence J. Magid, *San Jose Mercury News*

"Not only did all the existing Net books ignore Cyberspace's entertaining aspects, but they were process-oriented, not content-oriented. Why hadn't someone made a *TV Guide* for the Net? Wolff recognized an opportunity for a new book, and his group wrote *Net Guide*."—Mark Frauenfelder, *Wired*

"Couch potatoes have *TV Guide*. Now Net surfers have *Net Guide*."—*Orange County Register*

"*Net Guide* is one of the best efforts to provide a hot-spot guide to going online."—*Knoxville News-Sentinel*

"Assolutamente indispensabile!"—*L'Espresso*, Italy

Praise for **net games**

"A valuable guide for anyone interested in the recreational uses of personal computers and modems."—Peter H. Lewis, *The New York Times*

"*Net Games* is a good map of the playing fields of Netdom."—*Newsweek*

"This guide to games people play in the ever-expanding Cyberspace shows you exactly where to go."—*Entertainment Weekly*

"The second book in a very good series from Wolff and Random House."—Bob Schwabach, syndicated columnist

"Hot addresses!"—*USA Weekend*

"Move over Parker Brothers and Nintendo— games are now available online. There's something in *Net Games* for everyone from cross-word-puzzle addicts to *Dungeons & Dragons* fans."—*Reference Books Bulletin*

What are you waiting for?

Net Books!

net guide™

net games™

net chat™

net money™

Coming soon

net tech™

net sports™

net trek™

netmoney™

Your Guide to the
Personal Finance Revolution
on the Information Highway

A Michael Wolff Book

Kelly Maloni, Ben Greenman,
and Kristin Miller

For free updates call 1-800-NET-1133
or visit our Website at http://www.ypn.com/

RANDOM HOUSE
ELECTRONIC PUBLISHING

MICHAEL
WOLFF
& COMPANY, INC.
DIGITAL
PUBLISHING

New York

The Net Books series is a co-publishing venture of Michael Wolff & Company, Inc., 1633 Broadway, 27th Floor, New York, NY 10019, and Random House Electronic Publishing, a division of Random House, Inc., 201 East 50th Street, New York, NY 10022.

Net Money has been wholly created and produced by Michael Wolff & Company, Inc. *Net Guide, Net Games, Net Chat, Net Money, Net Tech, Net Sports,* NetHead, NetSpeak, and CyberPower are trademarks of Michael Wolff & Company, Inc. All design and production has been done by means of desktop-publishing technology. The text is set in the typefaces Garamond, customized Futura, Zapf Dingbats, Franklin Gothic, and Pike.

Published simultaneously in the U.S. by Random House, NY, and Michael Wolff & Company, Inc., and in Canada by Random House of Canada, Ltd.

0 9 8 7 6 5 4 3 2 1

ISBN 0-679-75808-9

The author and publisher have used their best efforts in preparing this book. However, the author and publisher make no warranties of any kind, express or implied, with regard to the documentation contained in this book, and specifically disclaim, without limitation, any implied warranties of merchantability and fitness for a particular purpose with respect to listings in the book, or the techniques described in the book. In no event shall the author or publisher be responsible or liable for any loss of profit or any other commercial damages, including but not limited to special, incidental, consequential, or any other damages in connection with or arising out of furnishing, performance, or use of this book.

All of the photographs and illustrations in this book have been obtained from online sources, and have been included to demonstrate the variety of work that is available on the Net. The caption with each photograph or illustration identifies its online source. Text and images available over the Internet and other online services may be subject to copyright and other rights owned by third parties. Online availability of text and images does not imply that they may be reused without the permission of rights holders, although the Copyright Act does permit certain unauthorized reuse as fair use under 17 U.S.C. §107. Care should be taken to ensure that all necessary rights are cleared prior to reusing material distributed over the Internet and other online services. Information about reuse is available from the institutions that make their materials available online.

Trademarks

A number of entered words in which we have reason to believe trademark, service mark, or other proprietary rights may exist have been designated as such by use of initial capitalization. However, no attempt has been made to designate as trademarks or service marks all personal-computer words or terms in which proprietary rights might exist. The inclusion, exclusion, or definition of a word or term is not intended to affect, or to express any judgment on, the validity or legal status of any proprietary right which may be claimed in that word or term.

Manufactured in the United States of America

New York   Toronto   London   Sydney   Auckland

A Michael Wolff Book

Michael Wolff
President and Editor in Chief

Peter Rutten
Creative Director

Kelly Maloni
Managing Editor

Senior Editors: Ben Greenman, Kristin Miller

Art Director: Jeff Hearn

Research Editors: Bill Folsom, David Heller, Robert Kenney,

Ali Lemer, Tristan Louis, Kendra Wilhelm

Editorial Assistant: Stephanie Engel

Contributing Editors: Suzanne Charlé, Nathaniel Wice

Technical Editor: David Wood

Copy Editors: Caleb Crain, S. Kirk Walsh

Chief Technology Officer: Stan Norton

Marketing Manager: Bill Folsom

Special thanks:
Random House Electronic Publishing—Kenzi Sugihara, Tracy Smith,
Dennis Eulau, Mark Dazzo, Alison Biggert, Robin McCorry

Alison Anthoine at Kay Collyer & Boose

Peter Ginsberg at Curtis Brown Ltd.

And, more than ever, Aggy Aed

The editors of *Net Money* can be reached at Michael Wolff & Company, Inc., 1633 Broadway, 27th Floor,
New York, NY 10019, or by voice call at 212-841-1572, fax at 212-841-1539, or email at editors@ypn.com.

Contents

Contents

Part 3. Shopping

Part 4. Investment

Part 5. Careers

Part 6. Business

Appendices

FAQ

1. Is there really a "personal finance revolution" going on out there?

Well, the way you do your banking, pay your bills, get loans, buy houses, shop, find a job, and invest your money will change. The possibilities and advantages of the networked world will alter the way we think about and deal with our financial lives as profoundly as the introduction of consumer banking, mass credit cards, and mutual funds. That is, the information, speed, and convenience previously available only to the very wealthy will now be available to all of us. Yes, it's a revolution.

2. But is it for me?

If you want to get your career on track, balance your checkbook, invest your savings, run your home budget with Quicken, set up a business, help your kids pick a college, or figure out how you're going to pay for the college they pick, then it's for you. All you need is a computer and a modem.

3. Are you saying that I won't need a bank, or broker, or even a credit card anymore?

What we're saying is that the very nature of banks, brokerages, and virtually all other financial institutions has changed. Brick-and-steel institutions with swinging doors and marble lobbies, rude receptionists, and irritable vice presidents will become electronic entitites. They and their products will be more like Microsoft, for better or worse, than like a mighty edifice on Wall Street or a drive-up window in the mall. In other words, your primary relationship with financial institutions and financial mechanisms of all types will be electronic—software on your home computer communicating and interacting with software on other computers. With the vast resources of the Net, banking, investing, bill paying, and tax paying will be as quick and easy as word processing.

4. Where does this take place? What is "the Net," anyway?

The Net is the electronic medium spawned by the millions of computers linked (that is, networked) together throughout the world. Known as Cyberspace, the Information Highway, or the Infobahn, the Net encompasses the Internet, a

ONLINE SERVICES

America Online:
- 800-827-6364 (voice)
- Monthly fee: $9.95
- Free monthly hours: 5
- Hourly fees: $3.50
- Email: joinaol@aol.com

CompuServe:
- 800-848-8199 (voice)
- Monthly fees: $8.95, first month free (standard); $2.50 (alternative)
- Free monthly hours: unlimited basic (standard); none (alternative)
- Hourly fees: $4.80 for 300, 1200, and 2400 baud, and $9.60 for 9600 baud (standard); $6.30 for 300 baud, $12.80 for 1200/2400 baud, and $22.80 for 9600 baud (alternative)
- Email: 70006.101@ compuserve.com

Delphi:
- 800-695-4005 (voice)
- Monthly fees: $10 (10/4 plan); $20 (20/20 plan)
- Free monthly hours: 4 (10/4 plan); 20 (20/20 plan)
- Hourly fees: $4 (10/4 plan); $1.80 (20/20 plan), $9 surcharge during prime-time hours
- Setup: $19 (20/20 plan);
- Full internet access, additional $3/mo.
- Email: info@delphi.com

eWORLD:
- 800-775-4556
- Monthly fees: $8.95 (includes 2 off-prime hours)
- Hourly rates: $4.95 off-prime, $7.90 prime time. →

global, noncommercial system with more than 30 million computers communicating through it; the commercial online services like CompuServe, America Online, and Prodigy; the thousands of local and regional bulletin-board services (BBSs); the networks of discussion groups, like FidoNet, that are carried out over BBSs; and the discussion groups known as Usenet that traverse the Internet. More and more, the Internet unites all the diverse locations and formats that make up the Net.

5. I don't know. It sounds very high-tech. I'm not good with computers. What if I hit the wrong button?

Then you've bought that Catalina mansion. Just kidding. The truth is that almost all the services have sophisticated systems to prevent accidental transactions. In other words, you can usually change your mind before you make a mansion-sized mistake.

- Email: eworld.mktg@ applelink.apple.com

GEnie:
- 800-638-9636 (voice)
- Monthly fee: $8.95
- Free monthly hours: 4
- Hourly fees: $3 (off-prime) or $9.50 (prime-time) for 2400 baud; $9 (off-prime) or $12.50 (prime-time) for 9600 baud
- Email: feedback@genie. geis.com

Prodigy:
- 800-PRODIGY
- Value Plan I: $14.95/month includes unlimited core services; 5 hours in plus services, which consist of the bulletin boards, EAASY Sabre, Dow Jones Co. News, and stock quotes; and 30 email messages; additional email cost 25¢ per message; additional 'plus' hours cost $2.95 each.
- Alternate Plan I: $7.95/month includes 2 hours of core or plus services; additional hours (core or plus) are $2.95/hour; email costs 25¢ per message sent.
- Alternate Plan II: $19.95/month includes 8 hours of core services; plus services cost an additional $2.95/hour; email costs 25¢ per message sent.
- Alternate Plan BB: $29.95/month includes 25 hours core and plus services; additional hours are $2.95/hour; email costs 25¢ per message sent.

6. All this money floating around— all of *my* money—is it safe? What about receipts and records?

Electronic business practices will work only if consumers have a high degree of confidence in them. For instance, there is a theoretical risk in passing a credit card over a network in an unencrypted (unencoded) form. And while it's not a large risk, care should be taken in how you pass your card number. Giving account information on the phone is still more secure than over a network, and inputting the number into a well-designed commercial Net site is safer than using email. Indeed, one of the major challenges facing electronic businesses is the perfection of systems that protect the integrity of online transactions. As for receipts and records, the electronic world promises to make such paper trails automatic; even now you can easily print a record of any transaction. For now, many Net services conduct initial transactions by phone, after which they issue customer identification numbers that serve as billing accounts for all future business.

SOFTWARE

Dow Jones:
800-815-5100 (voice)
- Software: Market Analyzer Plus 2.0 ($499 for Windows, $349 for Mac, $149 for Spreadsheet Link); Market Manager Plus ($299); News Retrieval ($19.95/year; $1.50/1,000 characters, although retrieval prices are higher for some services); Market Monitor ($29.95/month; 8 free non-prime hours/month, 6¢ each additional minute; $1.50/1,000 characters prime-time).

WealthBuilder:
800-521-2471 (voice)
- Software: Wealth Builder ($49.95)
- Online service: Platinum plan ($19.95/month for all services); Gold plan ($12.95/month for mutual fund, CD, money market, and stock quotes only). →

7. What about the rip-off artists? Aren't they flocking to Cyberspace?

No doubt. But they'll have to fight for turf alongside businesses like AT&T, Microsoft, FTD, Warner Bros., and IBM—to name just a few of the more or less trustworthy companies crowding into Cyberspace.

8. Okay. Say I'm going on an interview and I need some information about a company. What's the drill?

Try Hoover's Handbook Company Profiles, which appear on a number of different services and furnish detailed information on thousands of companies. You can impress your prospective employer with your knowledge about the company's history, earnings, and stock performance. In addition, Hoover's analyzes each company's practices, reputation, and prospects. Remember: a nice suit and a generous smile aren't the only necessary preparations for a good interview.

9. I'm thinking about buying bonds, but I don't want to use a broker. Can I do it myself?

Sure. There are a handful of discount brokers—including CompuServe's QuickWay and Prodigy's PCFN—that have extensive online services. Just set up an account, and then select the stocks you want to buy. In most cases you'll also have access to online resources for stock analysis and forecasting.

Quicken:
800-433-8810 (voice)
- Software: Quicken ($49.95)
- Online service: 3 free uses, $2.50/quote for next 6, 50¢/quote each additional
- Special offers: Online service is free with membership to CompuServe or Prodigy.

Charles Schwab StreetSmart:
800-334-4455 (voice)
- Software: Charles Schwab StreetSmart ($59)
- Stock quotes: first 100 free; 100 free for every online trade made; additional quotes cost $1.45/min. prime-time and 35¢/min. nonprime
- MarketScope ($1.20/min. prime-time, 80¢/min. nonprime)
- Company Reports ($4.50 each)

CheckFree:
800-882-5280 (voice)
- Software: CheckFree ($14.95)

10. And how about taxes? I keep hearing about electronic filing.

Online filing is very real, and very easy. The IRS maintains a bulletin board for electronic assistance, and you can order forms through email, print the forms you download, and use them when you mail in your return. And there are even some services that let you file electronically—just email your returns. So when April 15 starts to roll around, don't worry. Just harness the power of home computing, and pay the tax man confidently and conveniently.

11. Can going online help me get a job in San Francisco? I'd really like to work at that *Wired* magazine.

The Net has hundreds of resources for job-searching, from national classified pools to online employment services—including Bay Area listings (ba.jobs.offered and ba.jobs.misc newsgroups) and the classified section of the *San Jose Mercury News*. In addition, dozens of companies advertise their vacant positions electronically. And if you're not entirely certain that you want to work for a cool magazine, you can even take advantage of the online career counseling services. You never know—*Field & Stream* might be more your style.

SENDING EMAIL

I'm on a commercial service. How do I send Internet email? Each of the major commercial services offers Internet email, with slight variations in form.

From CompuServe
Enter the CompuServe mail area by choosing the **go** command from the menu and typing **mail** (if you don't have CompuServe's Information Manager software, type **go mail**). If you want to send a message to someone on another commercial service, your email will be routed through the Internet, so you must address it with the prefix **internet:**. Mail to John Doe at America Online, for instance, would be addressed internet:jdoe@aol.com; to John Doe at YPN, it would be addressed internet:jdoe@ ypn.com.

To CompuServe
Use the addressee's CompuServe ID number. If John Doe's ID is 12345,678, you'll address mail to 12345.678@ compuserve. com. Make sure you replace the comma in the CompuServe ID with a period.

From America Online
Use AOL's Internet mail gateway (keyword: **internet**). Then address and send mail as you normally would on any other Internet site, using the jdoe@ service.com address style.

To America Online
Address email to jdoe@aol.com.

→

12. You know, I've been thinking about doing some consulting from home. What does the Net have for me?

If you work from home, either full-time or after hours, you can find information and help at any time of day or night on the Net. For instance, the Working From Home Forum on CompuServe provides invaluable advice about setting up a home office and developing clients. But perhaps more importantly, the Net provides the home worker with his own company librarian, legal advisor, travel agent—and other hardworking staff previously available only to the big boys.

13. What kind of money are we talking here, by the way?

Most of the places that are described in this book either have no charge beyond Internet connection fees or are part of basic services on commerical networks like AOL, Prodigy, eWorld, or CompuServe. There are, of course, premium options that carry a cost above and beyond basic service, and we have marked those services with a dollar sign. In most cases, even these premium services are reasonably priced, and efficient use of services will keep your costs down. But remember to

From GEnie
Use the keyword **mail** and address email to jdoe@service.com@inet#. GEnie's use of two @ symbols is an exception to Internet addressing convention.

To GEnie
Address email to jdoe@genie.geis.com.

From Delphi
Use the command **go mail**, then, at the prompt, type **mail** again. Address mail to internet "jdoe@service.com" (make sure to include the quotation marks).

To Delphi
Address email to jdoe@delphi.com.

From eWorld
Use the command go email, compose your message, address message to jdoe@service.com, and click on the Send Now button.

To eWorld
Address email to jdoe@eworld.com.

From Prodigy
To send email from Prodigy, first download Prodigy's Mail Manager by using the command **jump: mail manager**. Address mail to jdoe@service.com. Mail Manager is currently available for DOS and Windows only. A Mac version is due soon.

To Prodigy
Address email using the addressee's user ID. For John Doe (user ID: ABCD12A), for example, you would address it abcd12a@prodigy.com.

examine costs carefully before plunging into a service. The Net changes.

14. I'm game. What do I need to get started?

A computer and a modem, and a few tricks to find your way around.

15. Can you help me decide what computer and modem I'll need?

If you've bought a computer fairly recently, it's likely that it came with everything you need. But let's assume you have only a PC. In that case you'll also need to get a modem, which will allow your computer to communicate over the phone. So-called 14.4 modems, which transfer data at speeds up to 14,400 bits per second (bps), have become the latest standard. You should be able to get one for less than $150. (Within a year, however, 14,400 bps will feel like a crawl next to faster speeds of 28,800 bps and higher.) Next, you need a communications program to control the modem. This software will probably come free with your modem, your PC, or—if you're going to sign up somewhere—your online service. Otherwise, you can buy it off the shelf for under $25. Finally, you'll want a telephone line (or maybe even two if you plan on tying up the line a couple of hours per day).

FINANCIAL BBS

DSC:
- 215-674-9290 (voice)
- 215-443-7390 (modem)
- Basic membership: $20, three months
- Internet Membership: $35, three months
- Telnet: dsc.voicenet.com

Exec-PC
- 800-EXECPC (voice)
- 414-789-4360 (modem)
- Basic membership: $25, three months
- Email: info@execpc.com

PC Ohio
- 216-291-3307 (voice)
- 216-381-3320 (modem)
- Memberships: $52–$139, one year
- Email: info@pcohio.com

---

16. I'm ready. What kind of account should I get?

You'll definitely want to be able to get email; you'll probably want wide access to the Internet, and, especially for business and and financial concerns, membership in a commerical service.

Here are some of your access choices:

Email Gateway

This is the most basic access you can get. It lets you send and receive messages to and from anyone, anywhere, anytime on the Net. Email gateways are often available via work, school, or the other services listed here.

Commercial Services

Priciest but often easiest, these services have a wealth of material for the financial Net-surfer. The big ones are America Online, CompuServe, and Prodigy. Also popular are GEnie, Delphi, and eWorld. Commercial services are cyber city-states. The large ones have more "residents" (members) than most U.S. cities—enough users, in other words, to support lively discussions among their membership, and enough resources to make a visit worthwhile. They generally require their own special software, which you can buy at any local computer store or by calling the numbers listed in this book. (Hint: Look for the frequent starter-kit giveaways.) AOL, CompuServe, Prodigy, Delphi, and (as of January 1995) GEnie all provide access to many if not all of Usenet's more than 10,000 newsgroups, and through email you can subscribe to any of the mailing-list discussions. Delphi provides access to the Internet's IRC channels.

> ### IP SOFTWARE
>
> Most "serial" dial-up connections to the Internet treat your fancy desktop computer as a dumb terminal that requires a lot of typed-out commands. An IP connection, whether through a direct hookup like Ethernet or a dial-up over phone lines, turns your computer into a node on the Net instead of a one-step-removed terminal connection. With an IP link, you can run slick point-and-click programs—often many at once. Macintosh users will need MacTCP and, depending on the kind of IP service you're getting, either Interslip or the more advanced MacPPP. Windows users will need the latest version of WinSock. (The latest versions of programs that run over WinSock can be found at ftp.cica.indiana.edu.) Two all-in-one packages of Internet software that you might want to consider for Windows are Chameleon and WinQVT. Your best best for these programs is to get your online service to give you these programs preconfigured, as the IP address can be mind-boggling to set up.

Internet Providers

There are a growing number of full-service Internet providers (which means they offer email, IRC, FTP, telnet, gopher, WWW, and Usenet access), including Your Personal Network (YPN), run by the editors of this book. In practical terms, the Internet enables you to connect with the Neptune Travel Network, shop in online malls, or chat about market forces in the misc.invest newsgroup. A dial-up SLIP (serial line Internet protocol) or PPP (point-to-point protocol) account is the most fun you can have through a modem. It is a special service offered by some Internet providers that gets you significantly faster access and the ability to use point-and-click programs for Windows, Macintosh, and other platforms.

Stand-Alone Software Packages

Because the financial resources of commercial services are a relatively small portion of their overall offerings, Net newcomers looking for a way into electronic business may be better served by a stand-alone software package designed specifically for business needs. From Dow Jones News/Retrieval to Wealth Builder, from Charles Schwab StreetSmart to Quicken Online, these packages are concentrated financial applications.

BBSs

BBSs range from mom-and-pop hobbyist computer bulletin boards to large professional services. What the small ones lack in size they often make up for in affordability and homeyness. In fact, many users prefer these scenic roads over the Info Highway. Many of the large BBSs (DSC-BBS, PC-

---

NEWSREADERS

To read the newsgroups you use a program called a reader, a standard offering on most online services. There are several types of readers—some let you follow message threads; others organize messages chronologically. You can also use a reader to customize the newsgroup menu to include only the newsgroups you're interested in.

Newswatcher
(Mac) Fancy newsreader. Whole newsgroups can be saved locally in a single file, by article, or by thread. Multiple binaries can be automatically decoded—making it possible to grab all of alt.binaries.pictures.supermodels with a couple of clicks. Requires an IP connection.

Nuntius
(Mac) Comparable to Newswatcher, except it can multi-task. Some people prefer the way Nuntius grabs the full text of threads; others hate waiting to read the first message. Nuntius also stores newsgroup subjects on your computer—this chews up disk space but accelerates searches through old messages. Requires an IP connection.

Trumpet
(Windows) The most popular Windows newsreader. Thread by subject, date, or author. Like Newswatcher, batch binary extraction. WinNV is also widely used. Available by anonymous FTP from ftp.utas. edu.au in /pc/trumpet/win trump. Requires an IP connection. →

Ohio, and Exec-PC come to mind) are as rich and diverse as the commercial services. BBSs are easy to get started with, and if you find one with Internet access or an email gateway, you get the best of local color and global reach. You'll find BBSs throughout this book. You can also locate local BBSs through the Usenet discussion groups alt.bbs.lists and comp.bbs.misc, the BBS forums of the commercial services, and regional and national BBS lists kept in the file libraries of many BBSs. Once you've found a local BBS, contact the sysop to inquire about the echoes (or conferences) you want. These are the BBS world's equivalent to the Internet's newsgroups. With echoes, you're talking not only to the people on your particular BBS but also to everyone on a BBS that carries the echo (in other words, a universe of millions). Even if the discussion of your choice is not on their board yet, many sysops are glad to add an echo that a paying customer has requested. Many, if not most, local BBSs now offer Internet email, as well as live chat, file libraries, and some quirky database, program, or directory unique to their little corner of Cyberspace.

Tin
(Unix) Intuitive Unix newsreader that works especially well for scanning newsgroups. You can maintain a subscription list, decode binaries, and search the full text of individual newsgroups. With its help files and easy-to-use menus, this is our favorite Unix newsreader.

nn (Unix) and rn (Unix)
Complex newsreaders (Network News and Read News) favored by Unix-heads.

trn (Unix)
Maps subjects within newsgroups.

Direct Network Connection

Look, Ma Bell: no phone lines! The direct network connection is the fast track of college students, computer scientists, and a growing number of employees of high-tech businesses. It puts the user right on the Net, bypassing the phone connections. In other words, it's a damned sight faster.

17. How exactly do I send an email?

With email, you can talk to anyone on a commercial service, Internet site, or Internet-linked BBS, as well as to those people connected to the Net via email gateways, SLIP, and direct network connections.

Email addresses have a universal syntax called an Internet address. An Internet address is broken down into four parts: the user's name (e.g., Michael), the @ symbol, the computer and/or company name, and what kind of Internet address it is: **net** for network, **com** for a commercial enterprise—as with Your Personal Network (ypn.com) and America Online (aol.com)—**edu** for educational institutions, **gov** for government sites, **mil** for military facilities, and **org** for nonprofit and other private organizations. For instance, the owner of this company, who'd rather be playing Doom and MUSHing than interacting with flesh-and-blood human beings—and whose late-night Big-Mac-besotted excursions through the deepest reaches of the Net are legendary among bit-stream geeks—would therefore be mwolff@ypn.com.

18. What about the Web, which I've been hearing so much about?

The World Wide Web is a hypertext-based information structure that now dominates Internet navigation. The Web is like a house where every room has doors to every other room—or, more accurately, like the interconnections in the human brain. Highlighted words in a document link to other documents that reside on the same machine or on a computer anywhere in the world. You only have to click on the appropriate word or phrase—the Web does the rest. With invisible navigation, you can jump from Scott Yanoff's list of business sites to the insurance-oriented ARIAWeb, and from ARIAWeb to a list of risk-management professionals worldwide.

MAIL READERS

Eudora
(Mac and Windows) If the host for your email supports the POP protocol, you're in luck. Eudora makes email even easier than it already was. The commercial upgrade to the free version includes message-filtering for automatically sorting incoming mail, but drops the fun dialog messages (if you start typing without an open window, Eudora beeps, "Unfortunately, no one is listening to keystrokes at the moment. You may as well stop typing". The Windows version requires an IP connection; the Mac version does not.

Pine
(Unix) Menu-driven with a full-screen editor and spell-check. Support of the MIME "metamail" format means that you can "attach" binary files within a letter.

Elm
(Unix, DOS, Windows, OS/2) Programmable "user agent" reader that can also sort, forward, and auto-reply. It does not include its own editor.

Mail
(Unix) As the name suggests, a no-frills mail program.

All the while you've FTPed, telnetted, and gophered with nary a thought to case-sensitive Unix commands or addresses.

Your dial-up Internet provider undoubtedly offers programs to access the Web. Lynx and WWW are pretty much the standard offerings. Usually you choose them by typing **lynx** and **www** and then **<return>**. What you'll get is a "page" with some of the text highlighted. These are the links. Choose a link, hit the return key, and you're off.

DOWNLOADING WEB BROWSERS

Sites at which you can find Web browsers for downloading, sorted by platform:

Windows:	Mac:
CICA—University of Indiana Windows Archive ftp://ftp.cica.indiana.edu:/pub/pc/win3/winsock/ mirror site is at ftp://ftp.cdrom.com:/.5/cica/winsock/	**MacWeb by Einet** ftp.einet.net:/einet/mac/macweb/
NCSA Mosaic for Windows ftp.NCSA.uiuc.edu:/PC/Mosaic	**Netscape for Mac** ftp.mcom.com:/netscape/mac/ mirrored at. ftp.meer.net:/pub/Netscape/Mac/
WinWeb by Einet ftp.einet.net:/einet/pc/winweb/	**NCSA Mosaic for Mac** ftp.NCSA.uiuc.edu:/Mac/Mosaic/
Air Mosaic ftp.spry.com:/AirMosaicDemo/	**University of Texas Mac Archive** ftp://ftp.utexas.edu:/pub/mac/tcpip/
Internet Works by Booklink (lite edition only) ftp.booklink.com:/lite/	
Netscape for Windows ftp.mcom.com:/netscape/windows/ mirrored at ftp.meer.net:/pub/Netscape/Windows/	

If you know exactly where you want to go and don't want to meander through the information, you can type a Web page's address, known as a URL (uniform resource locator), many of which you'll find in this book. With the emergence of new and sophisticated so-called Web browsers (with a graphical point-and-click interface) like Mosaic and NetScape, the Web is starting to look the way it was envisioned—pictures, colored icons, and appetizing text layouts. (See IP Software sidebar.)

19. And these newsgroups?

The most widely read bulletin boards are a group of some 10,000-plus "newsgroups" on the Internet, collectively known as Usenet. Usenet newsgroups travel the Internet, collecting thousands of messages a day from whoever wants to "post" to them. More than anything, the newsgroups are the collective, if sometimes Babel-like, voice of the Net—everything is discussed here. And we mean everything.

While delivered over the Internet, the Usenet collection of newsgroups are not technically part of the Internet. In order to read a newsgroup, you need to go where it is stored. Smaller BBSs that have news feeds sometimes store only a couple dozen newsgroups, while most Internet providers offer thousands. (If there's a group missing that you really want, ask your Internet provider to add the newsgroup back to the subscription list.)

The messages in a newsgroup, called "posts," are listed and numbered chronologically—in other words, in the order in which they were posted. Usenet is not distributed from one central location, which means that a posted message does not appear everywhere instantly. The speed of distribution partly depends on how often providers pick up and post Usenet messages. For a message to appear in every corner of the Net, you'll generally have to wait overnight. If you use the newsgroups a lot, you'll start to notice patterns where messages from some machines take five minutes to appear and others take a day.

You can scan a list of messages before deciding to read a particular message. If someone posts a message that prompts responses, the original and all follow-up messages are called a thread. The subject line of subsequent posts in the thread refers to the subject of the original. For example, if you were to post a message with the subject "how I lost all my money" in misc.invest, all responses would have the subject line "RE: how I lost all my money." In practice, however, topics in a thread tend to wander off in many directions.

20. Mailing lists?

Mailing lists are like newsgroups, except that they are distributed over the Internet email system. The fact that messages show up in your mailbox tends to make the discussion group more intimate, as does the proactive act of subscribing. Mailing lists are often more focused, and they're less vulnerable to irreverent and irrelevant contributions.

To subscribe to a mailing list, send an email to the mailing list's subscription address. Often you will need to include very specific information, which you will find in this book. To unsubscribe, send another message to that same address. If the mailing list is of the listserv or majordomo variety, you can usually unsubscribe by sending the command **signoff <listname>** in the message body. If the address of the mailing list instructs you to write a request to subscribe, then you will probably need to write a request to unsubscribe.

21. Echoes or conferences?

Local BBSs often carry what are known as echoes or conferences, which are part of messaging networks among BBSs. You'll find several of these networks mentioned throughout the book: FidoNet, RelayNet (RIME), JobNet, Ilink, Smartnet, and Intelec. There are hundreds of BBS conferences in Cyberspace, new ones are added daily, and no BBS carries them all—most don't even carry all the conferences on a single network. Check with local BBSs in your area code to see whether they have the network you want. If they do, but they don't carry the conference you're looking for, ask for it.

TELNETTING

To telnet, follow this simple four-step process:

1. Log in to your Internet site and locate the telnet program. Since telnet is a widely used feature, you will most likely find it in the main menu of your Internet access provider. On Delphi, for example, telnet is available in the main Internet menu. Just type **telnet.**

2. Once you've started the program, you should see a telnet prompt (for instance, telnet> or telnet:). Type **open <telnet address>**, replacing the bracketed text with the address of the machine you want to reach. (Note: Some systems do not require you to type **open**. Also, don't type the brackets.) Let's say you want to go to CDNow!, one of the world's most extensive online music stores. CDNow! is at the address cdnow.com, so after the telnet prompt you would type **open cdnow.com**, or just **cdnow. com**. Some telnet addresses contain port numbers, which are included after the site address and separated by a space →

Most sysops will gladly add a conference for a paying customer.

22. And telnet, FTP, gopher? Can you spell it out for me?

Telnet:

When you telnet, you're logging in to another computer or network somewhere else on the Internet. You then have access to the programs running on the remote computer. If the site is running a library catalog, you can search the catalog. If it's running a BBS, you can chat with others logged in. And if it's running a news service, you can have access to all the features of that service. In the world of electronic business, most of the telnetting you'll be doing will deliver you to huge bulletin boards and commercial services—FedWorld, the clearinghouse of Federal BBSs, is available through telnet, as are many of the large online stores.

3. The telnet program will connect you to the remote computer—in our example, the CDNow! server. Once you're connected, you'll see a prompt. Type the remote computer's log-in information as listed in the *Net Money* entry. The prompt may be as simple as **login** followed by another prompt for a password, or it may ask for information like a character's name, a gender, or the type of creature you'd like to play. If no log-in is needed, the Net Money entry will not list one. Oh, and you may be asked about the type of terminal you're using. If you're unsure, vt-100 is a safe bet.
4. You're logged in. Now just follow the instructions on the screen, which will differ with every telnet site.

FTP:

FTP (file transfer protocol) is a program that allows you to copy a file from another Internet-connected computer to your own. Hundreds of computers on the Internet allow "anonymous FTP." In other words, you don't need a password to access them. The range of material available is extraordinary—from books to free software to pictures to all types of financial data! More and more, FTP sites are being accessed from the Web, allowing Net users to view documents before retrieving them. To convert an FTP address to a URL, type **ftp://<ftp server><ftp path>**.

Gopher:

A gopher is a program that turns Internet addresses into menu options.

Gophers can perform many Internet functions, including telnetting and downloading files. Gopher addresses throughout this book are useful for finding collections of information and collections of telnet links to business sites. Gopher addresses require a port number, and most gopher programs automatically default to the standard setting of 70 unless otherwise instructed. In this book, any deviations from the standard port number are included in gopher addresses.

23. Any suggestions for dipping my toes in the water?

Why not just open the book to a page and try the first thing you see? Maybe you'll end up at the U.S. Patent Office reading about in-flight beverage dispensers, checking stock prices on QuoteCom, or buying a picante sauce from Hot Hot Hot. Don't get stuck where you started, though; there are tons of sites and services to check out before picking favorites.

24. I'm sold! Anything I need to know about how this book works?

If you know what kind of financial services you need, turn to the Net Money Index, where every subject and place in the book is listed alphabetical-

---

HOW TO DOWNLOAD

How do I download from a commercial service?
The download command on each of the commercial services may differ slightly depending on the type of computer you use, but in most instances file downloads work as follows:

On **America Online**, once you locate the file you want, select the file name so that it's highlighted. Then select one of two buttons: **download now**, or **download later**. If you choose **download later**, the file will be added to a list of files, all of which you can download when you're done with your America Online session.

On **CompuServe**, if you're browsing a library list (using CompuServe's Information Manager), you can highlight a file you want and select the **retrieve** button to download it immediately. If you want to download it later, select the box next to the file name, then select **yes** when you leave the forum and a window will appear that says download marked files? (If you don't have Information Manager, type **down** and **[return]** at the prompt following the file description.)

On **Delphi**, after you read a file description in the file or database area, there are four commands available—next, **down**, xm, and list. Type down and **[return]** to download the file.

→

Frequently Asked Questions

ly. Of course, you can browse Net Money at your leisure, checking out services and resources as you go.

The book is divided into six parts:

- 1. Day-To-Day
- 2. Milestones
- 3. Shopping
- 4. Investment
- 5. Careers
- 6. Business

Each part is broken down by subject. Under Milestones, you'll find categories on Real Estate, College Costs, and Retirement Planning; and Investment includes topics on Company News, the SEC, Bonds, Mutual Funds, and Online Brokers. In most cases, we've even gone one step further and created subheaders for our topics—Day-To-Day's Insurance category, for example, is divided into sections such as Life Insurance, Health Insurance, and Insurance and the Law.

All entries in Net Money have a name, description, and address. The site name appears first in boldface. If the entry is a mailing list, "(ml)" immediately follows; if a newsgroup, "(ng)"; if a BBS echo, "(echo)"; and if a BBS, "(bbs)." The description of the site follows.

After the description, complete address information is provided. A red check mark identifies the name of the network. When you see an arrow, this means that you have another step ahead of you, such as typing a command, searching for a file, subscribing to a mailing list, or typing a Web address (called a URL). Additional check marks

On **GEnie**, after you've chosen a file to download, select download a file from the RoundTable library menu. When you see the prompt enter the download request: type the file name and **[return]**. At the next prompt, which asks you to confirm your download, type **d** and **[return]** to download the file. At the next prompt, you'll be asked to choose a download protocol; your best choice, if available with your communications software, is Z-modem (number 4), so type **4** and **[return]**.

How do I download from the Internet?

Using FTP (file transfer protocol). Internet FTP sites open to the public (known as anonymous FTP sites) appear throughout this book, offering dozens of financial and business documents.

To FTP:

1. Log in to your Internet site. Then start the FTP program at that site—in most cases, by typing **ftp** or by choosing it from an Internet menu.
2. When you see the FTP prompt, type **open <ftp. address>** to connect to the other computer. The FTP Directory of Public Financial and Market Information, for example, is at the address dg.rtp.dg.com, so you would type **open dg.rtp.dg.com**. (By the way, sometimes you'll be asked for just the FTP site name, which means you wouldn't type **open**.)
3. Most FTP sites offer "anonymous login," which means you won't need a personal account

→

indicate the other networks through which the site is accessible; triple dots indicate another address on the same network; and more arrows mean more steps.

An address is context-sensitive—in other words, it follows the logic of the particular network. So, if the entry includes a Website, the address following the arrow would be a URL that you would type on the command line of your Web browser. If it is a mailing list, the address would be an email address followed by instructions on the exact form of the email message. An entry that includes an FTP, telnet, or gopher address would provide a log-in sequence and a directory path or menu path when necessary.

In a commercial service address, the arrow is followed by the service's transfer word (e.g., keyword, go word, or jump word), which will take you to the site. More arrows lead you along a path to the specific area on the site. IRC addresses indicate what you must type to get to the channel you want once you've connected to the IRC program.

The name of a newsgroup entry or BBS echo is also its address, so there is no address information other than the network for these types of sites. (You'll locate the newsgroup or echo at your access provider or BBS.)

The notation for BBS addresses differs slightly from that for the other sites. The address for a BBS is its modem number (or numbers).

or password to access the files. When you connect to an anonymous FTP machine, you will be asked for your name with the prompt **name:**. Type **anonymous** after the prompt. Next you'll be asked for your password with the prompt **password:**. Type your email address.

4. Once you're logged in to an FTP site, you can change directories by typing **cd <directory name>**. For example, the FTP Directory of Public Financial and Market Information at dg.rtp.dg.com is in /pub/misc.invest. After login, type **cd /pub/misc.invest** to change to the directory. (To move back up through the directory path you came down, you type **cdup** or **chdirup**). You must move up one directory at a time.

5. To transfer files from the FTP site to your "home" or "files" directory at your Internet site, use the get command. For example, in the FTP Directory of Public Financial and Market Information, you may run across a brilliant new market theory. Retrieve it by typing **get brilliant theory** and **[return]**. The distinction between the upper- and lowercase in directory and file names is important. Type a lowercase letter when you should have typed uppercase and you'll leave empty-handed.

25. I love making money, but what if I want to have some fun on the Net?

Try *Net Guide*, *Net Games*, and *Net Chat*! You should find them in your bookstore right beside *Net Money*. Keep an eye out for *Net Sports*, *Net Trek*, *Net Tech*, and *Net Music*—they're coming soon.

Part 1

Day-to-Day

Budgets & organization

There's no denying the vast array of online resources for the personal financier. In fact,

there are so many services and databases dealing with money management that it's nearly impossible to pick a single point of entry. As a result, we've selected several. AOL's **Money Matters** offers a good introduction to home budgeting, with useful tips and random talk on everything from college savings to carpooling. The **Get Organized Forum** on Delphi helps you put your day in order. **Health, Home, Family** pools the organizational strategies of harried adults across the country, addressing such topics as grocery shopping and morning jogs. And the **Personal Net Worth Program** helps you calculate your assets.

Father Knows Best—*downloaded from America Online's ABC Forum.*

Your Money An introduction to the world of finance, designed to answer the most basic questions about credit, insurance, real estate, retirement planning, investments, education planning, and scams. Each topic has a message board for discussion and questions, an FAQ, and a growing collection of articles on the topic written by the host, Richard A. Allridge, a certified financial planner. ✓ **AMERICA ONLINE** →*keyword* yourmoney

one is somewhat disorganized in its design. Nonethless, it's a good place to go to help give order to your life. Files, like the Beginner's Guide to Getting Organized, can be downloaded. There's a real-time conference, and in the message area, the organized and disorganized compare notes on topics such as decluttering, day planners, and the age-old challenge of preparing for a good dinner party. ✓ **DELPHI**→*go* custom 222

Health, Home, Family One of the most persistent pitfalls is time: How can you juggle the demands of a toddler with a full-time job? What to do when there aren't enough hours in the day? Visit this conference to learn the organizational strategies of other harried adults. ✓ **AMERICA ONLINE**→*keyword* exchange→Home/Health/ Careers→ Health/Home/Family

On the Net

Across the board

Money Matters Come here for home budgeting and consumer chatter. The forum advocates down-to-earth economic responsibility. Members praise frugality and exchange cost-cutting hints, worry over the safety of safe deposit boxes, and question the practices of church accounting. ✓ **AMERICA ONLINE**→*keyword* exchange→Home/Health/Careers→ Money Matters

Asset calculators

The Personal Net Worth Program This service calculates your worth by asking extensive questions about assets and liabilities. In addition, it projects your future net worth assuming a certain rate of growth. The service is free unless you want a printed report mailed to you for $3.50. ✓ **COMPUSERVE**→*go* hom-16

Personal

Get Organized Forum Like other Delphi custom forums, this

New Age Network Control of your life is impossible without positive thinking and regular meditation. This network contains files for downloading, both text and graphics, as well as a message board where other New Age devotees describe their experiences with healing from the inside. So what's a good way to start the day? Try this: "Mend a quarrel. Dismiss a suspicion and replace it with trust." ✓ **DELPHI**→*go* gro new

Stress Management Read about commuter stress, jet lag, office aggravation, and—got a sec?—there's even a section on time management. ✓ **AMERICA ONLINE**→*keyword* health→Lifestyles & Wellness→ Stress Management

Personal information manager shareware

2Do Personal Task Manager Personal information manager. ✓**INTERNET**→*ftp* ftp.cica.indiana. edu→anonymous→<your email address>→/pub/pc/win3/util→ 2dov11.zip (Windows)

Above & Beyond v3.0 PIM. Features pop-up alarms, week/ month to do lists, timers, task tracking, application launching, and more. Shareware. ✓**EXEC-PC**→File Collection Menu→MS Windows→*Download a file:* ABV30.ZIP ✓**AMERICA ONLINE**→*keyword* mbs→Software Libraries→Applications→AB.ZIP (Windows)

Account Manager 1.3 Track time spent on work projects and bill clients. ✓**INTERNET**→*ftp* ftp.cica. indiana.edu→anonymous→<your email address>→/pub/pc/win3 /util→acctmn13.zip (Windows)

Active Life 1.5 All-purpose scheduler and calendar with alarms. ✓**INTERNET**→*ftp* ftp.cica. indiana.edu→anonymous→<your email address>→/pub/pc/win3 /util→alwin15.zip (Windows)

Address Book 3.6.9 Classic address book application with good printout capabilities. Dial numbers, print envelopes and phone lists, and log phone calls. ✓**AMERICA ONLINE**→*keyword* mbs→ Software Libraries→Applications→ Address Book 3.6.9 (Macintosh)

AddressBook 1.3 All-purpose address organizer offers file association and auto sorting. ✓**INTERNET** →*ftp* ftp.cica.indiana.edu→anony mous→<your email address>→ /pub/pc/win3/util→adrbk13u.zip (Windows)

Around the House v2.02

Complete home and personal info manager. Track names, phone numbers, grocery lists, household maintenance, and other domestic information. Keeps track of appointments, income and expenses, inventory; it also has a word processor and prints reports. ✓**PC OHIO**→d→*Download a file:* ATH202.ZIP (DOS)

Auspice v3.51 This application will remind you about important things to do, by displaying the reminder, calendar, warning date, and event time. ✓**INTERNET**→*ftp* mac.archive.umich.edu→anony mous→<your email address>→ /mac/util/organization→auspice3. 51.cpt.hqx (Macintosh)

Black Book PIM capable of displaying GIF and PIX images. ✓**EXEC-PC**→File Collection Menu→ Mahoney IBM Compatible DOS→ BLK_BOOK.ZIP (DOS)

Daily Deeds v1.2 Timelog to track and report your activities. ✓**INTERNET**→*ftp* mac.archive.umich. edu→anonymous→<your email address>→/mac/util/organization→ dailydeeds1.2.cpt.hqx (Macintosh)

DayCross Basic to-do calendar. ✓**INTERNET**→*ftp* ftp.cica.indiana. edu→anonymous→<your email address>→/pub/pc/win3/util→day cross.zip (Windows)

DeskTools v2.0 Personal info manager has addresses, calendar, alarm, lists; also prints mailing labels, business envelopes, and disk labels. ✓**INTERNET**→*ftp* mac.archive. umich.edu→anonymous→<your email address>→/mac/util/organi zation→desktools2.0.cpt. hqx (Macintosh)

Do It All! v3.02 Time management application helps make priorities and draw up schedules. ✓**INTERNET**→*ftp* sumex-aim.stan ford.edu→anonymous→<your email address>→/info-mac→do-it-all-302.hqx (Macintosh)

Guy Friday Free-form manager that interprets the information you store. Shareware. ✓**COMPU-SERVE**→*go* macap→Browse Libraries →Gen. Business/PIMS→GUYFRI. SEA (Macintosh)

Little Black Book v5.00 Address book and dialer with call logging, fast search, auto-dialer. Particularly good for people whose business extends beyond the U. S., it supports international dialing and address formats and prints pocket-sized book. ✓**PC OHIO**→ d→*Download a file:* LBB500.ZIP (DOS)

Log Book Manager Keeps equipment or activity logs. Can subdivide entries for greater organization. ✓**PC OHIO**→d→*Download a file:* LOGBOOK.ZIP (DOS)

Log Master v3.0b5 Easy to use but powerful program tracks hours and prints professional-looking bills. Multiple project files, workers, sort utility, and more. Shareware. ✓**INTERNET**→*ftp* sumex-aim.stanford.edu→anony mous→<your email address>→ /info-mac→log-master-30b5.hqx (Macintosh)

Meeting Maker v1.5 Demo Demo of leading group scheduler for Macintosh. Network application helps you plan, schedule, and confirm meetings for office workers. ✓**INTERNET**→*ftp* sumex-aim. stanford.edu→anonymous→<your

Personal information manager shareware (continued)

email address>→/info-mac→meeting-maker-15-demo.hqx (Macintosh)

Mom for Windows Personal information manager just for mom, with alarm, dialer, calendar and more. ✓**INTERNET**→*ftp* ftp.cica. indiana.edu→anonymous→<your email address>→/pub/pc/win3 /util→momwn20a.zip (Windows)

Nag Date reminder program. ✓**INTERNET**→*ftp* ftp.cica.indiana. edu→anonymous→<your email address>→/pub/pc/win3/util→ nag6.zip (Windows)

Need A full PIM, including address book, notetaker, journal, scheduler, and to do list. ✓**INTERNET**→*ftp* ftp.cica.indiana.edu→ anonymous→<your email address> →/pub/pc/win3/util→needv10b. zip (Windows)

Opportunity for Windows This complete personal information manager allows you to print labels and form letters. Data may be imported or exported. ✓**INTERNET**→*ftp* ftp.cica.indiana.edu→ anonymous→<your email address> →/pub/pc/win3/util→oppwin10. zip (Windows)

Organize! For those uncomfortable with the rigidity of many PIMs, this is a diary-like electronic journal with search capabilities. ✓**INTERNET**→*ftp* ftp.cica.indiana. edu→anonymous→<your email address>→/pub/pc/win3/util→ org162.zip (Windows)

PageMe v1.0 Paging/call notification system. ✓**PC OHIO**→d→ *Download a file:* PAGED10.ZIP (DOS)

Personal InfoBank Pro Personal information manager for use with FileMaker Pro. ✓**COMPUSERVE** →*go* macap→Browse Libraries→ Gen. Business/PIMS→PIPRO.SEA (Macintosh)

PersonalLog Keep an electronic diary to track important thoughts, events, or conversations. ✓**AMERICA ONLINE**→*keyword* mbs→Software Libraries→Applications→ PersonalLog.v162.sit (Macintosh)

The Phone Master Stores telephone numbers and may be set to notify you so you don't forget to make that important call. ✓**INTERNET**→*ftp* ftp.cica.indiana.edu→ anonymous→<your email address> →/pub/pc/win3/util→pmast17.zip (Windows)

Phonebook Manager Manger for your phonebook. ✓**INTERNET**→ *ftp* ftp.cica.indiana.edu→anonymous→<your email address>→ /pub/pc/win3/util→phoneman. zip (Windows)

PhoneView 1.0 Address and telephone database. ✓**INTERNET**→ *ftp* ftp.cica.indiana.edu→anonymous→<your email address>→ /pub/pc/win3/util→phnview.zip (Windows)

PhoneVu 1.1 Log phone conversations. ✓**INTERNET**→*ftp* ftp.cica. indiana.edu→anonymous→<your email address>→/pub/pc/win3 /util→phonev11.zip (Windows)

Private Secretary v2.2.3 Monitors the phone via modem, and pages you when calls come in. Shareware. ✓**INTERNET**→*ftp* sumex-aim.stanford.edu→anonymous→<y our email address>→/info-mac /app→private-secretary.hqx (Mac-

intosh)

Professional Address Manager Address book, envelope printer, and phone dialer. ✓**INTERNET**→*ftp* ftp.cica.indiana.edu→ anonymous→<your email address> →/pub/pc/win3/util→addres17. zip (Windows)

Rolodesk v5.01 Database DA for addresses, phone numbers, etc. ✓**INTERNET**→*ftp* sumex-aim.stanford.edu→anonymous→<your email address>→/info-mac/app→ rolo-desk-501.hqx (Macintosh)

Time & Chaos v4.04 PIM/ Contact Manager with calendars, "to do" lists, telephone books, etc. LAN compatible. Shareware. Requires VBRUN300.DLL ✓**EXEC-PC**→File Collection Menu→MS Windows→*Download a file:* T&C404. ZIP (Windows)

To Do! v3.2.1 DA keeps track of agendas, groups by priorities, and has extensive print capabilities. ✓**INTERNET**→*ftp* sumex-aim.stanford.edu→anonymous→<your email address>→/info-mac/app→to-do-321-da.hqx (Macintosh)

ToDo v7.11 Comprehensive personal information manager for consultants: track hours, clients, projects, more. Extensive built-in help. ✓**EXEC-PC**→File Collection Menu→Mahoney IBM Compatible DOS→TODO711.ZIP (DOS)

ToDoWin A to-do list manager utility program with a color-coding priority feature. ✓**INTERNET** →*ftp* ftp.cica.indiana.edu→anonymous→<your email address>→/ pub/pc/win3/util→todow105.zip (Windows)

Financial software

Spend a few minutes browsing in CompuServe's Mac Applications Forum or Windows

Shareware Forum. From accounting to market analysis, from portfolio management to loan calculation, you can download enough specialty software to make your life easier by degrees. Along with visits to such Net software clearinghouses as the **Info-Mac** archive and **SimTel**, you can start to build a home collection of financial applications. In addition, the online universe contains numerous sites for software support. In Prodigy's **Business Software** message board, for instance, home financiers can compare notes and trade troubleshooting tips on programs ranging from MS-Works to Excel. And with more than 18,000 technical and instructional documents on Microsoft-ware, **Microsoft Knowledge Base** creates a kind of heaven for the baffled home user.

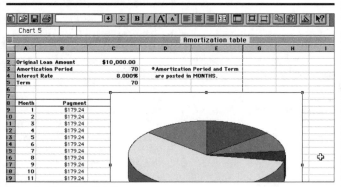

Screenshot from MicroSoft Excel.

On the Net

Across the board

BBS software If your primary interest is building your collection of financial- or business-related applications, you may want to subscribe to a BBS specializing in shareware. The larger BBSs have collections as extensive as those on the commercial services, at competitive prices. On most boards, the main menu has an option to go to the file collection. The collection is usually divided into several file directories: the BBS PC-Ohio, for instance, has 230 directories, including Finance-Accounting, Finance-Business. Finance-Personal, Finance-Taxes, Law/Legal, and Windows-Business. See the appendix for a list of business-related BBSs in your area code or the sidebar on page 27 for a selection of some of the country's biggest and best business BBSs.

PBS Professional Forum The Business & Finance library has an impressive range of general finance applications for both PCs and Macs, from payroll to inventory to address book software. In the forum's Professional library, you will find programs for home day-care providers, motel and inn owners, firefighters, and bicycle dealers, to name but a few. Resume-writing software is located in the Professional library as well. ✓ **COMPUSERVE**→*go* pbsprof→Libraries→

Business & Finance *and* Professional

Personal Finance Software Forum Offers a generous selection of financial software, with hundreds of programs relating to accounting, career and job hunting, financial planning, home management, investment, loan calculation and amortization, or-

> "In the PBS Professional library, you'll find programs for home day-care providers, motel and inn owners, firefighters, and bicycle dealers, to name but a few."

ganization, portfolio management, real estate, and taxes. AOL provides download assistance and reviews of especially popular programs. A software support section covers more than 50 companies whose wares range from market analyzers to personal organizers. Each company provides a corporate history and product list, and many have message boards for customers and technical FAQs. ✓**AMERICA ONLINE**→*keyword* pf software

DOS/Windows

Home and Hobby Helpers
How can you be organized? Let us count the ways. Here you'll find programs to organize food purchases and print out grocery lists (The Grocer), track your babysitters (Babysitter), log your jogs (The Runner's Log), and take inventory on your house (Organize Your Home). ✓**AMERICA ONLINE**→*keyword* pc software→Specialty Libraries/File Lists→Specialty Libraries→Home and Hobby Helpers

IBM Applications Forum
Business applications, personal accounting programs, personal information managers, database management systems, and word processors each have their own library in this massive forum for PC applications. Turn to the message boards to ask for recommendations on, for instance, technical analysis software, a job applicant program, or a mother's PIM (Mom for Windows). ✓**COMPUSERVE**→*go* ibmapp

IBM PC Software Library
An extensive collection of accounting, scheduling, personal management, and database shareware for PCs resides in the Applications library, but there are also quite a few program gems hiding in the Associa-

> **"One of the largest directories of software on the Net, this monstrosity is filled with finance and business applications for Windows users—you'll just have to sort through the hundreds of programs to find them."**

tion of Shareware Professionals (ASP) library. Perhaps the best way to find what you're looking for is to set ALL Libraries and search by program name or keyword (e.g., finance, tax, PIM). ✓**GENIE**→ *keyword* ibm→IBM PC Software Library→Set Software Library→Applications *or* ASP Shareware

PC Applications
The software libraries are jam-packed with business and financial applications for PCs. In the Productivity library, there are sections for Address & Phone applications and Desktop & Time programs (there's even a Mayan calendar). The Databases library has sections filled with templates and add-ons for major PC database languages including Clipper, dBASE, and Paradox, as well as an entire section devoted to Windows PIMS & Databases. The Financial library seems end-

less, with sections devoted to Home Financial, Investment, Quicken Support, and Windows Financial. Still browsing for new programs? Head for the Spreadsheets and Word Processing libraries with templates and utilities. The forum's active message boards make this site even richer, providing a constant flow of questions, answers, and feedback on the applications. ✓**AMERICA ONLINE**→*keyword* pc applications→Software Libraries

SimTel
From bond calculators to loan managers, the sites carry a wide range of personal finance and investment software for the DOS user. ✓**INTERNET** …→*ftp* oak.oakland.edu→anonymous→<your email address>→/SimTel/msdos/finance …→*ftp* ftp.funet.fi→anonymous→<your email address>→/pub/msdos/SimTel/finance

Windows
One of the largest directories of software on the Net, this monstrosity is filled with finance and business applications for Windows users—you'll just have to sort through the hundreds of programs to find them. ✓**INTERNET** …→*ftp* wuarchive.wustl.edu→anonymous→<your email address>→/systems/ibmpc/win3/util

BUSINESS BOARDS
Exec PC
414-789-4210
Free Financial Network
212-752-8660
HH Info-Net
203-738-0342
PC Ohio
216-381-3320
Pisces
312-281-6046
Software Creations
508-368-7139

...→*ftp* ftp.cica.indiana.edu→ anonymous→<your email address> →/pub/pc/win3/util ...→*ftp* mrc-next.cso.uiuc.edu→anonymous→<your email address>→/pub/win3 /util

Windows Forum As impressive a collection of Windows financial programs as you're likely to see, online or off. Head to the Applications library and get ready. There are sections for Excel, Paradox, MS Access, Ami Pro, and, hidden in the MORE folder, huge collections of software in the PIMS & Databases, Quattro, Quicken, Telecom, and Word for Windows sections. And, you still haven't heard about the mother lode of financial software: the Financial section. Need programs to track your investments, calculate your child support payments, or invoice your clients? They're here. ✓**AMERICA ONLINE**→ *keyword* win→Browse the Software Libraries→Applications

Windows RoundTable The count-down-to-the-weekend clock and the set of democracy documents in hypertext are exceptions in the Windows (Other Applications) library. The rule here is that anything goes, as long as its financial-, management-, or investment-related. There are the usual suspects: bill payment reminder programs, business card makers, stock and bond trackers, retirement programs, and mortgage analyzers. ✓**GENIE**→*keyword* windows→ Windows Software Libraries→Set Software Library→ Windows (Other Applications)

Windows Shareware Forum If you're in the market for a Windows business or finance application, check out the library of personal information managers (it's vast) and the Business/Finance library for job hunting, check balancing, decision mapping, and

> "Applications that sound alarms when you're due for an appointment, help you develop a business proposal, calculate your profits (or losses), give you the area code for any street in America, and track your portfolio are just a taste of what's available to the Mac owner on on Info-Mac."

stock tracking applications. ✓**COMPUSERVE**→*go* winshare

Macintosh

Business Software So you own a Macintosh and you want Canadian tax forms from 1992 and 1993 in Excel? And a FileMaker Pro database to track finances? An invoice template for Fourth Dimension? Ahh, and you need a personal information manager, a bond calculator, and a program to log job-hunting contacts. This library, while favoring Excel and FileMaker Pro, has a rich selection of Mac financial software. ✓**GENIE** →*keyword* mac→Macintosh Software Libraries→Set Software Li-

brary→Business

Info-Mac Applications that sound alarms when you're due for an appointment, help you develop a business proposal, calculate your profits (or losses), give you the area code for any street in America, and track your portfolio are just a taste of what's available to the Mac owner looking for finance programs at these sites. Since the finance applications are interspersed with other applications, you may want to download the abstracts file to help you identify the programs of interest. ✓**INTERNET** ...→*ftp* ftp.pht.com→anonymous→<your email address>→/mirrors/info-mac/app ...→*ftp* ftp.sunet.se→anonymous→<your email address>→/pub/mac/info-mac/app ...→*ftp* ftp.funet.fi→anonymous→<your email address>→/pub/mac/info-mac/app ...→*ftp* mrc-next.cso.uiuc.edu→anonymous→<your email address>→/pub/info-mac/app

Mac Applications Forum Like its PC counterpart, there are Macintosh libraries for spreadsheets, accounting, databases, and general business and PIM applications. Looking for tax templates, 401K planners, investment managers, auto leasing calculators, or Excel calendars? Drop by. ✓**COMPUSERVE**→*go* macapp

MBS Software Libraries There are several resources for financial software here: The Application library is loaded with applications to manage your mortgage, schedule your day, and log addresses and phone numbers, as well as one (Pogo Your Logo) to transform your company logo into a bouncing screen saver. The Spreadsheets, Templates/Misc. Files, and Business Utilities libraries are also filled with Mac programs. ✓**AMERICA**

ONLINE→*keyword* mbs→Browse the Software Libraries

Zmac Download & Support Forum Time managers and other "productivity" software selected by MacWEEK and MacUser editors. ✓**COMPUSERVE**→*go* zmc:download

Microsoft

Microsoft Knowledge Base Most of the 18,000 documents here are excerpted from user manuals and help sheets produced by Microsoft. Warning: there's a lot of information here. Searching for "Excel" finds more than a thousand articles. Changing the search to "Excel and export" narrows the choice to around 40 articles. ✓**AMERICA ONLINE**→*keyword* knowledge base

Program support

Business Software A huge message board with topics on programs ranging from Excel to Microsoft Access to Manage Your Money (MYM) to MSWorks. The board is most helpful for troubleshooting and software recommendations. ✓**PRODIGY**→*jump* computers support bb→Choose a Topic→Business Software

Financial Software This bulletin board is heavily focused on MECA's software products, particularly MYM. Peachtree and the Mutual Fund Tracker also have their own topics. ✓**PRODIGY**→*jump* computer bb→Choose a Topic→Financial Software

MECA Forum What do I do if I damage my data? What's internal error #12? And how do I tell MYM (Managing Your Money) that I've paid off the mortgage? A huge number of people use MECA's Taxcut and MYM soft-

MicroSoft founder Bill Gates—from favi43.informatik.uhl-erlangen.de

ware packages—and many of them show up here with their questions. ✓**COMPUSERVE**→*go* meca

Simply Money This software package contains several useful budgeting, investment management, and organizational features. The forum contains updates, demos, and documentation for the various versions of Simply Money. It's also a place where program users can post suggestions or complaints about the software. ✓**COMPUSERVE**→*go* simply

Spreadsheets

Lotus (echo) Gil wants Lotus 2.4 to print faster. Roderico needs a program to translate add-ins with an .ADN extension to an add-in with a .PCL extension. And Marcus is interested in opening his Lotus Windows files in Lotus DOS. Just sit back and watch the help roll in. ✓**RELAYNET**

Lotus123 (echo) Lotus-newbies congregate in this low volume conference, asking questions and trying to work through their transition from other spreadsheet programs. ✓**SMARTNET**

Microsoft Excel Forum Active

support forum for the popular spreadsheet program. From how to average subtotals to how to work with passwords on files, this is an excellent resource for Excel users to troubleshoot and pick up tips. The libraries, including one for the Mac and one for the PC, carry a mix of functional and bizarre files: baseball statistics or an amortization schedule, anyone? ✓**COMPUSERVE**→*go* excel

The World of Lotus A series of forums devoted to Lotus, including word processing, spreadsheet, technical, and German forums. The LDC Spreadsheet Forum is home to libraries and message boards devoted to advancing and troubleshooting use of Lotus 123. ✓**COMPUSERVE**→*go* lotus

> "Warning: there's a lot of information here. Searching for 'Excel' finds more than a thousand articles."

Personal finance shareware

Account Manager v1.1 File-Maker Pro templates to keep track of bank accounts, loan payments, credit card purchases, and the like. ✓**INTERNET**→*ftp* sumex-aim.stanford. edu→anonymous→<your email address>→/info-mac/app→fmpro_ accnt_mngr_11e.cpt.hqx (Macintosh)

Annuity Ace v1.02 Flexible program projects savings for deferred, immediate, and split annuities (savings, IRA, 401k, etc.). ✓**PC OHIO**→d→*Download a file:* ACE102.ZIP (DOS)

Budget Maker Helps you design a home budget. ✓**AMERICA ONLINE** →*keyword* win→*Search by file name:* BUDMKR11.ZIP (Windows)

Cash Control v1.0 This friendly but powerful checkbook program features split accounts, budget help, and check printing. Shareware. ✓**PC OHIO**→d→*Download a file:* CASHC.ZIP (DOS)

Cash For Kids Financial planner/manager for kids. ✓**INTERNET**→*ftp* oak.oakland.edu→ anonymous→<your email address> →/pub/msdos/finance→ CFK10T.ZIP (DOS)

Charge Account Management Program v1.11 Full-featured charge card manager. Enter, edit, or delete transactions. Numerous reports are available as well as up to 50 budget categories. ✓**PC OHIO**→d→*Download a file:* CHARGE.ZIP (DOS)

Checkbook Manager Multi-level checkbook register. ✓**AMERICA ONLINE**→*keyword* mbs→Software Libraries→Applications→CK2.2

Folder.sit (Macintosh)

Checkbook Plus v5.7 Full-feature cash management and budgeting program, which reconciles accounts and provides customized income statements. Features pull-down menus, help file, mouse support, calculators, and more. ✓**PC OHIO**→d→*Download a file:* CBPLUS57.ZIP (DOS)

Checkbook v1.7 Balance your checking accounts. ✓**INTERNET**→*ftp* mac.archive.umich.edu→/mac/util/ organization→checkbook1.7.sit. hqx (Macintosh)

ChequeBook Log bank transactions, check bank statement accuracy, and import or export data. Includes a calculator. Shareware. ✓**AMERICA ONLINE**→*keyword* win→ *Search by file name:* CHQ20U.ZIP (Windows)

CK 2.2 A checking account manager, which comes with extensive documentation and sample files. Shareware. ✓**INTERNET**→*ftp* sumex-aim.stanford.edu→anonymous→ <your email address>→/info-mac/ app→ck-22.hqx (Macintosh)

Cost of Living Adjuster v4.11 Do you make enough? Check with this program. Tables start at year 1900. ✓**PC OHIO**→d→*Download a file:* COLA411.ZIP (DOS)

Credit Card Plus 1.2 Organize your credit card information: numbers, interest rates, limits, bank info, and statement info. ✓**INTERNET**→*ftp* ftp.cica.indiana.edu →anonymous→<your email address>→/pub/pc/win3/util→ ccplus12.zip (Windows)

Credit Perfect Program to help

you repair and manage your credit. ✓**INTERNET**→*ftp* ftp.cica.indiana. edu→anonymous→<your email address>→/pub/pc/win3/util→ cred10.zip (Windows)

Debt Manager Finds best plan to pay off loans. ✓**INTERNET**→*ftp* oak.oakland.edu→anonymous →<your email address>→/pub /msdos/finance→DEBTMG13.ZIP (DOS)

Finance 1.0 Program for loan amortization. ✓**INTERNET**→*ftp* ftp.cica.indiana.edu→anonymous→ <your email address>→/pub/pc /win3/util→ financ.zip (Windows)

Finance 2.0 Tracks multiple bank accounts and a number of spending categories. ✓**COMPUSERVE** →*go* macap→Browse Libraries→Accounting/Finance→ FINANC.SIT (Macintosh)

Financial Freedom Organize savings and checking accounts. Also includes basic loan and interest analysis functions. ✓**EXEC-PC**→File Collection Menu→MS Windows→FFREED.ZIP (Windows)

HiFi v2.18 Financial planning and calculation tool with iconic, menu, button bar interfaces. Financial calculator, loan amortization, investment analysis, and more. Automatic charts and tables. Shareware. ✓**EXEC-PC**→File Collection Menu→*Search by file name:* HIFI218A.ZIP *and* HIFI218B. ZIP (Windows)

Home Accountant Track household expenses, budgets, and bank account and credit card activity. Generates several reports. Shareware. ✓**COMPUSERVE**→*go* confor→ Browse Libraries→Software Library

Personal finance shareware (continued)

→HOMEAC.ZIP (Windows)

Home Budget Finance Manager Budget and manage your home finances. ✓**INTERNET**→*ftp* ftp.cica.indiana.edu→anonymous→ <your email address>→/pub/pc /win3/util→hb20.zip (Windows)

Home Management II v2.11 Covers many of your financial needs. Includes modules for creating budgets, maintaining checking accounts and stock portfolios, and determining loan payments. Shareware. ✓**GENIE**→*keyword* invest →Investors' Software Libraries→ *Download a file:* HM2SHARE.ZIP (DOS)

KeepTrak v2.10 Home accounting program; includes Windows icons. Shareware. ✓**EXEC-PC**→File Collection Menu→Mahoney IBM Compatible DOS→ KEEPTRAK.ZIP (DOS)

Medical Insurance Data Tracker v3.1 Records personal medical expenses and generates lists for insurance companies. ✓**PC OHIO**→d→*Download a file:* MDINS31.ZIP (DOS)

MiniCoupon Coupon and shopping organizer. ✓**PC OHIO**→d→ *Download a file:* MINICOUP.ZIP (DOS)

Money Management Pro v1.2 Menu-driven program manages your finances. Includes pop-up calculator and calendar, loan and mortgage analysis, credit card manager, and error checking. Shareware. ✓**GENIE**→*keyword* invest→Investors' Software Libraries →*Download a file:* MONEYPRO.ZIP (DOS)

Money Matters v1.0 Computes, among other things, loans, depreciations, and investments. ✓**INTERNET**→*ftp* oak.oakland.edu→ anonymous→<your email address> →/pub/macintosh/appl→money matter.sit (Macintosh)

My Little Realm's Checking v2.5 Fast and easy data entry with macros helps you track tax deductions, business and household expenses, and more. Shareware. ✓**PC OHIO**→d→*Download a file:* MLRCHK25.ZIP (DOS)

O'Ledger Simple credit card and debit spread sheet editor. ✓**INTERNET**→*ftp* ftp.cica.indiana.edu→ anonymous→<your email address> →/pub/pc/win3/util→oledger.zip (Windows)

PayOff Calculate the best way to pay off your debt. ✓**INTERNET**→*ftp* ftp.cica.indiana.edu→anonymous→ <your email address>→/pub/ pc/win3/util→payoff22.zip (Windows)

Quick and Easy Finance v2.0 A complete finance software package. ✓**PC OHIO**→d→*Download a file:* QAEF2.ZIP (DOS)

Savings Account Management Program v1.0 Full-feature program tracks and organizes your savings account and prints reports. ✓**PC OHIO**→d→*Download a file:* SAVINGS.ZIP (DOS)

Smart Account This simple but powerful personal finance package supports direct debits, standing orders, and bank statement checkback. Shareware. ✓**EXEC-PC**→File Collection Menu→MS Windows→ SMTACC13.ZIP (Windows)

Talking Checkbook v5.04 Checkbook program for computers with Synthetic Speech Output. ✓**PC OHIO**→d→*Download a file:* CHECKS54.ZIP (DOS)

Track It! v1.02 Inventory your personal belongings with definable fields. Can create reports. ✓**EXEC-PC**→File Collection Menu→MS Windows→ TKH102.ZIP (Windows)

Wealth Management System Tracks savings, investments, retirement plans, mortgages, loans, and stocks and mutuals. ✓**INTERNET**→ ftp ftp.cica.indiana.edu→anony mous→<your email address>→ /pub/pc/win3/util→ winwealth.zip ✓**AMERICA ONLINE**→*keyword* win→ *Search by file name:* WMSD78.ZIP (Windows)

WinCheck A Windows checkbook program which manages checking, savings, and credit card accounts. ✓**INTERNET**→*ftp* ftp.cica. indiana.edu→anonymous→<your email address>→/pub/pc/win3 /util→winck30n.zip (Windows)

The Windows Home Accountant Track expenses, incomes, bank accounts, and credit card expenditures. ✓**INTERNET**→*ftp* ftp.cica. indiana.edu→anonymous→<your email address>→/pub/pc/win3 /util→homeacct.zip (Windows)

WinFin A collection of 18 small personal finance programs that let you analyze your retirement planning strategy, calculate your bond or CD earnings, or figure out your mortgage payments by filling in the appropriate forms. ✓**AMERICA ONLINE**→*keyword* win→*Search by file name:* WINFIN37.ZIP (Windows)

Quicken

The world of cars has its Ford Escorts and Tauruses. The world of film has its *Jurassic*

Park. And the world of financial software has *Quicken*, the monstrously popular money-management package that helps organize and analyze bank accounts, investments, and taxes. While the program isn't available online, there are plenty of places in Cyberspace to enrich and broaden your *Quicken* experience. If you want to talk about the program, ask questions or give answers, visit the **Quicken** discussion conferences on FidoNet and Smartnet; if you want to take advantage of freeware and shareware add-ons and tie-ins, drop by AOL's library of **Files for Quicken** on the Macintosh. And all Quickeners should check out CompuServe's **Intuit Forum**, which offers individual message boards for each platform and program version, as well as *Quicken*-related shareware and technical support.

Screenshot from Quicken for Macintosh

On the Net

Intuit Home Page Besides company news, history, and Intuit job opportunities, this Website features product descriptions (not very elaborate but helpful). ✓**INTERNET**→ *www* http://www.careermosaic. com/cm/intuit/intuit1.html

Quicken In the continuum of personal-finance management software, this is the be-all and the end-all, the alpha and omega. Quite simply, *Quicken* is the most popular personal-finance management program in the world, with a full complement of banking, budgeting, and organizing features.

Bill Gates liked the program so much he bought the company. *Quicken* revolves around the metaphor of a checkbook register no matter whether you're tracking a savings account, a credit card, a stock portfolio, or a mutual fund. The program is capable of remarkable organization and reporting functions once you adjust to keeping your accounts on the computer. Successive versions of the program have incorporated elaborate budgeting, retirement planning, and loan calculations.

Many people fall in love with this program, deriving untold pleasures from its multicolored income/expense pie charts. In conjunction with related programs, such as *CheckFree* and *MacInTax*, *Quicken* is also capable of electron-

ic bill paying, updating portfolio prices from an online service, and even paying taxes. If you don't have *Quicken*, you're in the same position as the people who laughed at radio or scoffed at TV—in short, about to be left behind. Voice call 800-624-9065 for more information.

comp.os.ms-windows.apps. financial (ng) *Quicken* and *Excel* dominate the discussion on this newsgroup. *Quicken* questions about savings bonds, rounding accuracy, technical support, and its compatibility with *TurboTax* are typical. ✓**USENET**

comp.sys.mac.apps (ng) More *Quicken* talk. ✓**USENET**

Files for Quicken on the Macintosh More than 15 shareware and freeware downloads for using *Quicken* on the Macintosh. There are programs to add 3-D icons to *Quicken*, to import stock quotes from AOL into *Quicken*, and some utilities for printing checks. ✓**AMERICA ONLINE**→*keyword* mac software

Intuit+ Forum Serves as the largest presence for *Quicken* on the Net with support and information on all Intuit products. The libraries are filled with free updates, shareware, archives of message topics, and tech support FAQs, with hundreds of files spread across libraries for *Quicken*/Mac, Small Business, and Online Services.

The majority of shareware centers around a few main functions: tax planning, incorporating downloaded quotes into *Quicken*, and converting *Quicken* files to and from other personal-finance software like *Managing Your Money*, *Dollars & Sense*, and *Money*. Intuit posts new product announcements, feature lists, and demos in the General Information section of the library. The message boards, divided by platform and program function, are also rich with information.

General Information

Everything from an Intuit Corporate bio to quick responses by the forum sysops on questions such as Can the CD-ROM version of *Quicken* run if the CD-ROM drive is later detached? (Yes, it can run from the hard disk, but you'll miss out on the "Ask the Experts" multimedia section.)

Quicken 4.0/Windows

Help puzzle out a work around for *Quicken*'s tendency to use an unreadable highlight color and watch requests for advice on importing old *Managing Your Money* data files turn into a lively debate over the relative merits of the two programs.

Quicken 1.0-3.0/Windows

Tech support for people still using old *Quicken* versions. Lots of good notes on shareware programs for incorporating downloaded stock quotes.

Quicken/DOS

Discuss the most recent version of *Quicken* for DOS. Also a good place to hear about features that have yet to be implemented on other platforms.

Suggestions

The single best place online to reach product-development people planning the next *Quicken*, but thanks to the vigilance of the sysops, this is also a dumping ground for some complaints noted in other topics (i.e. the slower speed of the Windows version).

Online Services

Want to compare notes on online banking services that work with *Quicken*? Or are you ready to stomp that modem that won't work with *QuickenQuotes*? Come here.

Quicken/Mac

The place for help with Mac *Quicken*.

Investments

Debate the most effective way to track your investment account in *Quicken*. Also lots of good suggestions for tracking mutual funds and getting updates of bond prices.

Other topics

Assorted topics that have their own bulletin boards: Quick-Books/DOS, QuickBooks/Windows, QuickPay, QuickInvoice, *Quicken* Companion, Intuit Talk, Small Business, and International. ✓**COMPUSERVE**→*go* intuit

Intuit Online If you need help with an Intuit product, finding it has never been so easy. There's a section where common questions for products such as *Quicken* or *QuickPay* are answered, as well as a Files and Software download area where members can retrieve tips, troubleshooting guides, instructions, and utilities for the Intuit product of their choice. The Intuit Financial BB is the hub of the area, with a huge message board devoted to member discussions and questions about the products. ✓**PRODIGY**→*jump* intuit

Quicken (echo) A group of about ten regulars and an equal number of constantly changing interlopers share their favorite strategies for shaving an extra day of float off the automatic payment of bills and sensibly tracking cash expenditures. If you're looking to compare notes on running the Windows version under IBM's Warp, you should know that there's an unusual concentration of OS/2 users here. ✓**FIDONET**

Quicken (echo) CPAs using QuickBooks, Windows users at home who wish they'd backed up those QDATA files, and friends helping friends who are plagued by "extraneous dots" on their invoice printing (answer: try experimenting with the print density setting) check into the conference regularly to swap advice. ✓**SMART-NET**

Quicken Support (PC) Archive of more than 50 shareware, free updaters, and freeware downloads for using *Quicken* under MS-DOS or Windows. Many of these shareware programs facilitate importing downloaded stock quotes into the older version of *Quicken* (the new version has the capability built in) or make it possible to print checks using *Quicken*. ✓**AMERICA ONLINE**→*keyword* pc applications→Browse the Software Libraries→Quicken Support

Banking on the future

One of the most powerful financial applications of networking technology, online bank-

ing allows you to pay your bills and monitor your accounts from the privacy of your own home. There are a number of ways to do it. You can use **CheckFree**, which delivers funds through the Federal Reserve system, or you can take your business to one of the dozens of big-name banks with online branches: Barnett Bank, Chemical Bank, Wells Fargo, and others. With double-blind passwords and special encryption, all your transactions are protected, but you might want to read more about electronic security issues in the **Online Banking FAQ**. Book passage for the future with **ecash**, an experiment in electronic currency. And even if you are neither a borrower nor a lender, you might still want to spend some time browsing in the **Banking and Credit Libraries** for bank ratings and analyses provided by private evaluation firms.

Screenshot from CheckFree

On the Net

Across the board

Banking and Credit Exchange credit horror stories—repossessed trucks on which all payments have been made—and offer advice. It's a good place to look for tips on the best credit-card rates or to discuss how best to save for your children's education and plans for inheritance. ✓**PRODIGY**→*jump* money talk bb→Choose a Topic→Banking and Credit

Banking and Credit Paralegals and credit counselors offer advice. Learn about credit "clearing scams," credit-card services, and the regulation of banking rates. Sysops provide lists of "credit-card secrets," nasty cheating practices to be on the look out for. If you have a specific institution that's giving you hassles, feel free to mention it by name to see if other travelers in Cyberspace have experienced similar dissatisfaction. ✓**COMPUSERVE**→ *go* conforum→Libraries *or* Messages →Banking & Credit

Hendy on Banking On the second and fourth Fridays of the month, syndicated columnist John Hendy summarizes banking news and gives advice on getting and maintaining a good credit rating. Hendy's advice on the best mortgages, savings plans, and credit programs is archived and searchable. ✓**PRODIGY**→*jump* hendy

Online Banking FAQ This short FAQ gives the basics about how to bank online, and while much of the information is specific to Prodigy, there is a lot of good advice about security issues. ✓**PRODIGY**→*jump* banking faq

CheckFree

CheckFree Maybe you're one of those people who always loses the credit-card bill, or runs out of checks, or pays late—a month seems so short these days, and those damned banks are always closing at 3:00 p.m. One of the fruits of the electronic age, *Check-Free* allows what seems like unconditional online bill payment, "any amount—to anyone—any bank, anywhere, any time." For the cost of start-up software, (currently under $15) and monthly charges ($9.95 per/month for 20 transactions or less with a $3.50 surcharge per ten additional transactions), *CheckFree* designs a home-electronic-payment system for you. Just enter the necessary information (amounts, accounts) and dial your local access number. Four business days later, *CheckFree* pays off your creditors. Because it accesses the Federal Reverse system, *CheckFree* can be used with any bank, and it includes elaborate security measures to insure that your financial information isn't filched from the phone lines.

The online services offer sample software for downloading, along with an FAQ that delves into such important issues as insufficient funds (in case you're curious, *CheckFree* will not fine you, but your bank still will). The program is compatible with many popular finance software packages including *Managing Your Money*, *Quicken*, *Microsoft Money*, and *Mac-Money*. *CheckFree* software is available for Mac, DOS, and Windows platforms, and you'll be mailed a local access number after you send in your registration. Voice call 1-800-882-5280 for more information. **$**

BillPay USA Prodigy is the only online service where *CheckFree* is operated online. Although called by a different name—BillPay USA—the features are the same. Monthly charges are billed to your Prodigy account. ✓**PRODIGY**→*jump* billpay **$**

CheckFree Support, product information, demos, and online software ordering for *CheckFree*. ✓**AMERICA ONLINE**→*keyword* checkfree ✓**COMPUSERVE**→*go* checkfree ✓**GENIE**→*keyword* checkfree

International banks

Bank of Ireland, Trinity Branch On the off chance that you hold an account at the Trinity Branch of the Bank of Ireland—or the new branch behind the Buttery—you can avail yourself of the institution's online presence. In addition to providing information on bank benefits, the BOI offers two online services. First, you can find out the current Irish pound exchange rates and have the Net do foreign-exchange calculations for you. And second, you can get a bank statement through Cyberspace. Anywhere in the world, just fill in your name and account type and the information comes back to you. ✓**INTERNET**→*www* http://www.webnet.ie/cust/ boi/index.html

Loans

The Best and Worst Ways to

Borrow Covers the pros and cons of all types of loans, and teaches you how to comparison shop to get the best value. Learn to borrow against your stocks with a margin loan, but beware the margin call when the market plunges. Use CDs, retirement plans, or life insurance for credit. And try to heed the advice to borrow wisely—the report warns against borrowing on credit cards or balloon mortgage plans. ✓**PRODIGY**→*jump* cr money

Picking a bank

Banking Libraries The FDIC publication *Bank Rating Analysis Service* can help you choose a bank. The file describes the CAMEL (capital, assets, management, earning, liquidity) system employed by private evaluation firms. ✓**COMPUSERVE**→*go* conforum →Libraries→Banking & Credit

PRODIGY BANKING	
The following banks are available nationally	
Banking Institution	*jump*
Barnett Bank	barnett bank
Boatmen's Bank	boatmens
Chemical Bank	chemical
Chevy Chase Bank	chevy chase
Delaware Trust	delaware trust
First PA Bank	first pa bank
Hamilton Bank	hamilton bank
Meridian Trust	meridian
MidLantic	midlantic
NBD Bancorp	nbd
New Jersey National Bank (NJNB)	njnb
PNC Bank (Pittsburgh National Corp.)	pnc bank
Wells Fargo	wells fargo
Wilmington Trust	wilmington trust
The following banks are available locally	
Banking Institution	*jump*
Bank One	bank one
Comerica	comerica
First Interstate of Denver	first interstate

CYBERPOWER! ™

Paying Your Bills

Once a few years ago I read this article that said that one day banks would be completely electronic. I can't tell you how much easier my life would be—I could just make sure that my parents have deposited my monthly allowance, and even pay off my MasterCard and Visa, from the relative safety of my dorm room. I live on West 114th Street, in New York City.

E ven on 114th Street, you're in luck, assuming that you subscribe to Prodigy. In the world of commercial online services, Prodigy gives you more bank for your buck, with more than 20 electronic banks. Many of the banks are "conditional deliverance" institutions, which means that their financial services are restricted by regional parameters. But since we live in an era of high-tech precision, there's no need to read disclaimers and terms to discover which of the online banks serve you. Just ask Prodigy to check—it knows where you're calling from and which banks service your area—and wait for the results.

If you do this, you'll find that New York's own Chemical Bank has an extensive online service known as Excel PC banking. If you are already a Chemical Bank customer, adding Excel PC service to your basic plan is as easy as touching a button; otherwise, the application process is longer and more involved. Once you have entered the world of Excel PC, though, you'll find that it was well worth the wait. From monitoring current balances to making monthly payments, financial transactions can be conducted entirely onscreen. Here's a brief review of the three main features of this banking service.

Account Balances
Of the various aspects of online banking, this is perhaps the simplest, but it's no

less convenient for its simplicity. After you enter your account number and password, you can review current information for any and all Chemical Bank accounts. Use the introductory balance screen for a quick check of account types, account numbers, and current balances, or select an individual account to retrieve more detailed information.

Statements

Give me liberty or give me death? No, not that kind of statement—a bank statement. If you select the Statements options from the Excel PC menu, pick a specific account, and then designate a starting date for account information, Excel PC will deliver a detailed record of your transactions, everything from transfers to payments to interest payments.

Bill Payments

While the other two aspects of electronic banking are passive features—they merely display information that you would otherwise read in a printed statement—the Bill Payment capability is something entirely different. With Excel PC QuickPay, you can schedule all regular payees—from landlords to utilities, and even your credit card companies—and then execute those transactions electronically. From the all-important Payments menu, you can check

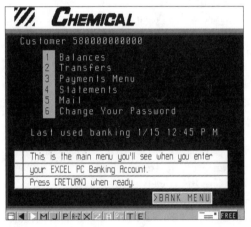

Excel screen on Prodigy

recurring, pending, and recent transactions; cancel pending payments between the time of scheduling and the scheduled payment date; and review the full history of the payments made to each payee.

Credit & debt

After you've read through the Frequently Asked Questions About Credit, you'll be full

of information about annual fees, billing errors, and payment plans. In fact, you may be so thrilled with your newfound knowledge that you'll want to run right out and apply for a card. Don't run out. Stay in, and apply for a **Chase Gold Visa** on Prodigy. If that's not futuristic enough for you, use CompuServe's **Visa Gold Card** service, which issues online account information that can be tracked and analyzed with **Quicken**, **Manage Your Money**, and other personal finance software packages. Falling behind in your payments? Check out the **Ten Steps to Improving Your Credit**, as well as similar articles in AOL's **Money, Debt, and Credit** library. And if all else fails, there's always **About Bankruptcy**, the valuable primer for personal financial collapse.

Chase Visa card—screenshot from Prodigy's Chase Gold Visa Feature

On the Net

Credit basics

Credit Libraries Here, you'll find Federal Trade Commission publications addressing issues such as how to get a credit history, repair bad credit, combat false credit reports, and avoid credit scams. The files Credit Card Blocking and Credit Repair Scams help you make sense of all those offers that arrive in the mail each day for "pre-approved credit." Also watch out for those "fix bad credit—remove bankruptcy" offers which seem like dreams come true to those with damaged credit. If you have been wrongly denied credit, the file How to Dispute Credit Report Errors describes what you need to do to fix it and who to contact for help. Citizens' rights under the Fair Credit Reporting Act, Equality in Lending and Truth in Lending Acts are clearly explained. The file Women and Credit Histories offers useful tips for fiancées, wives, divorcées, and widows for getting and keeping a credit record of their own. ✓**COMPUSERVE**→*go* conforum→Libraries→Banking & Credit

Frequently Asked Questions About Credit This comprehensive FAQ is garnered from the newsgroup misc.consumers, and covers topics ranging from the differences among various credit cards to understanding credit reports.

The FAQ also contains concise instructions for obtaining and revamping your credit report, battling billing errors, and making sure that your cards are working for you, not solely for the credit company. ✓**INTERNET**→*ftp* rtfm.mit.edu→anonymous→<your email address>→/pub/usenet-by-group/misc.answers→ consumer-credit-faq

Credit profiles

Internet Credit Bureau Though you're likely to be on the receiving end of credit checks, you can also initiate them. ICB will create a full credit profile for any individual or business, and the company can also track down missing persons or retrieve basic information about any Social Security Number. Simply fill out an online customer request form at the Web site or email it. ✓**INTERNET** ...→*www* http://www.satenet.org/credit/ ...→*email* icb@satelnet.org ✍ *Email a customer request*

TRW Credit Services Apply online to see your credit history, and for $44 a year TRW will update you whenever someone cracks into that credit-report vault. New bosses, prospective spouses—who knows who's looking into you? In addition, take the TRW online quiz and find out what your credit intelligence quotient is. According to this well-known credit reporting company, if you don't know what your credit report says about you—or the exact date of the last investigation into your credit history—you are woefully unprepared for modern life and the challenges of getting a loan. ✓**GE-**

NIE→*keyword* trwcredit **$** ✓**PRO-DIGY**→*jump* trw **$**

Credit cards

Chase Gold Visa To apply for a 10.8% variable rate Chase Gold Visa Card, fill out the application provided and email it back. If approved, you'll receive a no-annual-fee card with a credit limit up to $10,000 and a 3% over prime interest rate. ✓**PRODIGY**→*jump* chase

GM Card Apply online for a GM Mastercard that earns bonus money from General Motors when used. ✓**PRODIGY**→*jump* gm card

Premier Dining Club Become a card member of the Premier Dining Club and enjoy discounts at over 9,000 resturants. ✓**PRO-DIGY**→*jump* premier dining club ✓**COMPUSERVE**→*go* pd

Visa Gold Card CompuServe has a credit card—a normal Visa Gold Card with a twist. You can track your account online. The program works with Quicken, Manage Your Money (MYM), and other spreadsheets and word processors. The two card options which may be applied for online are the Classic Card and the Gold Card. Special Conductor software is required, and given to those approved for a card. ✓**COMPUSERVE**→ *go* card

Ecash

Ecash What is ecash? Well, it's electronic payment by email over the Internet that eliminates paper currency from the equation. It's a kind of virtual credit card. Have Chinese food delivered, and pay with ecash. Play a computer game, and pay with ecash. See an online therapist who works by real-time chat, and pay by ecash. Sounds like the future, doesn't it? Well, for

> **"'Ten Steps to Improving Your Credit' is trench warfare strategy for those with bad credit histories."**

the time being it is—unless you have an account at the First Digital Bank, which is owned and operated by the Dutch company DigiCash BV. If you do have a DigiCash account, you can withdraw money from your bank account and convert it immediately into ecash. But ecash is still in the trial stages; don't cut up your plastic yet. ✓**INTERNET**→*www* http://www.digicash.com

Credit repair

Best Rates Information on the best rates for consumer credit and banking: Bank Rate Monitor provides the names, addresses, and interest rates of banks with the best credit card deals; Consumer Financial Service charts the ten highest 7-day compound yields for money fund vehicles and the top 100 large banks in the top 10 markets for their CD and MMA rates. ✓**EWORLD**→*go* money matters→Best Rates

Money, Debt & Credit Features articles on "Establishing Credit" and "Cash management," an FAQ, and a message board where discussions range from "How do I repair my credit" to the benefits of the Diners Club credit card. ✓**AMERICA ONLINE**→*keyword* your-money→Money, Debt & Credit

Ten Steps to Improving Your

Credit For those who are not averse to using the credit laws to their own advantage, a user has uploaded "Ten Steps to Improving Your Credit." This is trench warfare strategy for those with bad credit histories. For example: "Since credit rating companies have only 30 days to verify a bad risk incident, keep questioning them until they miss the deadline." ✓**COMPUSERVE**→*go* con-forum→Libraries→Banking & Credit Libraries→Ten Steps to Improving Your Credit

Shareware

CreditPerfect Credit repair and management software. Prints credit report requests and helps you create letters in response to errors on your credit report. ✓**COM-PUSERVE**→*go* confor→Browse Libraries→Software Library→CREW 10.ZIP ✓**PC OHIO**→d→*Download a file:* CRED 10.ZIP ✓**AMERICA ON-LINE**→*keyword* win→ *Search by file name:* CREW101.ZIP (Windows)

The Debt Analyzer v1.24 Helps you reduce and eliminate debt by scheduling payments or consolidating loans. Up to 20 debts processed at once. ✓**PC OHIO**→d→*Download a file:* DBT 123.ZIP (DOS, Windows)

Debtfree Enter information about your loans and this program creates a loan reduction plan. ✓**AMERICA ONLINE**→*keyword* win→ *Search by file name:* DEBTFREE.ZIP (Windows)

LoanCalc Computes loan payment, declining balance, and equity schedules for fixed-rate loans. Shareware. ✓**INTERNET**→*ftp* mac.archive.umich.edu→/mac/util/organization→loancalc.sit.hqx (Macintosh)

Insurance

Insurance is risk and benefit, risk and benefit, and more risk and benefit, and the Net's

resources on the insurance industry include generous amounts of both elements. You want risk? Well, risk your naïveté by visiting Delphi's **Insurance and Financial Planning Conference**, which will acquaint you with some of the introductory issues of the insurance industry. Risk your patience by wading through the **Risk and Insurance Working Papers Archive**, filled with unwieldy titles ("A Reexamination of the Relationship between Preferences and Moment Orderings by Rational Risk Averse Investors") and arcane analysis. And finally, risk your ignorance by absorbing the useful insurance strategies discussed in **Consumer Brochures in Insurance** (how to select a policy, how to lower your premiums, how to cope with the unexpected). Then there are the benefits. Online insurance information is startling in both its breadth and depth, with contributions from the academic as well as the professional risk-management disciplines. So whether you want to cultivate that back-to-school feeling by reading

1928 Santa Paula flood—gopher://gopher.ucr.edu/Campus Events/California Museum of Pictures/Networkexhibitions

Teaching Notes on Courses in Risk and Insurance or keep tabs on the insurance industry with **clari.biz.industry.insurance**, whether you want to scrutinize **Recent Industry Financial Results** or conduct specific investigations into life, health, auto, and property insurance, the Net will reward your efforts. And if you think that the company that issued your policy is straying toward ethical shadows, stop by the **Insurance Fraud Research Register**.

On the Net

Across the board

ARIA Annual Conference Program Dense and deadening

risk-management jargon for the insurance professional. This 53-page document, which details the American Risk and Insurance Association's 1994 annual meeting in Toronto, is useful for any determined consumers who want to make sense of the current developments in academic and professional insurance. How are premiums determined? What can an insurance company do after a natural disaster? And what's the thinking on the viatical industry, which allows independent agents to pay cash for the life insurance policies of the terminally ill in exchange for beneficiary status? ✓**INTERNET**→ *www* http://riskweb.bus.utexas.edu/aria.htm

ARIAForum Covers assorted topics in the risk and insurance industry with both professional and academic orientations. ✓**INTERNET**→ *www* http://riskweb.bus.utexas.edu/ariaforum.html

Consumer Brochures in Insur-

ance Articles on topics ranging from home security basics to nine ways to lower your auto insurance costs to homeowner procedures after a natural disaster. ✓**INTER-NET**→*gopher* infx.infor.com:4200→ Consumer Brochures

Insurance and Financial Planning Conference This forum is split evenly between discussions of insurance, especially life and health insurance, and more general information on personal financial planning. As a result, it attracts both insurance professionals and personal consumers looking for the best rates and policies. ✓**DELPHI**→*go* cus 262

Insurance Discussion Collects a wide range of insurance-related comments and discussions, from detailed analyses of risk management legislation to tips on selecting an agent. If you have any insights into the life of life insurance, or you just want to complain about car insurance rates for adult males in the infamous 18-24 age bracket, this is a good place to start. ✓**PRODIGY**→*jump* money talk bb→Choose a Topic→Insurance

The Insurance Information Institute The collected publications of the Insurance Information Institute seek to boost the public's understanding of insurance—not only the economic theory behind the risk industry, but the legal regulations confining insurance companies. Consumers can read general brochures on such topics as "Home Security Basics" and "Insurance for Your Personal Possessions," as well as search a database of articles and related resources. ✓**INTERNET**→*gopher* infx.infor.com→ Insurance Information Institute-Publications

Insurance Planning In addition

to a fairly comprehensive FAQ, the area also carries an explanation of life insurance and a message board for discussing insurance issues. ✓**AMERICA ONLINE**→*keyword* yourmoney→Insurance Planning

List of Risk Theorists The next time you have a question about the insurance world, feel free to look up an expert in this document, which lists the various academic and professional members of the Risk Theory Society, along with their addresses, telephone numbers, and affiliations. ✓**INTERNET**→*www* http://riskweb.bus. utexas.edu/rts/1994member.html

Risk and Insurance Working Papers Archives A collection of abstracts and articles pertaining to actuarial matters. "A Reexamination of the Relationship between Preferences and Moment Orderings by Rational Risk Averse Investors"? "Causal Relationships Between Premiums and Losses, and Causes of the Underwriting Cycles"? Be still my beating heart. ✓**INTERNET**→*www* http://riskweb. bus.utexas.edu/rmi/workingpaper. html

RISKNet Mailing List (ml) With more than 400 subscribers worldwide, this electronic discussion list creates an ongoing symposium geared toward risk and insurance issues. Participants include academics from economics and business backgrounds, as well as actual actuarials. Also includes an archive that can be searched by author, topic, date, or thread. ✓**INTERNET**→*email* listproc@mcfeeley.cc. utexas.edu ✍ *Type in message body:* subscribe risknet <your full name> *Archives:* ✓**INTERNET**→*www* http:// www.crimson.com:80/risknet/hy per/

RTSWeb—The Risk Theory

Society (RTS) Does risk have a theory? Sure it does, or else most insurance companies wouldn't still be in business, let alone be raking in the big bucks. The Risk Theory Society is a small organization devoted to the study of both academic and practical insurance. The RTS's Web page discusses basic issues in insurance and risk, and offers links to many of the other insurance services on the Net. ✓**INTERNET**→*www* http://riskweb.bus. utexas.edu/rts/rtsweb.html

Car insurance

Auto Insurance Ratings Ratings, recommendations, and strategies for choosing the right auto insurance company. ✓**PRODIGY**→*jump* cr autos

Reporting an Automobile Accident Tip sheet on keeping cool in the wake of a smashup. Although information is specific to the Penn State campus, most of the recommendations are sound for everyone: "After the police investigation, your next call should be to your insurance agent who can assist you in arranging estimates and repairs and in completing insurance claim forms." ✓**INTERNET**→*gopher* info.psu.edu→University Life→University Life→Reporting An Automobile Accident

Health insurance

CR Health Insurance How does a hospital work? What exactly is covered by disability insurance? The Consumer Report on health insurance highlights an industry in transition, and tries to separate the rhetoric from the reality with advice, ratings, and recommendations. ✓**PRODIGY**→*jump* cr health insurance

Greg Conners Insurance Information from Greg Conners Insurance company about health insurance options for California residents. ✓**INTERNET**→*www* http://www.northcoast.com/unlimited/services_listing/greg_conners/gci.html

Health Reform & Insurance A library of introductory materials in the fields of health care and health insurance. Browse the glossary of health insurance terms, or conduct more specific research into HMOs, family care, coordinated care, long-term care, and disability insurance. Or if it's politics rather than policy you're looking for, read all about the issues rising out of the Clinton administration's failed attempt to reform national health care. From informed consent to managed competition, the buzzwords are all here, just waiting to be discovered. ✓**AMERICA ONLINE**→*keyword* health→Health Reform & Insurance

Long-Term Care Insurance This Web site answers the most common questions about long-term care, the difficult health-insurance decision more commonly (and less euphemistically) known as "putting Mom and Dad in a nursing home." In addition, it lists a set of support organizations and pamphlets that treat the issue in greater detail. ✓**INTERNET**→*www* http://www.service.com/answers/health_insurance.html

Medical & Health Services Information (BHPr-BBS) (bbs) This government BBS offers updates on a wide variety of health-care issues that overlap significantly with the health insurance industry. ☎→*dial* 703-321-8020→<your login>→<your password>→/go gateway→D→111 ✓**INTERNET**→*telnet* fedworld.gov→<your login>→<your password>→/go gateway→D→111

> "The first tip about shopping for life insurance, of course, is that you should start researching the matter before you're dead."

Medical Insurance Data Tracker v3.1 (DOS) With so many prescriptions and procedures, monitoring medical expenses is a difficult business. This program records personal medical expenses and generates forms that can be used in insurance claims. ✓**PC OHIO**→d→*Download a file:* MDINS31.ZIP

Home insurance

Essential Home Inventory Take inventory of the goods in your home for your insurance. ✓**INTERNET**→*ftp* ftp.cica.indiana.edu→anonymous→<your email address>→/pub/pc/win3/util→ehi10.zip, Windows

Home Inventory for Windows 3.1 Track personal property by insurance categories, personal categories, locations, and/or sub-locations. ✓**INTERNET**→*ftp* ftp.cica.indiana.edu→anonymous→<your email address>→/pub/pc/win3/util→jrehome.zip (Windows)

Homeowners' Insurance Explanations, ratings, and recommendations on everything from policy size to coverage type to specific homeowner's insurance companies. ✓**PRODIGY**→*jump* cr money

→Home Finance/Insurance

Personal Property Insurance Explains the ins and outs of personal property insurance for apartment dwellers. Is your building fire-resistant? Are you liable for injuries suffered by visitors to your residence? And should you use a direct or an independent agent to find a policy? ✓**INTERNET**→*gopher* info.psu.edu→Housing→Off Campus→Personal Property Insurance for Renters

Safeware Computer Insurance Insurance for computer owners. ✓**COMPUSERVE**→*go* saf ✓**GENIE**→*keyword* safeware

Track It! v1.02 Catalog your personal possessions and print reports. Shareware for Windows. ✓**EXEC PC**→file collection menu→MS Windows→TKH102.ZIP

Life insurance

CR Life Insurance The first tip about shopping for life insurance, of course, is that you should start researching the matter before you're dead. The Consumer Report on life insurance covers a wide range of life insurance topics, with articles on industry reform and sales practices, along with ratings and recommendations of major life-insurance companies. ✓**PRODIGY**→*jump* cr life insurance

Penn State TIPS: Shopping for Life Insurance Many universities have online reference centers for staff and students, and Penn State's is one of the best. Though this discussion of life insurance is aimed at students— "Most insurance companies realize that life insurance is expensive and holds a low priority for students"—this overview of the theory and reality of the industry is useful for anyone who is confused about how much coverage to take out. ✓INTERNET→*gopher* genesis.ait. psu.edu→Penn State Information→ University Life→Self Help: General →Shopping for Life Insurance

Online brokers

A to Z Insurance Life and medical insurance brokers, representing over 20 insurance companies. Application form is online. ✓IN-TERNET→*www* http://branch.com: 1080/legacy/legacy.html

Continental Insurancenter Offers automobile and homeowners policies, along with a wealth of online features that include policy quotes within 48 hours, claims filing, and policy changes. In addition, the service provides insurance tips for consumers. ✓COM-PUSERVE→*go* cic

One Call Insurance Residents of Massachusetts can take care of their insurance needs with One Call, which gives online premium estimates as well as furnishing policy applications. ✓INTERNET→*www* http://www.powerdog.com/One Call/

Industry news

clari.biz.industry.insurance (ng) Provides reports on various facets of the insurance industry, including the earnings of specific companies and the regulations guiding the risk-management business as a whole. ✓CLARINET

Financial Information on Insurance Companies From Allstate to to Aetna to Chubb, the major insurance corporations are all here, along with elementary directory information, and price and volume for any affiliated issues. ✓INTERNET→*www* http://pawws.se

capl.com/indus70.html

Insurance News Briefs For insurance news rendered in the shortest possible form, there's no place like USA Today. ✓EWORLD→*go* newsstand→USA Today Decisionlines→Insurance

Recent Industry Financial Results If you want to know how your insurance company's balance sheet reads after last year's hurricane, you'll want to check out this gopher site, which furnishes performance reports for the insurance industry. ✓INTERNET→*gopher* infx.in for.com:4200→Recent Industry Financial Results

In the classroom

Syllabi and Reading Lists for Courses in Risk and Insurance Each and every day, our nation's finest business-minded students are being initiated into the secrets of risk management. Don't get left behind. Instead, hop on over to this Website, which collects syllabi and reading lists from across the nation. ✓INTERNET→*www* http://riskweb.bus.utexas. edu/rmisyllabi.html

Teaching Notes for Courses in Risk and Insurance A collection of college lecture notes on risk and insurance courses. ✓IN-TERNET→*gopher* 128.83.218.12→ RISKGopher—The RISKNet (Risk and Insurance) Gopher→Teaching notes, syllabi, reading lists, software→Teaching Notes for Courses in Risk and Insurance

Insurance & law

The Insurance Fraud Research Register Conduct keyword searches of industry and government publications to determine if your neighbor's "accidental fire"

qualifies as insurance fraud, and learn about all the different ways dishonest people and dishonest companies can bilk each other out of millions. ✓INTERNET→*gopher* 128.83.218.12→RISKGopher—The RISKNet (Risk and Insurance) Gopher→Research Databases, Article Abstracts, Working Paper A→Risk and Insurance Abstracts and Working Papers→The Insurance Fraud Research Register

Legi-Slate Law Center The insurance industry is one of the most heavily regulated, and this site contains a wealth of information on every piece of insurance legislation currently pending in Congress. Though the service is available through subscription only (the mudhoney gopher is only a demo), the breadth of resources is stunning. Along with the full text of every bill, the service provides sponsorship information, remarks by supporting and dissenting Congressmen, a history of related legislation, and links to press clippings. Insurance topics include auto insurance, health insurance, life insurance, and liability, as well as less common risk industries such as bank insurance, crop insurance, flood insurance, and survivor old-age insurance. ✓INTERNET …→*gopher* mudhoney. micro.umn.edu 7000 …→*email* legislate@gopher.legislate.com ✍ *Write for help & support*

Regulators

Insurance Regulators If you want to know where to direct your questions about the insurance industry, consult this document, which offers a state-by-state list of insurance commissioners and other regulatory officials. ✓COM-PUSERVE→ius-1085→Insurance Regulators

Consumer power

In America, we're all consumers, and conspicuous ones at that, wolfing down alarming

amounts of goods and services. Like any smart consumers, though, we like to get our money's worth, and the broad spectrum of consumer resources available on the Net can help guarantee just that. Much of the information is research-based and even scholarly—for example, the **Journal of Consumer Research** investigates consumer behavior from a variety of perspectives, including macroeconomic, psychological, and sociological. If that's a little too rich for your blood, step back and review **General Consumer Information**, or go for a little entertainment with **Scams, Swindles, and Hoaxes**—some of the best of our time. **Legi-Slate** contains a vast database of recent legislation relating to consumer behavior. And the next time you bite into a hamburger and find a rat's tail staring back at you, hop right on over to the Website for the **U.S. Consumer Product Safety Commission**, which contains a comprehensive database of recent product recalls, as well as instructions for filing an online complaint.

Consumer Reports *screenshot—from AOL's Consumer Reports Forum*

On the Net

Across the board

clari.living.consumer (ng) Anyone who has ever watched in horror as their new car was recalled by its manufacturer, or felt the sting of an unfair return policy, will feel comfortable here. ✓**CLARINET**

CONSSCI (ml) A list for family and consumer economists, consumer educators, and consumer-affairs specialists. ✓**INTERNET**→ *email* listserv@ukcc.uky.edu ✍ *Type in message body:* subscribe conssci <your full name>

Consumer Forum With hundreds of postings on automobiles, banking, food and health, travel, laws, money savers, scams, and justified complaining, this forum runs the gamut of consumer concerns. Among the more interesting categories are Bargains & Offers and FightBack, the latter of which gives consumers a chance to vent their anger and conquer injustice.

✓**COMPUSERVE**→*go* consumer

Consumer Information Center (CIS-BBS) (bbs) Orginally created to provide the media with access to consumer-oriented press releases, this bulletin board has now evolved into a massive clearinghouse of consumer information, with not only consumer- news updates but also access to hundreds of free federal publications, such as *How to Buy Canned and Frozen Vegetables,* and *Child Health Guide.* ☎→*dial* 703-321-8020→<your login>→ <your password>→/go gate way→D→6 ✓**INTERNET**→*telnet* fed world.gov→<your login>→<your password>→/go gateway→D→6

Consumer_Rep (echo) From advice about the best credit cards to tips on how to save money when traveling, this discussion group is home to a community of money spenders and money savers. In this week's episode, Steve explains VCR repair, Brian debunks the Radio Shack electronic-security devices, and Barb, writing about pricing patterns at K-Mart, informs fellow shoppers that she has found that "some things are cheaper at one store, and other things are cheaper at another store!" ✓**FIDONET**

Consumer's Conference This conference treats a wide variety of consumer issues, not only reviewing and rating products, but also addressing more general issues about economic risks and responsibility. ✓**WELL**→g consumer

misc.consumers (ng) This newsgroup reads like one huge whine cellar, with hundreds of consumers from all walks of life complaining about airfares, lamenting the scourge of telemarketers, and discussing credit policies. While attitudes and tones vary wildly, everyone shares the desire to illuminate the often shadowy world of consumer spending—in short, to put their mouths where their money is. ✓**USENET**

Basics

Consumer Power If you want to complain about the way your dry cleaner ripped you off, or you need to have a charge removed from your American Express but don't know where to begin, check out CompuServe's consumer papers, which offer basic information on state consumer protection, credit, and product safety. ✓**COMPUSERVE**→*go* ius-34

General Consumer Information A library of basic consumer documents, including the Consumer Information Catalog, a consumer quiz, updated consumer information, and multiple documents outlining consumer resources. ✓**COMPUSERVE**→*go* consumer→Libraries→General Consumer Information

Children

misc.kids.consumers (ng) Though this newsgroup's name conjures up images of allowance management—"The Nickel: Don't Spend it All in One Place"—it is actually something different, a candid forum designed to address the financial needs of parents. And as the newsgroup proves time and time again, whether it's discussing the cost of biodegradable diapers or rating pull sleds, kids may be small, but they're not cheap. ✓**USENET**

"If you want to complain about the way your dry cleaner ripped you off, or you need to have a charge removed from your American Express but don't know where to begin, check out CompuServe's Consumer Power."

Electronics

Consumer Electronics Forum The electronics industry turns over so quickly that this year's hot product is often next year's doorstop. With the Consumer Electronics Forum, you can find out which speakers put the most boom in your bass, which VCRs have the best clarity, which CD-ROM players will enable you to meet the future head-on. In addition, the forum includes product descriptions and online technical support from such manufacturers as Videonics and Sennheiser. ✓**COMPUSERVE**→*go* ceforum

Food & drugs

FDA Info and Policies The service includes news releases, product approval lists, and summaries of investigations by the Food and Drug Administration, which is

charged with certifying all food products and pharmaceuticals before they hit the market. There are also selected full-text articles from the *FDA Consumer* magazine. ☎→*dial* 703-321-8020→<your log in>→<your password>→/go gateway→D→17 ✓**INTERNET**→*telnet* fed world.gov→<your login>→<your password>→/go gateway→D→17

News

clari.news.consumer (ng) There are plenty of considerations other than price that might guide your purchase of a new appliance—the environmental policies of the manufacturer, for instance, or performance reports from owners. This group is dedicated to news reports about consumer issues. ✓**CLARINET**

Consumer News A collection of articles on consumer subjects, including automotive purchases, travel costs, and personal credit. ✓**INTERNET**→*gopher* gopher.cic. net→Electronic Serials→General Subject Headings→Business→Consumer News (UIUC)

Consumer News An archive of consumer-related articles published in the *San Jose Mercury News* and maintained in AOL's Mercury Center. ✓**AMERICA ON-LINE**→*keyword* mercury→Consumer News

Consumer Reports The online full-text version of the country's premier source of consumer information rates everything from toasters to sports cars, always with an eye toward affordability, performance, and reliability. ✓**AMERICA ONLINE**→*keyword* consumer ✓**COMPUSERVE**→*go* csr

Journal of Consumer Research What is the psychological

affect of coupons? How much shopping do people do when they are waiting in line? What are the peak times for food shopping? Founded in 1974, the *Journal of Consumer Research* tries to answers these and other questions through scholarly research of consumer behavior. Digests of some journal articles can be found here, as well as electronic subscription forms. ✓**INTERNET**→*gopher* press-gopher.uchicago.edu→Journals from Chicago→JOURNALS IN BUSINESS AND ECONOMICS→JOURNAL OF CONSUMER RESEARCH

Regulation & laws

Consumer Agencies In the United States, consumers are protected by a wide variety of government and regulatory agencies, and this section of CompuServe's Information USA database lists consumer contacts for such issues as health inspection, land management, child support, aging, crime, and whistle blowing. ✓**COMPUSERVE**→*go* ius-1085

Consumer Products Safety Commission According to government statistics, in 1993 product flaws were responsible for some 30 million injuries and 20,000 deaths. With this service, consumers can learn about the national regulations for product safety and browse through years of databases of product recalls and investigations. (Newcomers to the CPSC may find the archives confusing.) Consumers can also file a product complaint online, by noting the particulars (date and location of the incident, a description of the incident, the type of consumer product involved, the manufacturer of the product, and the types of injuries incurred) and e-mailing the report. ✓**INTERNET** ...→*gopher* cpsc.gov ...→*email*

> "What is the psychological affect of coupons? How much shopping do people do when they are waiting in line? *The Journal of Consumer Research* tries to answers these and other questions."

cpsc/g=Arthur/i=K./s=McDonald/o=cpsc/ou1=cpsc-hq2@mhs.attmail.com ✍ *File a product complaint*

Legi-Slate The Consumer Information Center collects complete legislative information on all bills pertaining to consumer affairs, including sponsors, votes, press coverage, and congressional debate. Available by subscription only. ✓**INTERNET** ...→*gopher* mudhoney.micro.umn.edu 7000→Bills Sorted by Subject Key→Consumer Information Center ...→*email* legislate@gopher.legislate.com ✍ *Email for info*

Scams & schemes

Scams & Ripoffs The board provides a place for the fleeced to complain about their fleecing. The Warnings/ Scams library archives Federal Trade Commission documents on a wide variety of bunco jobs. ✓**COMPUSERVE**→*go* confor→messages *or* libraries→scams & ripoffs

Scams, Swindles, and Hoaxes This conference includes warnings about hoaxes-in-progress and fond reminiscence of swindles past. Along with investment caveats, there's some discussion of the figure of the flim flam man in American culture ("Rip-offs: From Melville to T-Rex") and some discussion of the psychological dimensions of dishonesty. ✓**WELL**→g scam

The environment

The EnviroProducts Directory Some companies are trying their best not to rape and pillage the ecosystem, and this directory pays tribute to them. Lists of products by name, company, and geographic region to help consumers find green companies and products. ✓**INTERNET**→*www* http://orca.envirolink.org/enviroproducts.html

Values

alt.consumers.free-stuff (ng) If you get something free, at no risk to your pocketbook or wallet, have you actually acquired anything at all? While you're waiting for the answer, you might want to visit this newsgroup, which dwells on the practical aspects of no-cost acquisition. What companies are running giveaway initiatives? What companies pretend to offer free services but load up on invisible charges? What are the best toys you can get from cereal these days? And does the Internet itself qualify as "free stuff"? ✓**USENET**

WinPrice v1.0 A comparison-shopping program that calculates the best unit price on varied quantities. Great for grocery shopping. Shareware for Windows. ✓**PC OHIO**→d→*Download a file:* PRICE 10.ZIP

Tykes as tycoons

Kids don't work, they don't pay taxes, and yet, they have disposable income. Amazing.

But as important as it might be to trust kids with an allowance, it's also important to help them understand fiscal responsibility. Investment and planned spending? Good. Three-day Milk-Duds benders? Bad. Help your progeny learn the value of a dollar with **Consumer Reports for Kids**, which not only rates toys and games but also addresses more general issues about family finance and filial accountability. And if Richie Rich won't sit still for a lecture, turn him on to **Interstellar Trader**, which teaches that economic principles don't stop at the borders of the planet Earth.

Macauley Culkin as Richie Rich— downloaded from CompuServe's Eforum

On the Net

Budgets

Cash for Kids v1.0t (Windows) With Cash for Kids, you can help your children learn how to save and budget money, track funds, and set spending goals. For ages 5 to 13. ✓**PC OHIO**→d→*Download a file:* CFK.ZIP

Careers

The History of Clarissa's Career Summaries of episodes in which Clarissa of the popular kid's TV show *Clarissa Explains It All*, explores career options. For in-

stance, in "Parents Who Say No," Clarissa gets a job at Baxter Beach carnival. ✓**INTERNET**→*www* http://www.ee.surrey.ac.uk/Personal/Clarissa/career.html

Consumer reports

Consumer Reports for Kids Both about kids and for kids, these consumer reports rate and recommend such products as toys, bikes, and board games. ✓**PRODIGY**→*jump* cr kids

Games

CIRCUS: Teach coins and change Targeted at younger children learning to recognize coins. When a child answers correctly, Flippy the Clown rewards him or her. Shareware for PCs. ✓**AMERICA ONLINE**→*keyword* pc software→

Browse the Software Libraries→ Specialty Libraries→Education→ *Search by file name:* CIRCUS.ZIP

Interstellar Trader Travel from planet to planet amassing wealth and power as you buy, sell, and trade goods. Designed to teach basic economic theories and mathematics. Macintosh shareware. ✓**AMERICA ONLINE**→*keyword* med→ Software Libraries→Software Search→*Search by file name:* Interstellar Trader.sea

Medieval Trader Still buying, selling, and trading, but this time you're a medieval trader wandering from village to village. Designed to teach basic economic theories and mathematics. Macintosh shareware. ✓**AMERICA ONLINE** →*keyword* med→Software Libraries →Software Search→*Search by file name:* Medieval Trader.sea

The Net

Kids Internet Delight Learning about the Net is a solid time investment for kids, and this site links to entertaining and educational Websites for children— from elementary schools online to a virtual dinosaur museum. ✓**INTERNET**→*www* http://www.clark.net /pub/journalism/kid.html

> "When a child answers correctly, Flippy the Clown rewards him or her."

Do it yourself

Tim Allen's reign on *Home Improvement* testifies to the popularity of do-it-yourself

shows. In fact, the Mr. Fixit type is an archetypal American hero—the upstanding citizen who can't see spending astronomical amounts on professional woodworking when he can just go down to the basement, sand the banister posts with his very own hands, and then report his carpentry victory to **rec.woodworking**. Need a new front door? Do it yourself. Want to put some chattahoochee on the patio? Do it yourself. From GEnie's **Home Improvement RoundTable**, which contains tips on home repair, to the **Consumer Electronics RoundTable**, which brings handymen into the world of high-technology, the Net's resources are plentiful. There are even a handful of Websites offering plans for home building or expansion, including blueprints for the magical **LAMA Elevating Mezzanine**.

Tim Allen of Home Improvement—*from America Online's NBC Forum*

On the Net

Across the board

alt.home.repair (ng) If your dream home is starting to seem like the disastrous house in the movie *The Money Pit*, you might want to post your laments on this newsgroup, where home-improvement experts will solve your particular dilemma or or, at the very least, soothe you with horror tales of their own. Wide-ranging and informative, this newsgroup should be mandatory reading for anyone who is thinking of tiling over that old floor or rewiring the guest room. ✓ **USENET**

Books That Work Intended to be a clearinghouse of articles relating to home repair, landscaping, and gardening although there's not much here now. In the future, the new site's architects hope to use it as a link to home repair and improvement sites on the Internet, and are currently soliciting suggestions by email. ✓ **INTERNET** ...→
www http://www.btw.com/ ...→

email webmaster@btw.com ✍
Email a suggestion

Handman (echo) Mike has a

> **"'I'm just trying to understand it,' your friend says, plaintively, as the bits and pieces of your laser-disc player lay strewn around him."**

problem with his central air conditioning. It seems that his dog chewed apart the low-voltage wires leading to the outside fan/compressor unit, and though the circuit breaker tripped, the reconnected circuit doesn't seem to be working. Can anyone offer him any advice? And speaking of advice, does anyone out there know anything about biodegradable caskets or painting boat hulls? ✓**RELAYNET**

Home Improvement & Repairs Forum Forum for the house proud (or wanna-be proud) includes a message board, documents for downloading, and a polling area in which home-repair nuts can ask questions of the entire forum group. ✓**DELPHI**→*go* custom 274

Home Improvement Round-Table A site for the home carpenters, plumbers, and painters who have decided they can do it better and cheaper than professionals. A whole workshop of categories of posted tips by and for handymen and handywomen: grandfather clocks, skylights, gutters, decks, retaining walls, and more tools than you could shake a claw hammer at. There is even a message board for environmental concerns related to home improvement. There's also a real-time chat room and a software downloading area. ✓**GENIE**→*key-word* diy

High-tech handymen

Consumer Electronics Round-Table Does everyone have that one friend who insists on tinkering with every high-tech appliance that crosses his path. "I'm just trying to understand it," he says plaintively, as the bits and pieces of your laser-disc player lay strewn around him in a semicircle. Get this friend to GEnie's Consumer Electronics RoundTable, which

dives headfirst into the arcane world of satellite dishes and Uniblitzes. If your friend can restrain himself from taking his computer apart, he might learn something. ✓**GENIE**→*keyword* ce

Plans for sale

The Advant Home Buy energy-efficient, environmentally-friendly home plans, including sketches. ✓**INTERNET**→*www* http://www.sccsi.com/Advant/homes.html

Archway Press A ten-book collection of over 500 house plans in country styles is on sale. ✓**INTERNET**→*www* http://branch.com:1080/archway/archway.html

The Domespace Home All-wood prefabricated dome-shaped structures, assembled by you or the supplier. Order online and then hang up the sampler: "There's No Place Like Dome." ✓**INTERNET**→*www* http://branch.com:1080/dome/dome.html

The LAMA Elevating Mezzanine Expand your living space with a strong, lightweight platform that can be raised or lowered at the touch of a button. The Mezzanine can be equipped with telephone jacks, electrical receptacles, halogen lights, and a remote control. Check out this electronic catalog of products. ✓**INTERNET**→*www* http://branch.com:1080/lama/lama.html

Woodworking

rec.woodworking (ng) A huge resource for woodworkers, with thousands of messages about stained maple, joiners, and tablesaws. One man even wants to know if he can dry his wood in a microwave. (He can.) ✓**USENET**

It's April 15!

Since it happens once a year, you have a habit of getting a little depressed when it

comes around, and using it to mark your inexorable crawl toward a deep gray grave. Your birthday? Nope. The income-tax filing deadline. And while paying taxes is never painless, the online taxation resources available to ordinary citizens cushion the blow significantly. Newcomers to the world of electronic taxes should start at **Tax Sites on the Net**, a wonderful Web page with links to tax-related mailing lists, newsgroups, and tax-form libraries. Or maybe you'd rather spend some time in **misc.taxes FAQ** and **Frequently Asked Questions**, two income-tax primers that cover everything from inheritance to itemizing. As the ides of April roll around, though, you'll want to be spending less time researching tax issues, and more time actually preparing your returns. To assist you in that task, **Taxing Times** has a huge catalog of tax forms that can either be downloaded or emailed to you, and the Internal Revenue Service itself maintains a document center (**IRS Tax Forms/Documents**). In addition, a number of services

Harold Lloyd—downloaded from CompuServe's Archive Forum

permit electronic filing of your return—check **Electronic Tax Filing Information** for details, or drop in on the **Information Reporting Program BBS**. When you're done writing that check to the tax man, read the amusing **Tax Trivia**.

On the Net

Across the board

Frequently Asked Questions Maintained by the Internal Revenue Service, this site asks and answers common tax questions, including "Do I have to fill out all the forms in my tax package," "Can I get the Earned Income Credit?" and the ever-popular "What is 'itemizing'?" ✓ **INTERNET→** *www* http://www.ustreas.gov/treasury /bureaus/irs/questns.html

Important Income Tax Dates for 1994 Don't get caught unaware. Use H & R Block's Income Tax calendar. ✓ **COMPUSERVE→***go* hrb

Income Tax Information A huge and frequently updated list of income tax resources on the

Net, this site not only lists sites for IRS forms, instructions, and publications, but links to newsgroups, statistical data, and government offices. ✓**INTERNET**→*www* http://ftp.netcom.com/pub/ftmexpat/html/taxsites.html

IRS Tele-Tax A phone service that provides recorded messages on more than 140 tax topics, Tele-Tax also has an introductory Web page, which includes a table of contents and a full list of local access numbers. ✓**INTERNET**→*www* http://www.ustreas.gov/treasury/bureaus/irs/teletax.html

misc.taxes FAQ Seeks to clarify basic tax problems and procedures through a series of questions and answers. ✓**INTERNET**→*ftp* rtfm.mit.edu→anonymous→<your email address>→/pub/usenet-by-group/misc.taxes

Tax Information By Category Whether you're a businessman, a farmer, a Navy SEAL, a landlord, or a retiree, you have your own set of tax rules and responsibilities, and H & R Block—the tax preparation giant that owns CompuServe—explains them all for you with this easy-to-use guide to basic tax information. ✓**COMPUSERVE**→*go* hrb

Taxes—IRS Information The tax portion of the immense Information USA library offers leads to clear and concise articles on topics such as tax loopholes, tax help, free tax preparation, and tax publications, as well as addresses and phone numbers for instructions on how to file by phone or computer. ✓**COMPUSERVE**→*go* ius-5494

Advice

Block on Taxes Julian Block, the tax specialist renowned for his "ability to translate complicated tax laws into plain English," offers tips and explains loopholes in the nightmarishly complex world of taxation. Prodigy's service comes complete with past columns and a photo of the estimable Mr. Block. ✓**PRODIGY**→*jump* block on taxes

CPA Online: Tax Questions Answered Find the CPA on your CPU with this service, which collects selected postings from misc.invest to create a resource book of tax queries, with detailed answers from a tax consultant. ✓**INTERNET**→*gopher* gopher.tc.umn.edu→Internet Services→List Servers→Law Lists→FEDTAX-L Archive

Chat

Investors Forum Curious about how your stock market losses affect your taxes? And what about those bonds in the closet? If you decide to cash them December 31 in the year prior to maturity, how are they taxed? Ask and ye shall be answered, if not always accurately. ✓**COMPUSERVE**→*go* investors→Financial Planning/Taxes

misc.taxes (ml/ng) This is the only Usenet newsgroup devoted entirely to taxation, and the participants don't waste any time in getting right to the heart of the matter, often with the online help of professional accountants. How does the government decide whether to grant an extension? What about home business expenses? If you buy baby furniture and lose the child in childbirth, can the crib be deducted? Hard questions, but asked and answered here. Archives of the group are available. ✓**USENET** ✓**INTERNET**→*email* list serv@shsu.edu ✉ *Type in message body:* subscribe fedtax-l <your first name> *Archives:* ✓**INTERNET**→*gopher* gopher.kentlaw.edu

→Internet Services→List Servers→Law Lists→ FEDTAX-L Archive

Tax & Accounting (echo) General discussion about tax and accounting issues, with considerable participation from professionals and a steady flow of questions from bewildered taxpayers. ✓**RELAYNET**→

Tax Bulletin Board When it comes time to pay the piper, you might as well have some commiseration, and you'll find it on AOL's tax bulletin board, which collects postings on everything from severance payment to inheritance taxes to tax preparation software. ✓**AMERICA ONLINE**→*keyword* tax

Tax Bulletin Board Addresses a wide range of tax topics, including psychological insights into why people don't like to pay taxes. In addition, it covers the mechanics of taxation, the ins and outs of tax law, and the advent of the 1040PC, the first form for online filing. ✓**GENIE**→*keyword* tax→Tax Bulletin Board

Tax Discussion From income taxes to capital gains taxes, from property taxes to corporate taxes, our government has plenty of ways to lighten our pockets, and most of them are discussed here. With that said, it should also be noted that traffic on the tax highway slows to a crawl out of season. ✓**PRODIGY**→*jump* money talk bb

Working From Home Forum Members of the work force who base their business in the home have a unique set of tax concerns, and this forum targets them directly. How can you apply for corporate status? If you work in two rooms can you deduct them both? Can you escape business taxes by filing personal bankruptcy? Mem-

CYBERPOWER!™

Filing Your Taxes

Have I got a problem. I had my tax return finished, and I made copies for my records, and then I left my file in a taxicab. I called the cab company, but it's gone. I still have the figures—in fact, I'm expecting a refund—but it's April 15, and I don't think I have time to start over. I've heard whispers about online filing, but I'm scared that it won't work for me. What can I do?

You should probably head over to CompuServe's tax area (keyword: taxes). Once you've arrived there, you'll find three different tax-related services—forms for downloading, tax software for downloading, and instructions for online filing. Forget about downloading forms—while these documents might have been useful to you back in February, when you would have had time to complete, print, and mail them, they're pretty much useless on the ides of April. Instead, head straight for the software area. Here, you'll find full versions of tax preparation programs like TaxCut and TurboTax. Download them at retail cost (between $20 and $40), and you should be able to create an electronic 1040 in a few short hours.

Once you have created your electronic return, brace yourself for the miracle of online filing. As miracles go, this one has elegant simplicity—in conjunction with the IRS, CompuServe has enabled citizens to electronically deliver their TaxCut or TurboTax documents. With CompuServe's special instructions, you'll be able to email your return to the IRS service center in Austin, Texas, the office responsible for handling all electronic returns. Keep in mind that this service only applies to taxpayers expecting refund checks; until Congress approves electronic filing of balance-due returns, or until the IRS takes credit cards, electronic filing is useless if you owe the Federal Government money.

If you qualify, electronic return has several advantages. It's fast. It's free. And then there's the convenience of a quick response. Within a few days of filing, electronic taxpayers will receive email notification that the IRS has received their return. If the return is accepted, the government will confirm the amount of the return; if it is rejected, the government will furnish reasons for the rejection. And depending on how you have requested your refund, you

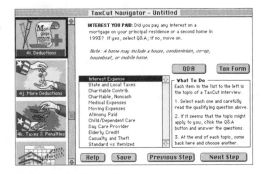

TaxCut for the Macintosh

may also receive information on direct deposit of the refund check.

Finally, a word of caution. Though electronic filing shrinks the paper trail, it cannot completely eliminate conventional documentation. While the tax process itself begins and ends online—you can download TaxCut, calculate your refund, and deliver the return without ever leaving Cyberspace—the law of the land still requires that a taxpayer signature accompany any tax return. For that reason, all electronic taxpayers are required to file IRS form 8453, which authorizes the electronic return. The 8453 includes a filing number assigned to your individual return by the IRS, and while completing the form is as simple as signing your name, don't forget to mail it—or your entire electronic return may be invalidated.

bers share advice and information. ✓**COMPUSERVE**→*go* working from home→Accounting /Tax

Forms

Government Publications Catalog Through the Government Publications Catalog, you can order any recent government report, form, or document. ✓**COMPUSERVE**→*go* gpo

IRS Tax Forms/Documents Co-sponsored by CompuServe and the IRS, this service provides online access to almost 500 federal tax forms, instructions, and publications. Forms are stored in PDF, a format than can be read with Adobe Acrobat Reader, and are accepted by the IRS at filing time. ✓**COMPUSERVE**→*go* taxforms

Tax Forms Through GEnie's tax forms service, you can obtain most Federal income tax forms, along with a selection of state documents. ✓**GENIE**→*keyword* tax

Tax Forms and Help via E-mail Whether you're looking for a T schedule or a W-3SS, a 706GS(T), or a run-of-the-mill old 1040, you'll want to visit this site, which explains how to order hundreds of tax forms through Email. If you don't have a full Internet connection, send Email to tax-forms@scubed.com for information. ✓**INTERNET** ...→*www* http://www.scubed.com:8001/tax/email.html ...→*email* tax-forms@scubed.com ✍ *Write for help & support*

Taxing Times Presented as a public service by Maxwell Labs, this is a repository of tax-related documents, including most state and federal income tax forms, instructions, and related publications. In addition, you can down-

load Canadian income tax forms and link to most of the important income tax sites on the Internet. ✓**INTERNET**→*www* http://www.scubed.com:8001/tax/tax.html

Online filing

Electronic Filing Be the first on your block to file your 1040PC forms online, then join other guinea pigs in discussing the pros and cons of computer taxation. ✓**COMPUSERVE**→*go* taxreturn

Electronic Tax Filing Information (1040 BBS) (bbs) Once upon a time, tax returns had to be hand-delivered. Then they were delivered by pony. Then the mailman took them to the IRS. Now the IRS is allowing taxpayers to pay the piper online, with the specially designed 1040PC form. The main bulletin board of this BBS contains extensive information about the 1040PC, along with a list of the electronic filing coordinator in each state. The IRS invites comments and sometimes permits users access to an online tax library. ☎→*dial* 202-927-4180→<your login>→<your password>→/go gateway→D→33 ✓**INTERNET**→*telnet* fedworld.gov→<your login>→<your password>→/go gateway→D→33

H&R Block Filing Service America's largest firm dealing with the preparation of federal, state, and local income tax returns, offers a wide range of tax services on CompuServe, including preparation. ✓**COMPUSERVE**→*go* hrb

Information Reporting Program BBS (bbs) File 1042S tax returns or download documents and forms that relate to returns, including 1099, 1098 and W2s. ☎→*dial* 304-263-2749

Intuit Tax Online BB A fairly new message board for TurboTax and MacInTax users. Electronic filing is its own topic. ✓**PRODIGY**→*jump* intuit tax bb

Magnetic Media Bulletin Board System (bbs) Run by the IRS, this Philadephia-based service allows taxpayers to file 1041, 1040 NR, and 941E forms online. ☎→*dial* 215-516-7625

Quicken Those filing electronically with Quicken will not deal directly with the IRS—instead, you create your tax return with either MacInTax or TurboTax, modem the return to Intuit, and the company forwards the electronic file to the IRS after reviewing them for formatting and accuracy. Quicken's online filing procedure has already helped more than 40 million taxpayers; state tax forms are also available. Voice call 800-624-9065 for more information. ✓**QUICKEN ONLINE**

U.S. Federal Tax Return Preparation Federal income tax instructions and related materials. ✓**INTERNET**→*gopher* pub.vse.cz→Public Domain Software and Internet Documents→Public domain software for MS DOS→SimTel MS-DOS collection (mirror)→177. taxes U.S. federal tax return preparation and related so.

State tax information

State Tax Information A gateway to online government information for most of the states in the Union; income tax information is easily retrievable from a general file or from state-by-state menus. ✓**INTERNET**→*gopher* marvel.loc. gov→Government Information→State and Local Government Information (U.S.)

Tax law

Congressional Bills A searchable database of all bills proposed by the 103rd Congress. ✓ **INTERNET**→*wais* wais://diamond.house.gov:210/USHOUSE_house_bill_text_103rd

Law Center Search through the database to find articles, decisions, and opinions concerning tax law, most of which are taken from Tax Notes Today. ✓ **GENIE**→*keyword* lawcenter **$**

Tax Legislation Database This database chronicles the passage of every tax bill proposed in Congress. The legislative sites touch on everything from overviews to abstracts and digests, committee referrals, committee schedules, recorded votes, remarks by members, committee reports, and relevant press coverage clipped from *The Washington Post*, the *National Journal*, and *Congressional Quarterly*. The scope of tax categories is truly impressive: business and corporate income; capital gains; gift, estate, and inheritance; income; property; sales, use, excise, and franchise. The gopher is only a demo. Email Legi-Slate for information about subscribing. ✓ **INTERNET** ...→*gopher* mudhoney.micro. umn.edu 7000 ...→*email* legislate @gopher.legislate.com ✍ *Email for information*

U.S. Code A full-text version of the U.S. Code, available for browsing or downloading. ✓ **INTERNET**→ *www* http://cpsr.org/pub/uscode

Villanova Tax Law Compendium This compendium of student tax papers elucidates such issues as the state income-tax responsibilities of non-resident professional athletes. ✓ **INTERNET** ...→*www* http://ming.law.vill.edu/taxcomp/taxcomp.html ...→*gopher* ming.law.vill.edu→The Villanova Tax Law Compendium ...→*ftp* ming.law.vill.edu→anonymous→ <your email address>→/pub/law /taxcomp

Tax stats

Public Taxpayer Statistical Information (IRS-SOI) The message on this BBS's home screen reads "even Bill Clinton pays taxes," and if you search long and hard enough in this vast storehouse of statistics, you'll be sure to find him, at least statistically. Along with hundreds of millions of other Americans, Bill and Hillary are represented in such absorbing reports as taxpayer usage study, state-to-state migration, individual statistical information, and county income data files. ☎→*dial* 703-321-8020 →<your login>→<your password>→/go gateway→D→104 ✓ **INTERNET** →*telnet* fedworld. gov→<your login>→ <your password>→/go gateway→ D →104

Software & support

Intuit Personal Tax Preparation Bulletin Board Formerly run by ChipSoft, the publisher of TurboTax and MacInTax before the company was bought by Intuit, this BBS offers tech support for the tax preparation programs. There is also a library of downloads on subjects like electronic filing and business taxes and a number of conferences for message-based discussions about tax and tax preparation issues. ☎ →*dial* 602-295-3261

MacInTax/TurboTax Created for use with Quicken, these programs—MacInTax for the Macintosh and TurboTax for the PC—have already aided with the electronic filings of more than 40 million income tax returns. The current versions can print out completed federal tax forms or prepare data for Quicken's electronic filing program. Both programs read Quicken data, rewarding those who have kept their accounts current all year, but they also work fine for taxpayers who have never before used Quicken. Voice call 800-624-9065 or 800-964-1040 for more information.

Simply Tax Offers updates, demos, and docs for Simply Tax, as well as comments from program users and manufacturers. ✓ **COMPUSERVE**→*go* simply

Tax Software Dozens of tax preparation and calculation programs. ✓ **GENIE**→*keyword* tax

TaxCut Software One of the most popular tax management programs on the market, this support forum offers product updates and pricing information along with technical advice. ✓ **COMPUSERVE**→*go* meca

Tax miscellany

Speakers' Service Hire an H & R Block expert to clarify taxing matters—and for free. ✓ **COMPUSERVE**→*go* mail→70007,4612 ✓ **INTERNET**→ *email* 70007.4612@ compuserve.com

Tax Trivia People in China paid their taxes with large sheets of pressed tea. Jivara tribesmen paid with shrunken heads. And scientists believe that there may be civilizations on other planets where taxes are paid simply by opening the eyes very, very wide. These and other fascinating facts about death's unavoidable partner are available as part of H & R Block's online tax service on CompuServe. ✓ **COMPUSERVE**→*go* hrb

Taxes shareware

1099s Made Easy Allows printing of 1099 tax forms on a LaserWriter II. Needs HyperCard. ✓**AMERICA ONLINE**→*keyword* pf software→Taxes→1099SMADEEASY. SEA (Macintosh)

1993 Tax Template (XL) Shareware spreadsheet for 1993 Tax Forms 1040, Schedules A, B, D and Minnesota M-1. Needs Excel 2.2 or newer. ✓**AMERICA ONLINE**→ *keyword* pf software→Taxes→XL 93 1040/ABD/M-1.SIT (Macintosh)

AM-Tax Tax preparation software for individual filing. ✓**INTERNET**→ *ftp* oak.oakland.edu→anonymous→ <your email address>→/pub/ msdos/taxes→AMTAX93.ZIP (DOS)

E-Tax Approved tax transmission program for modem, fax, or phone. Transmits directly to I.R.S.; checks returns for accuracy as well. (Does not prepare returns, though.) ✓**EXEC-PC**→File Collection Menu→Mahoney IBM Compatible DOS→ETAX.ZIP (DOS)

IRS Log v1.2 Keeps track of computer usage time for IRS reports. ✓**PC OHIO**→d→*Download a file:* IRSLOG 12.ZIP (DOS)

MFS v3.3 Married tax filing status analysis program. ✓**INTERNET**→ *ftp* oak.oakland.edu→anonymous→ <your email address>→/pub/ msdos/taxes→MFS3X3.ZIP (DOS)

O-Tax Form 1040 & schedule A/B income tax preparation program. ✓**INTERNET**→*ftp* oak. oakland.edu→anonymous→<your email address>→/pub/msdos/ taxes→OTAX93X1.ZIP (DOS)

Payroll Withholding Calcula-

tor v. 1.1 Shareware file which calcuates witholding tax for payroll, checks W-2s when preparing Income Taxes, and helps you figure for the best way to fill out W-4s at the beginning of each year. ✓**COMPUSERVE**→*go* work→Libraries →Accounting & Taxes→pay93.zip (DOS)

Quick Tax Estimator v. 1.12 S. Get a fast estimate of the total tax, earned income credit, child/dependent care credit, and your refund amount. ✓**COMPUSERVE**→*go* work→Libraries→Accounting & Taxes→QTAX.EXE (DOS)

QuickTax v1.08 Plans taxes to get the most from deductions, IRAs, savings plans, etc. Finds filing status and requirements, dependencies, withholding allowances, estimated tax. 1040 Tax Form Preparation Program ✓**EXEC-PC**→File Collection Menu→Mahoney IBM Compatible DOS→ QTAX08.ZIP (DOS)

Share-TAX/1040 v2.0 1040 form tax preparation program. Shareware. ✓**INTERNET**→*ftp* oak. oakland.edu→anonymous→<your email address>→/pub/msdos /taxes→STAX93.zip (DOS)

ShareTax 1040 Tax Form Preparation Program ✓**EXEC-PC**→File Collection Menu→Mahoney IBM Compatible DOS→ SHARETAX.ZIP ✓**INTERNET**→*ftp* oak.oakland.edu→ anonymous→<your email address> →/pub/msdos/taxes→STAX93.ZIP (DOS)

Tax Check v1.1 Fast and reliable estimates of owed federal taxes. Color or mono option. Easy to use. ✓**PC OHIO**→d→*Download a file:* TC93_11.ZIP (DOS)

Tax Fax Electronic tax filing by fax (form 1040EZ). ✓**INTERNET**→ *ftp* oak.oakland.edu→anonymous→ <your email address>→/pub /msdos/taxes→TAXFX93A.ZIP (DOS)

TaxList Organizer Organizes tax records. ✓**COMPUSERVE**→ ibmapp→Libraries→*Search for a file:* TL110.LZH (DOS)

Tax Sort v1.e Organize your income and expenses for April 15th. Prints reports. Get rid of that shoebox! ✓**PC OHIO**→d→*Download a file:* TAXSOR1E.ZIP (DOS)

Turbo Auto Log v1.01 Flexible program calculates auto logs for business tax purposes. Can be imported to spreadsheets or printed directly. ✓**EXEC PC**→File Collection Menu→Mahoney IBM Compatible DOS→ETAX.ZIP (DOS)

TValue Calculates amortization for leases and mortgages. ✓**EXEC-PC**→File Collection Menu→Mahoney IBM Compatible DOS→ TVALUE.EXE (DOS)

W3s Made Easy Program to help you prepare W3 tax forms. ✓**AMERICA ONLINE**→*keyword* pf software→Taxes→W3s Made Easy.sea (Macintosh)

Wages v1.00 Calculates hourly, weekly, monthly, or yearly wages. ✓**PC OHIO**→d→*Download a file:* WAGES100.ZIP (DOS)

WPro93S v0.94 1040 tax return preparation program comes with 52 forms, fee schedule, front page, calculator, and more. ✓**PC-OHIO**→d→*Download a file:* WPRO93S.ZIP (DOS)

Part 2

Milestones

Buying a car

If you're an aspiring pizza delivery woman with a newborn child and a deadbeat boy-

friend who was last seen in the Vegas pokey, car trouble is the worst nightmare imaginable. And when the car trouble is especially severe— i.e., you don't have one—the headaches can get bad. But don't fret. Never fear. Online automobile resources are here. Before you even reach for your checkbook, teach yourself the basics of automotive selection and financing with CompuServe's **Automobile Forum**, a roomy and high-performance area with a variety of car-related message boards. Then visit one of the online car lots— either **DealerNet** or **Webfoot's Used Car Lot**—to research models, options, and prices, along with service and parts. Grab a little consumer guidance from **Autovantage** and some road-test results from **Car and Driver**, and then drop by **rec.autos.marketplace** to check out the listings. And once you get that car, make sure you contact **SonicPRO** to order an alarm.

Rolls Royce—downloaded from http://www.sgi.com/grafical/gallery/rolls.jpg

Across the board

Automobile Forum One of the best online sources of general information about cars—with libraries and message boards on performance, safety, and insurance. What's the best used Nissan? Is the Taurus a good deal? Why does the Neon say "Hi" all the time? And why hasn't anyone invented a device to turn off a turn signal after 20 minutes of infernal blinking? ✓**COMPUSERVE**→*go* cars

Automotive Mailing Lists A complete list of all the automotive mailing lists on the Net with links to their archives. ✓**INTERNET**→*www* http://triumph.cs.utah.edu/lists.html

DealerNet "A world of personal transportation on your desktop," DealerNet links to dealers and showrooms for all types of autos. Search for parts, accessories, and affordable service. ✓**INTERNET**→ *www* http://www.dealernet.com/

Webfoot's Used Car Lot Collecting vintage Bentleys? Need a new headlight for your 1984 Honda? Webfoot's links to dozens of sites for used-car sales, used car parts, and general automotive in-

formation. ✓**INTERNET**→*www* http://pond.cso.uiuc.edu/ducky/cars/national.car.lot.html

Worldwide Car Network Chat with other car enthusiasts and hobbyists, about your choice of pre- and postwar automobiles, motorcycles, or pickup trucks. The Worldwide Car forum includes message boards on pricing, performance, and technology. If you contribute interesting material to the forum or pay a $49 fee, you join the Worldwide Car Network which provides online access to an international assortment of auto classifieds, auction announcements, car-show calendars, news, and car values and histories. ✓**COMPUSERVE**→*go* wcn $

Buying guides

Automobile Information Center Wholesale and retail prices of new, used, and collector automobiles from 1978 to the present will help you bargain with your local dealer. Or for a small fee, you can download information on over 50 different car-buying services to have the bargaining done for you. ✓**COMPUSERVE**→*go* ai

Autonet Learn to negotiate a lower price on a new car by knowing the difference between dealer invoice price, and the manufacturer's suggested price or download prices and specs on all new domestic and foreign cars, vans, and trucks (only $4 per report). The accuracy and completeness of the reports are checked, but they are not guaranteed. ✓**PRODIGY**→*jump* autonet **$**

AutoPages A comprehensive source of information about exotic and classic automobiles, with lists of dealers, information about manufacturers, articles, and reviews. ✓**INTERNET**→*www* http://www.clark.net/pub/networx/autopage/autopage.html

Autoquot-R Looking to buy a car made after 1980? Buy a full report that includes the year, make, base price, standard equipment and option packages, warranty information, and even the available colors of your car of choice. New and used car leasing, new car ordering and leasing services, and free-of-charge appraisals for used cars. ✓**COMPUSERVE**→*go* aq **$** ✓**GENIE**→*keyword* autoquot-r

Autovantage Do your research online before buying or leasing a new or used car. View summaries of new and used cars, including an overview of the base model, available options, recall history, and road-test highlights. Members can have Autovantage arrange details of the purchase of a car at a local dealer at an average savings of $2,000, and a savings of 20 percent at over 10,000 national service centers is also available for members. A yearly membership costs $49. ✓**PRODIGY**→*jump* auto-

vantage **$** ✓**COMPUSERVE**→*go* av ✓**GENIE**→*keyword* cars ✓**AMERICA ONLINE**→*keyword* autovantage ✓**DELPHI**→*go* shop auto

Consumer Reports Reports on road tests, new car profiles and ratings, reliability, and recall information, in addition to articles with titles such as "How to Drive Home a Bargain" and "Should You Lease?" Good basic information for the prospective buyer. ✓**AMERICA ONLINE**→*keyword* consumer reports ✓**COMPUSERVE**→*go* csr-1

New Car Showroom Find the car that's right for your needs. After comparing detailed lists of standard and optional features and dealer invoice prices, visit the showroom (for a small fee) to make better-educated car, van, and truck buying decisions. NHTSA crash test data, news briefs from the auto industry, and sales information aid your buying decision. ✓**COMPUSERVE**→*go* newcar

Car companies

Alfa Romeo All about the Italian car manufacturer, including mechanical issues, images, and resources for spare parts and used Alfas. If you're an owner, you can register your Alfa on the Who's Who of Alfa Romeo owners. ✓**INTERNET**→*www* http://amdahl1.cs.latrobe.edu.au:8080/~baragry/AlfaRomeo/HomePage.html

Cadillac Get information and free full-color catalogs of the new 1995 models, including the Seville STS, Eldorado Touring Coup, Deville Concours, and Northstar. Cadillac will even help you find a plan to finance your new car, and offer you 24-hour roadside service and trip-routing assistance. ✓**PRODIGY**→*jump* cadillac ✓**COMPUSERVE**→*go* cmc

Chrysler Information and brochures are available for new Chrysler products including the Cirrus, Concorde, Lebaron Convertible, New Yorker, Town & Country, and both the Plymouth Neon and Voyager. ✓**PRODIGY**→*jump* chrysler

Ford Once you've taken a new car for a test drive with the Ford Simulator 5.0 read about the credit program that best fits your needs and find the dealer nearest you with the local-dealer locator. If you've been using your Ford Citibank credit card, you can save up to $3,500 on your new Ford. Not only is there information, prices, and brochures on all 1995 models of Ford, Lincoln, and Mercury cars and trucks, but Ford also sells videos, software, and logo clothing and accessories. ✓**PRODIGY**→*jump* ford cars ✓**COMPUSERVE**→*go* fd

> "What's the best used Nissan? Is the Taurus a good deal? Why does the Neon say 'Hi' all the time? And why hasn't anyone invented a device to turn off a turn signal after 20 minutes of infernal blinking?"

Honda Order a free brochure and view information about the 1995 Honda lineup. ✓**PRODIGY**→*jump* honda

Mazda Request free brochures or browse information on the full line of Mazda cars, and locate the Mazda dealer nearest you. ✓**PRODIGY**→*jump* mazda

Pontiac Showroom Learn about Pontiac's "philosophy" of driving excitement by looking at the showroom of the most recent models, or by ordering a free brochure. If you have a General Motors Mastercard, you may already be earning up to $500–$1,000 a year toward a new car. Further help financing your new car can be found by looking at what are being referred to as the Smartlease and Smartbuy plans. ✓**COMPUSERVE**→*go* pon ✓**PRODIGY**→*jump* pontiac

Saturn Order free brochures on the latest Saturn models. In addition, the forum includes a bulletin board where Saturn owners chat about their cars. ✓**PRODIGY**→*jump* saturn

Toyota Information and I-love-what-you-do-for-me brochures about Toyota's most recent models. ✓**PRODIGY**→*jump* toyota

Magazines

Car and Driver The popular automotive magazine has gone online, with road tests, message forums, libraries, a store, an information center, and a Car and Driver chat area. The most recent issue of *Car and Driver* is also available. ✓**AMERICA ONLINE**→*keyword* car and driver

Road and Track Oriented primarily toward luxury and sports cars, Road and Track includes industry news and information on new products. The table of contents of the most current issue of *Road and Track* magazine is available, as are articles about how to get a bargain on a new car, road tests, and updates on new technology. The library contains photos and back issues of *Road and Track*. ✓**AMERICA ONLINE**→*keyword* road

Marketplace

ba.market.vehicles (ng) John wants a Porsche 911 SC 78–83; Bejan is selling a 1988 Jeep Cherokee Limited; and Mark's looking for a good mechanic to fix his Saab. What do they have in common? They live in the Bay Area. ✓**USENET**

nj.market.autos (ng) Cars for sale in New Jersey. ✓**USENET**

Palo Alto Weekly Classifieds/Auto Cars, trucks, motorcycles, RVs, and classic vehicles are offered for sale in the Palo Alto area. ✓**INTERNET**→*www* http://akebono.stanford.edu/yahoo/Business/Corporations/Automobiles/Classifieds/Palo_Alto_Weekly_Classifieds/

rec.autos.marketplace (ng) A Bentley in New York City, a Toyota in Pennsylvania, and a Honda in Connecticut are typical offerings in this high-volume auto classifieds newsgroup. ✓**USENET**

Used Cars for Sale Picture-perfect ads of used cars in the Seattle area. Currently lists only Fords and Volvos. ✓**INTERNET**→*www* http://www.seanet.com/Bazar/Cars/Used/Used_Cars. html

Motorcycles

Motorcycle Home Page If a box on four wheels is not your style, try out this site, which links to dozens of motorcycle brands—reviews, road tests, price guides, etc. ✓**INTERNET**→*www* http://cs.wpi.edu /~ravi/

Security systems

SonicPRO A car alarm system sales point. ✓**INTERNET**→*www* http://www.human.com/sonic/sonic.html

Simulators

Ford Simulator 5.0 A two-disk package that you can order online. Disk one, Window Sticker, lets you "spec out" a new Ford or Lincoln-Mercury, adding options and settling on a price for financing or leasing. Disk two, Showroom, allows you to spray paint your vehicle and play the Lake Wakatonka driving game, a computer simulation of steering, accelerating, gear shifting, and braking. ✓**COMPUSERVE**→*go* fd→Software→Software, Videos, and Sportswear→Fun & Informative Software **$**

Solar cars

Solar Car Home Page Are solar cars the wave of the future? Link to the University of Michigan Solar Car Team, Penn Solar Car Racing, and the Calsol Solar Car Project. ✓**INTERNET**→*www* http://akebono. stan ford.edu/yahoo/Entertain ment/Au tomobiles/Solar_Cars/

> "Read I-love-what-you-do-for-me brochures about Toyota's recent models."

Buying A Car Milestones

Electronic parking lot

alt.autos.antique (ng) ✓USENET

alt.autos.camaro.firebird (ng) ✓USENET

alt.cars.ford-probe (ng) ✓USENET

BMW (ml) ✓INTERNET→*email* bmw-request@balltown.cma.com ✍ *Write a request*

Classic Mustangs (ml) ✓INTERNET→*email* classic-mustangs-request@mustang.fc.hp.com ✍ *Write a request*

Honda-L (ml) ✓INTERNET→*email* listserv@brownvm.brown.edu ✍ *Type in message body:* subscribe honda-l <your full name>

Italian Cars (ml) ✓INTERNET→*email* italian-cars-request@balltown.cma.com ✍ *Write a request*

Land Rover Owner (ml) ✓INTERNET→*email* majordomo@chunnel.uk.stratus.com ✍ *Type in message body:* subscribe lro-digest <your full name>

Miata (ml) ✓INTERNET→*email* listserv@jhunix.hcf.jhu.edu ✍ *Write a request*

MR2 (ml) ✓INTERNET→*email* mr2-interest-request@validgh.com ✍ *Write a request*

Mustangs (ml) ✓INTERNET→*email* mustangs-request@cup.hp.com ✍ *Write a request*

Porsches (ml) ✓INTERNET→*email* porschephiles-request@tta.com ✍ *Write a request*

Quattro (Audi) (ml) ✓INTERNET→*email* quattro-owner@swiss.ans.net ✍ *Write a request*

RX7Club (ml) ✓INTERNET→*email* rx7club-admin@cbjjn.cb.att.com ✍ *Write a request*

The Saab Network (ml) ✓INTERNET→*email* saab@network.mhs.compuserve.com ✍ *Write a request*

Saturn (ml) ✓INTERNET→*email* saturn-request@oar.net ✍ *Write a request*

Supras (ml) ✓INTERNET→*email* supras-request@vicor.com ✍ *Write a request Archives:* ✓INTERNET→*ftp* viscorp.com→anonymous→<your email address>→/pub/supras

Toyota (ml) ✓INTERNET→*email* toyota-request@quack.kfu.com ✍ *Write a request*

Toyota Corolla (ml) ✓INTERNET→*email* corolla-request@mcs.net ✍ *Write a request*

Volvo-Net (ml) ✓INTERNET→*email* swedishbricks-request@me.rochester.edu ✍ *Write a request*

Real estate

If you're a first-time home buyer drowning in the sea of equity and easements, let the

world of electronic real estate keep your head above water. The **Real Estate Center** on Prodigy will assuage your fundamental doubts by teaching you how to calculate moving costs, negotiate with a broker, and select a good inspection agent. Then there's the matter of actually finding a new place. Start with **MLS— Sell, Buy, Rent, Exchange**, a nationwide listing of properties, or try the local classifieds. Prospective home owners drawing closer to the moment of purchase may want to dispense with the formalities and go right for **Mortgage Rates** and **Relocation Research**.

The Peer's House—downloaded from America Online's Graphix Exchange

On the Net

Across the board

Ask Our Broker The online broker is always available to address your real-estate queries. He will outline your chances of getting a home loan after bankruptcy, explain how to get the VA to finance closing costs, and even address whether refinancing is a good idea with current interest rates. Other experts in the real-estate field also lend their expertise. Appraisers suggest good equity buys—it appears that 7-Elevens usually go up in value—inspectors cue buyers on danger signs, and

other AOL members add their war stories and wise counsel. ✓**AMERICA ONLINE**→*keyword* real estate

Consumer Reports Real Estate A selection from *Consumer Reports* that aims to help home buyers get the best value for their money, covering all the different types of loans and payment plans and negotiation techniques. And if once isn't enough, there is the section on buying a vacation home— mortgage, tax, and equity issues for that cozy place in paradise. ✓**PRODIGY**→*jump* cr real estate

Home and Real Estate Round-Table Did you know that house sellers in Louisiana are not required to inform potential buyers if a house is haunted? Boo! Professional realtors and amateur home owners come together on the bulletin board to exchange information—everything from surreal stories about for-sale-by-owner debacles to tips on dealing with angry landlords to tax advice from a professional appraiser. The libraries contain several downloadable programs for managing your property

and creating amortization schedules. In addition, the forum contains home listings, although they are not very numerous. ✓**GENIE**→*keyword* home

misc.consumers.house (ng) While the bulk of threads in this newsgroup relate to home repair, you have to buy a home before you can fix it up, and many messages deal with that traumatic experience. The couple that lost their ideal home to the bankruptcy of the seller gets a sympathetic response from others stuck in the closing process. A woman refinancing her home is evicted by the first owner when he decides she is "in default during changeover." With tips on buying, avoiding penalties, and assessing value, this is a useful resource. ✓**USENET**

misc.invest.real-estate (ng) Discussion about real estate as an investment, including financing, restoration, and property leads. Government real-estate auctions are also announced here. ✓**USENET**

Real Estate Buying? Selling?

Real Estate **Milestones**

Renting? If you're in a house, apartment, condo, co-op, or any other paid shelter, you'll want to spend some time in this section, in which forum participants spend hour after hour talking over interest rates, housing starts, mortgages, inspections, and taxation. In addition, the forum has libraries with numerous programs for downloading—everything from real-estate transaction forms to rental-property management databases. ✓**COMPUSERVE**→*go* invforum→Real Estate

Real Estate Center A general guide to home buying that includes a home finder and a mortgage calculator. The main value of this service is its buying and selling tips. ✓**PRODIGY**→*jump* homes

Fannie Mae

Fannie Mae Online Some say Fannie Mae was the name of Harry Truman's favorite cow. Others say it's the Oak Ridge Boys' recent hit song. Wrong. It's the Federal National Mortgage Association— the congressionally created, shareholder-owned lending institution that targets low- to middle-income home buyers. Several Fannie Mae programs are described here, like those promoting rural home ownership, home buying for the self-employed, and community living for disabled adults. ✓**AMERICA ON-LINE**→*keyword* fannie mae

Industry exchange

clari.biz.industry.real-estate (ng) Follow the latest developments in the real-estate industry including housing starts, mergers and acquisitions of real-estate firms, government auctions, new legislation, and mortgage rates. ✓**CLARINET** $

> "Listings in CompuServe's Classifieds tend to get drowned in a sea of messages like 'dream apartments—no fee' and 'fix your credit—guaranteed.' But there are quite a few gems listed, such as the 15th-century thatched cottage in Buckinghamshire."

Commercial—Realestate (ml) Geared to the professional developer, broker, investor, owner, or management company dealing in commercial real estate. List members can post property advertisments and establish new business contacts. ✓**INTERNET**→*email* ted.kraus@property.com ✍ *Write a request*

Housing Starts Monthly updates on housing-start data. Also available are the data for housing units completed and housing vacancies. ✓**INTERNET**→*gopher* una.hh.lib.umich.edu→ebb→Housing starts <or> Housing units completed <or> Housing vacancies

Real Estate Network Information about the real-estate indus-

try—more for the agent than the buyer. ✓**INTERNET**→*www* http://www.csi.nb.ca/celerity/

Tenant-Net (ml) Official mailing list of Tenant Watch and the Division of Housing and Community Renewal (DHCR), representing more than two million rent-regulated tenants in New York State. ✓**INTERNET**→*email* jbfisher@pipeline.com ✍ *Write a request*

Listings

Classifieds–Real Estate/Mortgages Interested in an industrial site in the North Carolina research triangle? Looking for a luxury co-op on New York's Upper West Side—with a parking space, terrace, and a billiard room? No problem. Listings tend to get drowned in a sea of messages like "dream apartments—no fee" and "fix your credit—guaranteed." But there are quite a few gems listed, such as the 15th-century thatched cottage in Buckinghamshire with "all modern conveniences." Fees are calculated by line and duration of listing. ✓**COMPUSERVE**→*go* cla→Real Estate/Mortgages

Comstar Classified Search for a house, apartment, or roommate in the U.S. The service is free and easy to use. ✓**INTERNET**→*telnet* csii.com→star→Classified→Real Estate

For Sale By Owner Magazine Online and print magazine that lets home owners market their homes without a broker. By placing an ad, sellers can also order all kinds of home-selling aids, such as yard signs, brochure boxes, flyers, and blank contracts. The Santa Cruz area of California is the main focus, with some Idaho and Nevada listings. Browsing is free but listing your house will cost you from $18.50/month to $65/ month depending on the number of photos you want to display. ✓**INTERNET**→*www* http://www.human.com/mkt/fsbo/fsbo.html

GEMS—Global Real Estate Guide

International real-estate listings, including luxury properties in the Dominican Republic, Pacific Rim, and South Africa, as well as commercial and residential properties sorted by agent. GEMS is also host to the National Real Estate Service, which claims 15,000 commercial and residential ads. Fees for listing a house range from $10/month to $650/ month. ✓**INTERNET**→*www* http://www.gems.com/realestate/

GEnie's Real Estate Classifieds

If you're looking to sell a farm, or buy a house, or you want to rent office space or a vacation house at the beach, the three real-estate classified sections on GEnie are worth a try. ✓**GENIE**→*keyword* ads→Residential Rentals <or> Real Estate <or> Business & Business Real Estate→

Homes and Land

Homes and Land is an electronic magazine of nationwide real-estate listings. You can place an ad or browse through the listings. The system is easy to use—choose a geographical area and you will be given detailed listings. ✓**PRODIGY**→*jump* homes→ Listings

MLS—Sell, Buy, Rent, Exchange

A broad spectrum of properties is offered for sale here, from homes in Blue Hill, Maine (5 BR/ocean view), to Hilo, Hawaii (1 BR/dishwasher and carport). All entries contain information about property taxes, amenities, and utility rates. To list your home, fill out the online form and email it to MLS. There's no

Victorian home—downloaded from America Online's Architecture Forum.

charge. Rentals are also admissible, but not for periods less than a month. Brokers and salespeople may use the service if they identify themselves and follow special guidelines. ✓**AMERICA ONLINE**→*keyword* mls ✓**COMPUSERVE**→*go* mls

Real Estate Classifieds

Your classified will run 30 days in the consumer section for $5, and in the business section for $20. Both owners and agents list properties. Choose from a two-story log cabin in Alaska's Denali wilderness or a beachfront bungalow in the Bahamas. Every price range is covered. ✓**PRODIGY**→*jump* classifieds

Realty Referral Network

Find a real-estate agent in the area of your choice, including 5,000 cities in the U.S.A. and in Europe. ✓**INTERNET**→*www* http://mmink.cts.com/mmink/dossiers/rrn.html

World Real Estate Listing Service

Listings of houses in the United States and Canada. A 1,000-character ad for 90 days is free; there is a charge of $10.00 per picture. ✓**INTERNET**→*www* http://interchange.idc.uvic.ca/wrels/index.html

Listings: California

Cornish & Carey Country

Home listings and properties covering California's San Mateo and Santa Clara Counties. Listings are updated twice weekly. ✓**INTERNET**→ *www* http://www.baynet.com/cc/cchome.html

Four Circles Realty

Look at houses in San Francisco and the Bay Area by city, price range, or number of bedrooms and bathrooms. ✓**INTERNET**→*www* http://www.internet-is.com/re/index.html

Humboldt Mortgage Company

An advertisement for a mortgage company in Eureka, California, with links to general information about mortgage brokers and home-loan fees. ✓**INTERNET**→*www* http://www.northcoast.com/unlimited/services_listing/hm/hm.html

San Mateo Times Marketplace

Real-estate listings by township, primarily for San Mateo County, California. Each posting comes with a list of home features and photos. ✓**INTERNET**→*www* http://www.baynet.com/smtimes/market/list.html

Real Estate **Milestones**

Listings: Canada

Realty World Listings of Canadian properties. ✓**INTERNET**→*www* http://www.cygnus.nb.ca/mall/realestate.html

Listings: Chicago

Chicago Tribune—Real Estate Are you house hunting in the Chicago area? AOL has the full real-estate listings from the current week's *Chicago Tribune* online. You can search the listings or browse in the categories that interest you: Townhouses, Condos, Unfurnished Apartments for Rent, etc. To place an ad, you must voice call the *Trib* at 312-222-2222. ✓**AMERICA ON-LINE**→*keyword* trib ads→Real Estate

Listings: Colorado

Colorado Classified Listings for land and residential estates in Colorado, from studios to 100-acre ranches. ✓**INTERNET**→*gopher* usa.net→SPECIAL—Business Online→SPECIAL—Business and Real Estate Classifieds

Listings: D.C.

HomeBuyer's Fair Listings in the Washington, D.C. area, including a clickable map that allows you to specify smaller geographic areas to search. Also includes a mortgage calculator. ✓**INTERNET**→*www* http://www.homefair.com/

Listings: New Jersey

nj.market.housing (ng) Real-estate listings in the New Jersey area. ✓**USENET**

Listings: New York

New York State Housing Authority Gopher Carries news releases, policy statements, and fact sheets related to housing laws in the state of New York. ✓**INTERNET**→*gopher* gopher1.medlib.hscbklyn.edu→The Community→New York State Housing Information

nyc.market.housing (ng) Next to the *Village Voice*, this may be the best place to find a lead for a one-room apartment in the East Village, a share in Chelsea, or a roommate on the Upper East Side. ✓**USENET**

Texas

Austin Area Real Estate Do you want six bedrooms on Tarry Trail or seven on Weston Lane? Or how about that dream house on Shimmering Cove Road, the one with the exercise room, boat slip, and vine-covered pergola? Listings for residential properties in the Austin, TX, area, with descriptions,

---

REAL ESTATE BBSs

Homes Online, Inc.
216-562-4006
The Real Estate Connection
303-933-3372
California Home Buyers BBS
310-763-7866
Corporate Connection BBS
312-792-8292
London MicroNet BBS
519-451-4434
The Dealmakers On-line BBS
609-587-4651
Realpix BBS
702-566-6840
The Insider
713-784-8823
Real Estate Shop BBS
704-531-7375
MMIS Real Estate BBS
708-834-1450
The Dealmakers BBS
908-730-9002

---

prices, and photos ✓**INTERNET**→*www* http://www.gems.com/realestate/greg/7/r.r.7.0.html

Mortgages advice

Finding the Best Mortgage This article advises prospective homeowners to shop around for their mortgage—on any given day there is a 2 percent spread in rates, a differential which seems small but can add up to $200 a month over 20 or 30 years! The vocabulary of the mortgage is also clearly explained—what are term, points, APR, etc. All the variations of mortgage plans are detailed and accompanied by some average rate tables showing the comparative monthly payments for each form. ✓**PRODIGY**→*jump* cr money→Finding the Best Mortgage

Homeowners' Concerns You cut your piece of the American pie—you bought a home of your own. Now what do you do? The FTC has a series of publications designed to help home owners (and those who would be home owners) manage their debt and equity.

For first-timers, there is "Home Financing Primer," filled with suggestions about how to choose your lender, what different types of mortgages mean in interest, points, and principle. Second-stage owners should check out "Home Equity Credit Lines" and "Refinancing Your Home," which clearly explain the financial meat behind the fluffy TV spots promising to end payment worries with a second mortgage. Worksheets are included to help figure out if refinancing is the best solution.

And senior citizens with plenty of house but no cash to speak of might be fascinated to learn about "Reverse Mortgages," which allow them to gain monthly stipends, credit lines, or lump sums by taking a uninsured reverse mortgage. Pay it off at death or sale...or finance forward in a regular mortgage again! ✓**COMPUSERVE** →*go* con-for→Libraries Banking & Credit

HSH Rates & Indexes Loads of detail about the principles behind mortgage rates populate this rates service. The mystery behind adjustable rates and the treasury security index is solved, and there are even instructions for figuring rates yourself. The real bonus is an up-to-date comparative listing of interest rates, required down payments, points, and loan amounts for banks nationwide.

Ten-year adjustable-rate mortgages, for example, vary from 7.75 percent to 9.5 percent and zero to three points—a big difference to purchasers. The One-Year Treasury Security Index (T-Sec) is also calculated for the last year to help you chart ARM rates. These rates and indexes are furnished by HSH Associates Financial Publishers. ✓**AMERICA ONLINE**→*keyword* hsh

Mortgage Rates A brief introduction defines the types of mortgages—30-year fixed, 15-year fixed, jumbo (more than $203,150), negative amortization (deferred interest), and adjustable-rate mortgages (ARMs). Specialized loan programs like those from the Veterans Administration and the FHA are also detailed. With this information in hand, prospective home buyers can begin to explore the individual bank listings, which are updated on a daily basis. Each bank involved furnishes the current rate on most or all types of mortgages, contact information, and details on its lending program. ✓**AMERICA ONLINE**→*keyword* mortgage

Mortgages calculator

Mortgage Calculator Fill out an online questionnaire and analyze your mortgage options. ✓**INTERNET**→*www* http://ibc.wustl.edu/mort.html

Mortgages online

First Federal Savings Bank of Indiana Fixed-rate programs (15- and 30-year), adjustable-rate loans, jumbo loans, portfolio programs, and a biweekly mortgage-payment plan. ✓**INTERNET**→*www* http://branch.com:1080/first/first.html

Myers Equity Express Apply for a mortgage online, if you have a Web browser that allows you to fill out forms. Areas serviced are California, Arizona, Colorado, Idaho, Nevada, Oregon, Texas, Utah, and Washington. ✓**INTERNET** →*www* http://www.internet-is.com/myers/

Warehouse Mortgage Comprehensive range of financing products for residential, commercial, and business customers. ✓**INTERNET**→*www* http://www.internex.net/warehouse/home.html

Relocation Research What if the boss appeared at your door right now to tell you that you're being transferred to Peoria? There's a higher salary in the offing, sure, but is it worth it? What about housing costs, taxation, and utilities, not to mention crime rate, schools, hospitals, and community services? This service not only includes online information on contacting a relocation counselor, but prepares customized moving reports for $5.95 each. ✓**PRODIGY**→*jump* homefinder **$** ✓**COMPUSERVE**→*go* rl-4

Real Estate Shareware **Milestones**

Real estate shareware

Amortize It! v2.0 Flexible and friendly loan analyzer. Includes calculators for loans, refinancing, interest due, etc. International currencies and dates supported. ✓**PC OHIO**→d→*Download a file:* AMOIT20.ZIP (DOS)

Complex v2.01 Managing program for condo and co-op apartments. Database for occupant records, balloting (weighted or not), calculations for maintence fees. ✓**PC OHIO**→d→*Download a file:* CMPLX201.ZIP (DOS)

Excel Home Finance v1.0 Microsoft Excel spreadsheet calculates outstanding balance vs. time for home loans. Also looks at costs in buying and refinancing. ✓**IN-TERNET** →*ftp* sumex-aim.stanford. edu→anonymous→<your email address>→/info-mac/app→excel-home-finance-10.hqx (Macintosh)

Home Basis Record Manager v1.5 Keeps track of cost of houses and condominiums. Identifies more than 40 events that raise or lower basis. Supports laser printers. ✓**PC OHIO**→d→*Download a file:* HBRM15.ZIP (DOS)

Home Finance Microsoft Excel file that calculates the finance charges on your home. ✓**INTERNET** →*ftp* mac.archive.umich.edu→anonymous→<your email address>→/mac/util/organization→home finance.sit.hqx (Macintosh)

The Home Inspector Electronic home buying check lists and information to help you evaluate whether you've found home-sweet-home: Does the property have a basement? How's the plumbing? And the heating? Is there any closet space? ✓**AMERICA**

ONLINE→*keyword* real estate→Real Estate Library→PC Library→HOME INSP.ZIP (DOS)

House Calculates the mortgage amount (and payments) you'll probably be approved for based on your income and debts. ✓**AMERICA ONLINE**→*keyword* win→*Search by file name:* HOUSE.ZIP (Windows)

Loan Not only calculates mortgage payments, but compares loan options and figures out tax benefits. Shareware. ✓**AMERICA ONLINE** →*keyword* real estate→Real Estate Library→Mac Library→Loan.sit (Macintosh)

MacAmortize Creates amortized payment schedules that can be printed and saved. Displays multiple payment schedules. Shareware. ✓**COMPUSERVE**→*go* macap→Browse Libraries→Accounting/Finance→AMORT.SIT (Macintosh)

Mortgage Analyst v1.0 Analyzes scenarios in selecting loans and accelerated payment methods. Calculates Adjustable Rate Mortgages and displays payments graphically or by list. Shareware. ✓**GENIE**→*keyword* invest→Investors' Software Libraries→*Download a file:* MORTANAL.ZIP (Windows)

Mortgage Maker v1.01 Estimates monthly payments and closing costs for home mortgages. "Backsolving" feature lets you figure how much you can spend. Extensive documentation gives mortgage advice as well. ✓**INTERNET**→*ftp* sumexaim.stanford.edu→anonymous→<your email add- ress>→/info-mac/app→mortgage-maker-101. hqx (Macintosh)

Prepayment Planner Want to

know how much you'll save if you prepay your loan? Program calculates savings in interest payments and in length of loan payment. ✓**AMERICA ONLINE**→*keyword* real estate→Real Estate Library→PC Library→LOAN110.ZIP (DOS)

Quality Management System v3.1 This accounting system for property management handles accounts payable and receivable, disbursements, etc. Includes memo writer. ✓**PC OHIO**→d→*Download a file:* QMU.ZIP (DOS)

Realview Real Estate display/retrieval system helps realtors showcase listings with photos. Listings can be selected by criteria such as cost, number of bedrooms, and the like. Requires SuperVGA display. ✓**PC OHIO**→d→*Download a file:* REALTY1.ZIP *and* REALTY2. ZIP *and* REALTY3.ZIP (DOS)

Rent Wizard Application to assist you in keeping accurate records of your property transactions. Use the program to complete tax forms, summarize your investments, and print a lease. Shareware. ✓**AMERICA ONLINE**→*keyword* win→*Search by file name:* RENTWZD10.ZIP (Windows)

Rental Manager Program to manage as many as 600 rental units. Data tracking can include rent, maintenance, and other charges. The program can generate several types of reports, including expense calculations, lease terminations, and turnover rates, to name only a few. Shareware. ✓**AMERICA ONLINE**→*keyword* real estate→Real EstateLibrary→PC Library→MANAGER4.EXE (DOS)

Choosing a college

I'd like you to meet Mr. Educated American Teenager. Ed, as he's known for short,

has just started his senior year in high school, and he's a little worried about where he should attend college. He lives on the East Coast but he loves the West. He has good enough SAT scores for Pomona, but isn't that sanguine about Stanford. And then there are the concerns of Ed's parents—they're a little uncertain about elite private institutions, having sent a daughter through four years of college only to have her become a playwright and tattoo artist. To the Eds of this world, to the Mr. and Ms. Teenagers, we have only this to say: the Net! The **U.S. News College Fair Forum** provides detailed profiles of hundreds of American colleges and universities, not only from guidance counselors, but from fellow students and commiserating parents. The **Princeton Review WWW Server** furnishes practical advice on test-taking, admissions, and financial aid. And **Netcruiser Selected College Tours** uses the power of modern microprocessing to create virtual tours of Dartmouth, UNC, the University of Nevada, and the University of Utah.

Yale University—http://www.yale.edu/

On the Net

Across the board

College Board Sponsored by that testing institution that most high school students dread, the College Board's online presence is dedicated to helping find the right college: from "Tips on Choosing a College" (which includes how-to articles that consider issues ranging from student life to expense) to "Financial Aid Information" (a walk-through of the difficult application process, including types of aid, funding alternatives, and the financial aid rationale).

Students are a volatile bunch, though, and sometimes they have questions that can't be answered by prepared documents. That's where Ask the College Board comes in: it's a full-service message board that invites any and all questions from parents, high-school students, middle schoolers, and teachers wondering about admission requirements, testing strategies, and the kind of volunteer work that "looks good" to admissions boards. And, of course,

test dates are always posted here.

The College Board also sells its test-preparation materials and college guides through the College Store (Mastercard and Visa accepted) and provides a free version of the *College Handbook*, which includes brief descriptions of all 2,500 participating institutions, their entrance requirements, finan-

> **"Ask the College Board is a full-service message board that invites any and all questions from parents, high-school students, middle schoolers, and teachers."**

cial statistics, degrees offered, and other pertinent information, such as sports programs and gender ratio. ✓**AMERICA ONLINE**→*keyword* college board

Colleges & Universities Planning for an education is much more than finances. While the Colleges & Universities category does cover financial aid, the most active topics are those for students and parents trying to figure out which college to choose (there seems to be an alum from every college here) and for grad students talking about their programs. ✓**GENIE**→*keyword* ert→Education Bulletin Board→Colleges & Universities

Education Forum The forum is geared toward teachers and guidance counselors, making it a good site for informed answers to college planning queries. The Community College/Higher Education section also caters to professionals who can help with graduate school questions. ✓**COMPUSERVE**→*go* edforum

misc.education (ng) Frequented by both teachers and parents, the group offers guidance on how to best prepare students for college and standardized testing, as well as hosting interesting debates on issues like multiculturalism and compulsory schooling. ✓**USENET**

Princeton Review WWW Server Getting tested, getting in, and getting money. This site contains detailed descriptions of the content of all the standardized admissions tests—from the PSAT to the MCAT—and instructions on how best to prepare for these exams. The basics of financial aid are also covered: the forms that are necessary, the information that's required, and the way to read the resulting needs assessments. After

From the Cornell-Student Life home page—http://www.cornell.edu/student.html

reviewing the basics, the Princeton people list the options for funding and explain how to use grants, scholarships, work-study, loans, and savings to pay for schools you might otherwise have considered out of your financial reach. ✓**INTERNET**→*www* http://www.review.com/

Student's Forum In the Lounge, you'll find a lot of encouragement from other high-school students as you set your hopes on the college of your choice and then wait for the April mailman. ✓**COMPUSERVE** →*go* student

U.S. News College Fair Forum In the Guidance Counselor section, professionals from selected schools offer realistic advice. In Student to Student, high-school and college students meet to discuss the pros and cons of schools or the benefits of "the Greek System." And in the Alumni section, past collegiates wax nostalgic, still wrapped in the flag of their alma mater. For more detailed information about colleges, check out the forum's libraries, which contain rankings and descriptions based on *U.S. News*'s yearly evaluations (top ten for liberal arts, Western

liberal arts, national universities). Even this section has an interactive component—Talk Back to Us, in which members of university communities defend their school's reputation against the nefarious distortions of rankings. ✓**COMPUSERVE** →*go* usncollege

> "Demystify the college selection process with the Princeton Review, which evaluates colleges and rates them in categories like social life, extracurricular activities, academics, and even politics."

Guides & rankings

Peterson's College Guide Compare undergraduate programs using data on faculty, departments, and cost. The selectivity of each institution is weighed against the success of its graduates (i.e. the employment rate of graduates).

Peterson's summarizes the strengths and weaknesses of each undergraduate program to make selection easier, and the database can be searched by location, major, or school name. Meanwhile, the Peterson's Guide creates another comparative shopping problem with two identical online versions that differ vastly in cost. Expensive on GEnie; free on CompuServe. Go figure. ✓**GENIE**→ *keyword* college **$** ✓**COMPUSERVE**→ *go* petersons

---

Princeton Review Informed Parents Demystify the college selection process with the Princeton Review, which evaluates colleges and rates them in categories like social life, extracurricular activities, academics, and even politics. Guides are available on "Getting Into College" and "Paying for College," as well as a "Parental Guidance" feature that outlines when to start planning for college, how to help your children decide without pressure, and how to encourage your kids to do their homework. ✓**AMERICA ONLINE**→*keyword* education→Princeton Rev/Informed Parent

Home schoolers

misc.education.home-school. misc (ng) How do you get your home-schooled child through standardized testing and into college? This newsgroup is home to a large number of parents who have invested time and research in schooling their child and who ex-

change ideas and advice about the process. The FAQ provides an annotated bibliography and addresses for other Net resources. ✓**USE-NET**

Testing, testing

Exam Prep Center Preparing for a standardized college admissions test (PSAT, SAT, etc.)? Post your questions on the message board or ask to join an online tutoring session. Requests for help will be forwarded to an instructor who will then contact you. ✓**AMERICA ONLINE**→*keyword* exam prep

Tours

Colleges & Universities If a college has an online presence, you can probably get there from this site—one of the premier gateways to college information on the Net, this site not only links to individual colleges and universities but also connects to a large amount of faculty and student-body home pages, a universal university phone directory, scholarship information, job listings, and the U.S. Department of Education. ✓**INTERNET**→*www* http://white.nosc.mil/htlan/imagemap/PEHP_College? 155,40

Netcruiser Selected College Tours Take virtual tours of Dartmouth, the University of North Carolina at Chapel Hill, the University of Nevada, and the University of Utah. And while the tours don't provide a whole lot of accurate ambience—no beer, no boring lectures, no moments of thwarted romance—they're undoubtly the next best thing to being there. ✓**INTERNET**→*www* http://www.netcom.com.netcom/ctour.html

Colleges Online

Colleges are on the Net with their course catalogs, campus maps, faculty and student directories, admissions procedures, financial aid policies, and guides to student life. Here is an extensive list of Net addresses for American colleges.

Abilene Christian University
http://bible.acu.edu/

Acadia University
http://www.acadiau.ca/

Albertson College of Idaho
http://www.acofi.edu/

Albion College
http://www.albion.edu/

American University
http://www.american.edu/

Amherst College
http://www.amherst.edu/

Andrews University
http://www.cs.andrews.edu/index.html

Appalachian State University
http://www.acs.appstate.edu/

Arizona State University
http://www.asu.edu/

Auburn University
http://www.auburn.edu/

Ball State University
http://virgo.bsu.edu:8080/

Bates College
http://abacus.bates.edu/

Baylor University
http://www.baylor.edu/

Beloit College
http://stu.beloit.edu/1

Boise State University
http://gozer.idbsu.edu/Index.html

Boston College
http://infoeagle.bc.edu/

Boston University
http://www.bu.edu/

Bowdoin College
http://www.bowdoin.edu/

Bradley University
http://www.bradley.edu/

Bridgewater College
http://www.bridgewater.edu/

Brigham Young University
http://www.cs.byu.edu/byu-home.html

Brown University
http://www.brown.edu/

Bucknell University
http://www.bucknell.edu/

California Institute of Technology
http://www.caltech.edu/

Duke University logo—from http://www.duke.edu/

California State University, Chico
http://www.csuchico.edu/

California State University, Hayward
http://www.mcs.csuhayward.edu/

California State University, Long Beach
http://www.csulb.edu/

California State University, Northridge
http://www.csun.edu/

California State University, San Marcos
http://coyote.csusm.edu/

California State University, Fullerton
http://www.fullerton.edu/

Calvin College
http://www.calvin.edu/

Carleton College
http://www.carleton.edu/

Carnegie Mellon University
http://www.cmu.edu/

Carroll College
http://carroll1.cc.edu/

Case Western Reserve University
http://www.cwru.edu/

Cerritos College
http://www.cerritos.edu/

City University of New York (CUNY)
http://www.cuny.edu/

Colleges Online (continued)

University of California at Berkeley—
http://www.berkeley.edu/

City University of New York, Graduate School and University Center
http://www.gs.cuny.edu/

Clarkson University
http://fire.clarkson.edu/
CUhomepage.html

Clemson University
http://www.clemson.edu/home.
html

Cleveland State University
http://www.csuohio.edu/

Coe College
http://www.coe.edu/

Colby College
http://www.colby.edu/

Colgate University
http://cs.colgate.edu/

Colorado State University
http://www.colostate.edu/

Columbia University
http://www.columbia.edu/

Cornell College, Iowa
http://www.cornell-iowa.edu/

Cornell University
http://www.cornell.edu/

Creighton University
http://bluejay.creighton.edu/

Dakota State University
http://www.dsu.edu/

Dalhousie University
http://www.cs.dal.ca/home.html

Dartmouth College
http://www.dartmouth.edu/

Denison University
http://louie.cc.denison.edu/

DePaul University
http://www.depaul.edu/

Dixie College
http://sci.dixie.edu/

Drexel University
http://www.drexel.edu/

Duke University
http://www.duke.edu/

Duquesne University
http://www.duq.edu/

East Stroudsburg University
http://www.esu.edu/

Emory University
http://www.cc.emory.edu/
welcome.html

Florida Atlantic University
http://rs6000.adm.fau.edu/
fau.home

Florida International U.
http://nomadd.fiu.edu/

Florida State University
http://sis.fsu.edu/

Franklin & Marshall College
http://www.fandm.edu/

Gallaudet University
http://www.gallaudet.edu/

George Mason University
http://www.gmu.edu/

George Washington U.
http://gwis.circ.gwu.edu/

Georgetown University
http://www.georgetown.edu/
guhome.html

Georgia State University
http://www.gsu.edu/

Georgia Tech
http://www.gatech.edu/

Gustavus Adolphus College
http://www.gac.edu/

Hamilton College
gopher://gopher.earlham.edu/1

Hamline University
http://www.hamline.edu/

Hampshire College
http://www.hampshire.edu/

Hanover College
http://www.hanover.edu/

Harvard University
http://golgi.harvard.edu/harvard.
html

Harvey Mudd College
http://www.hmc.edu/

Hendrix College
http://192.131.98.11/

Colleges Online (continued)

Hobart & William Smith Colleges
http://hws3.hws.edu:9000/

Hofstra University
http://www.hofstra.edu/

Howard University
http://www.howard.edu/

Idaho State University
http://www.isu.edu/

Illinois State University
http://www.ilstu.edu/

Indiana University
http://www.cs.indiana.edu/

Indiana University of Pennsylvania
http://www.lib.iup.edu/

Iowa State University
http://www.iastate.edu/

Jacksonville State University
http://jsucc.jsu.edu/home.html

Johns Hopkins University
http://www.jhu.edu/

Kalamazoo College
http://kzoo.edu/

Kansas State University
http://www.ksu.edu/

Keene State College
http://kilburn.keene.edu/

Kent State University
http://www.kent.edu/

Kenyon College
gopher://gopher.kenyon.edu/1

Lehigh University
http://www.lehigh.edu/

Louisiana State University
http://unix1.sncc.lsu.edu/

Loyola College
http://www.loyola.edu/

Massachusetts Institute of Technology
http://web.mit.edu/

Miami University of Ohio
http://www.muohio.edu/

Michigan State University
http://web.msu.edu/

Middlebury College
http://www.middlebury.edu/

Mississippi State University
http://www.msstate.edu/

Missouri University
http://musie.phlab.missouri.edu/

Montclair State University
http://www.smns.montclair.edu/

Mount Allison University
gopher://gopher.mta.ca/

Mount Holyoke College
gopher://gopher.mtholyoke.edu/1

Princeton University—http://www.princeton.edu/

National University
http://nunic.nu.edu/

New Mexico State U.
http://www.nmsu.edu/

New York University
http://www.nyu.edu/

North Carolina State U.
http://www.ncsu.edu/

Northeastern University
http://www.ccs.neu.edu/

Northwestern University
http://www.acns.nwu.edu/

Oakland University
http://www.acs.oakland.edu/

Oberlin College
http://www.oberlin.edu/

Occidental College
http://www.oxy.edu/

Ohio State University
http://www.acs.ohio-state.edu/

Ohio Wesleyan University
http://192.68.223.4:8000/

Oklahoma State University
http://www.okstate.edu/

Oregon State University
http://www.orst.edu/

Pennsylvania State University
http://www.psu.edu/

Plymouth State College
http://www.plymouth.edu/

Pomona College
http://www.pomona.claremont.edu/

Colleges Online (continued)

Princeton University
http://www.princeton.edu/

Purdue University
http://www.cs.purdue.edu/

Reed College
http://www.reed.edu/

Rensselaer Polytechnic Inst.
http://www.rpi.edu/

Rice University
http://riceinfo.rice.edu/

Rutgers University
http://www.rutgers.edu/

San Diego State University
http://www.sdsu.edu/

San Francisco State U.
http://sfsuvax1.sfsu.edu/

Seattle Pacific University
http://www.spu.edu/

Skidmore College
http://foureyes.skidmore.edu/
welcome-to-foureyes.html

Sonoma State University
http://www.sonoma.edu/

Southwestern College
http://swc.cc.ca.us/

St. Joseph's College
http://scarecrow.saintjoe.edu/

St. Joseph's University
http://www.sju.edu/

Stanford University
http://www.stanford.edu/

State University of New York—SUNY at Binghamton
http://www.binghamton.edu/

State University of New York—SUNY at Brockport
http://www.acs.brockport.edu/

State University of New York—SUNY at Buffalo
http://www.acsu.buffalo.edu/

State University of New York—SUNY at Geneseo
http://mosaic.cc.geneseo.edu/

State University of New York—SUNY at Oneonta
http://137.141.153.38/

State University of New York—SUNY at Plattsburgh
http://bio420.hawk.plattsburgh.edu/

State University of New York—SUNY at Potsdam
http://www.potsdam.edu/

State University of New York—SUNY at Stony Brook
http://www.sunysb.edu/

Swarthmore College
http://www.swarthmore.edu/

Syracuse University
http://www.syr.edu/

Temple University
http://astro.ocis.temple.edu/

Texas A&M University
http://www.tamu.edu/

Trinity College
http://www.trincoll.edu/

Tufts University
http://www.cs.tufts.edu/

Tulane University
http://www.tulane.edu/

Union College
gopher://gopher.union.edu/1

United States Department of Education
http://www.ed.gov/

United States Military Academy
http://euler.math.usma.edu/
Introduction.html

University of Alabama
http://www.sa.ua.edu/

University of Alaska
http://www.alaska.edu/

University of Arizona
http://www.arizona.edu/

University of Arkansas
http://cotton.uamont.edu/

University of California at Berkeley
http://www.berkeley.edu/

University of California at Davis
http://www.cs.ucdavis.edu/
homepage.html

University of California at Irvine
http://www.ics.uci.edu/
ICShome.html

University of California at Los Angeles
http://www.ucla.edu/intro.html

University of California at Riverside
http://www.ucr.edu/

University of California at San Diego
http://www.ucsd.edu/

Colleges Online (continued)

University of California at San Francisco
http://www.ucsf.edu/

University of California at Santa Barbara
http://id-www.ucsb.edu/

University of California at Santa Cruz
http://ftp.ucsc.edu/index.html

University of Chicago
http://www.uchicago.edu/

University of Cincinnati
http://www.uc.edu/

University of Colorado at Boulder
http://www.colorado.edu/

University of Connecticut
http://www.uconn.edu/

University of Delaware
http://www.udel.edu/

University of Florida
http://www.ufl.edu/

University of Georgia
http://www.uga.edu/

University of Hawaii
gopher://gopher.Hawaii.edu/1

University of Houston
http://www.uh.edu/

University of Idaho
http://www.uidaho.edu/

U. of Illinois at Chicago
http://www.uic.edu/

U. of Illinois at Urbana-Champaign
http://www.uiuc.edu/

University of Iowa
http://www.isca.uiowa.edu/

University of Kansas
http://www.tisl.ukans.edu/

University of Kentucky
http://www.uky.edu/

University of Maine
http://www.maine.edu/

University of Maryland
http://www.umd.edu/

University of Massachusetts at Amherst
http://www.cs.umass.edu/rcfdocs/newhome/index.html

University of Massachusetts System
http://www.umassp.edu/

University of Miami
http://www.ir.miami.edu/

U. of Michigan, Ann Arbor
http://www.umich.edu/

U. of Michigan, Dearborn
http://www.umd.umich.edu/

University of Minnesota
http://www.umn.edu/

University of Mississippi
http://www.olemiss.edu/

University of Missouri
http://www.missouri.edu/

University of Missouri at Kansas City
http://www.umkc.edu/

University of Missouri at Rolla
http://www.umr.edu/

University of Nebraska at Lincoln
http://www.unl.edu/

University of Nebraska at Omaha
http://www.unomaha.edu/

University of Nevada Las Vegas
http://www.nscee.edu/

University of New Hampshire
http://www.unh.edu/

University of New Mexico
http://www.unm.edu/

University of North Carolina General Administration
http://uncecs.edu/

University of North Carolina at Chapel Hill
http://sunsite.unc.edu/

University of North Carolina at Charlotte
http://unccvm.uncc.edu/

University of North Texas
http://www.unt.edu/

University of Notre Dame
http://www.nd.edu/

University of Oklahoma
http://www.uoknor.edu/

University of Oregon
http://www.uoregon.edu/home.html

University of Pennsylvania
http://www.upenn.edu/

University of Pittsburgh
http://www.pitt.edu/

Colleges Online (continued)

University of Portland
http://hood.uofport.edu:8080/

University of Rochester
http://www.cs.rochester.edu/

University of San Diego
gopher://teetot.acusd.edu/1

University of San Francisco
http://www.usfca.edu/

University of South Carolina
http://www.csd.scarolina.edu/

U. of Southern California
http://cwis.usc.edu/

U. of Tennessee at Knoxville
http://www.utk.edu/

University of Texas at Austin
http://wwwhost.cc.utexas.edu/

**University of Texas
at Brownsville**
http://mercury.utb.edu/

University of Texas at Dallas
http://www.utdallas.edu/

**University of Texas
at Houston**
http://www.uth.tmc.edu/

**University of Texas
at San Antonio**
http://www.utsa.edu/

University of the South
http://www.sewanee.edu/

U. of the Virgin Islands
http://mola.uvi.edu:80/

University of Utah
http://www.utah.edu/

University of Vermont
http://www.uvm.edu/

University of Virginia
http://jefferson.village.virginia.edu/

University of Washington
http://alfred.u.washington.edu:8080/

**University of Wisconsin
at Eau Claire**
http://www.uwec.edu/

**University of Wisconsin
at Madison**
http://info.gradsch.wisc.edu/

**University of Wisconsin
at Milwaukee**
http://www.uwm.edu/

**University of Wisconsin
at Platteville**
http://www.uwplatt.edu/

**University of Wisconsin
at Stevens Point**
http://www.uwsp.edu/

**University of Wisconsin
at Wasau—Marathon Center**
http://oingomth.uwc.edu/

University of Wyoming
http://www.uwyo.edu/

Utah State University
http://www.usu.edu/

Vanderbilt University
http://www.vanderbilt.edu/

Wake Forest University
http://www.wfu.edu/
www-data/start.html

Washington College
http://www.washcoll.edu/

**Washington & Lee
University**
http://liberty.uc.wlu.edu/

**Washington University
in St. Louis**
http://www.wustl.edu/

Wellesley College
http://pebbles.wellesley.edu/

Wesleyan University
http://emu.con.wesleyan.edu/

Wheaton College
gopher://gopher.wheaton.edu/1

Willamette University
http://www.willamette.edu/

Williams College
http://otis.cc.williams.edu/

**Worcester Polytechnic
Institute**
http://realsoon.wpi.edu:8080/

Yale University
http://www.yale.edu/

Stanford University—from http://www.stanford.edu/

Paying for college

What price education? Well, a pretty high price, especially if you're thinking of logging

your bright college time in a private institution. But don't despair: there are dozens of good sources for college funding, and most of them are accessible through the Net. The basic resources divide evenly into those that discuss savings strategies (such as **Saving for College**, in the **Fidelity On-Line Investor Center**), and those that detail available financial aid (such as **The ABCs of Financial Aid** and the **Annotated Bibliography of Financial Aid Resource Materials**). In addition, there are detailed treatments of specific options such as **U.S. Series EE Savings Bonds for College** and dozens and dozens of listings dealing with grants, fellowships, government assistance, and foundation aid. Check out **the Grant Getter's Guide to the Internet**, the **National Endowment for the Humanities**, and **Grants and Fellowships**. And if you've already received an offer from a university and want to learn more about its requirements and restrictions, tap into a nationwide network of financial aid offices with **Financial Aid Offices**.

Dartmouth College—http://www.dartmouth.edu/

On the Net

Across the board

ABCs of Financial Aid If there's a formula for getting into college and securing funding, the Reference Press may very well know it. This area on eWorld offers detailed checklists of what parents and students should be doing academically and financially to prepare for college, and the advice begins with the first day of ninth grade. But, their most extensive explanations are reserved for getting college, federal, and state financial aid. An informative FAQ teaches families how to search for aid, while other articles offer suggestions on alternative funding measures and cost-cutting strategies. A financial aid checklist helps parents prepare for filling out the complicated forms. And the help doesn't stop when the application is filed. The Reference Press team also teaches parents and students

how to compare aid packages, and they have online representatives available for answering specfic questions. ✓**EWORLD**→*go* rsp→The ABCs of Financial Aid

Annotated Bibliography of Financial Aid Resource Materials A guide to resources that will get you through the college process without selling the house and car. Both government and private sources are listed and evaluated. ✓**INTERNET**→ *www* http://www. cs.emu.edu:8001/afs/cmu.edu.user /mkant/ftp/FinAid/ann...bib.ps

Fidelity On-Line Investor Center: Saving for College Fidelity wants to sell its college savings plans, and in order to do so the company has provided parents with a college-cost calculator designed to shock them into saving. All you need to do is plug in your child's age and whether he or she plans to attend a public or private institution. Voilà! the heart-stopping damage. If your nine-year-old wants to go to Vassar, for example, you will need a total of $110,688 in just nine short years. The next screen tells you how much you should start saving. Assuming an 8 percent return, the figures are $713 monthly or $8,555 annually for a sum total of $55,344. Frightened yet? ✓ **PRODIGY**→*jump* fidelity

Financial Aid News A library of information about the state of financial aid, with articles about the best college buys, college aid scams, and SAT scoring, as well as rankings of colleges in aid-related categories—for example, which colleges saw the biggest tuition increases last year and which continue to give the most need-based assistance. ✓ **EWORLD** *go* rsp→Financial Aid News

Saving for College If you have a newborn and you want that child to attend college, take a deep breath. By the time the tyke is 18, you will need between $95,000 and $290,000 for four years of university education. If your child is already in elementary school, your projected savings are slightly less, but still imposing: parents of an eight-year-old hoping for a private institution should be socking away almost $7,000 each year. This report lessens the nightmare, laying out the best types of investment, evaluating bonds and other programs especially designed for college savings, and clearly explaining taxation issues. The kid may be drooling now, but in 15 years she'll be ready for Yale. Will you be? ✓ **PRODIGY**→*jump* cr money→Saving for College

Q&A

ASKERIC The federally funded Educational Resources Information Center (ERIC) is an immense clearinghouse for educational information. ASKERIC, its online presence, is a helpful virtual library that points fund seekers in the direction of relevant information, publications on education, and discussions of college testing and admissions. ✓ **INTERNET**→*www* http://eryx.syr.edu

Education Planning A simple but informative introduction (in the form of a FAQ, articles, and message board) to legal gift giving to children, trust funds, and tax shelters. Learn the nitty-gritty of college savings as parents try to grapple with the most pertinent question of all: how much is enough? The feature also carries a link to the message board Ask the College Board, where anxious students and parents get advice directly from the College Board, along with a link to the 2,500 institutions profiled in the searchable version of the *College Handbook*. ✓ **AMERICA ONLINE**→*keyword* your money→Education Planning

U.S. News College Fair Forum The equivocal financial status of middle-class kids may be the most prevalent theme of discussion in this forum, but it's not the only topic in the air. When a divorced parent asks for advice about filling out financial aid applications, others in similar situations respond. And, when someone asks for ideas for funding a Russian exchange student, the forum is flooded with responses. U.S. News has staff online to help answer financial aid questions and provide information on grants and scholarships. They'll also point you in the direction of more detailed sources. All options are explored here, from gaining "independent status" to staying in state for payment breaks. ✓ **COMPUSERVE** →*go* usncollege→Messages and Libraries→Financial Aid

Financial aid offices

Financial Aid Offices Links to the financial aid and admissions offices of several American colleges and universities. You can also access information on scholarships, fellowships, and grants, or retrieve a bibliography of resources for offline reading on college funding. ✓ **INTERNET**→*www* http://www.cs.cmu.edu:8001/afs/cs.cmu.edu/user/mkant/Public/FinAid/finaid.html

Government aid

Catalogue of Federal Domestic Assistance Almost every government agency, from the Depart-

> "All you need to do is plug in your child's age and whether he or she plans to attend a public or private institution. Voilà! the heart-stopping damage. If your nine-year-old wants to go to Vassar, for example, you will need a total of $110,688 in just nine short years."

ment of Transportation to the Department of Energy, funds scholarships. No matter what your academic interest (mining, nursing, international business, or dance) or personal background (are you a minority student, a first-generation citizen, disabled, or a returning student?), the federal government more than likely has a scholarship that's up your alley. The Catalogue of Federal Domestic Assistance provides detailed information on requirements, application procedures, and contacts for scholarships. ✓**INTERNET**→*gopher* gopher.rtd.utk.edu→Federal Government Information→Catalogue of Federal Domestic Assistance→Scholarships

FEDIX/MOLIS—Federal Information Exchange, Inc. FEDIX provides information on the scholarships and grants offered by several U.S. government agencies. MOLIS, the Minority On-line Information Service, lists scholarship sources for minority students. ✓**INTERNET** ...→*www* http://web.fie.com ...→*www* gopher://fedix.fie.com

State Agency Address Book Find the telephone numbers of each state's education, disability, and veterans agencies—they're excellent sources of local educational funding information. ✓**EWORLD**→*go* rsp→State Agency Address Book

U.S. Department of Education This is the home page of the Department of Education, and a main source for information about federal funding opportunities. Use the option "A Researcher's Guide to the U.S. Department of Education" to search for grants and fellowships. ✓**INTERNET**→*www* http://www.edu.gov

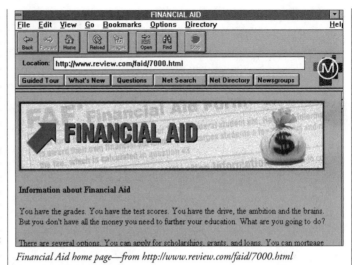

Financial Aid home page—from http://www.review.com/faid/7000.html

Grad students only

Funding Graduate School If there is anything harder than paying for college, it's paying for graduate school. This is a list of grad school funding options. ✓**INTERNET** →*www* http://www.cs.emu.edu:8001/afs/cmu.edu.user/mkant/ftp/FinAid/html/fellowships

Potential Sources of Funding for Graduate Students A list of major fellowships for graduate students, including contact names and addresses, eligibility requirements, deadlines, and, most important, scholarship amounts. ✓**INTERNET**→*www* http://bunny.cs.uiuc.edu/funding/generalinfo/gradStudents.txt

Minorities

African Studies Grants and Fellowships (UPenn) The University of Pennsylvania's African Studies Department publishes a list of scholarships and awards available to minority students studying Africa or African Americans. This gopher lists the awards and offers information about the

Nestlé minority scholarships database. ✓**INTERNET**→*gopher* gopher-penninfo.upenn.edu 71→Interdisciplinary Programs→African Studies→Grants and Fellowships

Latino Scholarships and Grants (UCLA) The Chicano Studies Center at UCLA maintains an extensive listing of funding opportunities. ✓**INTERNET**→*www* http://lmrinet.gse.ucsb.edu→Grants, Fellowships & Employment

Minority Scholarships and Fellowships (UCSC) No matter what kind of program you're in, there's probably financial aid for which you are eligible. Search financial aid opportunities by school, state, degree program, or sponsoring institution. ✓**INTERNET**→*www* http://web.fie.com/htbin/ cashe.pl

Planning ahead

College Calculator What's the magic figure you should invest to be able to afford a college education for your children? This Excel spreadsheet estimates the figure for both public and private school tuitions. ✓**COMPUSERVE**→*go* excel→Libraries→Excel for the Mac→COL-CAL.ZIP

U.S. Series EE Savings Bonds for College An Excel spreadsheet that determines the future value of bonds you are now saving for your child's college tuition and calculates the taxable savings return. For Excel 3.0 or higher. ✓**COMPUSERVE**→*go* excel→Libraries→Excel for the Mac→ EECOLL.XLS

Scholarships

CASHE Scholarship Information The "College Aid Sources for Higher Education" program is a for-profit enterprise with a database of over 150,000 awards of financial support at its fingertips. Simply fill out a questionnaire, and for $30 the service will generate a report with all the appropriate aid sources. The rest is up to you. ✓**GENIE**→*keyword* cashe $

Contests Are you good at chess? Do you have a talent for creative writing? If you'd like to beef up a college application and pocket some scholarship cash, consider entering a national competition. Grade- and high-school students can search for the competition that's right for them on this Website. ✓**INTERNET**→*www* http://www. cs.emu.edu:8001/afs/cmu.edu.user /mkant/Public/FinAid/finaid.html

Financial Aid Library Did you know about the *Journalism Internship Guide*, the *Armenian American Almanac*, or the *Guide to Literary Prizes, Grants and Awards in Britain and Ireland*? To open up the frantic funding search beyond the massive scholarship databases featured in its online database, the Reference Press provides descriptions of hundreds of offline, eclectic publications about grants, internships, scholarships, and

> "Free College Money! Ask Lesko, and you'll find out that military academies, state governments, and Uncle Sam are all rich sources of aid. Lesko describes hundreds of the aid packages available."

awards. ✓**EWORLD**→*go* rsp→Financial Aid Library

Foundation Center If the resources on the Net are not enough, the Foundation Center—a nationwide network of libraries specializing in finding money for students—lists its many locations and contact numbers, and provides a summary of its resources. ✓**INTERNET**→*gopher* itsa.ucsf.edu→ Researcher Tools→The Foundation Center

Free College Money Free college money! Free college money! According to Information U.S.A. guru Matthew Lesko, students just need to know where to look and whom to ask. Ask Lesko, and you'll find out that military academies, state governments, and Uncle Sam are all rich sources of aid. Lesko describes hundreds of the aid packages available, providing information such as addresses, telephone numbers, contacts, and

program or grant requirements. ✓**COMPUSERVE**→*go* ius-25613

Fulbright Scholar Program A description of Fulbright grants for lecturing and research in the coming year. Keep abreast of deadlines and this year's favored fields of study. ✓**INTERNET**→*gopher* gate.oxy. edu→Grants, Fellowships, Academic Positions and Summer Institute→ Fulbright Scholar Program

Grant Getter's Guide to the Internet A detailed guide to finding federal funding on the Net. Information on education resources on the Net and an annotated bibliography of other Internet guides are also included. ✓**INTERNET**→*gopher* uidaho.edu→Science, Research, & Grant Information→Grant Information→A Grant Getter's Guide to the Internet

Grants and Fellowships If you're looking for college and research funding, this may be the place to start. Heavy hitters like the American Philosophical Society, the Ford Foundation, and the National Science Foundation provide information on their grants and fellowships, as do other organizations such as the American Antiquarian Society, the American Center for Research in Egypt, and the Center for Lesbian and Gay Studies. ✓**INTERNET**→*gopher* gate. oxy.edu→Grants, Fellowships, Academic Positions and Summer Institute→Pre- and Post-Doctoral Fellowships

National Endowment for the Humanities A listing of grants being offered by the National Endowment for the Humanities. ✓**INTERNET**→*gopher* gate.oxy.edu→ Grants, Fellowships, Academic Positions and Summer Institute→National Endowment for the Humanities

National Science Foundation
A searchable database of award abstracts from the National Science Foundation. Listings include application deadlines, contacts, and requirements. ✓ **INTERNET**→*gopher* stis.nsf.gov→Index to NSF Award Abstracts

RSP Funding Focus With four separate databases created by the Reference Press, this service lists hundreds of scholarship and grant opportunities for undergraduates, graduates, and researchers. This is the most comprehensive collection of scholarship information in Cyberspace to date, and one of the easiest to use. Each database is categorized for minorities, women, veterans, the disabled, and students interested in studying abroad. A sample search on undergraduate aid for women turns up funding opportunities ranging from America's Junior Miss to the Clare Boothe Luce scholarships for women in engineering. Remember—it's harder than ever to pay for an education and this service will help you leave no funding stone unturned. ✓ **EWORLD**→*go* rsp→Dollar for Study, Research & Creative Activities

Scholarships and Grants A gateway to educational funding sources, including the Grant Getter's Guide, the Catalogue of Federal Assistance, and FEDIX. For science scholars and researchers, the site links to the National Institutes of Health, the National Science Foundation, and the Science and Technology Service. The online version of the *Scientist* is also available here. ✓ **INTERNET**→*gopher* riceinfo.rice.edu→Research Interests and Opportunities

Scholarships, Fellowships, and Grants A collection of fellowship opportunities prepared by major universities. The fellowship listings may be repetitious, but it is nevertheless worthwhile to study each school's catalog for little-known yet lucrative programs. Keep in mind that the clearinghouse nature of the project yields uneven results: while some universities merely list opportunities, others have taken the time to build searchable databases. The University of Kansas, for instance, has a particularly useful listing, with fellowships organized by deadline. ✓ **INTERNET**→*www* http://www.cs. emu.edu:8001/afs/cmu.edu.user/ mkant/ftp/FinAid/html/fellowships

Study Abroad Fellowships/ Scholarships for U.S. Students (UPenn) If you're determined to go abroad for your junior year in college, but need help paying for it, this gopher lists fellowships intended to help you expand your horizons. Some are only relevant to Penn students, but others are open to all comers. Rest assured: there are other scholarships besides the Rotary and Fulbright. Just take a look. ✓ **INTERNET**→*gopher* gopher://gopher-penn info.upenn.edu:71/1M%20penn info-srv.upenn.edu%209000% 206873%20Campus_Activities

Women

Fellowships/Scholarships for Women (Albany) While far from exhaustive, these two lists provide a significant number of sources of educational funding for women. The Albany list is organized by grant—ranging from National Science Foundation grants for biology to Wellesley College music fellowships. The Minnesota listing includes information on such programs as the Congressional Fellowships for Women in Public Policy and the National Association of Mexican-American Women. ✓ **INTERNET** ...→*gopher* leah.albany.edu→Academic Departments and Programs→Women's Studies→Scholarships—Awards— StudentOpportunities ...→*gopher* rodent.cis.umn.edu 11112→Women in Science and Engineering (WISE)→ Scholarships, Grants and Financial Support

Tapping Internet Resources for Women in Computing TAP (The Ada Project) offers an extensive listing of scholarships and fellowships for women in computer science and engineering. Includes a list of support organizations for women in the sciences. ✓ **INTERNET** →*www* http://www.ccs.yale.edu/ HTML/YALE/CS/HyPlans/tap/tap. html

> "RSP Funding Focus is the most comprehensive collection of scholarship information in Cyberspace to date, and one of the easiest to use. Each database is categorized for minorities, women, veterans, the disabled, and students interested in studying abroad."

College life

So, you've been admitted to the college of your choice, or the college of your second

choice, and now you're starting to get nervous about what campus life will bring. Will there be lots of work? Lots of sex? Lots of drugs? Lots of rock-and-roll? All of the above, hopefully, and in a package so kinetic and chaotic that it will keep you energized for years. Start on **soc.college** to find out what undergrads are overexerted about these days, and then continue on to **alt.folklore.college** to disabuse yourself of misconceptions about the college process. (Yes, Virginia, there really is an honor clause.) If you've already arrived on campus and you've immediately generated an intense dislike for your bunkmate, you might want to think about posting to **alt.flame. roommate**, and Greeks of all stripes can work their Panhellenic magic on **alt. college.fraternities** and **alt.college.sororities**.

On the Net

Across the board

alt.college.fraternities (ng) In addition to old-boy greetings and meetings, this newsgroup hosts debates on the institution itself. Hazing, the single-sex policy, and date

College fun—downloaded from CompuServe's Bettmann Archive

rape are consistently hot topics, and you may even run into someone unself-conscious enough to defend one of the three. ✓**USENET**

alt.college.sororities (ng) Less vocal than the fraternities newsgroup, the distaff half of the Greek newsgroups consists of friendly contact between "sisters"—both college students and alums. ✓**USENET**

alt.flame.roommate (ng) Practical and serious discussions are not the rule. While this newsgroup does occasionally address such real problems as the Roommate Who Will Not Pay Her Share, the Roommate Who Will Not Clean the Bathroom, and the Roommate Who Will Not Spend One Second Without Her Annoying Boyfriend Rick, many of the postings are consumed by hollow rage, filled with the sort of baseless griping that any student knows all too well. Still, roommate bashing is an unavoidable part of college life, and all members of the college set should know about this electronic opportunity to mock your

bunkmate mercilessly. ✓**USENET**

alt.folklore.college (ng) Do you really get a 4.0 if your roommate dies during the term? For answers to this and other myths of college life, just dive into this newsgroup. In addition to charting past folklore, the group invites participants to contribute new experiences to the annals of college folklore. Some of them are so extreme (sex in a carillon tower that drowned out the bells) that they sound like lies, but that's the beauty of the Net: epistemologically bankrupt, it makes every story an equal. ✓**USENET**

> "People seem more than willing to share test-taking strategies and tips about little-known funding sources."

College Life **Milestones**

College BB The bulletin board leader posts pertinent news, and his picks for best college values and most promising majors in the Academics topic. There is a mixture of college chatter and serious information-seeking on this board. In topics like Financial Aid, Admissions Testing, and Choosing a School, parents and kids seek, and receive, advice. People seem more than willing to share test-taking strategies and tips about little-known funding sources. College students bond with one another about required reading (not *Ulysses* again!) and job prospects. And confused sophomores get help from students who say, "go with your heart—be an art major" and parents pushing law school. ✓**PRODIGY**→*jump* college bb

College Students Serious discussions on college life and getting the most out of an education. Nontraditional students (read: older than 18, probably with kids) exchange survival strategies; concerned state-school students discuss school reputation with their compatriots at smaller private institutions; and everyone worries about how to pay for all this knowledge. ✓**GENIE**→*keyword* ert→Education Bulletin Board→Set Category→Colleges & Universities →College Students

soc.college (ng) There are always hundreds of messages on this newsgroup devoted to "the fine art of procrastination" and other weighty college issues. Despite the slacker veneer, this newsgroup is also useful for guerrilla research: just ask questions about a school of your choice and then lurk in the shadows, listening to the opinions of students who know the answers. Between their alternately jaded and naïve insights and the glossy, misleading college brochure

you've received in the mail, you may actually start to get a clearer picture of the place. The group's FAQ is a how-to guide to finding student's email addresses. ✓**USENET** *FAQ:* ✓**INTERNET**→*ftp* rtfm.mit.edu→ anonymous→<your email address> →/pub/usenet-by-group/soc.college/

Keeping in touch

Links to Colleges and Universities These pages provide links to a large number of prominent colleges and universities worldwide. (See pages 72–77 for addresses to the Websites of American colleges and universities.) ✓**INTERNET** ...→*www* http://white.nosc.mil/ht-lan/imagemap/PEHP_College?155,40 ...→*www* http://wwwhost.ccutexas.edu/world.univ.html ...→*www* http://www.clasu-fl.edu/CLAS/american-universities.html ...→*www* http://www.dartmouth.edu/Pages/other-Schools.html ...→*www* http://www.mit.edu:8001/people/cdemello/univ.html

Universities by Country Link to academic institutions worldwide, including universities in Croatia, Thailand, the U.K. and the United States. ✓**INTERNET**→ *www* http://akebono.stanford.edu/yahoo/Education/Universities

University Telephone Search A gopher index of university phone books that you can search. Less user-friendly than the White Pages, it offers the advantage of searching all institutions for those unsure of affiliations. ✓**INTERNET**→*gopher* gopher.nd.edu→Non-Notre Dame Information Sources→Phone Books→Other Institutions

White Pages Need to find someone at the Sorbonne, Yale, Keo University, Western Australia

University, or Los Alamos National Laboratory? This service enables you to choose the institution and then search phone directories by last name. If your target is listed, you get not only email addresses, but phone numbers and snail mail addresses as well. You can use this service to contact professors or admissions staff members at most universities. ✓**INTERNET**→ *www* http://fiaher,ncsa.uiuc.edu:8080/cgi-bin/phfd

---

Grad school & beyond

If the mortarboard fits, wear it—and keep wearing it, and wearing it, and wearing

it. Graduating college is a wonderful experience, certainly, but it's not the end of the world. And for many people, it's not even the end of the educational world. Law school, medical school, master's degrees, doctorates —these lofty diplomas beckon with promises of better jobs, higher pay, intensified prestige, and also a little learning here and there. If you're in a graduate program, or thinking about it, don't forget the Net. Online academic resources address a broad spectrum of graduate topics, including the best programs in various disciplines (**Graduate School Rankings**), a detailed guide to business school (**B-School Confidential**), and a law school mailing list (**bit.listserv.lawsch-l**). And for a more general discussion of graduate-school days keep your eyes on **soc. college.grad**.

On the Net

Across the board

soc.college.grad, soc.college. gradinfo (ng) Funny—all anyone here seems to care about is choosing and getting into a graduate program. Faculty members and

Columbia University Law Library—downloaded from http://www.columbia.edu/

grad students who visit the forum are usually receptive to questions from prospective applicants. ✓**USENET**

Guides & rankings

Graduate School Rankings Drawn from *U.S. News & World Report*'s 1994 rankings, this list ranks the top 50 graduate programs in law, business, medical, engineering, fine arts, and social work. Medical and engineering schools are also listed by excellence in specialties. The ranking criteria for each category—selectivity, placement success, faculty resources, and reputation—are clearly explained. ✓**INTERNET**→ *www* http://www.cs.cmu.edu: 8001/afs/cs.cmu.edu/user/lan day/pub/www/school-rankings.txt

Peterson's Graduate School Guide Search a database for domestic and international graduate programs. Profiles include information on costs, programs, faculty, student body, and facilities. ✓**GENIE**→ *keyword* gradline **$**

Business school

B-School Confidential A guide to business school that walks you through making the decision to

> "B-School Confidential is a guide to business school that walks you through making the decision to go, choosing a school, getting through the year, building a social life, and succeeding at your first job."

go, choosing a school, getting through the year, building a social life, and succeeding at your first job; it's informal and informative. ✓**INTERNET**→*www* http://161.21.2.29/bsc/bsc.html

bit.listserv.mba-l (ng) When Dartmouth dropped in *Business Week*'s ranking of M.B.A. programs, list members wanted to know the scoop. That burning desire for the truth abated when one subscriber noted that grads still make "$95K, 4th highest." From GMAT scores to course requirements to business school standings, the list reflects the anxieties and occasional avarice of students in a professional grad program. ✓**USENET**

Business Schools A worldwide list of business schools with Web and/or gopher presence, including Harvard, Wharton, Cornell, Dartmouth, and the estimable Helsinki Business Polytechnic. ✓**INTERNET**→ *www* http://akebono.stanford.edu/yahoo/Business/Business_Schools/

Law school

bit.listserv.lawsch-l (ml) One guy's searching for law schools with good programs in patent law. Another's begging for outlining tips. And then there's the student trying to figure out what a professor who just moved from Stanford to Chicago-Kent might ask on the final exam. While the current law students prepare themselves for a life of paperwork and litigation, undergrads flood the forum asking for feedback on their LSAT scores. ✓**INTERNET**→*email* listserv@american.edu ✍ *Type in message body:* subscribe lawsch-l <your full name>

Law RoundTable *The Paper Chase* has moved to Cyberspace—

in fact, it's in the Law Student Study Hall (category 5) of GEnie's Law bulletin board. Get help with your torts paper, vent your anxiety about the constitutional law professor, or debate the chances of finding a Wall Street job in the '90s. Elsewhere in the category, students offer one another pointers on choosing the best school and confronting the LSATs. And finally, the law students and lawyers proffer more or less sound advice for those contemplating America's most popular profession. ✓**GENIE**→*keyword* law→Law Bulletin Board

Medical school

Medical RoundTable The knee bone's connected to the thigh bone....Doctors in training and student nurses use this bulletin board to commiserate, connect, and converse with others undergoing rigorous medical programs. Advice on the best way of getting through the 48-hour shifts and the MCATs is freely offered, and career planning in the form of specialty debates is a common theme. Those considering the challenge of med school will find college-course suggestions and strategies for getting into a program in the United States. ✓**GENIE** →*keyword* medical→Medical Bulletin Board

Adult education

misc.education.adult FAQ Lists sources of education and job-training opportunities for adults. The telephone numbers and addresses of sponsoring organizations and publications are also included. ✓**INTERNET**→*ftp* rtfm.mit.edu→ anonymous→<your email address> →/pub/usenet-by-group/misc.education.adult

What are MBA interviews like?

"I had an interview with the Tuck School in February. The interview was comparable to job interviews (I had two each with The Boston Consulting Group and McKinsey). In contrast to the consultants, there were of course no cases which I had to solve. The interview lasted 40 minutes. Warming up (small talk about weather, my journey). Why do you want to become an MBA? Why at Dartmouth College? What are your goals? Then she answered my questions. A short discussion followed.

"The preparation is comparable to that for a job interview, also. Get the university's brochure, write down questions you have about the MBA program or about the MBA in general. But don't ask simple questions that could be answered by reading the brochure. Better ask for details of the curriculum, about the dorms... You should know the answers to the questions I mentioned above. But don't read from a sheet of paper!"
—from **bit.listserv.mba-l**

Making travel easy

Ah, the exhilaration of travel. New places. New faces. The unavoidable ulcer that you'll

develop from dealing with the hassles of booking flights, renting cars, reserving hotels, and dealing with unexpected cold snaps and typhoons. With the Net, though, all this stress will book a one-way trip out of your body, and the myriad online resources for making travel arrangements will have you smiling. First, there's **Eaasy Sabre**, the premier travel booking service in the world, with access to hundreds of airlines and thousands of hotels. Buy a plane ticket, pay for a hotel room, all online! Travelers sniffing out cheap fares should point their proboscis toward **Bargain Finders**, and then visit the **rec.travel library** to learn a little about their affordable destination. Before you leave, visit GEnie's **Travel RoundTable** to pick up tips and hotspots, and get a weather report from **Weather/Travel Information**. And if you're a fan of rail travel, don't forget to check out the **European Railway Schedules** for fares and times from rail lines across the continent. Remember—the trains in Spain run mainly in the rain.

Cruise ship—downloaded from America Online's Pictures of the World Forum

On the Net

Before you travel

Business Travel Tips Frequent business travelers will find this collection of articles useful for taking some of the sting out of hitting the road. The Budget Tips section keeps track of the best incentive programs and booking services, and the service also ranks hotels based on the perks they provide for business travelers. In addition, there's a Business Travel News database, which compiles press articles about changing travel conditions—everything from visa restrictions and fare fluctuations to car-rental policies. ✓**EWORLD**→*go* wwyh→Business Travel Tips

GNN Travel Center Interviews, articles, news, and resources that cover all areas of travel. Includes direct links to dozens of specialty guides, and travel-related Websites as well as instructions for subscribing to GNN's Travel Center newsletter, which contains updates on new Websites. ✓**INTERNET**→ *www* http://nearnet.gnn.com/ gnn/meta/travel/index.html

Internet Travel Mall (ITM) ITM is still in its infancy, but the concept of an electronic travel-brochure service is a promising one. Let's say you want to go to Fredericksburg, Texas. With online navigation tools, you can explore places to stay on your trip into the Lone Star State, and learn about the region from the publicity materials of each hotel or lodge.

The Web page for the Inn on the Creek Bed & Breakfast, for instance, includes rates, accommodations, and breakfast schedules, and describes the history of the area. And if it's Utah and not Texas that you're traveling to, you might be interested in information about a paragliding school just outside of Salt Lake City. For the time being, the pickings are a little slim, but more attractions will certainly be added.

The mall also contains dozens of useful 800 numbers, including listings for airlines, rental-car companies, motorcoach lines, international rail lines, cruise lines, and hotel/motel/resort chains. And finally, there is a miscellaneous travel library that includes such documents as an explanation of rental-car companies' age requirements and a glossary of airline terminology. ✓**INTERNET**→*www* http://io.com:8001/

rec.travel library This site offers a connection to a number of interesting archives. You can search for travel information by country and wind up with a profile written by a recent visitor. Or you can choose one of the more specific categories—clothing-optional beaches, bookstores, ski resorts. Whether you're interested in browsing travel recommendations from the Centers for Disease Control or checking out the financial profiles of foreign nations in the CIA World Factbook, the travel library has something for you. General FAQs lean toward time-tested travel topics such as exchange rates and intelligent packing. ✓**INTERNET** ...→*ftp* ftp.cc.umanitoba.ca→/rec-travel ...→*www* http://www.digi-mark.net/rec-travel

rec.travel.marketplace (ng) You know that section in the *New York Times* devoted to good deals and good advice on travel accommodations? Well, this is much better. Ask about international air fares, and travel agencies will post their best offers. Inquire about a cheap hotel in Amsterdam and you'll get a recommendation ("BOB's Youth Hostel if you don't mind a bunch of students who just like to kick back and get stoned!"). Discount fares, time shares, and apartment sublets are posted regularly. Bangkok or Paris, anyone? ✓**USENET**

rec.travel.misc (ng) This is a traveler's hangout—search for an apartment share in Paris, seek advice about a travel agent who

wants cash up front, or get feedback on the advantages and disadvantages of hostels. ✓**USENET** *FAQ:* ✓**INTERNET**→*ftp* rtfm.mit.edu→anonymous→<your email address> →/pub/usenet-by-hierarchy/rec/travel/misc

Tourism Offices Worldwide Directory Whether you're traveling as a tourist, a student, or a businessperson, a reliable source for currency, hotel, restaurant, and transportation information is usually the local tourist office. Search by country name for addresses and telephone numbers. ✓**INTERNET**→ *www* http://www.mbnet.mb.ca/travel/tourism-offices.html

Travel RoundTable Bulletin boards contain discussions on every destination imaginable—not only Europe and the Caribbean, but also the Middle East and the Far East, as well as some hidden treasures within our own national borders. In addition, users can download travel journals, articles, and maps from the travel libraries. ✓**GENIE**→*keyword* travel

> "On Delphi's Worldline you plug in a country name and information on local customs, business hours, currency, taxis, and tipping policies will be delivered to your screen."

The Traveler's Checklist Homepage Catalog of hard-to-find travel accessories, including a handy reference page that explains the ins and outs of using your electrical appliances on foreign voltage and the various adapters needed. ✓**INTERNET**→*www* http://www.ag.com/Travelers/Checklist/homepage

Worldline Globe-trotters should certainly be aware of this excellent source. Simply plug in a country name and information on local customs, business hours, currency, taxis, and tipping policies will be delivered to your screen. In addition, Worldline includes online phrase books for major foreign languages. And if you really get in trouble, the database lists addresses and phone numbers for U.S. consulates and embassies worldwide. ✓**DELPHI**→*go* trav news→world

Online booking

Eaasy Sabre Developed by American Airlines, Eaasy Sabre is the big dog of the online travel services, with access to 600 airlines (300 with online booking), 18,000 hotels, and 45 car-rental companies worldwide. The service is something of a task at first— new users must fill out brief registration forms, after which they are issued user ID cards and instructed to choose two passwords (twice as good as one password for insuring the security of any plans you might make). From there, though, it's like a magic carpet ride.

To book a flight, simply select the Flights menu, enter your destination, and then wait as Sabre retrieves all appropriate routes. The Fare command brings up a screen with round-trip and one-way prices for each flight, along with any restrictions, and if you select the Bargain Hunter option, the computer will filter for the lowest fares. Once you have settled on an itinerary and airline, just confirm the reservation. The process of reserving rental cars and hotel rooms is just as easy.

Designed originally for travel agents, Sabre has added a slightly friendlier version for the uninitiated; frequent travelers who know travel codes (quick—what's the standard abbreviation for Midway Airport in Chicago?) may want to stick with the Fasttrack option. ✓**AMERICA ONLINE**→ *keyword* sabre ✓**COMPUSERVE**→*go* sabre ✓**EWORLD** →*go* sabre ✓**DELPHI**→*go* trav→air→ sabre ✓**GENIE**→ *keyword* sabre ✓**PRODIGY**→*jump* eaasy sabre

PC Travel Check airline fares and schedules, make reservations, and purchase tickets online with a major credit card (a credit card is required to search fare and schedule information although no charges are incurred unless you elect to buy a ticket). PC Travel will deliver your ticket via overnight FedEx. ✓**INTERNET**→*www* pctravel. com

Travel Agents Online This loosely affiliated organization of Internet-accessible travel agents provides one-stop shopping for online assistance and even travel discounts. The Hotels_Plus service, for example, has access to 4,000 hotel and 1,600 car-rental locations throughout the world; other specialized agencies can help you take advantage of cheap fares to Eastern Europe or the South Pacific, or book a hotel for your Mexican honeymoon. ✓**INTERNET**→ *www* http://cc.umanitoba.ca/rec-travel/travel-agents.html

TravelShopper Browse through airline listings, compare prices, or even make a reservation with this

Downhill skier—downloaded from America Online's Macintosh Graphics Forum.

online service. Simply choose a departure point, destination, and travel dates, and TravelShopper will generate a list of all available flights. Then fill out a brief personal profile to determine fare eligibility, select the cheapest flight still remaining, and book your tickets. Because the service is affiliated with TWA and Northwest, you must be flying one of these carriers to receive the tickets by direct mail. Otherwise, your tickets will be mailed to a nearby affiliated travel agent or lie in wait for you at the airport. ✓**COMPUSERVE**→ *go* worldcim ✓**DELPHI**→*go* trav air→ travelshopper

Travel clubs

Traveler's Advantage This travel club advertises 50 percent discounts on hotels and discounts of up to 50 percent on "hot ticket" promotions. Updates on the latest special values on cruises and package vacations are also posted here. And as an added incentive, Traveler's Advantage gives an extra discount of 5 percent on every part of your trip that you book through Prodigy's online services.

For $1 you can have a three-month trial; the yearly fee is $49. ✓**PRODIGY**→*jump* travelers **$**

VIP Club For a yearly fee of $34, this members-only service entitles you to book flights, cars, hotels, tours, and cruises online—and gives discounts for all transactions. VIP members not only have access to special rates and immediate booking, but also earn discounts on any Sabre bookings. ✓**DELPHI**→ *go* trav vip **$**

Air travel

Aviation Weather Reports A complete airline weather service, with updates on snowstorms, fog, icy conditions, and even hot hail. ✓**COMPUSERVE**→*go* weather→Aviation

Bargain Finders Search by country, city, and region for the lowest fares available. The fares are only indexed by destination, so not all listed flights will be of use, but they'll certainly be cheap—Bargain Finders is a whiz at turning up reductions of 8 percent on same-day tickets or dirt-cheap

CYBERPOWER!™

Planning A Trip

My husband and I have been married for six years, and we have a four-year-old daughter. This spring is the first time since Stacy was born that both Rick and I have been able to get time off from work, and we want to try for a week in the islands, maybe Jamaica. I used to work in a travel agency here in Boston, so I know a little bit about making reservations and bookings. I'd like to buy my plane tickets online. Can I?

An easy answer: EAASY Sabre. Developed by American Airlines, Eaasy Sabre is available on virtually every commercial online service. We'll use eWorld's version (keyword: Sabre) as an example. The main Sabre Reservation Menu contains a variety of options, including flights/availability, fare information, hotels, and rental cars. This is the most important screen in Sabre, and if you ever stray from it, you can return by typing "/Res" at any command prompt.

When you enter the Flights/Availability menu, you'll be asked to input your city of origin, your destination, a departure date, and a preferred arrival time. Let's try May 31, and see if we can get you to Jamaica before noon. According to Sabre, there are no direct morning flights from Boston's Logan Airport to Kingston Airport, but there are roughly a dozen routes with plane changes in New York and Miami. Some take off at unreasonable hours—who wants to be sitting in the airport at 5 a.m.?—but then there's American Airlines flight 671 (departs Logan at 7:00 a.m., arrives in Miami at 10:28 a.m.), which connects with American flight 211 (departs Miami at 11:10 a.m., arrives in Kingston at 11:57 a.m.). You'll be on the island in time for a jerk chicken lunch. (If you still remember codes from your travel agent days, you can retrieve flight options with a single command line that includes cities of origin and departure, date of travel, preferred time of departure, number of passengers, and preferred airline—in short, BOS, KIN, MAY31, 700A, 3, AA.)

Next, you'll need to figure your fare. After you select your preferred route from the list of flights, you'll be asked to indicate what type of fare you are seeking—full coach, cheapest available one way, or round trip. When Sabre retrieves possible return flights, pick one—there's another set of American flights that looks good (American 1736 leaving Kingston for Miami at 2:57 p.m. and connecting with American 298, which departs Miami for Boston at 7:20 p.m.)—and ask for the cheapest available round trip. Here's the final damage for two adults and one child: round-trip fares of $403.95 for you and your husband, and $312.95 for your daughter, for a total cost of $1120.85. Search for other Bargain Finder fares if you like, but nothing else comes close; in fact, Sabre will be happy to tell you that you have saved $868 from regular coach fare. With your Sabre account, you can pay by credit card, and tickets will be delivered free via U.S. Mail or Federal Express.

Feeling heady from your successful airline booking? With EAASY Sabre, your power doesn't stop at the jetway door. You can search for a hotel by location, price range, chain, and accomodation, and pick between the town establishments—Jamaica Pegasus ($180/night) and Wyndham Kingston ($190/night)—and that Jamaica Palace resort in Port Antonio

Eaasy Sabre screen from eWorld

($170/night) that your husband's best friend has been raving about. Don't forget to rent your car through Sabre and search for special bargains. And finally, remember to have a great time—drinks on the beach, Majek Fashek in the air. Irie!

round-trips to London. Some carriers let you order tickets through the service, while others require a travel agent or Sabre to confirm the fare. ✓**DELPHI**→*go* trav air→bar

Canadian Airlines No online booking yet, but flight schedules, and assorted other information from one of Canada's premier carriers. ✓**INTERNET**→*www* http:// www.CdnAir.CA/

Guide to Airline Service This quick and handy database collects information on the policies, latest price cuts, and incentive programs of all major air carriers. Simply enter a carrier's name to retrieve information on such topics as VIP clubs, vacation promotions, business benefits, and even baggage allowances. ✓**DELPHI**→*go* trav air→ guide

Official Airline Guide Full lists of all airline flights, schedules, and fares. The service is rather pricey, with access running $10/hour during off-peak hours and soaring to $28/hour in the heart of the business day. Still, the resources are impressive: for any route, the OAG displays all flights and combinations of flights currently available, along with all possible fares. If your choice is available, you can book it immediately. Hotels and motels can also be reserved through the OAG, and the guide offers a number of specialized databases on cruises, skiing, resorts, discount travel, frequent-flyer programs, and weather. ✓**COM-PUSERVE**→*go* oag $ ✓**DELPHI**→*go* trav air→oag $ ✓**GENIE**→*keyword* oag

rec.travel.air (ng) Collecting hundreds of messages per week, this newsgroup serves as travel classified ad board, travel advisor, and travel magazine. Regulars sell their airline tickets, ask for airline

> **"For any route, the Official Airline Guide displays all flights and combinations of flights currently available, along with all possible fares. If your choice is available, you can book it immediately."**

recommendations, debate smoking restrictions, and post their adventures. ✓**USENET** *FAQ:* ✓**INTERNET** →*ftp* rtfm.mit.edu→anonymous→ <your email address>→/pub/ usenet-by-hierarchy/rec/travel/air

rec.travel library—air travel Need bulk tickets? Want to know how to avoid jet lag? Curious which airline has the best frequent-flyer perks? This collection of FAQs and articles from rec.travel collects the airborne experiences and wisdom of the well-traveled. And remember—when using this library, all seatbacks must be in the upright position. ✓**INTERNET**→*ftp* ftp.cc.umanitoba.ca→/rec-travel/air-travel

WinFly v1.0b Mile-tracking database for frequent flyers. Shareware for Windows. ✓**PC OHIO**→d→ *Download a file:* WINFLY.ZIP

Car travel

Guide to Car Rental Costs Though the information offered

in this searchable database is limited to new promotion news, members of Delphi's VIP travel club ($34/year) have access to an online reservation network linked to major car-rental agencies worldwide. Search by company or location. ✓**DELPHI**→*go* trav car $

TripMaker Demo Rand McNally's TripMaker plans car trips anywhere in the United States, Mexico, or Canada, with more than 640,000 miles of road and more than 125,000 cities committed to memory. Download the demo, and if you like the program, order the real version with the online form. ✓**COMPUSERVE**→*go* travel software→Libraries→*Search for a file:* TDEMO. ZIP

Cruises

Compu-Cruise by Rosenbluth With hundreds of itineraries and an online reservation capability, Rosenbluth's is one of the most sophisticated online cruise brokers. Earn a free cruise, download cruise graphics, and learn all about why people like to spend days and days in big boats drinking, eating, and dancing. ✓**COMPUSERVE**→*go* ros-35

Cruises One of the best online sources for information about cruises and cruise packages. Profiles of cruise lines, ships, and cruise routes, in addition to CruiSearch, a database that allows you to select a cruise by location or duration. Members of Delphi's VIP club receive all kinds of cruise discounts. ✓**DELPHI**→*go* trav cruis

rec.travel.cruises (ng) Cruise recommendations, ticket sales, and travel-agent advertisements fill the group. ✓**USENET**

Train

European Railway Schedules

Isn't train travel romantic? In Europe, riding the rails can often save time and multiply your destination options. Deutsche Bahn AG and CompuServe have joined forces to provide this extensive booking and browsing service for European railways. Learn about all available trains, their services (sleeper car, dinettes), and prices. Consult the station appendix to find out if you can rent a car, or at the very least expect a fleet of taxis, when you arrive. At this time you can only book if your travel plans include Germany, but schedule information is transnational. ✓**COMPUSERVE**→*go* railway

rec.travel.library—train travel

Riding Amtrak in the near future? How about the Finnish or German rail systems? Well, take heart—the schedules of all three are now available online. The Amtrak listings are maintained by a private Web user, and while they may not always be current, they're excellent for general planning. The German listing also includes fare, fly & ride, and station locale information. ✓**INTERNET** →*ftp* ftp.cc.umanitoba.ca→anonymous/<your email address>→/rec-travel/train-travel

Hotels & lodging

AA Accommodations (UK)

The British Automobile Club maintains this extensive database of hotels, guest houses, inns, farmhouse accommodation, and camping and caravan sites. Each entry is based on an actual visit to the site, and attempts to capture the flavor of the place, down to descriptions of antique fireplaces and the specials of the house kitchen. Hygienically tetchy Americans will be happy to learn that special "ser-

Coliseum—downloaded from America Online's Pictures of the World Forum.

vices" like showers and in-room baths are noted. You can search the entries by type of accommodation, city, postal code, or price range. ✓**COMPUSERVE**→*go* ukac-comm

ABC Worldwide Hotel Guide

If you ever need to find a hotel in Ulan Bator, Mongolia, this would be the place to check. This large database (7,000 listings) can be searched by country, city, or hotel name. While no price information is included, other useful tidbits for the business traveler (fax numbers, credit card acceptance, meeting rooms availability) are noted in each entry, along with a general description of hotel services, neighborhood, and "type of clientele." ✓**COMPUSERVE**→*go* abc

Bed & Breakfast Guide Increasingly, business travelers are opting for a more intimate hotel experience, and especially frequent business travelers, who are turning to B&Bs for a little R&R. This guide lists more than 1,000 B&Bs in the U.S. and Canada and links to 108 B&B reservations agents with over 11,000 guest homes on file. Reasonable rates remain a priority for the compilers of this service. ✓**AMERICA ONLINE**→*keyword* b&b

Guide to Hotel Chains A simple search retrieves basic information on most major hotel chains—not only rack rates and services, but incentive programs and bargain packages. Members of Delphi's VIP travel club ($34 per year) enjoy savings of up to 30 percent at hotels worldwide. ✓**DELPHI**→*go* trav hotel

Hilltop House Bed and breakfast inn in the heart of Napa-Sonoma wine country, set atop the Mayacamas Mountains on 135 acres of unspoiled wilderness. ✓**INTERNET**→ *www* http://www.baynet.com/bb/bb1.html

Neptune—Travel Industry Network Not a conventional travel agency, Neptune is a discount booking service that forwards reservations to individual hotels. The network currently links to Miami and Orlando, and plans to add links to Paris, London, Jerusalem, Atlanta, and Austin, Texas. ✓**INTERNET**→*www* http://www.neptune.com

Prodigy Inn Directory This convenient service allows you to find an inn by location. Selecting domestic or international inns, and then narrowing your search further, you can access a map detailing all major roads and cities. Then choose a city or a local attraction (national park, college) and a list of nearby inns appears. Each B&B entry contains its map coordinates, information on rates, services, child and smoking policies, and a description of the ambience. The information in this accommodations database has been provided by the innkeepers themselves, so prices should be current, even if descriptions may tend toward the picturesque. ✓**PRODIGY**→*jump* inns

Quest Hotel This club entitles card members to 50 percent discounts on 1,500 hotels worldwide for a yearly fee of $29.95. Simply scan their directory of hotels and book by telephone. ✓ **PRODIGY** →*jump* quest

Saint Lucia Vacation Rental Saint Lucia, West Indies, location: three bedrooms, two baths, kitchen, dining room, living room, porch with view, three-minute walk to beach, five-minute walk to tennis courts, nine-hole golf course, horseback riding. Maid included in rental price. You get the picture. ✓ **INTERNET**→*www* http://branch. com:1080/lucia/lucia.html

Restaurants

Zagat's Restaurant Survey Concise descriptions of fine dining establishments across the country—not only basic information, but descriptions of cuisine, quality ratings, and pricing guides. Special features such as singing waiters and private rooms are duly noted. Zagat's covers all major U.S. cities, and most guides can be searched by neighborhood, type of cuisine, and price range. ✓ **COMPUSERVE**→*go* tra-30 ✓ **PRODIGY**→*jump* zagats

Software support

Travel Software Support Forum Presently devoted to Rand McNally's TripMaker, which plans car trips anywhere in North America, the forum also includes a message board for discussion of the program's benefits and detriments. More vendors are expected. ✓ **COMPUSERVE**→*go* travel software

Weather

International City Forecasts High and low temps in Amman. Rain in Casablanca. Retrieve

> **"Zagat's Restaurant Survey features concise descriptions of fine dining establishments across the country—special features, such as singing waiters and private rooms, are duly noted."**

three-day forecasts on hundreds of major cities worldwide. ✓ **PRODIGY** →*jump* a-z int'l weather

U.S. City Forecasts Weather reports for hundreds of U.S. cities, along with a U.S. map and reports on ski conditions, beaches and boating, and fall foliage, where applicable. ✓ **PRODIGY**→*jump* a-z us weather

Weather Report Weather reports for most major cities in the United States, including national maps, radar, etc. ✓ **COMPUSERVE**→*go* weather

Weather Underground Includes extensive weather reports for the U.S. and Canada, as well as special reports for ski conditions and occasional occurrences such as hurricanes and earthquakes. Also covers selected international cities. ✓ **INTERNET** ...→*telnet* downwind. sprl.umich.edu ...→*telnet* measun. nrrc.ncsu.edu ...→*telnet* wind.atmos.uah.edu ...→*telnet* uscsu.colorado.edu

Weather/Travel Information Who needs Willard Scott? Bryant Gumbel, perhaps, and Katie Couric, certainly, and maybe the thousands of Americans who want to celebrate their hundredth birthdays with a roly-poly ambassador of meteorological goodwill. In fact, he's probably a national treasure. But that's not exactly the point. This is: through this gateway, any ordinary citizen can access dozens of weather services originating from the United States and Canada. Some provide simple forecasts for your destination, and others require graphics capability to display their interactive weather maps. ✓ **INTERNET** →*www* http://www.uiuc.ca:70 /1/weather

Youth travel

College Travel International (CTI) If you're under 25 and traveling, CTI offers information about discount airline tickets, Eurail passes, and travel packages. You can order your American Youth Hostel card online and retrieve information on hostels, an archive of newsletters about college travel discounts, State Department Travel Advisories, and all sorts of coupons for travel discounts. ✓ **INTERNET** ...→*telnet* prairienet.org→*visitor* ...→*email* wolvie@prairienet.org ✍ *Write for help & support*

Internet Guide to Hostelling A valuable resource for backpackers and budget travelers alike with listings for more than a hundred hostels worldwide, tips for traveling cheaply through North America, and answers to the most pressing questions: i.e. what exactly is a sleep-sheet? ✓ **INTERNET**→ *www* http://www.digimark.net/rec-travel/hostels/index. html

Travel guides

Whether you're planning on wandering the Lisbon beaches or camping out in the Austra-

lian outback, your point of departure should be the **GNN Travel Center Region/Country/City/State Guides**, a Web page that links to hundreds and hundreds of fascinating travel guides. There's **Paris**, a magnificent site with links to city history, the Louvre, and a detailed map of the Metro/RER. Or maybe you'd prefer **Jerusalem Mosaic**, or **Travel Britain Online**, or **Welcome to South Africa**. And if you do your research well enough, you can stay home and still have plenty to talk about.

Parliament—ftp://ftp.sunet.se/pub/pictures/views/london.gif

Across the board

Fodor's World View These online versions of the popular Fodor's guidebooks furnish generous information on hotels, restaurants, and culture across the world. With both full-text entries and search capabilities keyed to price range, service type, and location, this is a very comprehensive database—a sample search of restaurant listings by location and cuisine turned up the only Mexican restaurant in Edinburgh (Viva Haggis?). For a fee ($9.95 for one destination, $6.95 for additional two), Fodor's will prepare a personal travel update—just plug in your travel dates online and within

48 hours the company will mail or fax a brochure detailing local events occurring during your trip. ✓EWORLD→*go* fodors

GNN Travel Center Region/ Country/City/State Guides
Traveler's Advisory: Begin your research here. GNN's collection of world travel guides is the travel hub to end all travel hubs. Alaska? Antarctica? Aruba? Austria? Austin, Texas? No problem. And that's just a smattering of the A-list. The resources connected to this site are truly staggering. From the France home page, you can link to the Louvre, learn about the history of Paris, and spend time on the Riviera. Peru's Web page has an interactive map and information on all major cities. And the Kuwait site includes Kuwaiti recipes that you can whip up at the Gulf War Fifth Anniversary Bash. If you're thinking about tak-

ing a trip, and your plans don't remove you from the planet Earth, this is absolutely mandatory. ✓**INTERNET**→*www* http://nearnet.gnn. com/gnn/meta/travel/res/countries.html

rec.travel.usa-canada (ng)

> "If you're thinking about taking a trip, and your plans don't remove you from the planet Earth, GNN Travel Center is absolutely mandatory."

The land between the redwood forests and the Gulf Stream waters, is the traveler's destination of choice here. Oh, Canada is also covered. There are problems with Best Westerns, a wish for more Grand Canyon activities, and exasperation with the cost of renting a car in New York. And that's just the beginning. You should hear what they're saying about tacky tourist towns. ✓**USENET**

Regional & City Guides Regional and city travel guides have been culled from Prodigy member surveys, with a bit of "expert" travel advice thrown in. Choose a destination from the menu to find out what the locals really like to do (or at least what they are willing to share with others online). ✓**PRODIGY**→*jump* travel

Travels with Samantha A winner in the 1994 Best of the Web contest, this North American travelogue includes more than 250 annotated images. ✓**INTERNET**→*www* http://www-swiss.ai.mit.edu /samantha/travels-with-samantha. html

U.S. CityLink Whether you're interested in Cincinnati or Charlotte, New York City or Boston, this is the site for you, with links to dozens of home pages for U.S. cities. While some contain only rudimentary information, others are more extensive—the page for Staunton, Virginia, for instance, has extensive accommodation and attraction listings, including a wealth of materials on the Woodrow Wilson birthplace and museum. ✓**INTERNET**→*www* http:// www.NeoSoft.com:80/citylink/

Virtual Tourist Connects to a number of national and international travel guides, most of which have cultural summaries, local

> **"Virtual Tourist connects to a number of national and international travel guides, most of which have cultural summaries, local weather, and travel cost estimates."**

weather, and travel cost estimates. Information is indexed both graphically and textually, and ranges from resource guides and maps to country information. The Japanese site includes an audio file of the national anthem. ✓**INTERNET** →*www* http://wings.buffalo.edu/ world/

Weissman's Travel Reports Off to visit a new place? These travel profiles will help you know what to expect upon arrival. You can access Weissman's short descriptions of U.S. and international destinations, along with instructions on how to order more detailed reports that contain pertinent information on lodging, eating, money matters, and vital regional dos and don'ts. The cost is either $8.95 or $5.95 per report, depending on its length. ✓**AMERICA ONLINE**→*keyword* travel→Traveler's Corner→Weissman's Travel Reports $ ✓**EWORLD**→*go* travelers→Weissmann Travel Reports

Asia

rec.travel.asia (ng) Teaching in Taiwan, hotel hunting in Japan, doing business in Vietnam, and

more are all covered in this newsgroup devoted to traveling in Asia. ✓**USENET**

Australia

Guide to Australia An excellent site that contains comprehensive information on Oz—not just an Australian culture FAQ, but weather, rail schedules, premier attractions, and national history. ✓**INTERNET**→*www* http://www.csu. edu.au/education/australia.html

Europe

Air France While you cannot yet book an Air France flight through this service, you can find out about all current flights and special programs. ✓**COMPUSERVE**→*go* af

Paris An electronic guide to Paris, including images of and links to information about cafés, expositions, tourist sites, and stores. The site also includes a Paris Glossary that describes each arrondissement, links to Paris schools, and accesses a searchable English-French dictionary of 75,000 words. And then there are the Metro maps. ✓**INTERNET**→*www* http://meteora.ucsd. edu/~norman/paris/

rec.travel.europe (ng) Where are the best sights in Norway? What are good restaurants for Christmas dinner in London? And, how easy is it to make train reservations in Europe? Ask and you shall be answered. ✓**USENET** *FAQ:* ✓**INTERNET**→*ftp* rtfm.mit.edu→ anonymous→<your email address> →/pub/usenet-by-hierarchy/rec/ travel/europe

Travel Britain Online A service of the British Tourist Authority, Travel Britain Online is an up-to-the-minute guide to "events, anniversaries, customs, carnivals and fairs, dance, drama, exhibitions, music, shows, and sport." Each listing includes admission prices. And the UK What's On guide even lists the movies currently playing in London cinemas. ✓**COMPUSERVE**→*go* tbonline

UK Accommodation & Travel Services This service contains a number of useful features for tourists in the United Kingdom. The Automobile Club's ratings of restaurants may help you avoid the notorious plague of the English— bad food, for instance, not just bangers and mash but those omnipresent mushy peas. In fact, each restaurant entry is extremely detailed, down to price range, seating capacity, the best entrees, and even the best sauces. In addition, the service rates British hotels and inns, golf courses, and outings. And soon to come: AA Roadwatch, an up-to-the-minute advisory service for all British roadways. ✓**COMPUSERVE**→*go* ukaccomm

Florida

Destination Florida Thanks to its theme parks, sun, sea, and space center, Florida has always been a hot spot for visitors from around the world. Now, you can search a large database of travel accommodations for the Sunshine State, and purchase tickets to hundreds of cultural and sporting events through an online link to Ticketmaster. ✓**COMPUSERVE**→*go* florida

Israel

Jerusalem Mosaic Maps of Jerusalem. History of Jerusalem. Attractions of Jerusalem. A complete guide to one of the world's most historic cities. ✓**INTERNET**→ *www* http://shum.cc.huji.ac.il /jeru/jerusalem.html

Cozumel—downloaded from GEnie's Travel RoundTable

Mexico

Mexico-L (ml) Mexico is one of the most popular destinations for U.S. tourists and this mailing list discusses the highlights of the nation, from Mexico City to Mayan ruins. ✓**INTERNET**→*email* listserv@ tecmtyvm.mty.itesm.mx ✍ *Type in message body:* subscribe mexico-l <your full name>

Redwood country

Redwood Country Unlimited Access tourist information (maps, images, sight-seeing recommendations, and information about accommodations), a product directory, a services listing, news, and a guide to cultural events in northern California. ✓**INTERNET**→*www* http://www.northcoast.com/unlimited/unlimited.html

Ski country

Ski Resort Guide Capsule summaries of more than 200 ski resorts. There's something for everyone, from the double-black-dia-

mond expert to the newcomer who doesn't know the difference between a stem christie and Agatha Christie. ✓**PRODIGY**→*jump* ski resort guide

South Africa

Welcome to South Africa Lots of talk about natural beauty, cultural resources, and legalized gambling. ✓**INTERNET**→*www* http://osprey.unisa.ac.za/0/docs/south-africa.html

> **"What are good restaurants for Christmas dinner in London? Ask rec.travel.europe and you shall be answered."**

Retirement

What happens when you stop earning a salary? What are

the psychological and physical costs that accompany, or even intensify, the economic sacrifices? GEnie and AOL both have message boards devoted specifically to **Retirement Planning**, and there's even a **Consumer Reports Retirement** section on Prodigy that weighs the comparative benefits of Keoghs, SEPs, IRAs, and pension formulas. In addition, the government's presence on the Net ensures plenty of resources pertaining to Social Security, including **Social Security Administration FAQ** and **Social Security Retirement Benefits**. And if you just want to talk about the ups and downs of retirement life, check out AOL's **SeniorNet Forum**, CompuServe's **Retirement Living Forum**, or Prodigy's **Seniors BB**.

Couple walking—from America Online's Pictures of the World Forum.

questions. Seniors also discuss the difficult business of surviving on a fixed income in the 90s, and in the Finance topic a son warns others about an investment scam that drained his mother's savings. A retiree wants to stay active, and asks if remaining employed will reduce his Social Security payments. And finally, there's the stock club, a group of seniors interested in playing the stock market who exchange investment tips here daily. ✓**PRODIGY**→*jump* aarp ✓**AMERICA ONLINE**→*keyword* aarp

---

Retirement Calculator Retirement may be decades away, but have you started planning yet? This Excel spreadsheet estimates how much you should be saving weekly. ✓**COMPUSERVE**→*go* excel→ Libraries→Excel for the Mac→ RE-TIRE

Retirement Living Forum This forum provides retirement advice in two formats. First, there are the libraries, which contain a wealth of information for downloading. There's the Pension Rights Center,

with its files on pension plans and the Employee Retirement Income Security Act (ERISA); H&R Block's tax information for seniors; primers on mutual funds and IRAs; and Social Security libraries filled with useful programs on benefit calculation, disability and survivor benefits, and benefit adjustments. In the forum itself, participants pose specific questions about retirement issues and are answered by online experts and other retirees. ✓**COMPUSERVE**→*go* senior

---

Seniors BB Seniors meet here to address their special concerns, financial and otherwise. What's the best place to retire? Well, Fort Lauderdale seems to be out, and Costa Rica and Aruba are on the rise—although helpful Georgians point out that there is no tax on pensions in the Peach State. While retirement may seem like a dream

On the Net

Across the board

AARP Bulletin Board The American Association of Retired People runs this bulletin board, and sponsors a special financial counseling service from the Scudder company. Simply choose the Talk to Scudder topic to ask your

> **"What's the best place to retire? Well, Fort Lauderdale seems to be out, and Costa Rica and Aruba are on the rise—although helpful Georgians point out that there is no tax on pensions in the Peach State."**

come true—beer and TV all after-noon—there are also plenty of psychological, financial, and medical fears associated with the process, and the forum also serves to deal with those. One of the biggest topics of discussion on this board, in fact, is long-term health care, and the role of the senior-citizen lobby in the evolving national health care debate. ✓ **PRODIGY**→ *jump* seniors

SeniorNet Forum Seniors exchange investment advice and strategize together about money matters in the investment and finance section of the forum. Although they may be living on fixed incomes, most of the regulars here seem to be practiced, savvy investors, market vets who monitor their stocks, bonds, and mutuals every day of the trading week. Two widows discuss the wisdom of moving from high-yield money markets to more conservative funds; two elderly men compare stock tips. Not all decisions depend on a financial bottom line; one father bought IBM stock because all his kids work there. ✓ **AMERICA ON-LINE**→ *keyword* seniornet

Retirement benefits

Fidelity On-Line Investment Center Fidelity offers an online calculation of retirement benefits. First, prepare yourself by collecting the necessary information, and then follow the easy-to-understand process of estimating your retirement costs, sources of retirement income, your current assets, and your projected minimum savings. Fidelity, of course, also presents its own investment strategies. ✓ **PRODIGY**→ *jump* fidelity

Retirement planning

Consumer Reports Retire-

ment *Consumer Reports* knows two things. First, that Social Security isn't the only way to make it through the retirement years; second, that not every plan is perfect for every person. In these reports, the magazine's writers scrutinize Keoghs, SEPs, IRAs, and a variety of pension formulas, charting their benefits and detriments for different types of retirees. This series of reports also helps retirement-plan consumers keep up with the changing tax laws governing savings and pension, and the changing government regulations for long-term health-care coverage. ✓ **PRODIGY**→ *jump* cr retirement

Kiplinger's Library This collection of articles from *Kiplinger's Personal Finance* magazine includes a number of valuable tips for retirement planning. The thrust of the articles seems to be that it's never too early to select your retirement savings package and pension plan, and the Closing in on Retirement section drives this point home by illustrating how far in advance the process should begin. Other articles contain guidelines for choosing the right retirement spot, tying up loose financial ends, figuring living expenses, and even planning what to do with all your extra time. The forum cautions retirees not to miscalculate how long savings will last, and proposes alternate methods for funding retirement—particularly CDs, stocks, treasuries, and bonds. ✓ **PRODIGY**→ *jump* kiplinger's

misc.taxes FAQ When the regulars of this newsgroup are not lamenting new taxes or exchanging proven strategies for dodging the tax man altogether, they discuss practical taxation questions, and much of the discussion revolves around retirement savings,

particularly the relative benefits of Keoghs and 403(b)s, and the ins and outs of estate taxes. The FAQ is particularly informative. ✓ **INTERNET**→ *www* http://www.kentlaw.edu:70/execo:-t+misc.taxes:/bin2/httpnews

Money Talk BB There are several topics on this bulletin board that will be of interest to those considering their retirement options. In the Financial Planning section, Prodigy participants engage in ongoing debate over the value of living trusts and the best ways to avoid exorbitant estate taxes. The forum also keeps a financial expert on staff to field difficult questions about IRAs and 401(k)s. Don't fear the future. Conquer it. ✓ **PRODIGY**→ *jump* money

> "The more we hear that the Social Security system will be bankrupt by the time the Baby Boomers hit 65, the more working people start to fret about their futures. How best to combat these fears? Start by reading GEnie's Retirement Planning."

Retirement Accounts This is primarily an advertising facility for a number of banks and investment services—Dean Witter hawks IRAs and Boatman's Bank tries to convince you of the importance of MMAs. After you have perused the consumer information in other online services, return here with your newfound knowledge and order brochures on specific retirement plans. ✓**PRODIGY**→*jump* retirement accounts

Retirement Planning The more we hear that the Social Security system will be bankrupt by the time the Baby Boomers hit 65, the more working people start to fret about their futures. How best to combat these fears? Start by reading this bulletin board, which outlines the basics of pension plans, IRA accounts, and 401(k)s. ✓**GENIE**→*keyword* invest→Investors' Bulletin Board→Set Category→Retirement Planning (category 20)

Retirement Planning Come here with your retirement questions. The message board is a great place to ask for help with your 401(k) or to discuss your child's retirement planning, but be sure to check the Retirement FAQ first—forum members have already asked and answered questions about the number of times an IRA account may be changed each year, the rules about taxing social security, and the investments you can't make with an IRA account. ✓**AMERICA ONLINE**→*keyword* yourmoney→Retirement Planning

Social security

Social Security Administration FAQ The questions may be simple. I lost my Social Security card—how do I get another one? Or they may be complex. How exactly are my benefits calculated?

This FAQ attempts to tackle all these issues. The major benefits programs are clearly explained, along with how to apply for and receive your due. Related issues like additional deductions and family eligibility are addressed, and you can learn how to get a free personal earnings and benefit estimate to help plan for retirement shortfall. ✓**INTERNET**→*gopher* gopher.ssa.gov→P-Frequently Asked Questions (FAQs)

Social Security News The Social Security Administration furnishes a good deal of information about its programs at this site. To keep on top of Congress's constant adjustments of benefits, the government publishes a news summary with details of all cost-of-living increases, along with the complete text of all Social Security–related legislation like the Social Security Domestic Employee Reform Act of 1994. Finally, there are numerous summaries of international agreements, such as the recent cooperative benefits pact with Greece. The monthly SSA newsletter—filled with research articles on retirement and the American populace—rounds out the service. ✓**INTERNET**→*www* http://www.ssa.gov/ssa_news.html

Social Security Retirement Benefits Several important Social Security articles and guides are stored at this site. "What You Need to Know about Retirement" helps workers begin to think about the future. Those planning to retire early can find out when the money starts flowing in "When You Get Your Benefits." And precise (or avaricious) citizens can calculate the payback from 45 years of FICA paycheck withdrawals with "How to Figure Your Social Security Benefit." If the amount you ascertained from the calcula-

tions seems inadequate, or you happen to like working, read "How Work Affects Retirement Plans" to learn how ceaseless industry affects benefits. There is also a document here addressing the notorious "notch" that creates a benefit imbalance that works against citizens born between 1917 and 1920. ✓**INTERNET**→*gopher* gopher.ssa.gov→E-Retirement Benefits

Your will

Where there's a will, there are relatives. And anyone who

has ever written a will, or benefited from one, will be thrilled to learn of the wealth of resources available on the Net. Unsure how to begin the process? Download a **Sample Will**. Worried that you may have forgotten something in your own will? Check out the tips in the **Will-Writing Checklist**. If you would like to make a strong final impression on your inheritors, you may find inspiration in the **Last Will and Testament of Jacqueline Onassis**, available for download from CompuServe.

On the Net

Across the board

Wills, Trusts, and Estates In the special help section of the Wills, Trusts, and Estates category, a legal expert answers technical questions about everything from avoiding inheritance taxes to challenging Great-Uncle Sebastian's will (the poor old sap left everything to the ACLU). Other hot topics are the pros and cons of living trusts and living wills. And in the Heirs or Hostages section, the beneficiaries talk back. Contains software that lets you write a will at home without a lawyer. ✓**GENIE**→*keyword* law→Law Bulletin Board→Set Category→Wills, Trusts, and Estates (category 19)

Howard Hughes—downloaded from CompuServe's Archive Forum

Celebrity wills

Last Will and Testament of Jacqueline Kennedy Onassis Compare your assets with those of the former first lady, or check to see if Jackie O left anything to you. ✓**COMPUSERVE**→*go* legal→Browse Libraries→General→*Download a file:* JACKIO.ZIP

Estate planning

Estate Planning What can you do if you become the beneficiary of property you don't want? Consult the Estate Planning FAQ in the Your Money forum ("You may issue a disclaimer which is an unqualified refusal by a potential beneficiary to accept proceed."). And if you want feedback on the will you've just written? Stop by the message boards here. There are also articles on drafting a will and creating trusts. ✓**AMERICA ONLINE**→ *keyword* yourmoney→Estate Planning

Living wills

Legal Issues The library of these forums contains living-will forms that are legal and binding in a number of states. Other articles address probate issues. In the Legal forum, online lawyers answer questions about living wills, as well as other estate-planning topics. ✓**COMPUSERVE** ...→*go* lawsig →Libraries ...→*go* retirement →Browse Libraries→Legal Issues

Will writing

Sample Will It's a classic—"I, YOUR NAME HERE, being of sound mind and memory, do hereby make, publish and declare this to be my Last Will and Testament...." This downloadable will template is good for those without complex financial assets, or complicated postmortem wishes. Two witnesses and backup executors are essential. So go and "give, devise and bequeath unto others." The will form is the property of Legal Shareware (LegalSWare@aol.com) and if used requires a $19.00 fee. ✓**AMERICA ONLINE**→*keyword* mbs→Software Libraries→*Search by file name:* WILL_93.TXT

Will-Writing Checklist You can't take it with you, but you also can't know exactly what's going to happen when you leave it behind. With the complicated estate-planning laws and regulations, wills today aren't just about Grandmother's silver tea service and a trunkful of Confederate currency. This checklist prompts the would-be will writer to inventory all assets, from real and personal property to life insurance and real estate. And once you have a clearer idea of what you have, it is easier to decide how to divide the spoils. ✓**GENIE**→*keyword* law→Law Library →Set Software Library→All Libraries (category 12)→*Download a file:* 49

Part 3

Shopping

Electronic marketplace

First, man exchanged sticks for berries. Then came capitalism. Then strip malls. Then

the Home Shopping Network. And now, there's online shopping. New and improved, fully operational, future-perfect, and good-to-go, electronic commerce harnesses the power of your home computer in the service of old-fashioned consumerism. From pet toys to sex toys, notions to hand lotions, haute cuisine to hot sauce, online shopping services bring the world to your fingertips. Need Russian fine art? Try **Muscovy Imports**. Want to hire a private detective? Check out **InPhoto Surveillance**. And if you're in the mood for a political gift, there's always **Setting the Record Straight—Bill Clinton and Gennifer Flowers**, transcripts of the phone conversations between the President and his alleged paramour. From the corporate tie-ins on major commercial services to the myriad companies with gophers and Websites, the Net is fast becoming one of the country's busiest marketplaces.

The Mall of America—downloaded from CompuServe's Graphics Forum

On the Net

Malls & catalogs

Catalog Collection Custom-built golf clubs from Austads, unique gifts from Hammacher-Schlemmer, clothes from Land's End, housewares from Spiegel, and more. ✓**PRODIGY**→*jump* catalog collection

Concord Direct Over 50 available catalogs to order from order. Titles include J. Crew, the Boston Museum of Fine Arts, Nordic-Track, the Star Base Columbus Star Trek Catalog, and Everything Automotive. ✓**COMPUSERVE**→*go* ca

eMall An interesting mix of 'eShops', including Santa's Hangout, Spice Merchant, Springs of Life (new age books & gifts), Harvest Burgers (vegetarian patties), Rowena's Gift Cakes, Rob-1 Motorsports (auto accessories), Capulin Coffee and Chile Today—Hot Tamale (imported peppers and hot sauces). There's also a link to a travel guide to the Big Apple—Explore! New York—complete with Broadway listings. You can order products online via the Web page, email, toll-free fax, or toll-free voice. ✓**INTERNET**→*www* http://emall.com/Home.html

Global Commerce Link The A–to–Z listing of companies and their Web pages—which you can search or browse—is the big draw of this site. From the American Lamb Council to AT&T, big and small businesses are brought together here. Peruse their catalogs, read about their products and company history, and even join them by putting your business in the directory. The site also includes pages with links to Web browser and decompression software, and an extensive listing of other Internet sites, including those related to business and finance: the more Net savvy its customers, the better. ✓**INTERNET**→

www http://www.commerce.com

Global Network Navigator (GNN) Shopping One of the most beautifully designed shopping areas on the Web. Look for NordicTrack and the Lonely Planet Travel Guides, as well as a large selection of computer-related products. ✓**INTERNET**...→*www* http://gnn.interpath.net/gnn/gnn. html ...→*www* http://www.digital. com/gnn/gnn.html

Home Shopping Values An online division of TV's Home Shopping Network that sells clothing, jewlery, housewares, and electronics. ✓**COMPUSERVE**→*go* hsv ✓**PRODIGY**→*jump* hsc outlet net

IMALL: The Electronic Mall on the Internet Runs free classified ads—from autos to employment to collectibles—that are active for two weeks before automatically being removed. Those interested in a product featured in the classifieds, are usually given an email address to contact the seller. Not only does this classifieds megalopolis feature its own listings, it also links to more than two dozen Usenet newsgroups that feature classifieds. Although well organized, many of the categories at the fairly new site are still empty. Similarly, the mall area which runs daily sales and features online ordering (well, you still have to fax in your credit-card number) is not very well stocked yet. ✓**INTERNET**→ *www* http://www.imall.com/home page.html

J. C. Penny Clothing, electronics, and housewares are available through J. C. Penny's online catalog. ✓**PRODIGY**→*jump* jc penny ✓**COMPUSERVE**→*go* jcp

The Mall Over a hundred stores reside on CompuServe, and the

> **"A simple interface on Delphi's 'Shopping' lets you choose from a selection of standard online shopping services: flowers, computer products, entertainment media, books, and even coffee beans."**

mall enables users to get a directory of the merchants, send feedback about their experiences, and search for products. Most merchants accept one of the major credit cards. ✓**COMPUSERVE**→*go* mall

The Mall The Mall has over 40 merchants offering gifts, compact discs, coffee, flowers, electronics, hobby supplies, computer software, and astrology materials store. Merchants take major credit cards, and a number of them also ship to Canada and Japan. Interested in selling your merchandise online? Select Feedback & Mall Information and enter an application.✓**GENIE**→*keyword* geniemall→ Enter GEnie Mall

The Marketplace A small shopping area that includes a flower shop, online bookstore, computer store, and a gateway to the Shopper's Advantage Club. ✓**AMERICA ONLINE**→*keyword* marketplace

Sears Clothing, electronics, and housewares may be ordered from the Sears online catalog. ✓**PRODIGY**→*jump* sears ✓**COMPUSERVE**→ *go* sr

Shopper's Advantage/Comp-u-store A selection of over 250,000 products direct from the manufacturer, ranging from home electronics to jewelry to cosmetics. Gateways to this electronic store are available from several of the commercial services. No fees are rendered on top of your online services' basic costs unless you wish to join the Shopper's Advantage Club. Membership does have its advantages—lower merchandise costs. To browse (and even buy) without being a club member, be sure to select the option of entering as a non member. Merchandise is delivered via UPS. ✓**AMERICA ONLINE**→*keyword* compustore ✓**COMPUSERVE**→*go* sac ✓**DELPHI**→*go* shop compustore ✓**GENIE**→*keyword* cus

Shopping A simple interface lets you choose from a selection of standard online shopping services and products: flowers, computer products, entertainment media, books, and even coffee beans. ✓**DELPHI**→*go* shop

Shopping Prodigy boasts a large array of shopping options, including some big names: You can browse through abridged catalogs from Spiegel, Hammacher Schlemmer, Lands' End, and Sears (naturally), or select general categories of stores such as "Entertainment," "Computers," and "Travel." ✓**PRODIGY**→*jump* shopping

Spiegel Request a Spiegel catalog or order online clothing, electronics, and housewares. ✓**PRODIGY** →*jump* spiegel

Sunglasses, Shavers and More Sunglasses by Ray-Ban, travel clocks by Braun, pens by Cross, and in-line skates by Ultra Wheels. ✓ **COMPUSERVE**→*go* sun ✓ **GENIE**→*keyword* shades-more

Addiction treatment

Stop Smoking Center Stop smoking with this special program, which teaches self-control without the aid of hypnosis, drugs, chewing gum, patches, or cigarette substitutes. ✓ **INTERNET**→ *www* http://branch.com:1080 /smoking/smoking.html

Archiving

Digital Dynamics Inc. Complete CD-ROM production company, offering corporate data archiving, electronic catalog publishing, indexing, imaging and OCR scanning, multimedia development, mastering and duplication, and data conversion from most sources and formats. ✓ **INTERNET**→*www* http://branch.com:1080 /dd/dd.html

Art

Art Gallery Both open edition prints and limited edition (signed and unsigned) prints for the home or office. Downloadable Windows-based catalog for offline viewing. ✓ **INTERNET**→*gopher* ftp.std. com→vendors→ArtGallery

The Electric Gallery Digital representations of naive and primitive art from around the world. As of this writing, Haitian art is being featured. ✓ **INTERNET**→*www* http: //www.egallery.com/egallery/

Metropolitan Museum of Art Reproductions, publications, and other unique gift items from the Metropolitan Museum of Art.

Mammoth Records Web page—http://www.nando.net:80/mammoth/

Members receive a 10 percent discount. ✓ **COMPUSERVE**→*go* mma

Muscovy Imports Contemporary Russian fine art, including oil paintings, bronze sculpture, jewelry, and art objects. ✓ **INTERNET**→ *www* http://branch.com:1080 /muscovy/muscovy.html

Sandra Morton Fine Arts Features paintings from Bali. ✓ **INTERNET**→*www* http://www.tagsys. com/Ads/Morton/index.html

Arts & crafts

Crafter's Showcase A selection of handmade craft items from Northern California, including dolls, carousels, and cat plaques. ✓ **INTERNET**→*www* http://www. northcoast.com/unlimited/product_directory/cs/cs.html

Audio

BBC Music Monthly A catalog of new and old classical music releases and a full-length CD is sent to subscribers each month. ✓ **COM-**PUSERVE→*go* bcm

BMG Music Service CDs and cassette tapes of all genres can be purchased. ✓ **COMPUSERVE**→*go* cd

Books on Tape Over 3,000 audio book titles to rent or buy. ✓ **COMPUSERVE**→*go* bot

Breakfast Records Independent record label begun by the members of Orbit. Several other alternative rock groups are also featured, complete with band bios, music samples, tour schedules, band photos, and album covers. Several cassette tapes available for purchase. ✓ **INTERNET**...→*www* http://breakfast.com:2500/ ...→*gopher* gopher.breakfast.com 2501

CDnow! Over 140,000 CDs, cassettes, and mini-discs which can be delivered, for a price, to most countries in the world. There is also a toll-free number to handle no-questions-asked returns. ✓ **IN-**TERNET→*www* http://cdnow.com/

Columbia House The Compact Disc Club carries thousands of popular music titles. ✓**PRODIGY**→*jump* columbia house ✓**COMPUSERVE**→*go* ch

Entertainment Works Thousands of music CDs and VHS movie titles for sale. ✓**COMPUSERVE**→*go* ewk ✓**GENIE**→*keyword* music+videos

Justice Records A small, multigenre independent record label selling tapes and CDs online. ✓**COMPUSERVE**→*go* jr

Mammoth Records Independent record label specializing in alternative rock. Order albums directly or peruse band profiles, album covers, tour dates, music samples (including full-length singles), and reviews. ✓**INTERNET**→ *www* http://www.nando.net/mam moth/

Musicworks! Order CDs and tapes from a large catalog of classical and modern recordings. ✓**PRODIGY**→*jump* musicworks

Narada Productions An independent music label specializing in instrumental new music. CDs, cassettes, and sheet-music books are available. ✓**COMPUSERVE**→*go* np

Noteworthy Music Thousands of CDs and videos covering over 20 musical styles, such as big band, bluegrass, cajun/zydeco, classical, Christian, country, gospel, jazz, rap, and reggae. Search the catalog by artist, album title, song title, genre, or record label. ✓**INTERNET**→*www* http://www. netmarket.com/noteworthy/bin/ma in/:st=0ngxih35hg|3 ✓**GENIE**→*keyword* noteworthy

Setting the Record Straight - Bill Clinton and Gennifer Flowers Two-cassette tape set with accompanying 80-page book documenting this one-hour phone conversation between Wild Bill and Ms. Flowers. Download samples prior to ordering via mail order. ✓**INTERNET**→*www* http://www. sccsi.com/2gee/bill.html

Balloons

PC Balloons Order balloon bouquets for delivery. ✓**PRODIGY**→ *jump* pc balloons

Bicycles

Didi's Shack of Wheels Get a good wheel deal from this Arizona bike shop, which sells bicycle accessories. ✓**INTERNET**→*www* http:// jemez.nursing.arizona.edu/~ kendelm/didi.html

Spring City Cycle Co. Order bicycle parts and accessories. ✓**INTERNET**→*www* http://iquest.com/~top cycle/

Books

Book Stacks Unlimited (bbs) Search for books by author, title, ISBN, or keyword. Over 270,000 titles available. ☎→*dial* 216-861-0469 ✓**INTERNET**→*telnet* books.com

Books & Guides Need help navigating the Internet? Several how-to Net books are featured, including *Net Guide*. ✓**DELPHI**→*go* sho books

CompuBooks Over 3,800 computer-book titles are available for 15 percent off the publisher's price. If you need help in selecting a title, ask the technical staff. ✓**COMPUSERVE**→*go* cbk

Future Fantasy Bookstore Besides offering science fiction, fantasy, and mystery novels, including signed copies of books that you may preorder, Future Fantasy sells related paraphernalia, such as role-playing games and T-shirts. Covers of books may be viewed, and excerpts are here for the reading. There are also Web links to related sites. ✓**INTERNET**→ *www* http:// www.commerce.digi tal.com/palo-alto/FutureFantasy/ home.html

HarperCollins Online Choose from over 17,000 book titles and more than 1,000 new books a

Net Books Web page—http://www.ypn.com/

year. ✓**COMPUSERVE**→*go* har

Internet Book Shop This site, which focuses on academic and journal publishers, can be searched by subject, title, author, publisher, and ISBN. You may join their mailing list, specifying which of 1,000 categories interest you. ✓**INTERNET**→ *www* http://www.demon.co.uk/ bookshop/ibs.html

Judaism: The Online Bookstore Both online and print versions of their Judaica catalogs are available via this gopher. ✓**INTERNET** →*gopher* cgisj.cgi.com→ Bookstore

Library of Science Over 200 science-related books from several leading publishers. *Journey to the Ants*, anyone? ✓**COMPUSERVE**→*go* los

McGraw Hill Book Company Books from the publishing giant. New titles are discounted by 20 percent. ✓**COMPUSERVE**→*go* mh

Microsoft Press Books for computer users of all skill levels. ✓**COMPUSERVE**→*go* msp

Moe's Book Shop A used bookstore that also carries remainders and new titles at 10 percent off. They'll try to locate any book you want—just ask. Several email catalogs are available, including ones on African art, pop culture, and cookbooks. ✓**INTERNET**→*www* http://sunsite.unc.edu/ibic/Moeshome.html

Online Bookstore Hundreds of general-interest and computer books at discounts to 25 percent. ✓**AMERICA ONLINE**→*keyword* bookstore

Online BookStore You can buy electronic versions of current books, as well as printed books, books on disk, and—if you please—lobsters. The catalog includes sample texts, pictures, and videos. ✓**INTERNET**→ *www* http://marketplace.com/0/ obs/obshome.html

PTR Prentice Hall Computer science, engineering, and business books. ✓**COMPUSERVE**→*go* ptr

Random House Electronic Publishing Excerpts from the latest cutting-edge computer books published by Random House's Electronic Publishing division. Discounts available for online ordering. ✓**COMPUSERVE**→*go* random

Read USA Mail Order Desktop reference books and hardware and software guides. ✓**DELPHI**→*go* sho read

The Reference Press Bookstore This business information provider—publishers of the Hoover's Handbook series—develops reference books and electronic products for both the domestic and international markets. Their full catalog of reference books includes downloadable fax order forms and descriptions of each product. ✓**INTERNET** ...→*gopher* gopher.hoovers.com ...→*www* http: //www.hoovers.com

Small Computer Book Club Books about personal computers, including multimedia, word processing, and spreadsheet programs. ✓**COMPUSERVE**→*go* bk

Softpro Books Over 4,000 computer-related titles that encompass both hardware and software, the business side of the computer industry, and humor (Dilbert books). ✓**INTERNET**→*www* http:// xor.com:80/softpro/

Time Warner Electronic Publishing Books of every genre with a special books-of-the-month feature. ✓**COMPUSERVE**→*go* twb

UB and US-Books and Things Publisher and distributor of books that are written by, for, or about African peoples. Over 1,000 titles on topics including religion, psychology, history, poetry, health and nutrition, biography, essays/ leaders/politics, and finance and business. ✓**INTERNET**→*www* http:// www.ip.net/shops/UB_and_US-Books_and_Things/

Toucan Chocolates—http://branch.com: 1080/toucan/toucan.html

Electronic malls online

The Internet Store Logo at http://www. medium.com/store1m.html

BizNet Shopping Center ✓IN-TERNET→*www* http://www.bnt. com/shopping.html

Branch Mall ✓INTERNET→*www* http://server.branch.com/

BPA-EDELWEB Cybershop ✓INTERNET→*www* http://champagne.inria.fr/digishop/entrance. html

The Commerce Center ✓INTER-NET→*www* http://www.infi.net/ commerce.html

CTSNET Marketplace ✓INTER-NET→*www* http://www.cts.com:80 /cts/market/

CyberDEALS ✓INTERNET→*www* http://cyberdeals.com/

CyberMall ✓INTERNET→*www* http://www.nstn.ca/

CyberStore ✓INTERNET→*gopher* gopher.gate.net→Marketplace--"The CyberStore on the Shore"

DigiCash Cybershop ✓INTER-NET→*www* http://www.digicash. com/digishop/shopmain.html

Downtown Anywhere ✓IN-TERNET→*www* http://www.awa. com/

GEMS - Product & Service Showcase ✓INTERNET→*www*

http://www.gems.com/show case/index.html

Global-X-Change Market-place ✓INTERNET→*www* http:// www.globalx.net/gxc/marketp. html

The Human Factor's Open Market ✓INTERNET→*www* http:// www.human.com/index.html

Internet Direct's Online Shop-ping/Business Server ✓INTER-NET→*www* http://www.indirect. com/buss.html

Internet Shopkeeper ✓INTER-NET→*www* http://www.ip.net/ cgi-bin/shopkeeper

The Internet Solution ✓INTER-NET→*www* http://www.is.co.za/ services.html

The Internet Store ✓INTER-NET→*www* http://www.medium. com/store 1m.html

The Internet Storefront ✓IN-TERNET→*www* http://storefront. xor.com/

MarketBase(tm) Online Cat-alog of Goods and Services ✓INTERNET→*gopher* mb.com

MarketPlace ✓INTERNET→*www* http://marketplace.com/

Matrix Marketplace ✓INTER-NET→*www* http://www.internex. net/market.html

NetCenter—The Mall ✓INTER-NET→*www* http://netcenter.com/ netcentr/mall/index.html

NetMarket ✓INTERNET→*www* http://www.netmarket.com/

The PICnet E-Mall ✓INTERNET→ *www* http://www.pic.net/lobby/ lobby.html

Oslonett Marketplace ✓INTER-NET→*www* http://www.oslonett. no/html/adv/ON-market.html

Shopping 2000 ✓INTERNET→ *www* http://www.shopping2000. com/

Shops On The World ✓INTER-NET→*gopher* ftp.std.com→Shops on The World

STUFF.com ✓INTERNET→*www* http://www.stuff.com/

TAG Online Mall ✓INTERNET →*www* http://www.tagsys.com/ Ads/

Telerama Shopping Plaza ✓INTERNET→*gopher* ivory.lm.com→ Shopping Plaza: Businesses and Services

The Village Mall ✓INTERNET→ *www* http://crusher.bev.net/mall/

Virtual Advertising adfx (tm) ✓INTERNET→ *www* http://www. shore.net/~adfx/adfx.mall.html

Worldwide Marketplace ✓IN-TERNET→*www* http://www.cygnus. nb.ca/

"Surf the Net" T-shirt available at http://www.stuff.com.

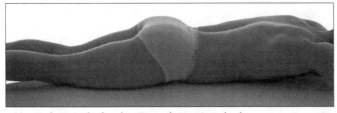

2(x)ist Underwear ad—from http://www.digex.net/2xist.html

Wiley Professional Books Save 10 percent when you use your credit card in ordering titles on topics including computers, business, engineering, science, and law. ✓**COMPUSERVE**→*go* jw

Chocolate & candy

Chocoholics Spreadable bittersweet chocolate in a jar. ✓**INTERNET**→*www* http://www.northcoast.com/unlimited/product_directory/chocoholics/chocoholics.html

Krema-NutButtersNutsCandyGifts Gourmet nuts and nut butter. ✓**INTERNET**→*www* http://www.ip.net/shops/Krema-NutButtersNutsCandyGifts/

Sweet Enchantment Unique candy assortments, including the Halloween Licorice Hand. ✓**INTERNET**→*www* http://www.wilder.com/sweet/sweet.html

Toucan Chocolates Four-, ten-, and twenty-piece assortments of milk and dark chocolates with tropical nuts. Part of the proceeds from every box sold goes to Cultural Survival, Inc., a group that works with indigenous peoples to preserve the rain forests. ✓**INTERNET**→*www* http://branch.com:1080/toucan/toucan.html

GEnie Classified Ads Class reunions, personals, rooms for rent, car and computer listings, and job announcements are all listed here. Costs of placing an ad are minimal—although there's an additional cost if you post anonymously. ✓**GENIE**→*keyword* ads **$**

Clothing

2(x)ist Underwear All types of men's underwear, complete with pictures of the various products: boxers, thongs, briefs, T-shirts, and long underwear. ✓**INTERNET**→*www* http://www.digex.net/2xist.html

Americana Clothing Sporty clothing brands such as Levi's, Dockers, and Champion. ✓**COMPUSERVE**→*go* ac

Brooks Brothers Clothing from New York's classic purveyor of Oxford shirts, double-breasted blazers, and wing tips. ✓**COMPUSERVE**→*go* br

Dianne's Casual Creations Coordinated casual clothes, wearable art, and accessories for adults and children. ✓**INTERNET**→*www* http://www.ip.net/shops/DiannesCasualCreations/

L'eggs L'eggs, Bali, and Hanes hoisery. ✓**PRODIGY**→*jump* leggs ✓**COMPUSERVE**→*go* lh

Lands' End Request a catalog from this well-known mail order company. ✓**PRODIGY**→*jump* lands end ✓**COMPUSERVE**→*go* la ✓**GENIE**→*keyword* landsend

Nine Lives Women's Clothing

Consignment Store Women's pre-owned clothing. Name brands include Anne Klein, Liz Claiborne, Donna Karan, etc. Multiple methods of searching inventory are available, as well as "personal shopping assistants." ✓**INTERNET**→*www* http://chezhal.slip.net com.com/

Paul Fredrick Men's shirts and accessories from the Paul Fredrick catalog online. ✓**PRODIGY**→*jump* paul fredrick ✓**COMPUSERVE**→*go* pfs

Stonewall Partners Cotton shirts with a red ribbon embroidered over the heart. Five percent of the proceeds goes to your favorite AIDS charity. ✓**INTERNET**→*www* http://branch.com:1080/united/united.html

Stuart McGuire Shoes Dress, executive, and casual shoes for men. ✓**COMPUSERVE**→*go* shoes

The Sunglass Shop Popular brands of sunglasses including Ray-Ban, Serengheti, and Porsche. ✓**PRODIGY**→*jump* the sunglass shop

The Warehouse Tuxedos Sells, well, tuxedos. ✓**INTERNET**→*www*

Stonewall Partners—www http://branch.com:1080 /united/united.html

http://branch.com:1080/tuxedo/tuxedo.html

Coffee

Capulin Coffee Gourmet coffee, grown using environmentally sustainable methods. "Capulin" means that water has not been used in processing, thereby preserving original flavors and alkaloids. ✓**INTERNET**→*www* http://eMall.Com/AshCreek/AshCreek1.html

Coffee Anyone? Coffees, teas, chocolate, mugs, and other accessories. ✓**COMPUSERVE**→*go* cof ✓**GENIE**→*keyword* coffee ✓**DELPHI**→*go* shop coffee

Green Mountain Coffee Roasters Over 70 varieties of coffee from all over the world. ✓**COMPUSERVE**→*go* gmr

Collectibles

Sports Cards and More Complete year sets for various manufacturers of baseball, basketball, hockey, and football trading cards. Some premium price single cards, too. ✓**INTERNET**→*www* http://www.icw.com/sports/sports.html

Corporate identity

America Online Store America Online logo sweatshirts, tour guides, mugs, and other products. ✓**AMERICA ONLINE**→*keyword* america online store

CompuServe Store Official CompuServe merchandise, ranging from user guides and membership kits to T-shirts and posters. ✓**COMPUSERVE**→*go* ord-29

The GEnie Merchandise Store T-shirts, decals, key rings, mugs, polo shirts, and other logo prod-

AOL T-shirts—from the America Online Store

ucts. ✓**GENIE**→*keyword* geniestore

Glossbrenner's Master Guide to GEnie Learn time saving shortcuts and get the most out of your GEnie subscription. ✓**GENIE**→*keyword* order →Order Glossbrenner's Master Guide to GEnie

Prodigy Shop Order Prodigy logo items. ✓**PRODIGY**→*jump* prodigy shop

Computer stuff

Absolut Museum Three-disk set of memorable Absolut Vodka ads—more than 200 paintings, photos, and fashion designs. Procedes benefit Amfar. Email for ordering info. Available for IBM compatibles. ✓**COMPUSERVE**→*go* abs

Apple Computer Inc. Filled with press releases, company news, and technical fact sheets, the site also has a catalog of new products and customer-support information. ✓**INTERNET**→*www* http://www.apple.com

Broderbund Software Educational and game-oriented software, such as *Myst, Print Shop Deluxe, Carmen Junior Detective,* and the *New Kid on the Block.* ✓**COM-**

PUSERVE→*go* bb

CD Publishing Corporation's CD-ROM Products Catalog Several Net products are available, including packet drivers, NetNews (a subscription-oriented archive of USENET feeds updated weekly), NetGems (including the source code for the X Windows system, version 11, release 5), and system administration and security tools. ✓**INTERNET**→*gopher* gopher.cdpublishing.com→catalog

Computer Express Over 2,000 game, business, and education software titles for IBM and Macintosh, including *Doom II, Colonization,* and *Lotus Smartsuite.* ✓**PRODIGY**→*jump* computer express ✓**COMPUSERVE**→*go* express ✓**AMERICA ONLINE**→*keyword* shopping ✓**DELPHI**→*go* shop com ✓**INTERNET**...→*www* http://cexpress.com:2700/...→*gopher* cexpress.com 2600

Computer Solutions Full-service computer store that provides hardware, software, training and networking solutions to businesses, educational institutions, and individuals. ✓**INTERNET**→*gopher* ftp.std.com→vendors→compsol

CyberGroup Internet books, training and consulting services, server installation, configuration, and support. Public and in-house courses ranging from Internet Technology Briefings to hands-on courses dealing with WWW server construction. ✓**INTERNET**→*www* http://www.ip.net/shops/CyberGroup/

Dalco Computer Electronics PC components and supplies ranging from monitors to modems. ✓**COMPUSERVE**→*go* da

Digital PC Store A catalog of

PC hardware and accessories, including printers, communication software, monitors, and software. Visit the graphical showcase, but to order you must voice call the toll-free number given. ✓**COMPUSERVE**→*go* dd

Direct Micro Mailing List Savings on microcomputer accessories for mailing-list members. ✓**GENIE**→ *keyword* directmicro

Download Superstore Software ranging from *Egyptian Clip Art* to *Chinease* (a Chinese writing learning program). ✓**PRODIGY**→ *jump* download superstore

Essential Data, Inc. Peripherals for PCs, including modems, storage products, multimedia, and power products. In addition to quantity discounts, the company also offers discounts for prepaid or wire-transferred payments. International customers are welcome. ✓**INTERNET**→*gopher* marketplace. com→essential.data

Exec/Direct Hardware, software, CD-ROM players, games, and books. For information and discussion on products, check out the linked PC World Forum. ✓**COMPUSERVE**→*go* pwm

FCR Software, Inc. Network, routing, and WAN software for standard "off the shelf" computers such as the IBM PC, Apple Macintosh, and Sun Workstations. Current products include PPP for the Macintosh, ARA for UNIX, PPP for UNIX, and a portable routing platform. ✓**INTERNET**→ *www* http://www.wilder.com /homepage.html

IBM An elaborate electronic catalog with IBM company news and detailed product descriptions and pictures. From the products page,

> **"DRNY Ventures sells the Lazyciser: an exercise device for those with no desire to 'feel the burn'—tones and strengthens major muscle groups with resistance training."**

you can link to listings about PCs, midrange computers, networking software, and more IBM computer merchandise. The site also features lists of 800 numbers for technical support and ordering, and links to PC shareware archives and PC magazines with a Net presence. No online ordering. ✓**INTERNET**→ *www* http://www.ibm.com

IBM PC Direct Order a PC online. IBM owns Prodigy and Prodigy sells IBM products—amazing. ✓**PRODIGY**→*jump* ibm pc direct

IBM Personal Software Products IBM software products. ✓**COMPUSERVE**→*go* ip

Internet Shopping Network Over 20,000 products from over 1,000 vendors are available after registering your credit-card info via an 800 number. Mainly computer hardware, software, peripherals, and accessories. Full graphics or text-only interfaces for slow connections. ✓**INTERNET**→ *www* http://shop.internet.net/

Intuit Home Page Besides company news, history, and Intuit job opportunities, this Website features product descriptions (not very elaborate but helpful). ✓**INTERNET**→ *www* http://www.career-mosaic.com/cm/intuit/intuit1.html

JDR Microdevices Over 4,500 PC products and electronic components to choose from. ✓**COMPUSERVE**→*go* jdr

Komando Mall Computer accessories, supplies, publications, and software. ✓**AMERICA ONLINE**→ *keyword* komando

MacWarehouse Macintosh hardware and software clearinghouse. ✓**COMPUSERVE**→*go* mw

MacZone/PC Zone PC and Macintosh equipment clearinghouse. ✓**COMPUSERVE**→*go* mz ✓**E-WORLD**→ *go* maczone (for Macs)

MaryMac Industries The complete line of Tandy computer products. ✓**GENIE**→*keyword* mary-mac

Micro Star Software Software club that specializes in new Windows shareware programs, educational programs for kids from 4 to 14, desktop-publishing collections, games, and DOS programs. ✓**INTERNET**→ *www* http://www. awa.com:/bh/microstar/msclub.ht ml

MicroWarehouse Hardware and software for PCs. ✓**COMPUSERVE**→*go* mcw

Mission Control Software IBM games, CD-ROMs, and accessories. ✓**COMPUSERVE**→*go* mcs ✓**GENIE**→*keyword* mc-software

MR Mac Software Network and communications-related software for Macintosh computers. Demos are available for all software products. ✓**INTERNET**→*www* http://www.ip.net/shops/MR_Mac_Software/

Network Express An ISDN router manufacturer that offers networking solutions, with a special emphasis on ISDN connections. ✓**INTERNET**→*www* http://branch.com:1080/netexpress/netexpress.html

Omni Technology Hardware and software for PCs. ✓**GENIE**→*keyword* omni

On Disk Monthly Subscribe and receive new software every month in categories ranging from finance to entertainment. ✓**PRODIGY**→*jump* on disk monthly

Parsons Technology Software packages on various topics: finance and productivity, the church and the bible, golf, and geneaology. ✓**COMPUSERVE**→*go* pa ✓**GENIE**→*keyword* parsons ✓**DELPHI**→*go* sho par

PC Catalog Another catalog of PC software and computer-related merchandise, including motherboards, modems, and memory. ✓**PRODIGY**→*jump* pc catalog ✓**COMPUSERVE**→*go* pca ✓**AMERICA ONLINE**→*keyword* pc catalog ✓**GENIE**→*keyword* pc catalog

Power Express Battery Catalog Sells high capacity battery packs, improved battery chargers and conditioners, original and OEM-compatible batteries, battery management software, and power-saving accessories. ✓**INTERNET**→*www* http://www.baynet.com/power/list.html

R. Frazier, Inc. Disposal of outdated and unwanted computer and electronic systems in a man-

ner that is environmentally sound and economically viable. ✓**INTERNET**→*www* http://www.biznet.com.blacksburg.va.us/~rfrazier/index.html

Shareware Club Join the Shareware Club and receive a monthly batch of shareware. ✓**PRODIGY**→*jump* shareware club $

Shareware Depot Substantially discounted software. ✓**PRODIGY**→*jump* shareware depot ✓**COMPUSERVE**→*go* sd

Softdisk Publishing Discounted software. ✓**COMPUSERVE**→*go* sp ✓**GENIE**→*keyword* softdisk

SOFTEX Programming utilities, tutorials, spreadsheets, and entertainment software. ✓**COMPUSERVE**→*go* sfx-4

Software Etc. Order from the software guide of this computer chain store—anything from games to word-processing programs. ✓**PRODIGY**→*jump* software etc

UNIROM All types of CD-ROMs at discount prices: business, children's entertainment, education, games, maps and travel, medical, music, reference, shareware, and adult. ✓**INTERNET**→*gopher* marketplace.com→ unirom

XOR Network Engineering, Inc. Full range of network services, including network engineering, system administration, network integration, software development, information services development, and Internet training. ✓**INTERNET**→*www* http://plaza.xor.com/xor/index.html

Contact lenses

Contact Lens Save up to 60 percent on your next contact lens

IBM Computer from the IBM Web page—http://www.ibm.com

purchase. ✓**PRODIGY**→*jump* contact lens ✓**COMPUSERVE**→*go* cl ✓**GENIE**→*keyword* contact

Lens Express Contact lenses and designer sunglasses. You have to have a current prescription. ✓**COMPUSERVE**→*go* len

Educational aids

Doctor Duey's Wacky Web Pages Selection of non traditional, humorous science teaching aids. ✓**INTERNET**→*www* http://scitech.lm.com/

Electronics

Colonel Video and Audio Home-electronic products, including brands such as Sony, Panasonic, Kenwood, and Hitachi. ✓**COMPUSERVE**→*go* cva

Escort Store An electronics company whose products are only available online. Products include laser detectors and cordless phones. ✓**COMPUSERVE**→*go* escort

Hybrid Technical Systems Technically oriented books and videos as well as software, air conditioners, and audio equipment. ✓**COMPUSERVE**→*go* hts

Engineering services

Anderson & Associates, Inc. A full range of services, from planning and analysis to design and implementation. The firm focuses on civil, environmental and transportation engineering, planning, landscape architecture, and surveying. ✓**INTERNET**→*www* http://www.biznet.com.blacksburg.va.us/~anderson/

Durability, Inc. Develop new products and technologies for the analysis, design, and testing of high performance engineering materials. ✓**INTERNET**→*www* http://www.biznet.com.blacksburg.va.us/~durability/

Exercise equipment

DRNY Ventures Sells the Lazyciser: an exercise device for those with no desire to "feel the burn"—tones and strengthens major muscle groups with resistance training. ✓**INTERNET**→*www* http://branch.com:1080/lazy/lazy.html

Fantasy

Dancing Dragon Designs More than 400 items from the world's only all-dragon catalog. Merchandise on sale includes collectibles, books, posters, puzzles, masks, sculptures, jewelry, T-shirts, artifacts, personal, and household items. ✓**INTERNET**→*www* http://www.northcoast.com/unlimited/product_directory/dancing_dragon/dancing_dragon.html

Flowers

800-Flowers and 800-Gifthouse Flowers and gifts for all

Sloppy Joe Fixin's—http://emall.com/Harvest/Harvest.html

occasions. ✓**COMPUSERVE**→*go* gm

800-The-Rose All manner of floral gifts, plus balloons and stuffed animals, are available through an international network of 25,000 florists. Orders placed prior to 1 p.m. EST are guaranteed to arrive the same day (within the U.S. only). ✓**INTERNET**→*www* http://www.netmarket.com/flowers/bin/main/:st=0ngxih35hg|3

Absolutely Fresh Flowers Florist specializing in overnight delivery of large bunches of multi-colored miniature carnations. ✓**INTERNET**→*www* http://crash.cts.com/~flowers/

The Flower Stop Flowers delivered anywhere in the United States. ✓**AMERICA ONLINE**→*keyword* flower shop ✓**GENIE**→*keyword* ldroses ✓**DELPHI**→*go* sho lon

FTD Online Order the featured FTD bouquet, or select your own arrangment by viewing photos of the arrangements—a unique option on CompuServe. ✓**COMPUSERVE**→*go* ftd

Grant's Florist & Greenhouse FTD delivery of a full range of fresh flowers and plants. The site contains pictures of arrangements for sale, as well as a handy email-based reminder service to help you keep track of your gift-giving needs. ✓**INTERNET**→*www* http://florist.com:1080/flowers/flowers.html

Lane & Lenge Fresh-cut flowers, potted plants, and special arrangements for delivery throughout the world. ✓**INTERNET**→*www* http://plaza.xor.com/lane/start/index.html

PC Flowers Flowers delivered anywhere in the United States, from FTD florists. ✓**PRODIGY**→*jump* pc flowers

Walter Knoll Florist Plants, flowers, fruits, and balloons delivered within 24 hours of your order. ✓**COMPUSERVE**→*go* wk ✓**GENIE**→*keyword* knoll

Food

Adventures in Food Win a selection of gourmet foods specially selected to match your zodiac sign, or choose your own selection of gourmet goodies. ✓**COMPUSERVE**→*go* aif

Cheeseboard Gourmet cheeses, pastas, and pates. If you need help with your selection try the items recommended for your zodiac sign. ✓**PRODIGY**→*jump* cheeseboard

Figi's Get a free gift when ordering from Figi's selection of edible gifts, featuring nuts, candy, dried fruit, and more. ✓**COMPUSERVE**→*go* fg

Florida Fruit Shippers Grapefruit, oranges, and tropical fruit.

✓**COMPUSERVE**→*go* ffs

Fruit Baskets - From Pemberton Orchards Order fruit via email, fax, or a toll-free number. Shipments sent anywhere in the continental U.S., as well as overnight if ordered prior to 1 p.m. EST. ✓**INTERNET**→*gopher* ftp.std.com→vendors→fruit.baskets

Gimmee Jimmy's Cookies Cookies for every occasion, with flavors like peanut-butter chip, coconut pecan, and chocolate chip. ✓**COMPUSERVE**→*go* gim ✓**GENIE**→ *keyword* cookies

Grant's Health Products Various health aids: honeybee pollen, royal jelly, propolis, green barley, aloe-vera drink. ✓**INTERNET**→*www* http://branch.com:1080/health/health.html

Harvest Burgers Harvest Burgers contain 100 percent vegetable protein (16 grams per serving), about 75 percent less fat than traditional meat patties, and about 54 percent fewer calories. ✓**INTERNET**→*www* http://eMall.Com/Harvest/Harvest1.html

Omaha Steaks Choose from steak, pork, lamb, seafood, poultry, desserts, and the recipe of the month. ✓**COMPUSERVE**→*go* os

Rowena's Gift Cakes Almond, orange, and lemon pound cakes, plus gift-basket assortments. ✓**INTERNET**→*www* http://eMall.Com/Rowena/Rowena1.html

Taste Unlmtd-Savory Sauces Gourmet sauces: Rao's Homemade Marinara Sauce, Chittenden Kitchen's Cranberry Yummie!, and more. ✓**INTERNET**→*www* http://www.ip.net/shops/Taste_Unlmtd-Savory_Sauces/

> "Order and view the infamously trashy Spencer Gifts products, including the now-legendary lava lamp."

Taste Unlmtd-Simple Pleasures Traditional cheese-and-nut gift packs, including the ubiquitous Cheeseball. ✓**INTERNET**→*www* http://www.ip.net/shops/Taste_Unlmtd-Simple_Pleasures/

Virginia Diner Nuts, candies, hams, and more. ✓**COMPUSERVE**→*go* va

Gadgets & gizmos

Anchiano Computer Eyewear Glasses to protect you against the glare of the computer screen. ✓**INTERNET**→*www* http://branch.com:1080/eyewear/eyewear.html

Hammacher Schlemmer Unique items and gadgets from this well-known catalog can now be ordered online. ✓**PRODIGY**→*jump* hammacher schlemmer ✓**COMPUSERVE**→*go* hs

Solar Panel Power Portable solar panel that can substitute for batteries in many devices like radios, CD players, and toys that run on C and D batteries. ✓**INTERNET**→*www* http://www.wilder.com/solar.html

TMASecurityCorp Security products including defense sprays, electronic stun devices, personal and home alarms, surveillance/ counter surveillance equipment, and more. ✓**INTERNET**→*www* http://www.ip.net/shops/TMASecurityCorp/

Gift shops

Alaskan Peddler Alaskan T-shirts, jewelry, smoked salmon, and more. ✓**COMPUSERVE**→*go* ak

Brenton Harbor Gift Services Gifts, books, flags, you name it. ✓**COMPUSERVE**→*go* bh

CBS Online Store Looking for a *Young and the Restless* baby bib? A *Northern Exposure* sweatshirt? A *60 Minutes* coffee mug? These and other CBS-related items are available. ✓**PRODIGY**→*jump* cbs online

Find a Gift Gift ideas for men, women, and children. Can be searched by subject if you have your own gift ideas. ✓**PRODIGY**→*jump* find a gift

Gift Sender Hundreds of gift ideas ranging from bonsai trees to gourmet fruit baskets. ✓**COMPUSERVE**→*go* gs

Just Terrific Gifts Need a corporate gift idea? A bon voyage gift basket? Order a unique gift basket to be shipped anywhere in the continental United States. ✓**GENIE**→*keyword* gifts

Spencer Gifts Order and view the infamously trashy Spencer Gifts products, including the now-legendary lava lamp. You can also search a directory for the location of the nearest Spencer Gifts store and share your feedback with management. ✓**INTERNET**→*www* http://www.btg.com/spencer

Gunsmithing

Scott, McDougall, and Asso-

Lava lamps—from Spencer Gifts
http://www.btg.com/spencer

ciates A gunsmithing, firearm training, and firearm investigation outfit located in Cotati, California, this company maintains an extensive online catalog of its services, which range from looking into safety malfunctions to training upstanding citizens in the proper use of a 1911-type-single-action .45 Read the online information or send email to macscott@crl.com. √**INTERNET**→*ftp* ftp.crl.com→anonymous→<your email address>→/users/ro/mac scott/firearms

Home breweries

Charleston Beer Works Suppliers of home-brewing equipment, hops, and malts. √**INTERNET**→*www* http://www.sims.net/organizations/chasbeerworks/chasbeerworks.html

D Distributing Home brewery in a bag! A brew sack of malt extract that allows you to brew pub-style beer in the privacy of your own home. Order online. √**INTERNET**→*www* http://www.human.com/mkt/ddist/

Home furnishings

Bassett Furniture Order furniture without ever leaving home. √**COMPUSERVE**→*go* bfc

Marrakesh Express Moroccan rug and pillow shop. √**INTERNET**→*www* http://uslink.net/ddavis/

THINK BIG! WorldStore Oversize novelty items such as 6-foot rulers, 5-foot-tall pencils, humongous crayons, towering toothbrushes, and giant baby bottles. √**INTERNET**→*www* http://www.ip.net/shops/WorldStore-THINK_BIG/

Hot sauce

Atlanta Chile Company Hot sauce, tortilla chips, nuts, drink mixes, and cookbooks. √**INTERNET**→*www* http://www.bizweb.com/chile.html

Chile Today Hot Tamale Chile and hot sauce facts and figures, as well as an online catalog to order the burning condiments. √**INTERNET**→*www* http://eMail.com/Chile/Chile1.html

Hot Hot Hot Some like it hot, some like it hotter, and some like it so hot that steam pours out their ears. A veritable museum of scorched mouths. In addition to a lavish online catalog, the company publishes its own Hot Sauce FAQ, and every month one sauce is elevated to the top of the pack for special selection status. Will it be Ring of Fire, Burn Baby Burn, or the Torrid Texas Tongue-Twister? Stay tuned. √**INTERNET**→*www* http://www.presence.com/hot

Household items

Placesettings China, crystal, and silver from many well-known companies, including Dansk, Mikasa, Noritake, and Wedgewood. An online bridal registry service is also available. √**PRODIGY**→*jump* placesettings

TuppNet Buy Tupperware on the Net. Parties are held on IRC every Wednesday at 6 p.m. PDT. Catalogs, including image catalogs, and order forms can be downloaded. Then, just email in your order. √**INTERNET** ...→*ftp* ftp.netcom.com→anonymous→<your email address>→/pub/tuppnet ...→*irc* /server David.CA.US.undernet.org 6667→/channel #TuppNet ...→*email* tuppnet@netcom.com ✍ *Email with order*

Jewelry

Colorburst Studios Catalog,

CYBERPOWER! ™

Let's Go Shopping

I love my computer, but it's old. Real old. It coughs. It sputters. It reminisces. It's not the CPU it used to be. Before it rides off into the final sunset, I want to use it for one last mission—to buy a new computer. Can I shop for a new computer online? And is the irony too cruel, to have a dying machine dispute its obsolescence by finding its own replacement?

Well, we can't help you gauge the cruelty of the irony, but we can assure you that your computer, no matter how decrepit, is perfectly capable of helping you shop for a new computer. Direct the old geezer to Delphi's Comp-U-Store (go shop comp), which is organized like a huge department store—everything from baby toys to bathroom fixtures, cameras to china. And even computers. First call up the main shopping directory with the TO DEPT command, and then select the computer category. Once you're inside the massive retail brain of the Comp-U-Store, making online purchases is so easy that Gramps won't even get winded. Narrow your purchase by manufacturer, model name, and even price range (separate the low and high boundaries with a semicolon), and then just sit back and wait for the results. Feel free to have a short but heartfelt talk with your old computer during the product search. Explain that he's served you well, that times change, that we all must move on eventually. And when the Comp-U-Store returns its results—a new PowerBook 150 for $1,418.20, including the shipping cost—try to restrain yourself from howling with delight.

Because half-hearted cruelty is no cruelty at all, you might want to consider sending your old machine to the big Trash Icon in the sky with a heightened awareness of its own uselessness. If so, add insult to injury by checking out the Internet Shopping Network (http://www.internet.net), which claims to be the world's largest mall devoted to computer products. While your old computer looks on helplessly—while it becomes implicated more and more deeply in its own demise—buy up all the finest accessories for your new PowerBook. The huge master catalog of the Internet Shopping Network is divided by platform and category, and if you like, you can even use ISN Power Searching to narrow the field by product name, company name, minimum and maximum price, and category parameters. Searching for relatively cheap Mac PowerBook accessories turns up a PowerBook Security Kit ($48.25), a long-life battery ($47.67), and a notebook keypad ($94.14). Buy them all.

Finally, head over to the state-of-the-art electronic mall known only as Shopping 2000 (http://www.shopping2000.com), where you'll find multimedia catalogs for a variety of stores, including JC Penny, Tweed, and Tower Records. The Tower Records catalog features album cov-

Shopping 2000 Home page

ers and audio samples from selected LPs, including Aaliyah's hip-hop happening *Age Ain't Nothing But a Number*. Instruct your old computer to download the sample; with every received byte, you'll test the age-old theory that machines can't cry.

with photos, of handmade jewelry. ✓**INTERNET**→*www* http://www.tele port.com/~paulec/catalog.html

Earrings by Lisa! Illustrated catalog of earrings. ✓**INTERNET**→ *www* http://mmink.cts.com/mmink /kiosks/earrings/earrings.html

Jewelry by Diana Kane Designer jewelry. ✓**INTERNET**→*www* http://www.tagsys.com:80/Ads/Di anaKane/

Milne Jewelry Handmade southwestern silver and turquoise jewelry. ✓**INTERNET**→*www* http:// www.branch.com/milne/Milne01. html

Kitchen products

Chef's Catalog Over 1,000 kitchen products including a food dehydrator, a gingerbread-house mold, a Belgian waffler, a frozen-yogurt and ice-cream maker. ✓**COMPUSERVE**→*go* cc

Magazines

Magazine Deals Subscribe to any of the 300 magazine choices from Publisher's Clearing House. ✓**PRODIGY**→*jump* magazine deals

Monogramming

Penny Wise Custom Print Shop Monogram items from baseball caps to letter openers. ✓**COMPUSERVE**→*go* pwp

New Age

The Crystal Portal Tarot decks, T-shirts, and books and videos on the likes of Celtic lore, Eastern spirituality, Norse mythology, shamanism, magick and wicca. ✓**INTERNET**→*www* http://cyber sight.com/cportal/cphome.htm

White Dolphin Books Thousands of New Age resources, including books, tapes, CDs, videos, CD-ROMs, meditation supplies, and gift items. Indexed by subject. ✓**INTERNET**→*www* http://www. northcoast.com/unlimited/prod uct_directory/white_dolphin/white _dolphin.html

Office supplies

PC Pens Pens, art and drafting supplies. ✓**PRODIGY**→*jump* pc pens

Penny Wise Office Products Office products from paper to diskettes to pencil sharpeners. ✓**COMPUSERVE**→*go* pw ✓**AMERICA ONLINE**→*keyword* penny ✓**GENIE**→ *keyword* pennywise

U.S. Stamps Postage stamps from the United States Postal Service. ✓**PRODIGY**→*jump* us stamps

Pet supplies

IAMS Company Dog and cat food. ✓**COMPUSERVE**→*go* iam

ImageMaker's Gifts for Dog Lovers Handmade items geared to canine groupies: quilts, boxer shorts, fabric, tote bags, aprons, refrigerator magnets, and more. ✓**INTERNET**→*www* http://fender.on ramp.net/imagemaker/

Unique Concepts, Inc. Dog or cat treat-of-the-month club, featuring homemade, all-natural foods. ✓**INTERNET**→*www* http:// branch.com:1080/treats/treats.html

Pharmacies

Court Pharmacy A fully stocked drugstore online with products ranging from hair- and skin-care products to photo supplies. Fill prescriptions and even ask advice via email from Tom the pharma-

Big Baby Bottle—http: //www.ip. net/shops/WorldStore-THINK_BIG/

cist. ✓**GENIE**→*keyword* pharmacy

Phone services

AT&T Online Store AT&T merchadise: telephones to fax modems. ✓**COMPUSERVE**→*go* dp

Hello Direct Order telephone productivity tools, including a 900 MHz cordless headset. ✓**INTER-NET**→*www* http://www.hello-direct. com/hd/

Private investigations

InPhoto Surveillance A fully licensed detective agency with representatives within a three-hour drive of 85 percent of the United States. The company's website contains an library about surveillance—from the legal and ethical dimensions of the practice to help in reading results. And if the flat-foot finds the hubby with a floozy, you can upload the incriminating photos for all the world to see. ✓**INTERNET**→*www* http://www.inter

access.com/users/rjones/

Sex

Condom Country Catalog of prophylactics and assorted sexual accessories, narrated by the Condom Cowboy. Also includes a penis-size chart, condom history, condom jokes, condom instructions, and public service announcements on AIDS and STDs. ✓**INTERNET**→*www* http://www.ag. com/Condom/Country

JT Toys All manner of sexual aids, clothes, books, how-to videos, and more. A particularly deep inventory of bondage tools. ✓**INTERNET**→ *gopher* ftp.std.com→vendors→jttoys

SeXXy Software Adult software and CD-ROMs primarily for PC-compatible computers. ✓**INTERNET**→*gopher* ftp.std.com→vendors→sexxy software

Songs

Send a Song Songa via telephone can be sent to a friend or loved one. Choices are listed by subject such as Birthday, Love, and Missing You. ✓**PRODIGY**→ *jump* send a song

Sports equipment

Austads Golf Custom-built golf clubs, as well as clothing, balls, and accessories. ✓**PRODIGY**→*jump* austads golf ✓**COMPUSERVE**→*go* au

The Racquet Workshop Full line of tennis gear. ✓**INTERNET**→ *www* http://arganet.tenagra.com/ Racquet_Workshop/Workshop. html

Subculture

Fringeware, Inc. Online Catalog An extremely diverse catalog

The Internet Shopping Network Web page—http://www.internet.net/

of "fringeware," including a book series entitled "Timothy Leary's Greatest Hits," fertility planning software, and, for the truly retro, sterling silver cigarette holders. ✓**INTERNET**→*www* file://io.com /pub/fwi/HTML/prices.html

Telecommunications

AmeriCom Long Distance Service A complete telecommunications service site offering long distance and related products. A handy area code/country code finder program is linked to this site. ✓**INTERNET**→*www* http://www. xmission.com/~americom/

PhoneScapes Telephone calling card. ✓**INTERNET**→*www* http:// branch.com:1080/maxim/maxim. html

Talk N Toss The prepaid phone card. ✓**INTERNET**→*www* http:// branch.com:1080/talk/talk.html

Toys & games

3d0 Warez and More 3DO machines and CDs. Atari, Jaguar, Sega, and Nintendo platforms are

planned. ✓**INTERNET**→*www* http:// www.ip.net/shops/3d0_Warez_ and_More/

Burpco Burp Gun A blast from the past: the original Burp Gun (circa 1950), which shoots 15 ping-pong balls via air power. ✓**INTERNET**→*www* http://branch.com: 1080/burpco/burpco.html

C. C. Writer Gaming Supplies Strategy and fantasy gaming supplies. ✓**INTERNET**→*gopher* market place.com→ccwriter.com

Chips and Bits Subscription information for *Strategy Plus Magazine*, a gaming magazine, and discount game software for Genesis, Super Nintendo, New Geo, IBM, 3DO, and more. ✓**GENIE**→*keyword* chips

Epic MegaGames Download shareware versions of games for a small fee or order your own copy of commercial Epic games. Chat with other Epic MegaGames players in rooms of the forum. ✓**COMPUSERVE**→*go* emg

Gamelink CD-ROMs CD-

Anchiano Computer Eyewear—http:// branch.com:1080/eyewear/eyewear.html

ROM titles on a universe of topics: animals, art, business, children, cooking, dinosaurs, foreign languages, music, space, and sports. ✓**INTERNET**→*www* http:// www.awa.com:/mm/gamelink/ gamelink.html

Infinite Illusions The speciality here is juggling equipment, but you'll also find books, boomerangs, kites, and yo-yos. ✓**INTERNET**→*www* http://io.com/usr/infinite/index. html

Sierra Online Games from Sierra Online, such as Yserbius and Space Quest. ✓**COMPUSERVE**→*go* si

The Vermont Teddy Bear Co. Meet the bear of your dreams. ✓**INTERNET**→*www* http://www.service. digital.com/tdb/vtdbear.html

Trees

The Bonsai Boy of New York Each bonsai tree is potted in a glazed ceramic container and sent along with all the stuff that's needed for this miniaturist art. ✓**INTERNET**→*www* http://branch.com:1080 /bonsai/bonsai.html

Vacuum cleaners

Sweeps Vacuum & Repair Center Inc. Vacuum cleaners designed to minimize the amount and size of particles expelled into the room. Also available: a complete selection of all makes of vacuum cleaner bags and belts. ✓**INTERNET**→*www* http://branch.com:1080

/sweeps/sweeps.html

Videos

Corinth Video A master catalog of videos as well as a browseable catalog of dance, opera, theater, classic and foreign films, and classic television. Includes several movie- and video-related links to other Internet resources. ✓**INTERNET**→*www* http://www.awa.com:/softlock/ video/

Critics' Choice Video Choose from more than 2,000 movie titles and more than 42,000 videos. Laser disc and 8mm are available for some titles as well. ✓**COMPUSERVE**→*go* ccv

InfoVid Outlet: The Educational & How-To Video Warehouse Over 3,500 how-to videos on a wide range of subjects, including auto repair, aerobics, boating, and computers. ✓**INTERNET**→ *www* http://branch.com:1080/infovid/c 100.html

NOVA WGBH videos Videos from the PBS series. ✓**INTERNET**→ *www* http://branch.com:1080 /nova/nova.html

Video production

SassyProductions Provides Avid 8000 non linear editing services. ✓**INTERNET**→*www* http://www.ip. net/shops/SassyProductions/

Science Television Professional and educational videos for the scientific community. ✓**INTERNET**→ *www* http://www.service.com/stv/

Vitamins

SDV Vitamins Vitamins, herbal supplements, and vitamin-related information. ✓**COMPUSERVE**→*go* sdv

Vitamin Express Order health products and get information about vitamins and health and skin care. ✓**COMPUSERVE**→*go* hve ✓ **PRODIGY**→*jump* vitamin express

Vitamist All-natural oral sprays containing vitamins and minerals. ✓**INTERNET**→*www* http://www.icw. com/vitamist/vitamist.html

Windows

Anderson Windows Features a list of common questions—and answers—about windows and glass doors, as well as ideas for window design and a free brochure about the company. ✓**PRODIGY**→ *jump* anderson windows

Wine

Forest Hill Vineyard A large selection of award-winning California chardonnays. ✓**INTERNET**→*www* http://branch.com:1080/wine/ wine.html

> "InPhoto Surveillance is a fully licensed detective agency. And if the flatfoot finds the hubby with a floozy, you can upload the incriminating photos for all the world to see."

Classifieds

Online shopping takes two forms. On the one hand, there are the retail shops, which operate like regular stores: advertisements, prices, catalogs, and so on. Then, there are classified ads. Like their print counterparts, online classifieds are immensely valuable; unlike print ads, electronic listings are easy to navigate, with keyword searches that find and retrieve the ads you want to see. Jump into one of the classified clearinghouses—from CompuServe's **Classifieds** to AOL's **Classifieds Online**—to find information on tickets, jewelry, cars, pets, and anything else even vaguely negotiable. If you're in the San Jose area, zip over to the **Mercury Center**, which carries hundreds of ads each day in categories such as real estate, transportation, employment, and personals. And if you've narrowed down your search to a specific type of merchandise, make sure you don't forget about the various **rec.marketplace*** newsgroups and the miscellaneous classified sites; track down lenses and filters at AOL's **Photo Buy & Sell**, for instance, or collect Dead bootlegs at **Tape**

Chicago Tribune Online—screenshot from America Online

Heads. Virtually all of the classified services accept ads as well, and the price is usually right.

On the Net

Across the board

4-Sale (echo) Hoping to buy a 720K floppy drive or to sell an Atari Jaguar? The conference is flooded with hundreds of such offers. Unlike most parts of Cyberspace, telephone numbers are often publicly exchanged here. ✓**RELAYNET**

Buy-Sell (echo) An Energizer Bunny screensaver is selling for $10, IBM games are going for as low as $1, and modems are omnipresent on this low-volume classified's conference. ✓**ILINK**

Classifieds Reading the classifieds goes high tech. Search within a set of categories (real estate, employment, cars, travel, etc.) by the

age of the ad or ad number. You can automatically reply to an ad, create your own ad, or delete your ad. Ads meeting CompuServe's requirements are posted within 24 hours. Read help for fee and requirement information (accessed via the "?" with Information Manager). ✓**COMPUSERVE**→*go* classifieds

Classifieds Online Want to get rid of that extra modem or the 386 you no longer use since that purchase of the PowerPC? Open up to the classifieds on AOL. There are three boards devoted to computer trading, one to jobs, and another to general merchandise where everything that's not computer related is put on the block. Ads are free to place and get added to the boards instantly. While AOL does not formally review new ads, the Tradin' Talk message folder is worth reading to see what other AOL members are saying about the advertisers. ✓**AMERICA ONLINE**→*keyword* classifieds

ForSale (echo) 500 messages in two days is about average for this mega-active classifieds conference. While the great bulk are oriented toward computer equipment and software, cross-stitch patterns, and gaming supplies have a place here as well. ✓**FIDONET**

ForSale (echo) One guy's shopping for a present for his wife and another's interested in a good deal on a power Mac. At a rate of a couple hundred messages a week, the conference is active but not overwhelming. ✓**INTELEC**

GEnie Classified Ads Class reunions, personals, rooms for rent, car and computer listings, and job announcements are all listed here. Costs of placing an ad are minimal—although there's an additional cost if you post anonymously. ✓**GENIE**→*keyword* ads **$**

TPI Online Classifeds Members advertise their job openings, apartment rentals, investment opportunities, airline tickets, computer equipment, books, boats, and bicycles on this catch all classifieds board. Advertisements are listed by category; no ads for psychics, guns, or personal hygiene products permitted. Ads will be posted by 5 p.m. the next business day after submission. There are fees for placing but not responding to an ad. ✓**PRODIGY**→*jump* online classifeds→Read/Place Ads

Local listings

ba.market.misc (ng) If it's not a computer, you can probably sell, buy, or trade it here, especially if you're in the Bay area. Airline tickets, living room sets, concert tickets, fish tanks, and glow-in-the-dark powder have all been pushed. ✓**USENET**

Chicago Tribune Classifieds Browse or search car, help wanted, real estate, and other advertisements taken directly from the pages of the current week's *Chicago Tribune*. To place an ad, you must voice call the *Trib* at 312-222-2222. ✓**AMERICA ONLINE**→*keyword* trib ads

Mercury Center—Advertising Today's classifieds from the *San Jose Mercury News* are online and may be browsed or searched. There is also the Mall, where participating companies in the San Jose area have their own mini-forums, offering detailed descriptions of merchandise and an online order form. The Online Mini Market within the mall is another classified like section: "Adorable Maltese Needs Home"; "Best Singles Dateline Ever." You get the

> ## "I have a signed mint Wretched I'd like to trade for an Old Man of the Sea in similar condition."

picture. ✓**AMERICA ONLINE**→*keyword* mercury→Advertising

nj.forsale (ng) New Jersey Netters have their own electronic superstore with cars, exercise equipment, furniture, T-shirts, and more selling and trading here. ✓**USENET**

Arts & crafts

rec.crafts.marketplace (ng) Val is asking about a mail-order source for tumbled semi precious stones. Marlina is selling Brazilian embrodiery kits. The online, ongoing crafts fair gets several dozen messages per week. ✓**USENET**

Audio

alt.music.bootlegs (ng) Trade, buy, and sell bootleg tapes, videos, and CDs. Pearl Jam, Oingo Boingo, Tori Amos, Janet Jackson, Neil Young, and Bob Dylan fans are part of the tape (make that CD and video) trading frenzy of people here trying desperately to avoid missing out on the bootleg of a lifetime. ✓**USENET**

Dat Heads Hippy funk dominates, but recordings from bands of all music styles are traded here. ✓**INTERNET**→*email* dat-heads-request@virginia.edu ✍ *Write a request*

rec.music.makers.marketplace (ng) There is more traffic here than on the games market-

place newsgroups—and that's a lot of activity. From guitars to modular systems to saxophones, Netters are selling and buying instruments. ✓**USENET**

rec.music.marketplace (ng) Whether it's a bootleg or a seldomly used CD, music recordings are sold and traded here. Marillion, the Smashing Pumpkins, the Police, and Laurie Anderson probably aren't making any money off Net sales, but their fans are spending at a frantic rate. ✓**USENET**

Tape Heads Although originally created as a site where Grateful Dead fans could trade tapes, the list has exploded to include a diverse group of music fans trading and talking about taping. ✓**INTERNET**→*email* tape-heads-request@virginia.edu ✍ *Write a request*

Taper's Den AOL may well be the online service with the most devoted Grateful Dead fans. They're certainly some of the most active tape traders on the Net. From taping techniques to intergenerational tape trading, the forum is an excellent place to enter the trading scene. ✓**AMERICA ONLINE**→*keyword* dead→Grateful Dead Messaging→Taper's Den

Bicycles

rec.bicycles.marketplace (ng) If you have never heard of Campagnolo quill road pedals or XT crankarms or a '94 Gold Rush Replica, skip this group. On the other hand, a dedicated cyclist in the market for a new bike might want to browse the large list for sale here. ✓**USENET**

Books

rec.arts.books.marketplace (ng) Hunter Thompson books are sought, *Star Trek* books are for sale, bookstores are recommended for buying Lovecraft novels, and a signed first edition of *Neuromancer* is dangled on this electronic book fair. ✓**USENET**

Cameras

Photo Buy & Sell A swap and shop of tripods, enlargers, lenses, film hangers, and cameras. ✓**AMERICA ONLINE**→*keyword* kodak→Photo Buy/Sell

rec.photo.marketplace (ng) Camera equipment accounts for the majority of postings on this newsgroup although occasionally artists post information about their photographs. ✓**USENET**

Comics

rec.arts.comics.marketplace (ng) Sick of your *Daredevil* comic books? Sell 'em online. Desperate for a copy of *Spectre* from the 1960s? Trade for it. Auctions of comic books—sometimes collections of 100—are held all the time. ✓**USENET**

Computer stuff

ba.market.computers (ng) Surprise! There's a fast-moving market for computers and computer products in the Bay Area. ✓**USENET**

Computer marketplace newsgroups (ng) Newsgroups for buying and selling computers and computer-related products. See sidebar for a list of the groups. ✓**USENET**

Science fiction

rec.arts.sf.marketplace (ng) Anything's up for sale here, as long as it has a sci-fi theme. ✓**USENET**

Sex

alt.sex.erotica.marketplace (ng) All sorts of erotic play toys are hawked here—from home videos to gay movies to phone sex. ✓**USENET**

Toys & games

comp.sys.ibm.pc.games.marketplace (ng) A non-stop auction of IBM-compatible games. ✓**USENET**

rec.games.board.marketplace (ng) Serious collectors post lists of board games, desired and for sale. Messages often go into agonizing detail about the condition of games ("One of the large ships has a small piece of plastic missing from the back end") and the group has the atmosphere of an antique auction: competitive and obsessive. In fact, there are often bidding wars. (Right now, high bid for Milton Bradley's Broadsides and Boarding Parties is $40. Do I hear $45?) ✓**USENET**

rec.games.deckmaster.marketplace (ng) "I have a signed mint Wretched I'd like to trade for an Old Man of the Sea in similar condition," writes Willy from the University of California, Davis. Deckmaster cards, not classic books, are being traded and auctioned, and the demand is immense. ✓**USENET**

rec.games.frp.marketplace (ng) Haggle for spell books and the latest version of *Cyberpunk 2020*. ✓**USENET**

Video games

rec.games.video.marketplace (ng) Round-the-clock trading in video games. ✓**USENET**

Part 4

Investment

Investment basics

Nervous about buying that penny stock your brother recommends? Ashamed that you

don't know much about call options? Curious why your mutual funds aren't making as much money as you had hoped? The Net is full of valuable resources for novice investors, from Prodigy's **Investor's Glossary** to the extensive **Investment FAQ**. After a few hours browsing these resources, you'll know enough to speak intelligently to your stockbroker girlfriend or assess the recommendations and strategies in **Consumer Reports Investment**. And if not, don't hesitate to order in some extra help from AOL's **Reading List** of financial best-sellers.

New York City's Financial District—downloaded from America Online's Pictures of the World Forum

On the Net

Across the board

Consumer Reports Investments Advice for the layman on a variety of investment issues, such as "Allocating Your Investments," "Deferred Annuities and Mutual Funds," "How to Invest a Windfall," and "How to Spot an Investment Scam." ✓ **PRODIGY**→*jump* cr investments

Investment FAQ This mammoth Investment FAQ offers a concise introduction to investment in the electronic age, answering questions on stocks, bonds, options, mutuals, brokers, and markets. ✓ **INTERNET** ...→*www*

http://www.cis.ohio-state.edu/hypertext/faq/usenet/investment-faq/general/top.html...→*ftp* rtfm.mit.edu→ anonymous→<your email address>→/pub/usenet-by-group/misc.answers/investment-faq/general

Investment/Financial Services Learn where to find valuable information (primarily addresses and phone numbers of contact organizations) on an extensive number of financial topics, including stocks, bonds, and commodities. ✓ **COMPUSERVE**→*go* ius-5061

Investment Planning The FAQ and the introductory articles are almost exclusively about mutual funds; topics on the message board range from investment software to foreign stocks. You can also perform a full-text search on investment subjects. ✓ **AMERICA ONLINE**→*keyword* yourmoney→Investment Planning

The Reference Desk Post your business question and eWorld members or Reference Press librarians (publishers of Hoover's Handbooks) will help you find the answer. Categories include career and job searches, industry information, business trivia, market research, and company information. ✓ **EWORLD**→*go* refpress→The Reference Desk

Books

Business Resource Catalog A catalog of publications produced by the Reference Press. Online ordering is available. ✓ **EWORLD**→*go* refpress→Business Resource Catalog

Reading List An online store overseen by AOL's Decision Point Forum featuring a list of book and audiotape recommendations for investors and businesspeople. Books are sorted by level of expertise (beginner, intermediate, and expert); AOL subscribers can order them online at a discount. ✓**AMERICA ONLINE**→*keyword* dp→ Investment Books & Tapes

The Reference Press Bookstore This business information provider develops reference books and electronic products for both the domestic and international market. Their full catalog of reference books is online with descriptions of each product and downloadable fax order forms. ✓**INTERNET**→*gopher* gopher.hoovers.com

Terms

Investment Glossary Basic vocabulary for economics, general investment, investment instruments, mutual funds, stock analysis, and trading. ✓**AMERICA ONLINE**→*keyword* aaii→Reference Library→Reference Shelf→ Investment Glossary

Investor's Glossary If you're flummoxed by futures or baffled by bonds, you're not alone—the world of investment is a rather insular one, with an idiosyncratic language that can sound like secret code. ("Covered put," whispered the man in the black fedora.)

Even worse, simple concepts are often obfuscated by tortuous terminology. This glossary defines more than 200 terms from the world of options, markets, and brokers. Before you know it, you've become a person who talks confidently about the Alpha Equation or GTCs. ✓**PRODIGY**→*jump* investors glossary

Moneywords v3.5 Comprehensive and easy-to-read online glossary to business language with more than 2,600 definitions. Shareware for DOS. ✓**PC OHIO** →d→*Download a file:* MONY WD35.ZIP

INVESTOR'S GLOSSARY

Arbitrage—Profiting from differences in the price of a single security that is traded on more than one market.

Basis points—Refers to yield on bonds. Each percentage point of yield in bonds equals 100 basis points. If a bond yield changes from 7.25% to 7.39%, that's a rise of 14 basis points.

Call option—An option contract that gives the holder of the option the right (but not the obligation) to purchase, and obligates the writer to sell, a specified number of shares of the underlying stock at the given strike price, on or before the expiration date of the contract.

Depreciation—A noncash expense that provides a source of free cash flow. Amount allocated during the period to amortize the cost of acquiring long-term assets over the useful life of the assets.

Ex-dividend—Interval between the announcement and the payment of the next dividend. An investor who buys shares during that interval is not entitled to the dividend. A stock that has gone ex-dividend is marked with an x in newspaper listings.

Futures contract—Agreement to buy or sell a set number of shares of a specific stock in a designated future month at a price agreed upon by the buyer and seller. The contracts themselves are often traded on the futures market. A futures contract differs from an option because an option is the right to buy or sell, whereas a futures contract is the promise to actually make a transaction.

Initial public offering—A company's first sale of stock to the public. Securities offered in an IPO are often but not always those of young, small companies seeking outside equity capital and a public market for their stock. Investors purchasing stock in IPOs generally must be prepared to accept very large risks for the possibility of large gains.

Load fund—A mutual fund with shares sold at a price including a sales charge—typically 4% to 9.3% of the net amount indicated.

Margin account—A leveraged account where stocks can be purchased for a combination of cash and a loan. The loan in the margin account is collateralized by the stock and, if the value of the stock drops, the owner will be asked to either put in more cash, or sell a portion of the stock. This is all federally regulated.

Out-of-the-money—A call option is out-of-the-money if the strike price is greater than the market price of the underlying security. A put option is out-of-the-money if the strike price is less than the market price of the underlying security.

Price/earnings ration—Shows the "multiple" of earnings at which a stock sells. Determined by dividing the current price by current earnings per share (adjusted for stock splits). Earnings per share for the P/E ratio is determined by dividing earnings for the past 12 months by the number of common shares outstanding. Higher "multiple" means investors have higher expectations for future growth, and have bid up the stock's price.

—from Prodigy's **Investor's Glossary**

Thinking about investing

From GEnie's Investors' RoundTable to the massive Investment Conference on the

WELL, Cyberspace contains dozens of locations for investors to meet and talk about investment issues. Want to learn more about portfolio valuation? Curious about the history of the AMEX? Drop in and start chatting. If you'd rather follow the counsel of experts, check out **Market Beat** and **Brendan Boyd's Investment Digest** for basic investment tips and strategies. And, finally, those investors with a particular interest in the laws and regulations behind investment practices can browse the **Federal Securities Acts of 1933 and 1934**.

On the Net

Across the board

AAII Online Sponsored by the nonprofit American Association of Individual Investors and featuring hundreds of articles on investing basics. Articles are organized in folders on the forum's opening screen (International Investments, Insurance, Managing Your Portfolio, etc.), and the collection can be searched via an icon at the bottom of the forum. See the Reference Library for suggested financial reading, names of brokers, investment terms, and the like.

The Reference Shelf contains cut-to-the-bone surveys of soft-

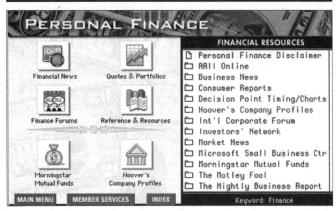

Personal Finance Screen—from America Online

ware, services, and discount brokers for computerized investing. The Software Library stores a growing archive of mostly public domain programs for managing investments, and is divided into such categories as Technical Analysis, Portfolio Management, and Fundamental Analysis.

Stock Selection and Computerized Investing dominate the AAII Message Area, but there are also busy threads on such subjects as dealing with brokers. ✓**AMERICA ONLINE**→ *keyword* aaii

Competitive Intelligence More of a primer than a resource for advanced investment strategy. Includes recommendations for business information—from magazines to newspapers to reference books to analysts' reports—and clear and concise explanations about business basics, from how a company goes public to the difference between stocks and bonds. ✓**EWORLD**→*go* refpress →Competitive Intelligence

Finance (echo) Join dozens of financially minded participants as they deflate each other's bad stock tips and try to explain complex in-

> "Join dozens of financially minded participants on Finance as they deflate each other's bad stock tips and try to explain complex investment formulas and pet theories about market balance."

vestment formulas and pet theories about market balance. ✓**RE-LAYNET**

FTP Directory of Public Financial and Market Information
Amateur financiers upload market analyses and reports, graphs and spreadsheets. Be warned—this information is public domain and guaranteed by no one. ✓**INTERNET**→*ftp* dg-rtp.dg.com→anonymous→<your email address>→/pub/misc.invest

Inside Investing A world of personal finance discussion. Great graphics and well organized. ✓**EWORLD**→*go* money matters→Inside Investing

Invest (echo) From technical analysis to corporate taxation, this forum offers a broad spectrum of investment topics; postings reflect various levels of expertise and insight. ✓**FIDONET**

Investment What's the best stock market software? What are the criminal codes pertaining to trader fraud? Will the NYSE ever be supplanted by another stock market? Whether participants are musing on the warp in world markets ("If I were running a company, I'd register on the Japanese stock exchange and let those crazy investors over there double my P/E overnight") or investigating cutting-edge investments like biotech stocks ("I would like to know what companies make the hardware for doing polymerase chain reaction work. Seems to me it's a major change in how we do biological work, that might be a growth business"). The information imparted here is almost always interesting and sometimes even useful. ✓**WELL**→*g* invest

Investor (echo) Though this con-

> **"The Money Talk Bulletin Board encourages discussion on investment theory, so feel free to test out your idea that the stock market falls after NFC victories in the Superbowl."**

ference is ostensibly devoted to investment strategy—especially technical analyses of stocks—it tends to slip into other areas of economics and finance. Participants have shown a special penchant for deriding ATMs. ✓**ILINK**

Investor's Forum The Investment Message Boards are filled with detailed user comments on individual stocks, as well as discussions about mutual funds and bonds, futures and commodities, brokers and advisors, and international investing. The forum includes an Investment Chat Room for real-time investment discussion, and libraries of financial documents and financial software. ✓**AMERICA ONLINE**→*keyword* invest

Investor's Network Welcome to AOL's stock club. Decision Point's Carl Swenlin hosts this forum, in which individual investors exchange wit, wisdom, and get-rich-quick schemes. Posts on the "Investing Today Message Board" lean toward highly specific strategies of technical analysis and market timing. There are also special

message boards for brokers, as well as those covering taxes, international investing, mutual funds, bonds, and individual stocks. Live weekly investment talks are held Sunday from 9 p.m. to 11 p.m. EST in the Investment Chat Room. ✓**AMERICA ONLINE**→*keyword* investor

Investors' Forum Whether you dabble in stocks and bonds or pour thousands annually into commodities and mutual funds, there's sure to be a discussion tailored to your needs.
Topics on the message boards range from Stocks/The Market to Options Trading to Newsletters/Theories. The forum also offers real-time conferences with various financial experts, a wide range of financial software for downloading, and an extensive library that archives newsletters and introductory documents. ✓**COMPUSERVE**→*go* invforum

Investors Forum As one of the custom forums which are "owned" by Delphi members or other companies, this forum is separated from the service's official groups, but its message boards, download areas, and real-time conferences are definitely worth checking out. The forum is not heavily trafficked, but there is valuable information on investment topics ranging from stock tips to an explanation of the CANSLIM acronym. ✓**DELPHI**→*go* custom 216

Investors' RoundTable Discussions on the finer points of making money cover everything from stocks and bonds to industrial news. Greenhorns and zillionaires speculate on the ebb and flow of market forces. The RoundTable provides a forum for topics such as investment software and investment clubs, and includes an extensive software downloading area. ✓**GENIE**→*keyword* invest

misc.invest (ng) Examines general investment topics, ranging from stocks and bonds to mutual funds to the vagaries of E-trade. If you want to discuss your retirement plans or complain about the mistreatment of the tobacco industry—"Congress and the anti-smoking lobby are driving the tobacco industry out of business in the U.S."—put your two cents in, and see what the yields are. A few committed newsgroup participants upload market reports—the same info that you're paying for on other services. ✓**USENET**

Money Talk Bulletin Board A prodigious financial chat resource, with ongoing talk about stocks, options, bonds, futures, and mutual funds. The board encourages discussion on investment theory, so feel free to test out your idea that the stock market falls after NFC victories in the Superbowl. ✓**PRODIGY**→*jump* money talk bb

National Association of Investors Corporation Forum The National Association of Investors Corporation is a nonprofit organization that promotes better investing through investor education and self-development. In other words, it caters to people looking to invest responsibly as a means to long-term stability, and not to get rich quick. As a result, the forum features down-to-earth talk about down-to-earth matters—for example, investing for college funds. Forum members recommend stocks, and discuss their picks in software and opinions on other financial matters. ✓**COMPUSERVE**→*go* naic

Nightly Business Report Online The online counterpart to

"They say the business of America is business, but this bulletin board argues that business is the business of the world, too. If you want to speculate on what effect IRA softening might have on U.K. markets or how Bosnia can possibly rebound from war, you'll find partners in rumination in International Business."

PBS's daily business news show features segment transcripts, a well-intentioned but relatively quiet message-based forum called Talking Business, a software library with a growing collection of sound clips and images from the show, and a guide to local airtimes and stations for the program.

One of the features, NBR in the Classroom, is aimed at schoolteachers looking to spread the economics gospel among the younger generation. Real-time chat confer-

ences hosted by on-air reporters and anchors are promised for the near future, and should enliven the dialogue. ✓**AMERICA ONLINE** →*keyword* nbr

International

International Business They say the business of America is business, but this bulletin board argues that business is the business of the world, too. If you want to speculate on what effect IRA softening might have on U.K. markets or how Bosnia can possibly rebound from war, you'll find partners in rumination. ✓**PRODIGY** →*jump* your business→Internat'l Business

misc.invest.canada (ng) Newsgroup participants worry over international financial relations—"When Canadian citizens (not resident in the U.S.) earn interest income from a U.S. bank, does the IRS report this information to Revenue Canada?" (no)—analyze Canadian stocks, and occasionally engage in small talk about ice hockey. ✓**USENET**

Legal issues

Federal Securities Acts of 1933 and 1934 If you want to know how the Securities and Exchange Commission is organized, or how the government goes about obtaining reimbursement of expenses for assisting foreign securities authorities, these documents will provide you with hours of legislative fun. ✓**INTERNET** ...→*www* http://www.law.uc.edu/CCL/33Act/index.html...→*www* http://www.law.uc.edu/CCL/34Act/index.html

Financial Executive Journal Published jointly by the Cornell Law School Legal Information Institute and the NASDAQ Stock Market, this journal addresses the finer points of financial law and regulations. ✓**INTERNET**→ *www* http://www.law.cornell.edu/ nasdaq/nasdtoc.html

LawTalk - Business Law and Personal Finance An extensive archive of articles on basic legal issues relating to investment decisions. ✓**INTERNET**→*www* http:// www.law.indiana.edu/law/biz law.html

Publications

Brendan Boyd's Investment Digest Financial analyst Brendan Boyd, whose columns are syndicated by UPI, writes this investment column for Prodigy. ✓**PRODIGY**→*jump* investment digest

eINVEST - Electronic Journal of Investing (ml) Addresses specific investment strategies and research methods. The list also features daily market updates and quotes courtesy of *Holt's Market Report.* ✓**INTERNET**→*email* listserv@ vm.temple.edu ✍ *Type in message body:* subscribe e_invest <your full name>

The Electronic Journal of Finance (ml) Whether you're a tentative investor or a wheeler-dealer, a young couple trying to buy a house or an old couple trying to buy a condo, this journal offers valuable insights for your financial future. ✓**INTERNET**→*email* listserv@ vm.temple.edu ✍ *Type in message body:* subscribe finance <your full name>

Individual Investor A monthly magazine that specializes in personal investments, chiefly stocks and mutual funds. Free online excerpts are available in the Electronic Newsstand, both from the current issue and from the magazine's archives. ✓**INTERNET**→*gopher* gopher.enews.com→Business Publications→Individual Investor

Internet Personal Finance Letter Under the guidance of editor Michael P. Griffin, this newsletter examines a variety of personal finance issues, including many investment topics. For market hobbyists and devoted investors, this newsletter is a helpful resource—clear without being simple minded, insightful without being condescending. ✓**INTERNET**→ *email* pfl-requet@umassd.edu ✍ *Type in message body:* subscribe pfl <your full name>

Journal of Financial Abstracts Though this electronic journal is intended for professional and academic use, much of the material is of interest to individual investors. The journal is archived in the Economics Department gopher at Washington University in St. Louis. ✓**INTERNET**→*email* MarrM@clemson.edu ✍ *Write a request*

Market Beat *The Los Angeles Times* is offering free electronic distribution of Tom Petruno's Market Beat column, which focuses on the needs and problems of "the do-it-yourself investor." ✓**INTERNET**→*email* petruno@netcom. com ✍ *Type in subject line:* subscribe

Worth Magazine Forum A companion forum to the online financial magazine, the *Worth* message board includes online features and news items, and also collects fairly casual postings from readers, often with an offbeat spin—for instance, how to choose a choice lobster. ✓**AMERICA ONLINE**→*keyword* worth

Investment shareware

Bond Evaluation Program Evaluates municipal and corporate bonds and calculates the return on investment. ✓**AMERICA ONLINE**→ *keyword* win→*Search by file name:* BEP 10.ZIP (Windows)

Bond Tracker 2.0 Track U.S. savings bonds. ✓**INTERNET**→*ftp* ftp.cica.indiana.edu→anonymous→ <your email address>→/pub/pc /win3/util→bonds20.zip (Windows)

Capital Investment simulation. ✓**EXEC-PC**→File Collection Menu→ Mahoney IBM Compatible DOS→ CAPITAL.ZIP (DOS)

Capital Gainz v3.2 Powerful and comprehensive portfolio manager for stocks, securities, and other money instruments. Calculate gain/loss, reinvest dividends, and record splits. Shareware. ✓**PC OHIO**→d→*Download a file:* CAPGNZA.ZIP *and* CAPGNZB. ZIP (DOS)

EEBond Savings bond database and valuation program. Determines value of Series EE and E bonds and U.S. Saving Notes. Shareware. ✓**PC OHIO**→d→*Download a file:* EEBNDW.ZIP (Windows)

EZStock v2.0 Track and analyze any investment or collectible: stocks, bonds, coins, baseball cards, etc. Built-in help, graphs, and mouse support. ✓**PC OHIO**→ d→*Download a file:* EZSTOCK2.ZIP (DOS)

The Feeling's Mutual Detailed information for more than 800 mutual funds. ✓**AMERICA ONLINE**→ *keyword* mbs→Software Libraries→ Applications→TFM.sea (Macintosh)

FileMaker U.S. Savings Bonds FileMaker Pro database calculates current value of EE or E bonds. ✓**INTERNET**→*ftp* mac. archive.umich.edu→anony mous→<your email address>→ /mac/util/organization→filemaker ussavingsbonds.cpt.hqx (Macintosh)

Financial Portfolio v3.1 Tracks accounts and investments, and calculates net worth. New version has redesigned interface and pop-up menus. Built-in help. ✓**INTER-NET**→*ftp* mac.archive.umich.edu →anonymous→<your email address>→/mac/util/organization→ financialportfolio3.1.sit.hqx (Macintosh)

Financial Portfolio v3.1 for Hypercard Same as Financial Portfolio v3.1, but in a Hypercard stack. ✓**INTERNET**→*ftp* mac.archive. umich.edu→anonymous→<your email address>→/app→financial-portfolio-31.hc.hqx (Macintosh)

Fund Manager A mutual fund investment application that categorizes your portfolio, maintains a transaction record, and calculates your gains and losses. ✓**COMPU-SERVE**→*go* invfor→Browse Libraries →Mutual Funds→FUND.7 (Macintosh)

Fund Manager v6.2 Tracks mutual funds. Outputs both numerical and graphical information. Shareware. ✓**GENIE**→*keyword* invest→Investors' Software Libraries →*Download a file:* FUNDMN62. ZIP (Windows)

FundExpert Manages a portfolio of mutual funds, stocks, and bonds. Records transactions, calculates returns, prepares IRS

Schedule D form, plots historical data, and includes a download feature for retrieving quotes from Prodigy and CompuServe. Shareware. ✓**AMERICA ONLINE**→*keyword* win→*Search by file name:* WFUN D44.ZIP (Windows)

The Investment Portfolio Manager Import data, calculate profit and total return, and produce charts. Shareware. ✓**COM-PUSERVE**→*go* invfor→Browse Libraries→Mutual Funds→VARINV. ZIP (DOS)

Investment Tracker v1.1 Hypercard 2.1 stack that tracks stocks, mutual funds, etc. Calculates average annual yield, tax basis, etc. ✓**INTERNET**→*ftp* mac. archive.umich.edu→anonymous→ <your email address>→/info-mac/app→investment-tracker-11-hc. hqx (Macintosh)

Money Math Tools for financial analysis, including an interest calculator, and analysis tools for CDs. ✓**INTERNET**→*ftp* ftp.cica. indiana.edu→anonymous→<your email address>→/pub/pc/win3 /util→momath.zip (Windows)

Mutual Fund Manager 2.0 Program to manage a mutual fund portfolio with complete transaction records and weekly charting reports. Shareware. ✓**COMPUSERVE** →*go* invfor→Browse Libraries→ Mutual Funds→MUTUAL.ZIP (DOS)

The Mutual Fund Tracker v3.6 Determines when to buy or sell mutual funds; hypothetical results available based on entered criteria. ✓**PC OHIO**→d→*Download a file:* MFTRAC36.ZIP ✓**COM-PUSERVE**→*go* invfor→Browse Libraries→MF TRAC.ZIP (DOS)

Investment shareware (continued)

OPPM 5.06 Sophisticated portfolio management software and charting program for stocks, bonds, mutuals, savings, and other assets. ✓ **COMPUSERVE**→*go* invfor→ Browse Libraries→Stocks/The Market→OPPM50.ZIP (DOS)

Parity v1.3 Comprehensive stock charting program with over 40 indicators, multiple charts and panes, user defined formulas, and import/export capabilities. Requires 80386 with 2MB, mouse and VGA. ✓ **GENIE**→*keyword* invest →Investors' Software Libraries→ *Download a file:* PRTY13D1.ZIP *and* PRTY13D2.ZIP *and* PARITY13.TXT (Windows)

PC Chart v1.5 Fully integrated technical analysis program for serious stock and commodity traders. Can download quotes from GEnie, CompuServe, America Online, etc. ✓ **GENIE**→*keyword* invest→Investors' Software Libraries →*Download a file:* PCHART15.ZIP (DOS)

Quote Tracker Choose the time during the day you want to see stock quotes and the program automatically checks into CompuServe and displays them. Program is also configurable to notify you about relevant company news. Demo version. ✓ **COMPUSERVE**→*go* invfor→Browse Libraries→Stocks/ The Market→QTDEMO.EXE (Windows)

RCFUNDS Intended specifically for the novice investor, this program tracks mutual fund transactions. ✓ **INTERNET**→*ftp* ftp.cica. indiana.edu→anonymous→<your email address>→/pub/pc/win3/ util→rcfunds.zip (Windows)

Simplified Investment Manager v2.01 Easy-to-use portfolio manager can graph value and gain. ✓ **EXEC-PC**→File Collection Menu→ Mahoney IBM Compatible DOS→ SIM201.EXE (DOS)

The Stock Analyst v1.10 Powerful, easy-to-use program is menu-driven—it features buy/sell analysis; line, bar, P/E charts; and support for up to 1,500 stocks. ✓ **PC OHIO**→d→*Download a file:* ANALYST.ZIP (DOS)

Stock Watcher Fetch and display stock prices at designated times. Shareware. ✓ **COMPUSERVE**→ *go* macap→Browse Libraries→Accounting/Finance→STOCKW.SEA (Macintosh)

Stocker Converts AOL's Stock Portfolio Display into format suitable for Quicken 4.0. ✓ **AMERICA ONLINE**→*keyword* mbs→Software Libraries→Applications→ Stocker_ .sea (Macintosh)

$tokTrax v4.28 With a database of over 8,000 company names and symbols, this stock portfolio/charting system can manage up to 200 portfolios. Translates stock data captured from GEnie, CompuServe, and other commercial services. ✓ **EXEC-PC**→File Collection Menu→ Mahoney IBM Compatible DOS→ STX428.ZIP (DOS)

Tradex A technical analysis and portfolio management program for the experienced analyst to evaluate historical prices and volumes. Shareware. ✓ **AMERICA ONLINE**→ *keyword* mbs→Software Libraries→ Applications→Tradex.sit (Macintosh)

Wall Street Simulator v1.0 Realistic simulation of a brokerage account: trade with real market prices. Analyze results and compare to other registered users. Shareware. When you register you will receive the manual, upgrades, and a semi-annual newsletter. ✓ **PC OHIO**→d→*Download a file:* WSSW10.ZIP (DOS)

Wall Street Tracker 7.1 A shareware program, that uses technical analysis to recommend buying, selling, or holding stocks. Supports report and charting reports as well as data retrieval via online services. ✓ **COMPUSERVE**→*go* invfor→Browse Libraries→Stocks/ The Market→WALLST.ZIP (DOS)

Wall $treet The Bottom Line v6.2 Popular and powerful investment managment program for stocks, bonds, precious stones and metals, etc. New version features ability to download from online services (Dow Jones, CompuServe, America Online, etc.). Shareware. ✓ **PC OHIO**→d→*Download a file:* WALLST62.ZIP (DOS)

WinBond v4.2 Tracks and evaluates Series EE bonds. Features import capabilities, multiple bond files, and more. Requires VBRUN 300.DLL. ✓ **AMERICA ONLINE**→*keyword* win→*Search by file name:* WBD42.ZIP (Windows)

WorthTrack 2.0 Download and file investment data such as quotes, news, company reports, and earnings projections. Program can monitor your portfolio and determine gain or loss. ✓ **COMPUSERVE**→*go* invfor→Browse Libraries→Stocks/The Market→ WORTH.ZIP (Windows)

Investment news

Did you hear what happened to Viacom yesterday? What are financial columnists saying

about the investment issues relevant to national health care? How will Rwandan unrest affect our national economy? Think of the Net as a gigantic newsstand waiting to answer these questions, as well as any other financial concerns you might have. From general-interest publications such as **Time** and **The New York Times** to wire services such as the **Associated Press** and **United Press International**, from online news networks such as **CNN** and **C-SPAN** to specialty financial publications and columns such as **Smart Money** and **Daily China Headline News**. Like print media, the online resources are diverse, detailed, and fascinating; unlike print media, it's easy to find what you're looking for.

On the Net

Financial columnists

Brendan Boyd's Money List
This factoid feature is compiled by financial columnist Brendan Boyd, who attempts to enrich (and, more likely, amuse) investors with fascinating financial facts. Do you know which soft drink sells the best in the United States? Can you

Newsboy—downloaded from Compu-Serve's Archive Photo Forum.

identify the richest nation in Europe? And how much do you think a grizzly bear's gallbladder is worth? ✓**PRODIGY**→*jump* money list

Smart Money Syndicated talk-show host Bruce Williams brings his avuncular manner and no-nonsense financial advice to the Net. If you are making less than $20,000 annually, should you buy a new Mercedes? Sir, don't get me started. ✓**AMERICA ONLINE**→*keyword* columnists→Lifestyles Columns →Smart Money

Susan Bondy on Money Do you know how to spot swindlers? Susan Bondy does. In her syndicated column, Bondy addresses a wide variety of consumer and financial issues. ✓**COMPUSERVE**→*go* columns→Susan Bondy on Money

Financial magazines

AI in Finance Addresses the application of artificial intelligence to financial industries, such as the stock market, banking, and insurance industries. ✓**INTERNET**→*gopher* gopher.enews.com→Magazines, Periodicals, and Journals→AI in Finance

BusinessWeek One of the best weekly sources for business and financial news; available with full-text searches dating back to 1985. ✓**GENIE**→*keyword* busweek $

The Economist News and commentary on world politics, finance, science, technology, and the arts. Includes analysis of world market trends, international trade, and the health of various currencies. ✓**INTERNET**→*gopher* gopher. enews.com→Business Publications→ The Economist

Fortune Magazine Online searching through all *Fortune* issues from 1985 until the present. ✓**GENIE**→*keyword* fortune $

GNN Personal Finance Center The GNN Personal Finance Center contains articles on a variety of personal-finance topics, including investment. ✓**INTERNET**→ *www* http://gnn.interpath.net/ gnn/meta/finance/index.html

Kiplinger's Personal Finance Magazine News and advice on a wide variety of personal finance topics. ✓**PRODIGY**→*jump* kiplinger's magazine

Louis Rukeyser's Wall Street Aimed at the financial Everyman, this publication dispenses with jargon and fancy charts, and cuts to the heart of the matter: What investments will work for people with limited resources and modest goals? If you want to increase your earnings with a minimum of risk, consider this publication. ✓**INTERNET**→*gopher* gopher.enews.com→ Business Publications→Louis Rukeyser's Wall Street

Money Magazine The ins and outs of personal wealth, with articles on a wide range of investment and budgeting topics. Online access varies according to service: GEnie allows for full-text search and retrieval from 1987 to the present, and Wealth Builder has both browsing and clipping features. ✓**GENIE**→*keyword* moneymag $ ✓**WEALTH BUILDER $**

Financial newspapers

Barrons Financial Weekly Dating back to 1987, Dow Jones' searchable Barrons archive is a

clari.biz
clari.biz.briefs
clari.biz.earnings
clari.biz.economy
clari.biz.economy.world
clari.biz.features
clari.biz.finance
clari.biz.mergers
clari.biz.misc
clari.biz.review
clari.biz.top
clari.biz.urgent
clari.biz.world_trade

comprehensive source of information on international investment, with weekly data and analysis of close-ended and open-end funds. In addition, the publication tracks the performance of world stock markets. ✓**DOW JONES NEWS/RETRIEVAL**→//news $

Wall Street Journal Online Offers the complete, searchable text of the *Wall Street Journal* and the *Asian Wall Street Journal*. ✓**DOW JONES NEWS/RETRIEVAL**→//news $

Financial wires

Business News Business news in various categories, including government and business, media, defense contracting, retail, and utilities. Reports are brief, favoring clarity over detail, and they're updated daily. ✓**AMERICA ONLINE**→*keyword* business news

Business News Summary Carries the current day's newsbriefs on a variety of business and investment topics, including domestic and international trade, corporate activity, and market news. ✓**PRODIGY**→*jump* quick business

Business Wire Business-related press releases—everything from personnel changes to corporate transactions to industry updates—are listed by date, but you can also search for specific companies by name or ticker symbol. ✓**COMPUSERVE**→*go* tbw ✓**DELPHI**→*go* bus bus ✓**DOW JONES NEWS/RETRIEVAL**→//wires $

Citibank Global Report Cosponsored by Citibank and CompuServe, this service provides market updates, country profiles, and corporate news from around the world. ✓**COMPUSERVE**→*go* cointl

ClariNet Business Newsgroups (ng) Taken as a set, the clari.biz newsgroups are like a wire service, with edited and moderated postings on a variety of domestic and international business topics. From the day's headlines (clari.biz.top) to the previous day's market activity (clari.biz.review) to the mergers of the moment (clari.biz.mergers). See sidebar. ✓**CLARINET $**

Daily China Headline News (j) Every issue of *Daily China Headline News* includes a few brief news articles, as well as a listing of the top business and investment headlines of the day. ✓**INTERNET**→*email* listserv@asiainfo.com ✉ *Type in message body:* subscribe headline <your full name>

DowVision Includes the full text of the *Wall Street Journal* as well as same-day text of the *New York*

Times News Service, the Dow Jones News Service, Dow Jones International News Service, and press-release services. Register: ✓**INTERNET**→*www* http://dowvision. wais.net **$** ✓**DOW JONES NEWS/RETRIEVAL**→//wires **$**

Economy Headlines This screen offers the day's economic headlines in menu form, and links to a variety of other screens that handle more specific topics, such as international business, company news, market updates, and economic indicators. ✓**PRODIGY**→*jump* economy headlines

Knight-Ridder Tribune Business News Business news from industry magazines (*Journal of Commerce, AdWeek, Traffic World, Air Commerce,* etc.) and 73 Knight-Ridder and Tribune newspapers around the country. A portion of Knight-Ridder's financial news is also available on a delayed basis. On AOL, Knight-Ridder's news is combined with news feeds from other services. ✓**EWORLD**→*go* krt ✓**AMERICA ONLINE**→*keyword* business news

Kyodo News International Search today's Japanese business news by company name, industry, news subject, market sector, geographical area, statistical category, or government agency. ✓**DOW JONES NEWS/RETRIEVAL**→//wires→ Kyodo News International **$**

PR Newswire Reprints of press releases from thousands of companies (including some that are less than newsworthy). Search by company name or ticker symbol. ✓**DELPHI**→*go* bus pr ✓**DOW JONES NEWS/RETRIEVAL**→//wires **$**

Reuter's Business and Financial News Financial dispatches covering not only general market information but also specific industries—including airlines, banking, information technology, pharmaceuticals, and telephones. ✓**DELPHI**→*go* bus reu

Reuters Business Briefs Business briefs from the previous day. ✓**EWORLD**→*go* eworld news

Top 10 Business News Stories Summaries of the day's top ten business news stories. ✓**EWORLD**→ *go* refpress→Top 10 Business News

UPI Business News Release Issues general business news releases, as well as stock and commodity reports. Rates and prices are updated half-hourly on market days. ✓**DELPHI**→*go* bus upi

Magazines & journals

Atlantic Monthly Online From time to time, publishes features on the state of the nation's—or the world's—economy. ✓**AMERICA ONLINE**→*keyword* atlantic

Foreign Affairs Coverage of global, political, and economic issues. ✓**INTERNET**→*gopher* gopher. enews.com→Magazines, Periodicals, and Journals→Foreign Affairs

National Review Conservative point of view on national and international politics, economics, and cultural trends. ✓**INTERNET** →*gopher* gopher.enews.com→Magazines, Periodicals, and Journals→ National Review

New Republic Addresses a wide variety of political, cultural, and economic issues. ✓**AMERICA ONLINE**→*keyword* new republic

Time Online America's most popular newsweekly has a regular section reporting on domestic and international economies and business, with occasional commentary on economic matters. GEnie archives all articles since 1985 in a searchable database. ✓**AMERICA ONLINE**→*keyword* time ✓**GENIE**→ *keyword* timemag

US News and World Report Offers weekly coverage of the domestic and world economies, as well as consumer-oriented features. ✓**COMPUSERVE**→*go* usnews

Network news

ABC News on Demand Not only publishes the day's top stories, but also summarizes the network's news magazines. Browse the headlines, dip into anchorman Peter Jennings' journal (the anchorman is frequently in a financial mood), or check Stephen Aug's Economic Report. ✓**AMERICA ONLINE**→*keyword* abcnews

> "Though the online *New York Times* is anchored by cultural coverage, the paper also reprints the day's top economic and financial news stories. This is only a selection, though, not all the news that's fit to upload."

C-SPAN Includes daily broadcast schedules and program summaries. ✓**AMERICA ONLINE**→*keyword* c-span

CNN Online Interactivity is the buzzword of choice in CNN's latest online venture, which includes a real-time talk show hosted by anchorperson Susan Rook. But the real meat of this service lies in its libraries, which contain transcripts of CNN's news clips and features. Relive the October '87 stock crash online. ✓**COMPUSERVE**→*go* cnnonline

Newspapers

Boston Globe Provides access to a full-text archive of every article published in Boston's premier daily newspaper from 1980 to the present. ✓**GENIE**→*keyword* bglobe **$**

Chicago Tribune The big paper from the Windy City has an exceptionally strong online doppel-gänger—a full-text version placed on America Online each and every day, along with a full-text searchable database on GEnie that dates back to 1985. Along with long-standing curmudgeons like Mike Royko and Bernie Lincicone, the paper offers extensive business coverage by local and syndicated columnists. ✓**AMERICA ONLINE**→*keyword* chicago tribune ✓**GENIE**→*keyword* chitrib

Detroit Free Press One of the Midwest's largest newspapers, the *Detroit Free Press* has special access to the auto industry and the labor movement. Full-text articles available. ✓**COMPUSERVE**→ *go* detroit **$**

Los Angeles Times The West Coast's finest newspaper is online on GEnie, with full-text articles from 1985 to the present. The *L.A. Times* is also online on Dow

Jones News/Retrieval, but not for browsing. Instead, it is part of DJNR's news wire service, which allows you to search by company name, industry, news subject, market sector, geographical area, statistical category, and government agency. ✓**GENIE**→*keyword* latimes **$** ✓**DOW JONES NEWS/RETRIEVAL**→ //wires→Today's Los Angeles Times (Washington Edition) **$**

New York Times Though the online *New York Times* is anchored by cultural coverage, the paper also reprints the day's top economic and financial news stories. This is only a selection, though, not all the news that's fit to upload. ✓**AMERICA ONLINE**→*keyword* times stories

San Francisco Chronicle The only online news coverage of the Bay Area, this service offers full-text search for all *Chronicle* articles published since 1988. ✓**GENIE**→ *keyword* sfchronicle **$**

San Jose Mercury News This northern California daily includes a fair amount of California business news—much of it highlighting West Coast industries such as computing. ✓**AMERICA ONLINE**→ *keyword* mercury center

USA Today Full-text articles since 1988 can be searched. ✓**GENIE**→*keyword* usatoday **$**

Washington Post GEnie provides full text of all *Post* articles since 1983. ✓**GENIE**→*keyword* dc-post **$**

Wire services

Associated Press Global Wires Access to several international AP wires, including AP France en Ligne, Deutsche Presse-Agentur Kurznachrichtendienst, and Australian Associated Press. ✓**COMPUSERVE**→*go* nws-73

Associated Press Online Latest news, along with weather, sports, national, international. Features include general financial briefs and hourly updates of the *Dow Jones* average. ✓**COMPUSERVE**→ *go* ap

PA News Detailed daily updates of the latest happenings from the United Kingdom, including news of Parliament, the City, the courts and, of course, the Royal Family. ✓**COMPUSERVE**→*go* pa

Reuters UK News Clips Furnishes up-to-the-minute news from "the city." ✓**COMPUSERVE**→*go* nws-73→Reuters UK News Clips

United Press International For headline news and stories that might not have made it into the pages of your daily paper. ✓**DELPHI** →*go* new int

NYT online logo—captured from America Online's New York Times *Online.*

Customized news

The working life is a busy life: meetings, deadlines, unexpected disasters. Some days

you don't even have time to read the newspaper. That's where online clipping services come in. For a small fee, services such as Dow Jones's **Clipping Service** and GEnie's **QuikNews** will collect the news you need and deliver it to you (electronically, of course) for your perusal. And then there are the databases you can search. From **Dialog** to **IQuest** to **Business Dateline**, these services comprise full-text versions of hundreds of publications that you can pull news from in a matter of seconds. **Dow Jones News/Retrieval**, the largest such service, has access to nearly 1,500 publications, and its sophisticated search features permit comprehensive research. Need to know a date for a company's IPO? Curious what was happening in the footwear industry during the Gulf War? There's no better—or faster—way to find out. Be warned, though: because of their incredible power, these services don't always come cheap, and if you're not economical in your searches, you can run up hundreds of dollars in charges.

Newspaper vending machines—from http://sunsite.unc.edu/otis/pers/Steffens_S.html

On the Net
Business databases

Business Database Plus Search and retrieve full-text articles from a database of more than 100 business magazines and industry newsletters. ✓**COMPUSERVE**→*go* busdb **$**

Business Dateline Search and retrieve full-text articles from a database of more than 115 regional business publications in the U.S. and Canada. Articles date back to 1985. ✓**COMPUSERVE**→*go* busdate

Canadian Business Center If you're thinking of doing business with a company north of the border, or you just want to research the past performance of a Canadian company, you might want to conduct your search within the confines of GEnie's Canadian Business Center, which contains full-text searches of Reuters news wire stories, plus basic financial information on thousands of Canadian companies. ✓**GENIE**→ *keyword* canbusiness **$**

Dow Jones News/Retrieval The top dog of the bunch, Dow Jones offers access to more than 50 corporate and industrial databases and more than 1,400 regional, national, and international publications. Publications take anywhere from a single day to eight weeks to appear on the service, but this may be the only place on earth where your waiting will be rewarded with eventual appearance of the *Allentown Morning Call*, the *Antiviral Agents Bulletin*, and the *Yuba-Sutter Appeal-Democrat*.

With myriad search features and report parameters, the service can answer extremely specific research questions: say, for instance, that you want to know if any companies involved in shrimping in southern Lousiana enjoyed massive profits during the late 1970s. Simply set up a query and wait while the DJNR superbrain locates your information. Bubba-Gump shrimp, anyone?

Rates vary from reasonable to exorbitant depending on the level of use, but personal investors might want to consider subscribing to the Dow Jones Market

Monitor, a simplified version of the News/Retrieval service which charges a flat fee for off-peak use. Voice call 800-522-3567 for more information. **$** ✓**INTERNET**→*telnet* djnr.dow jones.com **$**

Reference Center The Reference Center's Business holdings are deeper than the Marianas Trench, with more than 800 journals, newsletters, and bulletins. *American Business Law Journal? American Demographics? American Economist? American Import-Export Management?* All here. And that's only the beginning. But be warned—retrieval isn't cheap. ✓**GENIE**→*keyword* refcenter **$**

Clipping services

Clipping Service By far the most powerful financial news clipping service, Dow Jones lets you define ten daily news searches, and then monitors incoming news for articles that meet the requirements of those searches. Searches, which cover the entirety of the vast Dow Jones News/Retrieval database, can be customized by type of publication, range of dates, and content restrictions. ✓**DOW JONES NEWS/RETRIEVAL**→//clip **$**

Executive News Service With access to clips from the *Washington Post* and major wire services (AP, UPI, Reuters), this service provides general business news as well as news sorted by company ticker symbol. In addition, it offers a few perks—for instance, sorting stories into folders for later perusal. ✓**COMPUSERVE**→*go* ens **$**

Farcast Drawing on news feeds from the AP, UPI, PR Wire, and Businesssswire, this email service clips the articles you're interested in and sends them to your electronic mailbox. Choose up to 15

topics, select the news wires and publications you want searched, and indicate when you want the news delivered. At any time, you can send a query to the archives for full-text articles or a stock quote (just email the symbol). Flat monthly fees are charged. ✓**INTERNET**→*email* info@farcast.com ✍ *Email for automated info* **$**

GEnie QuikNews For the person who wants to follow a very select part of the news. This clipping service allows you to enter up to ten search terms, and then searches Reuters World Service, Reuters Business Reports, and Newsbytes. ✓**GENIE**→*keyword* quiknews **$**

NewsNet Enormous news wire and database service that claims to log more than 17,000 news items a day from 700 separate publications and 25 newswires. The hundred-plus-page Guide to News draws from major sources like Dun & Bradstreet, Investment Analy$t, Knight-Ridder/Tribune News Services, Reuters, TRW Business Profiles, and Standard & Poor's, plus legions of small newsletters including the *Counterterrorism & Security Report* and the *Clean Tech Innovator.* In addition to full-text searching, the database offers NewsFlash, an electronic clipping service that can deliver stories by satellite, FM-sideband, fax, or email. Voice call 800-952-0338 for more information. **$**

Personal Investing News Briefs For busy souls, *USA Today's* Decisionlines is a treasure chest, and the Personal Investing subsection a godsend, with vital information about the world's markets, issues, and economies. Every morning, the service delivers dozens of personal investing news briefs already sorted and tagged.

✓**EWORLD**→*go* usa today→Personal Investing

Personalized News Clipping Service Obtain clips from a variety of financial publications— from *Money* to the *Wall Street Journal* to the Reuters News Service—in accordance with your investment needs. Search by keyword and dates. ✓**WEALTHBUILDER$**

General databases

Bibliographic Citations Center With GEnie's vast Bibliographic Citations Center, you have the power of a reference library at your fingertips, and can retrieve citations on virtually any topic. ✓**GENIE**→*keyword* citations

BookShelf Sometimes the solution is a book. But what book? GEnie's BookShelf lets you narrow down the massive Books in Print database to find just the book you need, along with publisher information so that you can order the volume online. ✓**GENIE**→*keyword* bookshelf **$**

Dialog Provides access to summaries of more than 100,000 journals and the complete text from over 3,000 publications. Hundreds of separate databases are grouped in the Business subject area, including extensive Dun & Bradstreet, Standard & Poor's, Moody's, and Disclosure files on the finances of U.S. and international companies. The general Business & Industry subcategory contains dozens of databases from *Jane's Defense and Aerospace News* and *Bond Buyer* to delayed market quotes and *Commerce Business Daily.* The News subject area contains the full text of more than 50 U.S. papers, as well as the wire services of Knight-Ridder (Dialog's owner as of 1993), Reuters, and

UPI. There are equally encompassing science, law, and government areas. So-called supercategories for fishing expeditions through the Dialog databases include ALLBUSINESS and ALL-NEWS.

Business Connection

The Dialog Business Connection, a spin-off service, provides menu-driven searches on more than two million public and private companies. Databases include Dun & Bradstreet, Standard & Poor's, and Moody's. Main features include: Worldwide Corporate Intelligence for background info on companies' locations, financial positions, officers, directors, and products; U.S. Financial Screening by user-defined criteria like earnings or equipment capital; Products and Markets for market-share data, product-development activities, and manufacturers' trade names; Worldwide Sales Prospecting, with listings on more than 11.5 million companies by location, type of industry, and size; Travel Planning through the Official Airline Guide Electronic Edition's files on flights, fares, and hotels (includes online booking service); Dialog Business News Flash with Knight-Ridder and other news wire services; Dialog Alert Service for flagging new information on a particular company as it is added to the Dialog databases.

Corporate Connection

Another service, the Corporate Connection, features a menu-driven search designed for companies that want to make Dialog available to users who may not have the time to learn the regular search commands. The service includes a manager's kit for setting up a support person within the customer company.

Voice call Dialog (800-3-dialog)

to set up an a personal or corporate account or access the database through the GEnie gateway. ✓**GE-NIE**→*keyword* dialog **$**

Federal Center For comprehensive information on our nation's bureaucracy, search the full texts of the *Federal Register*, the Federal News Service, *Federal Research in Progress, Tax Notes Today*, and the *Washington Post*, as well as other publications. Who ever said that government had no accountability? ✓**GENIE**→*keyword* federalctr **$**

IQuest Access to over 800 databases spanning the worlds of government, news, entertainment, sports, and business. Most articles appear in three forms: single-line citations, paragraph-length abstracts, and full text. Information can be found via menu navigation or target searching. ✓**COMPU-SERVE**→*go* iquest **$**

Lexis/Nexis The mother of all legal and news database services. From legal records to the papers of record, it's all here. The listing of libraries takes up two full screens; the list of news sources runs 76 screens long. A number of these search libraries are tailored for investors.

The Company section contains thousands of in-depth company and industry research reports from leading investment banks and brokerage houses. The Business Reference library (Busref) is full of company directories, studies of business opportunities, and biographical information on political candidates, congressional members, international celebrities, business, religious, and political leaders. The Banks section boasts more than 40 full-text sources—including Investext reports—on the banking industry.

The Business Finance directory

(Busfin) provides wide coverage of both the general business press and industry-specific publications. Look here for sources on mergers and acquisitions. Finally, Current News (Curnws) offers an extremely large library which allows full-text searches of the last two years of all the news sources, and EdgarPlus provides the smoothest (and possibly most expensive) access to 10-K filings. For more information, voice call 1-800-346-9759. **$** *Info:* ✓**INTERNET** ...→*ftp* ftp.meaddata.com→anonymous→ <your email address> ...→*www* http://www.meaddata.com

News Source USA Search and retrieve articles from a wide selection of national and regional publications, including *Time, Business Week*, and dozens of daily newspapers ranging from the *Philadelphia Inquirer* to *USA Today*. ✓**COMPUSERVE**→*go* newsusa **$**

Newsstand Full-text search and retrieval features for dozens of daily newspapers (*Akron Beacon Journal* to the *Wichita Eagle*), hundreds of magazines (*Aging* to *Your Public Lands*), and thousands of newsletters (*Ad Solutions Report* to *Youth Market Alerts*). Searching terms follow Boolean logic. ✓**GENIE**→*keyword* newsstand **$**

International

U.K. Newspaper Library If you find yourself obsessed with UK news, fretting over the price of petrol or the FT-SE 100, you might want to put your mind at ease by reading through the British press. Contains searchable full-text versions of the *Daily Telegraph*, the *Financial Times*, the *Guardian*, the *Observer*, the *Independent*, and the *European*. ✓**COMPUSERVE**→*go* ukpapers **$**

Company research

Say you want to invest in a company, but you're just not sure if it's a good prospect.

The CEO recently died of a stroke, and there are persistent rumors that 5-percent owners are selling off their shares. And besides, you're not even sure what products this company manufactures. With access to private corporate research services, as well as government documents, the Net has ample charms for the corporate researcher. Take **Hoover's Company Profiles**, for instance, which provides comprehensive profiles on thousands of companies, or **Dun's Financial Records Plus**, which furnishes financial and operational data on almost a million businesses. Other services specialize in basic address and phone information (**BIZ*FILE**), corporate news (**Publications Online**), insider information (**Disclosure II**), and corporate credit (**TRW Business Profiles**). And if you want to learn more about companies across the world, try the **Australia/New Zealand Company Library**, the **Dun & Bradstreet European Company Profiles**, and the **UK Company Research Center**.

Hoover's logo—from http://www. hoovers.com

On the Net

Across the board

Company Analyzer Provides U.S. stock prices on 15-minute delay, as well as a detailed profile of each company selected, including price and volume history, dividend history, bond and option issues, financial statements, management discussion, officers, and salaries. The service also furnishes CUSIP numbers (Committee on Uniform Securities Identification Procedures), which are useful for other corporate databases. ✓**COMPUSERVE**→*go* analyzer **$**

Company Reports These reports include current quotes, latest corporate news, financial and market performance, earnings estimates, company and industry profiles, income statements, balance sheets, insider trading summaries, and investment research reports. ✓**DOW JONES NEWS/RETRIEVAL**→//quick **$**

Company Reports Delivers

company profiles with the following information: gross sales, valuation, profitability and growth numbers, balance sheet and income trends, earnings- and dividends-per-share estimates, 52-week price and volume charts, current news, quarterly data for the current year and annual data for the past five years, comparisons with the S&P 500 and industry average, institutional ownership, equity information, and company contacts. ✓**CHARLES SCHWAB STREETSMART $**

Company Screening Permits rapid searches through the Disclosure database of SEC filings: de-

"Rankings are fun. Who's the richest? Who's the most socially responsible? Where's the best place to work if you're gay? What are the 25 largest brokerage houses and the ten oldest companies in America? Check it out with Hoover's."

tailed financial data on more than 11,000 publicly traded American companies. ✓**COMPUSERVE**→*go* co-screen **$**

D&B Company Profiles Find basic business statistics such as net worth, corporate size, 52-week price, and profitability estimates from a database of 7 million U.S. companies. ✓**DOW JONES NEWS/ RETRIEVAL**→//dmi **$** ✓**GENIE**→*keyword* d&bprofiles **$**

Dun's Financial Records Plus Get comprehensive financial, historical, and operational information on almost a million public and private U.S. companies, as well as historical and operational data on almost a million more. Reports include detailed financial records for the past three years and company profiles that include ownership, subsidiary, and personnel information. ✓**DOW JONES NEWS/RETRIEVAL**→//db **$**

Hoover's Business Rankings Rankings are fun. Who's the richest? Who's the most socially responsible? Where's the best place to work if you're gay? What are the 25 largest brokerage houses and the 10 oldest companies in America? Check it out with Hoover's— number one in business rankings. ✓**AMERICA ONLINE**→*keyword* rankings

Hoover's Company Profiles Search the full text of *Hoover's Handbook* for detailed profiles of the largest and fastest growing companies, listed alphabetically, by industry, and by geographical location. Profiles are exhaustive, with information that includes assets, sales figures, number of employees, CEO and CFO salaries, and company products. In addition, the profiles feature long and gossipy descriptions of company history and culture. You can find out the location of the company offices, future goals or ongoing programs, and recent stock prices. Oh, and you can also get telephone, address, and fax information. For job seekers or investors, one of the first places to check. ✓**AMERICA ONLINE**→*keyword* company ✓**COMPUSERVE**→*go* hoover ✓**EWORLD**→*go* hoovers

Hoover's MasterList of Major Companies Capsule profiles of 7,500 of the largest public and private U.S. companies. Information includes name, address, phone and fax numbers, CEO, CFO, one-year sales figures, employment data, ticker symbol, a calendar of the fiscal year, and industry descriptor. MasterList will soon include coverage of European companies. ✓**EWORLD**→*go* masterlist

The International Corporate Forum Online Promising to bring you one step closer to the CEOs of public corporations, the ICF publishes online the prepared statements of leaders of public companies which, by and large, read like introductions to annual reports. You can submit questions to the participating CEOs and perhaps even get an answer. It's a limited notion of interactivity, but it's a start. ✓**AMERICA ONLINE**→*keyword* icf

S&P Online Distills the recent business histories of more than 5,000 companies to bring you essential information, including recent market activity, dividend information, product-line summaries, and earnings estimates. ✓**COMPUSERVE**→*go* s&p **$** ✓**DOW JONES NEWS/RETRIEVAL**→//sp **$**

The Texas 500 The electronic version of *Hoover's Guide to Major Texas Corporations*, containing directory information on 500 companies, as well as more detailed profiles on the 25 largest corporations, the 20 most promising ones, and the ten most Texan businesses (you'll have to graze here to find out just what "most Texan" means). Search by keyword or browse by topic. ✓**INTERNET**→*gopher* gopher.texas-one.org

Company news

Company News Search through the Dow Jones News Retrieval database for information on the company of your choice. If you don't know the exact name or ticker symbol, enter an approxima-

> "Interested in investing in that new designer toothbrush company, but nervous about the persistent rumor that its payables are running later and later? TRW Business Credit Profiles supplies detailed credit profiles for more than 2.5 million companies."

tion, and the service will list near-matches. Because Company News is available on so many services, search protocols may differ slightly; Charles Schwab's service, for example, uses simple point-and-click technology to retrieve its company news. ✓**DOW JONES NEWS/RETRIEVAL**→//company $ ✓**PRODIGY**→*jump* company news $ ✓**CHARLES SCHWAB STREETSMART** $

Publications Online A database of dozens of financial publications, journals, and company newsletters with information on industries, individual businesses, and initial public offerings (IPO). ✓**COMPUSERVE**→*go* pubonl $

Corporate credit

TRW Business Credit Profiles Interested in investing in that new designer toothbrush company, but nervous about the persistent rumor that its payables are running later and later? This service supplies detailed credit profiles (including company name, address, sales, employees, ownership, credit history, and the number of credit inquiries during the past nine months) for more than 2.5 million companies. Reports cost $29 each. ✓**GENIE**→*keyword* trw profiles $

TRW Business Profiles This massive credit and business database provides information on more than 13 million U.S. businesses, including ownership, credit histories, UCC filings, tax liens, judgments, and bankruptcies. ✓**COMPUSERVE**→*go* trwreport $

Corporate earnings

I/B/E/S The Institutional Brokers Estimate System provides earnings estimates on over 3,400 publicly traded corporations. ✓**COMPUSERVE**→*go* ibes $

> "Order reports from Corporate Ownership Watch on insider trading activity, 5 percent filings, as well as lists of the companies with the most insider selling and buying."

Zacks Corporate Earnings Estimator Enter a company's name or ticker symbol, and get recent earnings data and earnings projections, as well as the projected corporate growth rate and brokerage analysts' ratings. In addition, the service reports weekly earnings highlights and surprises. ✓**DOW JONES NEWS/RETRIEVAL**→//eps $

Directories

BIZ*FILE A huge online *Yellow Pages*, which indexes more than 10 million businesses in the United States and Canada. Search the index by company name, geographical location, telephone number, or type of business. ✓**COMPUSERVE**→*go* bizfile $

D&B U.S. Business Locator Search by name or geographic location to retrieve basic information about almost 9 million U.S. companies and professionals. ✓**GENIE**→*keyword* d&blocator $

Executive Desk Register of Public Corporations A database of U.S. public corporations

searchable by name, address, telephone number, ticker symbol, CEOs and CFOs, and exchange affiliation. ✓**DELPHI**→*go* bus reg

Thomas Register of North American Manufacturers Remember the scene in Henry James' *The Ambassadors*, in which Lambert Strether won't tell Maria Gostrey the flagship product of the Massachusetts company that has sent him to Paris in search of Chad Newsome? Today, Strether wouldn't stand a chance: All Maria would have to do is to run a search in this database of North American companies, products, and services. ✓**GENIE**→*keyword* tregister $

Dividends

Dividend Calculation Enter the ticker symbol of any publicly traded U.S. company and retrieve a complete record of all dividends paid to stockholders. ✓**COMPUSERVE**→*go* dividends

Insider information

Corporate Affiliates Research Center As a result of complex corporate structures, it's not always clear which fish is the big fish. This service allows you to input the name of any company; it will then list its subsidiaries, and its subsidiaries' subsidiaries, and so on. If the company is a subsidiary, the Research Center will list its parent company. The extensive database covers more than 80,000 parent companies and their corporate children. ✓**GENIE**→*keyword* affiliates $

Corporate Ownership Watch Order reports on insider-trading activity, 5 percent filings, as well as lists of the companies with the most insider selling and buying.

Searches can be conducted either by ticker symbol, company name, or the name of the filing party. ✓**DOW JONES NEWS/RETRIEVAL**→//watch **$**

Disclosure II Collates and indexes the reports filed by all publicly owned companies, and lists the names of officers and directors, subsidiaries, insider owners, institutional owners, and owners of more than 5 percent of the company's stock. ✓**COMPUSERVE**→*go* disclosure **$** ✓**DOW JONES NEWS/RETRIEVAL**→//dsclo **$**

Int'l companies

Australian/New Zealand Company Library Directory and financial information on almost 100,000 private and public companies in Australia and New Zealand. Drawing on such financial databases as Dun & Bradstreet's Australian and New Zealand listings and full-text news archives like Global Textline, the library permits searches by company name, geographic location, industry code, or keyword. ✓**COMPUSERVE**→*go* anzcompany **$**

Canadian Company Information Directory information on more than 350,000 Canadian companies. Updated quarterly, this database includes company names, addresses, and telephone numbers, as well as such rudimentary corporate information as sales figures, number of employees, and the names of chief executive officers. ✓**COMPUSERVE**→*go* cocan **$** ✓**GENIE**→*keyword* d&bcanada **$**

Citibank's Global Report Up-to-the-minute foreign exchange rates and spot commodity prices. ✓**COMPUSERVE**→*go* glorep

D&B Asia/Pacific Company

Profiles Contains key statistics (name, address, annual sales net worth, number of employees, and growth rate) for hundreds of thousands of companies in 40 Asian and Pacific countries. ✓**GENIE**→*keyword* d&basia **$**

D&B European Company Profiles This is a good starting point for background on 2 million European companies, with short corporate profiles including information on company personnel and earnings. ✓**GENIE**→*keyword* d&beurope **$**

D&B International Company Profiles Dun & Bradstreet's European and Asia/Pacific databases, plus financial information on hundreds of thousands of African and Indian companies. ✓**GENIE**→*keyword* d&bintl **$**

European Company Library With access to several worldwide corporate databases, this service supplies address, personnel, and financial information on more than 2 million European companies. ✓**COMPUSERVE**→*go* eurolib **$**

German Company Library Directory and financial information on roughly 50,000 German companies. ✓**COMPUSERVE**→*go* gerlib **$**

UK Company Research Center Directory and financial information on millions of U.K. companies, with gateways to databases such as Dun & Bradstreet's European Market Identifiers, the ICC British Company Directory, Jordan's Registered Companies, and Kompass UK. The service also accesses such financial databases as Extel Cards, Financial Times Analysis Reports, and Infocheck UK. Search by company name, geographic location, number of em-

ployees, or keyword. ✓**COMPUSERVE**→*go* couk **$**

WorldScope International Company Profiles Detailed financial reports—including directory information, earnings reports, and historical and financial summaries—on more than 6,000 foreign corporations. Searchable by ticker symbol or company name. ✓**DOW JONES NEWS/RETRIEVAL**→//worldscope

---

CYBERNOTES

25 Greatest Fortunes in the US:

		$Bill.
1	Walton family	23.0
2	Mars Family	9.6
3	Warren E. Buffett	8.3
4	Samuel Irving, Jr.	
	Donald E. Newhouse	7.0
5	William H. Gates III	6.2
6	John Werner Kluge	5.9
7	Sumner M. Redstone	5.6
8	Barbara C. Anthony	
	Anne Cox Chambers	4.8
9	Jay Arthur	
	Robert A. Pritzker	4.4
10	Keith Rupert Murdoch	4.0
11	Ted Arison	3.7
12	Ronald O. Perelman	3.6
13	Richard M. DeVos	
	Jay Van Andel	3.5
14	Sid Richardson	
	Lee Marshall Bass	3.5
15	Kirk Kerkorian	3.1
16	Charles de Ganahl	
	David Hamilton Koch	3.0
17	Paul G. Allen	2.9
18	David Packard	2.8
19	Henry Ross Perot	2.4
20	Henry Lea Hillman	2.4
21	Edgar Miles Bronfman	2.3
22	Ted Turner	2.2
23	Robert Muse Bass	2.2
24	Lester Crown & fam.	2.2
25	Walter H. Annenberg	2.1

—from **Hoover Rankings**

SEC filings & EDGAR

In this country, disclosure is the law—all publicly traded firms are required to file

detailed financial information with the Securities and Exchange Commission, including such information as insider trades, annual reports, and personnel information for top financial officers. And, thanks to the electronic age, these disclosure laws now work for you. Government reports are available to anyone with a modem. The Electronic Data Gathering and Retrieval program (EDGAR) allows unfettered access to the complete collections of SEC filings. Publicly available filings are archived at **Town Hall EDGAR**, **SEC Online**, and **Disclosure SEC**, which creates both company reports and ownership reports. And **Federal Filings Notification** even provides real-time reports of SEC filings. Be forewarned, though—the reports are sometimes long, dense, and even incomprehensible to anyone without an understanding of SEC procedure and filing codes.

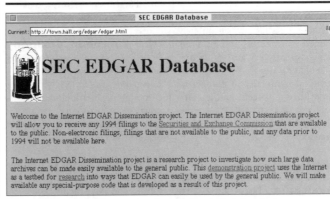

Town Hall EDGAR Web page—http://town.hall.org/edgar/edgar.html.

On the Net

Disclosure SEC Drawing on the vast SEC/EDGAR database, the service creates two sets of reports.

Company reports include income statements, balance sheets, and ratio reports from the past eight years, as well as quarterly income statements from the past five quarters. Ownership reports disclose management discussions and ownership information, corporate salaries, stock holdings of directors and principal shareholders, and the president's letter to shareholders. Search by ticker symbol or CUSIP number—and if you don't know either of these, you can look them up in an accompanying file. The full complement of company and ownership reports costs about $40. ✓**COMPUSERVE**→*go* dis **$**

Federal Filings Notification This service provides real-time notification of SEC filings, along with detailed analysis of the most important developments in each day's filing action. ✓**DOW JONES NEWS/RETRIEVAL**→//wires **$**

SEC Online Full text of all 10-K, 10-Q, 20-F, annual reports, and proxy filings can be searched either by keyword or by company name.

✓**DOW JONES NEWS/RETRIEVAL**→// sec **$**

Stern School EDGAR This experimental SEC database includes an introduction to securities filings, help documents, description and explanation of forms, and a sample 10-K to assist you in understanding the ins and outs of SEC documentation. In addition, the site contains the R. R. Donnelley Guide to filing SEC forms. ✓**INTERNET**→*www* http://edgar. stern.nyu.edu/

10-K Library Search this easy-to-use database of 2,000-plus SEC filings by company name. The reports have been stripped of the tags that normally fill 10-Ks, making them more readable. ✓**EWORLD** →*go* 10k

Town Hall EDGAR Includes all publicly available filings (10-K, 10-Q, 20-F), as well as notification of any SEC investigation. ✓**INTERNET**→*www* http://town.hall. org/edgar/edgar.html

Industry news & analysis

If you want your business news sorted by industry, you've come to the right place.

From the twenty-plus **clari. biz.industry** newsgroups—which track developments in industries such as aviation, construction, and tourism—to the projections, trend analyses, and statistics collected in **Hoover's Industry Profiles**, the Net contains dozens of useful resources for industry research. Need to learn more about aerospace investment? How about home electronics, radio broadcasting, or gasket manufacturing? Investors with a vested interest in a specific industry should take heart from specialty services such as **The Mining Channel** and **Investors in Space**.

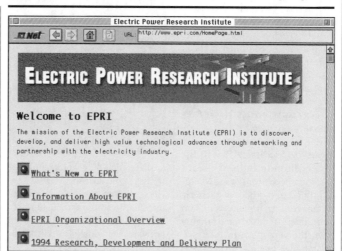

Electrical Power Research Institute Home page—http://www.epri.com/HomePage.html

On the Net

Across the board

clari.biz.industry* newsgroups (ng) If you want to check on the latest media merger or need to determine how new regulations affect grain silos, consult this family of newsgroups, which lists developments in a variety of fields, ranging from agriculture to aviation, manufacturing to mining. Divided by industry, these newsgroups are repositories for news releases from major wire services. See page seven for a list of the groups. ✓**CLARINET $**

Hoover's Industry Profiles Facts and figures on nearly 200 U.S. industries, including 30 service industries and some 150 manufacturing industries. Did you know that the health-care industry employed 2 million nurses and "generated more than $942.5 billion in expenditures in 1993"? Filled with projections, trend analysis, and statistics (supplies, expenditures, employee numbers), the reports are long and detailed. If you want a quick but smart rundown of issues and challenges facing an industry, the reports spell those out as well. ✓**AMERICA ON-LINE**→*keyword* industry profiles ✓**EWORLD**→*go* business sector

Industry Decisionlines For the busy executive or investor who needs to follow a specific industry but who can't spare the time to read the entire newspaper. Brought to you by *USA Today*. ✓**EWORLD**→*go* usa today

Industry News What's the future

"So much can happen in a quarter. The attentive investor needs daily doses of news and analysis. Quick Market Intelligence compiles daily industry reports from a variety of newspapers and magazines."

of coal? How many banks are established in an average week? Does the appliance industry seem to be suffering from an alarming amount of insider sell-offs? Find the answers here, under the specific industry or in one of the presorted Dow Jones categories (i.e. conglomerates, consumer cyclical, consumer noncyclical, technology). Service includes all sorts of dispatches, among them wire-service reports and SEC filing updates. ✓**DOW JONES NEWS/RE-TRIEVAL**→//industry **$**

Industry Statistics Part of the vast Economic Bulletin Board based at the University of Michigan, this site reproduces quarterly Commerce Department reports on more than 40 industries ranging from the aerospace industry to truck-trailer manufacturing. ✓**INTERNET**→*gopher* una.hh.lib.umich. edu→Industry Statistics

Media General Financial Services Company & Industry Data Comprehensive data on the performance of more than 50 industries, including closing prices, P/E ratios, and relative price indexes. ✓**DOW JONES NEWS/RE-TRIEVAL**→//mg **$**

Quick Market Intelligence The problem with most industry reports is that they're quarterly, and so much can happen in a quarter. To keep a finger on the pulse of an industry, the attentive investor needs daily doses of news and analysis. Here, comprehensive industry reports are compiled from a variety of newspapers and magazines, and updated daily. ✓**EWORLD**→*go* quick market

U.S. Industrial Outlook 1994 This site contains International Trade Administration forecasts for more than 30 major worldwide in-

> **"Not just a man in the moon, but a market. Investors in Space is devoted to discussions about investment opportunities in outer space."**

dustries, including wholesaling, retailing, coal mining, travel services, pharmaceuticals, space commerce, entertainment, insurance, and securities. ✓**INTERNET**→*gopher* unslvma.umsl.edu→The Library→ Government Information (US Federal & State Info & Docs)→U.S. Industrial Outlook-1994 (NTDB Version) (Statistics)

By industry

Business and Technology Particularly good for insights into high-tech and biotech industries. ✓**WELL**→gbiztech

Cowles/SIMBA Media Information Network First-class coverage of the media industry featuring the Cowles/SIMBA Media Daily, a summary of the day's mergers, expansions, contractions, hirings, and firings. More thorough coverage, organized by type of industry and subject, can be found in folders available from the opening screen, such as: Advertising, Book Publishing, Broadcast and Cable, Deals and Financials, Magazines, Media Notes, Media People, New Media, News From Cowles/SIMBA, Newspapers, Online Services, and the Internet. Several of the company's other

newsletters and trade publications are also available, including the *Electronic Education Report, Media Convergence Alert, Multimedia Business Report,* and *Electronic Marketplace Report.* The Bulletin Board is bustling with help-wanted and positions-wanted postings, as well as discussions on everything from electronic shopping to intellectual property law. Email feedback to SIMBA02@ aol.com. ✓**AMERICA ONLINE**→*keyword* simba

Electrical Utilities Funded by 700 member utilities, the Palo Alto–based Electric Power Research Institute (EPRI) manages more than 1,600 research projects throughout the world in the area of electricity generation and distribution. If you've wondered why utilities stocks are no longer considered the stable, income-producing investments they once were, the EPRI's reports and news clippings covering the industry are worth a look. ✓**INTERNET**→ *www* http:// www.epri.com/HomePage.html

clari.biz.industry

clari.biz.industry.agriculture
clari.biz.industry.automotive
clari.biz.industry.aviation
clari.biz.industry.banking
clari.biz.industry.broadcasting
clari.biz.industry.construction
clari.biz.industry.dry_goods
clari.biz.industry.energy
clari.biz.industry.food
clari.biz.industry.health
clari.biz.industry.insurance
clari.biz.industry.manufacturing
clari.biz.industry.mining
clari.biz.industry.print_media
clari.biz.industry.real_estate
clari.biz.industry.retail
clari.biz.industry.services
clari.biz.industry.tourism
clari.biz.industry.transportation

Inside Media Run by the industry biweekly *Inside Media*, this forum focuses primarily on print publishing and TV, although other forms of electronic media are tracked as well. The most popular topic is Media Rumor Mill, which is full of insider gossip from the world of magazine publishing and advertising. The forum provides database services for advertising professionals and industry news for the media investor. Searches of the full-text, three-year database start at $10 through the Inside

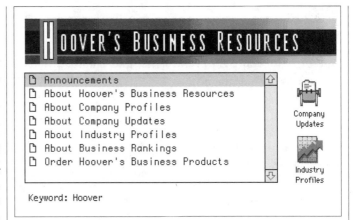

Hoover's Business Resources—screenshot from America Online

> **"Terrazo, tile, marble, and mosaic construction? 1743, of course. Men's and boy's neckwear? 2323. Rental of railroad cars? 4740. If none of this makes any sense, you clearly aren't familiar with Standard Industrial Classifications, government codes which divide the world of business into its constituent parts."**

Media Magazine Infobase, but there's also a standard AOL search of recent issues through the Search Inside Media icon. ✓**AMERICA ON-LINE**→*keyword* inside media→Inside Media

Investors in Space Not just a man in the moon, but a market. The list is devoted to discussions about emerging investment opportunities in outer space. Subscribers must be residents of the planet Earth. ✓**INTERNET**→*email* server@lunacity.com ✍ *Type in message body:* join space-investors

Mining Channel News and analysis about publicly traded mining companies and mining stocks. ✓**INTERNET**→*www* http://www.wimsey.com/Magnet/mc/index5.html

Newsbytes (ng) The world's largest news service devoted entirely to the computer industry. More than a dozen bureaus cover the microcomputer industry and consumer computing news. GEnie permits full-text search of articles from 1983 to the present. ✓**CLAR-INET**→clari.nb* $ ✓**GENIE**→ *keyword* newsbytes

SIC

Standard Industrial Classification Lookup Terrazo, tile, marble, and mosaic construction? 1743, of course. Men's and boy's neckwear? 2323. Rental of railroad cars? 4740. If none of this makes any sense, you clearly aren't familiar with Standard Industrial Classifications, government codes which divide the vast world of business into its constituent parts—taxonomizing everything from transporation to retail to financial services. Type a keyword for a list of pertinent SIC categories. ✓**INTERNET** ...→*gopher* gopher.lib.virginia.edu →Social Science Data Center→ General Social Sciences Resources→SIC and FIPS Code Finders→SIC Code Finder. or Search for SIC Codes (enter a SIC or keyword) <?>

Standard Industrial Classification Section Offers a link to the SIC search service, explains the SIC, and furnishes lists of codes which are updated annually. ✓**INTERNET**→*gopher* vaxvmsx.babson.edu→Business Resources→Standard Industrial Classification [SIC] Codes

Market reports & indices

Market watchers, both professional and amateur, flock to the Net with regularity, and

you can fly among them. If you want basic market information and rudimentary analysis, subscribe to **Holt's Market Report**, Prodigy's **Latest Market News**, and the set of seven **clari.biz. market.report newsgroups**. The New York Stock Exchange (NYSE), the American Stock Exchange (AMEX), and the Over-the-Counter stock exchange (NASDAQ) all have individual services devoted to their trades, and there are a number of concise reports available that treat the Dow Jones Industrial Average, including **Historical Dow Jones Averages**, **Dow Jones News and Analysis**, and **News-a-Tron Stock Index News and Analysis**. And devotees of the Chicago Board of Trade will want to check out the Website for the **Chicago Mercantile Exchange**, which includes historical information on the exchange along with price and volume data.

On the Net

Across the board

Clari.biz.market.report newsgroups (ng) Curious about

the recent rumors that caused Shanghai A stocks to plunge? Disturbed about the instability in Danish stocks? The clari.biz.market.report newsgroups cover worldwide market news, with separate newsgroups for Asia, Europe, and the United States. See sidebar for newsgroup list. ✓**CLARINET**

Current Market Snapshot Gives delayed news (highs, lows, lasts, and volume) of the Dow Jones, S&P 500, NASDAQ, and London Gold Market, as well as exchange rates for the yen, pound, and Deutsche Mark. ✓**COMPUSERVE**→*go* snapshot

Final Markets End-Of-Day Price Service The stats and just the stats, ma'am. Download the open, high, low, and settle prices of the major worldwide exchanges. Packages range in price from $20 for just the agricultural market to $50 for the American, European, Pacific, Agricultural, and Financial markets. Knight-Ridder also sells, but does not require, KR-Quote, a program that dials in each evening and downloads the data. Voice call 800-526-DATA for more information. **$**

Holt's Stock Market Reports A brief summary of activity from major U.S. and foreign markets—number and volume of issues traded on the U.S. exchanges, currency exchange rates, number of new highs and lows on the exchanges, gold and interest rate figures, and listings of the most active stocks. The Holt report has its own gopher site and appears daily on the misc.invest newsgroup, as well as

in the eINVEST mailing list. ✓**INTERNET**→*gopher* wuecon.wustl.edu:671→Holt's Stock Market Reports

Latest Market News Market updates in news-brief form, providing rudimentary analysis of current market activity. ✓**PRODIGY** → *jump* latest market news

Market Closing News Activity reports on the NYSE or AMEX are available as soon as trading closes. ✓**PRODIGY**→*jump* closing news

Markets at the Close Want to know how the Dow Jones did yesterday? How about the Comex gold market or the Long Bond? Service provides graphs for major markets followed by screens for selected exchanges. ✓**PRODIGY**→*jump* market close

Stock Market Highlights Exactly what its name suggest—a list of the most active issues, the largest gainers and losers, and the rising and falling stocks from the last trading day. ✓**COMPUSERVE**→*go* market

US Market Update If you need to know about the Dow Jones In-

clari.biz.market

clari.biz.market.news
clari.biz.market.report
clari.biz.market.report.asia
clari.biz.market.report.europe
clari.biz.market.report.top
clari.biz.market.report.usa
clari.biz.market.report.usa.nyse

dustrial Average, or the S&P 500, and you need to know now, this service reports and charts current statistics on both indexes. ✓**PRODI-GY**→*jump* us stocks

AMEX

AMEX at the Close The NYSE may get all the publicity, but there's plenty of money tied up in the American Stock Exchange as well, and this service provides price and volume information at the close of every trading day. ✓**PRODIGY**→*jump* amex close

AMEX Most Active Stocks Need to know the ten most active issues from the AMEX? You'll find the info here. ✓**PRODIGY**→*jump* amex active

Chicago Mercantile

Chicago Mercantile Exchange Owned by its members, whose exchange "seats" cost nearly a million dollars, Chicago's massive Merc is the world's largest marketplace, where billions of dollars are traded daily in futures and options on agricultural commodities, foreign currencies, interest rates, and stock indices. On the Web, though, the CME is just another home page, albeit one with background information on the exchange, a chart of membership prices, volume and trading information, and a description of the magnificent trading floor. ✓**INTERNET**→*www* http://www.interacess.com/users/wilbirk/

NASDAQ/OTC

NASDAQ at the Close Basic market info for NASDAQ's indices—the composite as well as industrials, insurance, banks, financial, and transportation. ✓**PRO-DIGY**→*jump* nasdaq close

NASDAQ Most Active Stocks A list of the ten most active NAS-DAQ issues from the previous day's trading. ✓**PRODIGY**→*jump* nasdaq active

NYSE/Dow Jones

Dow Jones Averages Publishes half-hourly updates of the Dow Jones industrial, transportation, utility, and stock averages. ✓**DELPHI**→*go* bus dow

Dow Jones News and Analysis A brief summary and analysis of the activity of the Dow Jones indices, updated daily. ✓**DELPHI**→*go* bus fin dow

Historical Dow Jones Averages Sure, everyone knows yesterday's market close, but how about the market close on this date in 1944? Find extensive historical data about the Dow Jones market indices here. ✓**DOW JONES NEWS/RETRIEVAL**→*//dja* $

Marketpulse Detailed real-time NYSE information: Identifies the most active issues and the greatest point, and percentage gainers and losers. ✓**DELPHI**→*go* bus mar $

News-a-Tron Stock Index News and Analysis Provides stock ratings from Trendvest. ✓**COMPUSERVE**→*go* nat $

NYSE at the Close Reports on the major indices at the close of the New York Stock Exchange. ✓**PRODIGY**→*jump* nyse close

NYSE Most Active Stocks This screen lists the ten most active issues in the previous day's trading on the New York Stock Exchange. ✓**PRODIGY**→*jump* nyse active

PAWWS Historical charts for both the S&P 500 index and the DJIA. ✓**INTERNET**→*www* http://www.secapl.com:80/pawws/

Standard & Poor's Summary Summary of the activity of the S&P 500 Stock index, updated daily. ✓**DELPHI**→*go* bus fin sta

International

World Market Update A clear and concise summary of all major world market indices, from the Nikkei to the Hang Seng to the Toronto Composite. ✓**PRODIGY**→*jump* world market update

Oslonett The traders at the Oslo Stock Exchange are no doubt quite tired of hearing jokes about frozen fish and used Fjords. For a modest subscription rate, this service offers stock quotes from the Oslo Exchange. ✓**INTERNET**→*www* http://www.oslonett.no/stocks/index.html $

Polish Stock Market Delayed financial results on Polish stocks and bonds, as well as an extensive archive of market data. You'll have to speak a little Polish to navigate, so here are some helpful tips: information from the Warsaw exchange is in the "PGPW - rynek ascji" directory, bonds are in "WGPW - ryneck obligacji," and financial results in "WGPW - walory." ✓**INTERNET** ...→*ftp* plearn.edu.pl→anonymous→<your email address>→/tessa.192→ SESJA* ...→*gopher* plearn.edu.pl:71→Teksty, dokum, opisy, listy dysk, gielda, itd→Ekonomia - gielda

Vienna Stock Exchange Daily price and volume information, as well as a large database of historical quotes from the past three months' trading at the Vienna stock market. ✓**INTERNET**→*telnet* fi-ivs01.tu-graz.ac.at→boerse

Getting stock quotes

So, you want to check on your stocks. Once upon a time, you had to wait for the next

morning's newspaper, or watch for a ticker flowing across your TV screen. In the computer age, though, stock information is at your fingertips. On the Net, you can download price and volume information from a variety of services. Most stock tickers are on 15-minute delay, although a few—**Signal** and Dow Jones News/Retrieval's **Real-Time Quotes** —report market shifts as they occur. Investors who want historical stock data have a wealth of options, from CompuServe's **Multiple Issue Historical Pricing** to the **Free Financial Network**. Most services report not only current share price, but also cash dividend per share, per cent yield, P/E ratio, closing price, earnings per share, sales in hundreds, net change, high, low, and close.

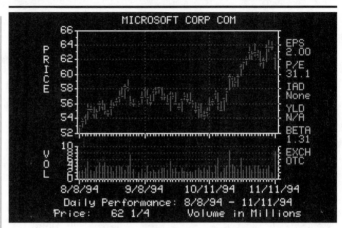

MicroSoft's share history from CompuServe's Securities Price & Volume Graph Forum

On the Net

Real-time tickers

Real-time Quotes Turn your computer into a ticker with Dow Jones News/Retrieval, which offers market trading prices for stocks from the New York, American, Pacific, and Chicago exchanges, and the NASDAQ National Market and small-cap issues. Composite quotes and averages from the New York, American, Chicago, Pacific, Philadelphia, Boston, and Cincinnati exchanges are also available. ✓**DOW JONES NEWS/RETRIEVAL**→//rtq **$**

Signal Forget about 15-minute delays—they're for laggards, slowpokes, lollygaggers, amateurs, and the little guy. Be a player! Signal provides real-time trading data for stocks, stock options, commodity futures, and market indices on all major exchanges. The accompanying *Trendsetter* software (*Pro Analyst* and *Hotline*) creates sophisticated technical analysis of the actual lots being traded, even as reports are captured over FM, cable, or satellite by the Signal receiver. The broadcast—which also includes Dow Jones News Headlines and News Alerts, Treasury Bond Service, and Signal trading advisories—takes about ten minutes to cycle through the more than 50,000 securities. New trades, however, are broadcast immediately, putting the full loop at about 20 minutes. All this technology doesn't come cheap. Basic receiver packages run upward of $200. Available for Macintosh and Windows. Voice call 415-571-1800 for more information. **$**

Daily quotes

Chemical Company Stock Prices Provides daily closing prices for 35 major chemical stocks. The service also furnishes historical quotes for the current year. ✓**INTERNET**→*www* http://hackberry.chem.niu.edu:70/1/Stock%2OPrices

Closing Stock Quotes Lists the high, lows, volumes, changes, and closes of the previous trading day for more than 6,000 publicly traded stocks, along with volumes, NAVs, and closing prices for major mutual funds. ✓**GENIE**→*keyword* quotes

CSI Data Retrieval Service Daily updates of prices for predefined portfolios, which range from Treasury bills and light crude oil to live cattle and orange juice. *QuickTrieve* modem-retrieval software available for Macintosh and MS-DOS. Voice call 800-274-4727 for more information about the service. **$**

Experimental Stock Market Data One of the most complete sources of stock market information available free online, the service furnishes same-day price and volume charts for 300 NYSE stocks, and provides a ticker symbol lookup feature. ✓**INTERNET**→ *www* http://www.ai.mit.edu/ stocks.html

Options Profile and Pricing This service requests an underlying common, and then retrieves a list of all related put-and-call options on major U.S. exchanges. Prices are listed on 15-minute delay. ✓**COMPUSERVE**→*go* oprice

Delayed tickers

Current Quotes Get prices for NYSE, AMEX, and NASDAQ issues, but be warned: delays of "at least 15 minutes" can stretch up to ninety minutes or even half a day. Quotes are listed by symbol only, and contain 52-week high and low, yield, and P/E ratio. ✓**AMERICA ONLINE**→*keyword* quotes

Current Stock Quotes Free stock quotes by ticker symbol on 15-minute delay. ✓**COMPUSERVE**→ *go* qquote

Current Stock Quotes Stock quotes by ticket symbol or partial company name on 15-minute delay for a charge of 7¢/issue. ✓**DELPHI**→*go* bus sto **$**

Current Stock Quotes Enter ticker symbol or company name to retrieve free stock quotes on 15-minute delay. ✓**PRODIGY**→*jump* quotes

Current Stock Quotes Get current quotes by ticker symbol on 15-minute delay. ✓**DOW JONES NEWS/RETRIEVAL**→//cqe **$**

Dial Data "If it's traded on an exchange, it's on our database." Intra-day and historical modem retrieval of market prices on stocks, bonds, options, mutual funds, commodity futures, commodity futures options, indexes, and index options. Monthly flatrates are available. Voice call 718-522-6886 for more information about the service. **$**

DTN Wall Street The Data Transmission Network supplies live quotes (15-minute delay) and financial news to a stand-alone videotext system that you rent. Basic service covers stocks, bonds, mutual and money market funds, indices, and futures contracts. Elective services include U.S. treasuries (bills, bonds, notes, and strips), U.S. agency and mortgage-backed securities (GNMA, FNMA, FHLM, FHLB, FFCB, FICO, SLMA, RFC), Canadian stocks, and an automatically updated *Standard & Poor's Stock Guide* Database. There is also a DTN-to-PC link that feeds several of the portfolio management programs available for the Mac and IBM-compatible with the service's 24-hour data, including a LAN application for Novell networks. Hard-core Internet aficionados may note that DTN is the supplier of quote information to the experimental Security APL Quote Server Website. **$** *Info:* ✓**INTERNET** →*www* http://www.secapl.com/ dtn/info/top.html

Farcast Besides offering a personalized clipping service that delivers news by email, Farcast provides stock quotes on demand. Email a ticker symbol and get back a quote. Flat monthly fees are charged. **$** *Info:* ✓**INTERNET**→*email* info@farcast.com *Email for automated info*

Market Quotes Offers price and volume for major indices and stocks by ticker symbol on 15-minute delay. ✓**EWORLD**→*go* market quotes

PAWWS The Portfolio Accounting World Wide from Security APL offers free quotes on 15-minute delay for U.S. stocks traded at the NYSE and AMEX, mutual funds, and money markets. ✓**INTERNET** …→*www* http://www. secapl.com:80/pawws/

QuoteCom Data Service Fifteen-minute delayed quotes from all major U.S. financial markets, as well as data sorting and charting capabilities. *Info:* ✓**INTERNET**→ *www* http://www.quote.com/help. html

TeleChart 2000 Retail software that gives you access to a bulletin-board service for downloading data on stocks and mutual funds, viewing graphs, and performing extensive technical analysis. As the name suggests, charting is the heart of the package, with a multitude of built-in indicators from relative strength graphs and On Balance Volume to MACD and Time Segmented Volume. Use the EasyScan feature to organize stocks and mutual funds by highly specific criteria, such as "short-term stochastic crossing 20 or 80"or "stocks above their 200 day price moving average." Historical data also available by disk. Requires MS-DOS. Voice call 800-

776-4940 for information. ☎→ *dial* 800-251-9103 $

Historical quotes

Historical Commodity Prices Look up any historical commodity price, by day, week, or month. ✓**COMPUSERVE**→*go* cprice

Historical Price and Volume Stats Retrieves historical price and volume information for stocks. ✓**COMPUSERVE**→*go* pristats

Historical Quotes An immense store of historical stock quotes. ✓**DOW JONES NEWS/RETRIEVAL**→ //hq

Historical Quotes from the Free Financial Network BBS Massive amounts of stock-quote data at affordable prices. ☎→*dial* 212-752-8660 $

Historical Quotes from PISCES BBS In addition to current and historical stock quotes, you'll find discussion forums on investment. At $80 a year, it's a reasonably priced service for the devoted investor. ☎→*dial* 312-281-6046 $

Media General Financial Services Company & Industry Data Comprehensive data on issue performance, including analysis of the last trading week, month, quarter, and year, and a comparison of issue performance with relevant market indicators. ✓**DOW JONES NEWS/RETRIEVAL**→ //mg $

MQdata Customized reports on historical stock prices or dividends drawn from CompuServe's Micro-Quote database. ✓**COMPUSERVE**→*go* mqdata

Multiple Issue Historical Pric-ing Charts the volume, close, average, highs and lows of any number of issues over a time period you select. ✓**COMPUSERVE**→*go* qsheet

Securities Price & Volume Graph The next time historical stock prices seem like a morass of numbers, try this service, which draws full-color GIF graphs of an issue's recent history. ✓**COMPUSERVE**→*go* trend

Securities Prices With access to a variety of financial databases, this service provides single-day quotes for single or multiple issues, as well as historical quote information. ✓**COMPUSERVE**→*go* mqint $

Single Issue Pricing History-Historical Price and Volume Stats Provides historical prices by day, week, or month, and includes CUSIP, exchange code, volume, and highs and lows. ✓**COMPUSERVE**→*go* prices

Tradeline Performance History One of the largest historical pricing databases available, with historical quotes and volume information on actively traded NYSE, AMEX, NASDAQ, and OTC securities. A screening feature lets subscribers select stocks, and the service's sophisticated data-retrieval options allow users to either plot onscreen charts or download the quotes to most types of offline charting software. ✓**DOW JONES NEWS/RETRIEVAL**→ //tradeline $ ✓**PRODIGY**→*jump* tradeline $

International

Canadian Stock Archives & Ticker Symbol Lists Historical quotes for over 300 Canadian stocks, plus a full list of Canadian ticker symbols. ✓**INTERNET**→*www* file://dg-rtp.dg.com/pub/misc. invest/Canadian

QuoteCom Data Service Historical stock reports and sophisticated searching tools for virtually all major securities exchanges in Canada, London, Continental Europe, and Asia. *Info:* ✓**INTERNET**→*www* http://www.quote. com/help.html

Small-Biz Electronic Network Data Line This bulletin board releases the daily Stat-Canada market report, which summarizes activity in various Canadian financial markets. ☎→*dial* 416-785-7915 $

Tradeline International Stock Quotes In addition to a vast amount of domestic market information, the service provides historical quotes and volume information for more than 25,000 international issues. ✓**PRODIGY**→*jump* tradeline $ ✓**DOW JONES NEWS/RETRIEVAL**→//tradeline $

UK Historical Stock Prices Retrieve stock prices from July 1990 to the present for more than 5,000 U.K. equity issues and more than 250 market indices. At no cost, access a list of ticker symbols and SEDOL numbers for companies. ✓**COMPUSERVE**→*go* efs-1 $

Symbol lookup

Market and Industry Index Symbol Lookup Frustrated in your search for an elusive ticker symbol? The symbols for issues from more than 800 market indices are provided through this service—not only domestic, but worldwide stock, bond, and commodity markets as well. ✓**COMPUSERVE**→*go* indicators

Advice & analysis

If you need help in deciding which stocks to keep and which ones to dump, which

issues will stay healthy and which will fall ill, you're not alone—especially on the Net. From **Inside Investing** to **Vestor Buy/Sell Market Reports**, from AOL's **The Motley Fool Investment Forum** to Prodigy's **Strategic Investor**, the online world offers more expert advice than you'll be able to absorb. While it's difficult to ascertain exactly what constitutes "expert" advice—some of the financial analysts volunteer their credentials; others are more reticent—there are a few general rules for selecting investment counselors. First, you'll want to decide if you prefer technical or fundamental analysis—in radically reductive terms, technical analysts (**Wall Street SOS Forum** and **Telescan**) deal only with the hard data of stock performance, while fundamental analysts (**S&P Online** and the aptly named **Fundamental Issue Analysis**) factor in such issues as company philosophy and public perception. And on the far edge of fundamental analysis, there are even some services that borrow paradigms from biology

Screenshot from eWorld's Money Matters Forum

and psychology, such as **NeuroQuant Profiles** and **Predicto**.

On the Net

Across the board

Colloquium A newsletter published by the Manhattan investment banking firm of Wertheim Schroder & Co. Tailored to meet the needs of professional investment managers, it nonetheless can be a good source of useful tips for individual investors. ✓**INTERNET**→ *www* http://www.hydra.com/ws/collo quium.html

Decision Point Daily analysis on 150 stocks, weekly charts on a variety of stocks, popular proprietary market indicators, and ample regular market commentary. To those uninitiated into the finer points of financial analysis, the reports of moderator Carl Swenlin might have a mazelike quality. Hang in there, though, and soon you'll be

talking about apparent and actual bottoms forming on the "Short-Term Volume Oscillator." Decision Point comes to life with a busy message-based forum (fundamentalists and techies trading I-told-you-so's), a real-time chat conference area, and a midsize library of charts and other data. Who knows, you might even enjoy Carl's right-wing political postscripts. ✓**AMERICA ONLINE**→*keyword* dp

Inside Investing For those seeking investment enlightenment, this service offers access to the investment strategies of top executives, reconstituted so that their thoughts can be understood by ordinary people. ✓**EWORLD**→*go* money matters→Inside Investing

Insider Information Find price forecasts on issues from the S&P 100, the S&P 500, and the Wilshire 5,000—more than 8,000 U.S. stocks in all. The newsletter claims that its accuracy "rivals that of Wall Street and corporate insiders," which is either a plus or a minus, depending on your past relations with Wall Street. Sample issues are free; after that, it'll cost you. ✓**INTERNET**→*email* subscribe@forecast.com ✍ *Type in message body:* <your full name> <your address> <your telephone number> <your email address> **$**

Investext Investment Reports Information on earnings, stock value, management changes, business climate changes, regulatory effects, competition, and new products. The service permits detailed searches of the database of more than 320,000 investment reports, and offers weekly market commentary and historical portfolios. ✓**COMPUSERVE**→*go* investext **$** ✓**DOW JONES NEWS/RETRIEVAL**→ //invest **$** ✓**GENIE**→*keyword* investment **$**

MarketScope An investment news and analysis feed that includes P/E ranges, economic outlooks, S&P recommendations by risk/reward goals, commentary on current market activity, company-specific dossiers, and earnings forecasts for 1,000-plus companies. MarketScope's "Touted in the Media" summarizes the business press. ✓**CHARLES SCHWAB STREETSMART $**

misc.invest.stocks (ng) Which stocks are blue chips? Which are cow chips? Should you keep your buy-and-sell tickets for tax purposes? When is the best time to short Boston Chicken? Questions range from the dead serious to the highly naive. (One man wonders if *Playboy*'s "Girls of the SEC" really work for the Securities and Exchange Commission.) ✓**USENET** *FAQ:* ✓**INTERNET**→*ftp* rtfm.mit.edu→ anonymous→<your email address> →/pub/usenet-by-group/misc. invest.stocks

The Motley Fool Investment Forum Friendly, down-to-earth investment advice delivered with a bad case of Dadaist hiccups. For instance, in this forum "foolish" is the greatest honorific for an insight or moneymaking stock trade. The hardworking staff, which includes a former writer from *Louis Rukeyser's Wall Street Week*, has created what some consider to be the finest online corrective to the macho mumbo jumbo that characterizes most stock-tip services. One highlight is the Novice Investor area, site of a small library of back-

ground reading for new investors; a Monthly Novice Quiz (with free online time as prizes); and a special message board area where no question goes unanswered no matter how foolish. Then, there's the Fool Portfolio, a fully managed, real-money online portfolio. Unlike most show portfolios, "intentions to buy, sell, or sell short a stock are announced the night before doing so." This makes it possible to follow right along with your own investments, rather than learn at the end of the day that you missed getting in on a rally or out of a crash. There's also an exuberant football pool during the NFL season; live conferences scheduled several times a week in Foolish Chat Central. ✓**AMERICA ONLINE**→ *keyword* fool

Professional Investor Report This newsletter not only summarizes business and trading news, and market data on active stocks, but also covers general activity of all major U.S. financial markets. ✓**DOW JONES NEWS/RETRIEVAL**→ //wires **$**

Strategic Investor An integrated investment management and analysis service which includes market reports, stock and mutual fund charts, as well as company profiles. The main draw of the service is Stock Hunter, a securities selection program that employs eight popular stock valuation models designed by professional money managers to suggest investment strategies. Less complicated than some of the other online stock analysis services, Strategic Investor is noteworthy for its commitment to graphic displays of financial information and its easy interface with other financial services. ✓**PRODIGY**→*jump* strategic investor **$**

> "One highlight of the Motley Fool Investment Forum is the Novice Investor area, site of a small library of background reading for new investors; a Monthly Novice Quiz (with free online time as prizes); and a special message board area where no question goes unanswered no matter how foolish."

Telescan Telescan's two halves, Analyzer and ProSearch, add up to a powerful tool for selecting and analyzing securities—perhaps more powerful than most brokers bother with. In addition to market quotes on 15-minute delay, the Telescan database contains historical price and volume data back to 1973; background fundamentals on all NYSE, AMEX, and NASDAQ stocks; news retrieval from more than 15 wire services; S&P Marketscope; insider-trading info; company profiles; earnings estimates and stock forecasts. The Analyzer has dozens of technical charting functions for graphing these data; ProSearch will sift through the same numbers looking for securities that meet technical or fundamental criteria (you can even back test the historical performance of the securities found in your searches). In sum, hard-core. Available for MS-DOS users. Voice call 800-324-4692 for more information. **$**

Top Advisors' Corner Lines up an array of newsletter samples from well-known financial advisors. Check out the New Guru Review area for advice from investment advisors still trying to establish themselves. ✓**AMERICA ON-LINE**→*keyword* advisor

Trendvest Market & Fund Ratings Look here for the ratings of stocks, bonds, commodities, and mutual funds—condensed analyses that are the financial world's equivalent of the star system for movie reviews. ✓**DELPHI**→ *go* bus tre **$**

Vestor Buy/Sell Recommendations This service integrates more than 30 stock analysis and evaluation programs to chart stocks, options, and futures, and offers financial recommendations on more than 6,000 stocks. ✓**COMPUSERVE**→*go* ves **$**

Windows on WallStreet Designed by MarketArts Inc., this software package for the personal investor automates data downloading from services such as CompuServe, Dial Data, and Dow Jones News/Retrieval; incorporates online research into a technical analysis program; and then charts the analysis. A spreadsheet program is included, as is a personal information manager component. Built into the software is the data

> **"With a fascinating combination of technical, fundamental, and even (gasp!) psychological data, the NeuroQuantifiers dare to predict the future performance of stocks, indices, and options."**

number for MarketArts Inc.'s BBS, which provides 24-hour-a-day technical support. Voice call 214-235-9594 for more information. **$**

Fundamental

Fundamental Issue Analysis Service to sort hundreds of thousands of issues by basic search terms (descriptions, company financial information, and earnings information). ✓**COMPUSERVE**→*go* iqint **$**

NeuroQuant Profiles Strange name, strange newsletter. Many other investment newsletters use state-of-the-art financial market prediction techniques. Neuro-Quant uses techniques that are even newer and shinier. With a fascinating combination of technical, fundamental, and even (gasp!) psychological data, the Neuro-Quantifiers dare to predict the future performance of stocks, indices, and options. ✓**INTERNET**→ *www* http://www.quote.com/

newsletters/neuroquant/ **$**

Predicto Financial analyst Bob Moore's investment predictions use Genetic Algorithm, which applies such biological processes as natural selection, sexual reproduction, inheritance, and mutation to financial markets in an attempt to evolve economic life. Think of a market as a bed of moss, and your dollars as tiny organisms struggling to find their place in this new ecosystem. ✓**INTERNET**→*www* http://www.quote.com/newsletters/predicto/ **$**

S&P Online Though it is more commonly known as a database for equity evaluation, this service also includes recommendations for long-term growth stocks and speculative/cyclical prospects. ✓**COMPUSERVE**→*go* S&P

Technical

The Investment ANALY$T Provides multiple services: issue pricing information (current and historical quotes for NYSE, AMEX, and NASDAQ stocks and mutual funds); stock performance analysis (price/volume charts, insider trades, buy/sell indicators, company news, and other indicators in easy-to-read chart or graph formats); stock screening and selection. (A sophisticated search program that cross-searches up to 135 different company characteristics to find companies most closely matching your selection criteria.) The ANALY$T also tracks portfolios, identifies market trends, monitors competitors, and checks insider movement. ✓**GENIE**→*keyword* analyst **$**

Investment Analysis Calculates the annualized returns for securities for any time period since 1982. ✓**COMPUSERVE**→*go* return **$**

Issue Examination Thumbnail sketches and searches of all types of issues, providing current prices, as well as exchange information, trading status, and historical prices. ✓**COMPUSERVE**→*go* examine

Market Analyzer PLUS This compact software package tracks and analyzes issues according to preset investment equations. It also retrieves price and volume information, and gauges the wisdom or folly of the investment. A formula library explains the investment equations, which range from stochiastics to Bollinger Bands. Voice call 800-522-3567 for more information.

misc.invest.technical (ng) Covers the multiple intersections of investments and technology—not only computer and high-tech stocks, but also developments in technical analysis. ✓**USENET**

Securities Screening If you know what kind of investments you want to make but don't know where to find them, this will help you narrow the field. Specify your needs in any of ten different categories (price, earnings, dividends, risk, capitalization, highs and lows, exchange, and industry), and the service will find the appropriate securities. ✓**COMPUSERVE**→*go* screen

Technical Analysis Furnishes technical opinions on all issues, including Innovest ratings and price projections. ✓**DOW JONES NEWS/RETRIEVAL**→*//*innovest **$**

Wall Street Edge You'll find basic financial information here: a market overview; quote information on stocks, options, and mutual funds; and a digest of a variety of financial analysis services and publications, including newsletters

and premium phone services. ✓**PRODIGY**→*jump* wall street edge **$**

Wall Street SOS and Wall Street SOS Options Alert Founded by Jeremy Gentry in 1970, Security Objectives Services offers two daily investment publications. Wall Street SOS lists data from SOS's exclusive Bull/Bear Index market analysis system along with detailed forecasts based on that data. Options Alert proposes buy-and-sell recommendations for options and stock-options markets. The online services also offer investment advice and portfolio management assistance. ✓**DELPHI**→*go* bus sto **$** ✓**GENIE**→*keyword* sos **$**

Wall Street SOS Forum In addition to Wall Street SOS and Wall Street SOS Options Alert, SOS Forum includes a variety of other publications and recommendations that follow the ROC (Return on Capital) method of common stock evaluation and the market timing system known as the Bull/Bear Index. In addition to an archive of the Bull/ Bear Index, the forum contains the daily SOS Top Stocks List, SOS Top Funds List, and the SOS Weekly Market Commentary, which con-

> **"Market Analyzer Plus's formula library explains the investment equations, which range from stochiastics to Bollinger Bands."**

centrates on the weekly performance and prophecies of Jeremy Gentry's market models. Investors who want to bite back can do so on the Wall Street SOS Board, which hosts investment chat on topics such as NAIC—Investment Clubs, Stocks, and Mutual Funds. ✓**AMERICA ONLINE**→*keyword* sos

Software support

Equis International Software Forum Provides technical support for EQUIS International's investment analysis products: Pulse Portfolio Management, MetaStock, MetaStock RT, The DownLoader, and The Technician. ✓**AMERICA ONLINE**→*keyword* equis

Linn Software Forum Linn Software is best known for TickerWatcher, an integrated application that provides market data collection, market monitoring, charting, portfolio management, technical analysis, and technical screening capabilities. This forum lets TickerWatcher users compare notes and ask questions of the technical support staff. ✓**AMERICA ONLINE**→*keyword* linnsoft

Omega Research Forum The pros and cons of Omega programs, like TradeStation and SuperCharts, are the order of the day on this forum, which also provides technical support for customers and demos for downloading. ✓**AMERICA ON-LINE**→*keyword* omega

Trendsetter Users Forum Trendsetter Software publishes financial market analysis products for the Mac, including Personal Hotline, Personal Analyst, and Professional Analyst. The forum includes product suggestions and discussion among customers, as well as software demos. ✓**AMERICA ONLINE**→*keyword* trendsetter

Monitoring mutual funds

So you've decided that mutual funds are the ticket to secure, well-managed investment.

Join the club. But before you join, make sure to read the **Mutual Fund FAQ** and **User's Guide to Mutual Funds**; they'll clear things up for the novice investor who doesn't know the difference between open-end and closed-end, load and no-load. Once you're up to speed on the lingo, you'll probably want to investigate the Net's resources for mutual fund tracking and analysis. From **NETworth** to **Morningstar Mutual Funds**, the online world offers numerous investment services oriented toward mutual funds. AOL's **Decision Point** provides daily analysis of more than 100 mutuals. And if you want to speak to a human voice, use **Toll-Free Numbers for Mutual Fund Companies** to find the appropriate number. Whether you're interested in aggressive growth funds or bond funds, you'll appreciate the Net, and the Net will appreciate you. In short, the feeling is mutual.

On the Net

Across the board

Decision Point Daily analysis on

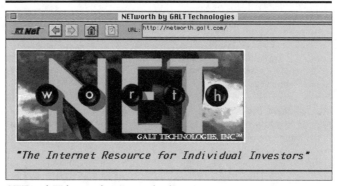

NETworth Web page—http://networth.galt.com/

160 mutual funds, weekly charts of a variety of mutual funds, and regular market commentary. ✓**AMERICA ONLINE**→*keyword* dp

Dreyfus Corp. Though its primary intent is to sell mutual funds to individual investors, the service also contains a section on mutual-fund analysis that assists prospective tycoons in understanding the basic strategies of mutual-funds investment. ✓**COMPUSERVE**→*go* dr

misc.invest.funds (ng) This newsgroup discusses any and all kinds of funds—college funds and mutual funds, gold funds, and 401(k) funds. Are load funds better in the long run? Can currency funds serve as an inflation hedge? And what about those infomercials for fidelity funds? Sometimes the postings get very specific—one man wants to know if his wife's company, a small nonprofit whose 403(b) plan is invested in a family of loaded mutuals, is paying too much to its administrator. But if you like to talk about annuities and no-load mutuals, the fund—er, fun—will never end. ✓**USENET**

FAQ: ✓**INTERNET**→*ftp* rtfm.mit. edu→anonymous→<your email address>→/pub/usenet-by-hierarchy/ misc/answers/investment-faq

Monocle A multi-feature mutual funds investment package, with over 1,000 daily price quotes, screening and ranking, technical analysis, and portfolio management. The effective interaction of graphic and textual elements and the easy access to extensive databases make it an excellent way to keep an eye on your mutual-fund investments. For DOS or Windows. Voice call 800-251-3863 for more information. **$**

Morningstar Mutual Funds The best-known independent company in the business of tracking mutual funds, ten-year-old Morningstar tracks the performance, operations, and analytical methodology of more than 5,000 mutual funds. The funds are ranked by more than 30 investment objectives, including "Top 25 Overall Mutual Funds," "Aggressive Growth," "Speciality-Natural Resources," and "Municipal

Bond-Single State." You can search most funds that Morningstar tracks. For real-time discussions, you're welcome to drop by the Lounge, but the bulk of mutual-fund talk happens on the message boards, which feature more than 50 topics, including Retirement, Fidelity Funds, 20th Century Funds, and Load vs. No-load Funds. ✓**AMERICA ONLINE**→ *keyword* morningstar

Mutual Fund Market Manager This set of documents addresses the concerns of mutual-funds investors, in particular such issues as fund selection and strategies for maximum security. ✓**INTERNET**→ *www* http://networth.galt.com/ www/home/mutual/mutualmn.html

NETworth: The Internet Resource for Individual Investors With tie-ins to financial analysis firms like Chicago-based Morningstar, the service allows users to download no-load mutual fund marketing information, prospectuses, and financial newsletters. With free quotes on over 4,500 mutual funds, as well as educational forums and industry news, the service provides a solid entry into the world of mutual funds. ✓**INTERNET**→ *www* http://networth.galt.com/

SOS Top Funds List A list of the day's top ten mutual-fund picks based on the technical analysis methods of the Security Objectives Services. ✓**AMERICA ONLINE**→ *keyword* sos→Daily Funds

Intro to mutuals

Mutual Fund FAQ Concise answers to 24 basic questions about mutual-funds investing. Is there any disadvantage to using a mutual fund? What is a socially responsible fund? ✓**INTERNET**→ *www*

http://gnn.interpath.net/gnn/meta /finance/res/mfq.html

Toll-free Numbers for Mutual Fund Companies From Acorn to Baird to Corcoran, a list of more than 250 toll-free numbers for mutual-fund companies. ✓**INTERNET**→ *www* http://gnn.interpath. net/gnn/meta/finance/res/800. html

User's Guide to Mutual Funds Twelve pages worth of abbreviations and definitions, from net asset value (NAV) to average weighted maturity. Handy for anyone starting to peer below the surface of mutual funds. ✓**AMERICA ONLINE**→ *keyword* morningstar→User's Guide

Current quotes

Current Mutual Quotes Current price quotes for all traded mutual funds. ✓**DOW JONES NEWS/RETRIEVAL**→//cqe $

Experimental Stock Market Data One of the best free sources of market information, with charts of price movement for major mutual funds. ✓**INTERNET**→ *www* http://www.ai.mit.edu/stocks.html

Mutual Funds Charts the last 30 days of the Lipper Growth Fund Index (a net asset, value-weighted index of the 30 largest growth mutuals), plus gives closing NAVs (net asset values) for ten of the largest U.S. equity mutual funds. ✓**PRODIGY**→ *jump* mutual funds

Mutual Quotes Offers price and volume for major mutual funds by ticker symbol on 15-minute delay. ✓**EWORLD**→ *go* market quotes

PAWWS The Portfolio Accounting World Wide from Security APL offers free quotes (15-minute

delay) for U.S. mutual funds. ✓**INTERNET**→ *www* http://www.secapl. com:80/pawws/

Quotes Get free quotes on selected mutual funds. The 15-minute delay, however, can stretch into a significantly longer period of time. ✓**AMERICA ONLINE**→ *keyword* quotes

Tracking mutuals

Donoghue's Money Fund Report Reports and analysis for government-only money funds, tax-free money funds, and general purpose money funds. ✓**DELPHI**→ *go* bus mon $

Fast EDGAR's Mutual Funds Reporting Part of the EDGAR Project at NYU, this service provides prospectuses and semiannual reports for major mutual funds. ✓**INTERNET**→ *www* http://edgar. stern.nyu.edu/mutual.html

FundWatch Online Screens and sorts over 1,900 mutual funds and provides extensive information on funds by ticker symbol. The service is updated with new ratings, ranking, and performance information each month. ✓**COMPUSERVE** → *go* moneymag

Highest Federally Insured CD Rate Creates reports for liquid money market accounts, CD and small minimum balance accounts, jumbo CDs, and money market mutual funds, as well as serving as a rate almanac. ✓**COMPUSERVE**→ *go* rategram $

Mutual Funds Performance Report If you want to check on the past performance of various mutual funds, you'll find all the necessary information here— prospectuses, prices, and so forth—along with analysis. ✓**DOW JONES NEWS/RETRIEVAL**→//funds $

Evaluating bonds

Subordinated bonds, asset-backed bonds, mortgage-backed bonds, floating-rate bonds,

convertible bonds, zero-coupon bonds, and callable bonds. If this is all mumbo jumbo to you, check out **Basic Information About Bonds** and **Bonds Made Easy**, two useful introductions to the bond world. Then check out bond prices and ratings with services such as **Tradeline** and **Current Bond Quotes**.

On the Net

Across the board

clari.biz.market.misc (ng) News releases and information on assorted financial markets, including the bond market. ✓**CLARINET $**

Intro to bonds

Basic Information About Bonds The Bond Funds section of Prodigy's Consumer Reports Investment dictionary provides basic information about bond performance in recent years—not only what gains bondholders can expect, but also the drawbacks of bond-based investment. ✓**PRODIGY** →*jump* cr investments→ Bond Funds

Bonds Made Easy Cast as a dialogue between a novice investor and a veteran of the bond wars, this document explains such basic but vital issues as market values, maturity, prevailing interest, and the relationship between bonds and interest rates. ✓**COMPUSERVE**→ *go* invforum→Libraries→Bonds/

Junk bond king Michael Milken—from CompuServe's Bettmann Archive

Fixed Income→ BONDS.THD

Bond prices

Bond Prices and Ratings It couldn't be simpler: Enter the ticker symbol or CUSIP number of one or more issuing companies, and this service will list all bonds (with ticket symbols and CUSIP numbers), issue type, and issue date, identifier number, price, and yield, as well as the Standard & Poor's and Moody's ratings. ✓**COMPUSERVE**→*go* bonds **$**

Current Bond Quotes Furnishes detailed bond quotes, including the previous day's closing price, current open, high, low, and last price, and cumulative trading volume for an issue. ✓**DOW JONES NEWS/RETRIEVAL**→//cqe **$**

Key Rates and Bonds This page summarizes U.S. credit markets by displaying a variety of rates, including the prime rate; various T-bills, T-notes, and T-bonds; and Dow Jones bond indices. In addition, it charts the

Federal funds rate for the past 30 days. ✓**PRODIGY**→*jump* key rates & bonds

PAWWS The Portfolio Accounting World Wide from Security APL offers free quotes (15-minute delay) for U.S. bonds traded on the NYSE and AMEX. ✓**INTERNET** →*www* http://www.secapl.com: 80/pawws/

Tradeline Historical quotes and volume information for a variety of bond issues. ✓**DOW JONES NEWS/RETRIEVAL**→//tradeline **$** ✓**PRODIGY**→*jump* tradeline **$**

> "Cast as a dialogue between a novice investor and a veteran of the bond wars, Bonds Made Easy explains such basic but vital issues as market values, maturity, prevailing interest, and the relationship between bonds and interest rates."

Commodities market

From clari.biz.market.commodities—which provides regular updates on the commodi-

ties market—to **Commodity Quotes**, the Net offers a wide variety of valuable services for the investor interested in commodities. If you're one of those investors who follows the glitter, there are also many resources directed specifically at the gold market, from **World Gold** and **Gold Prices** to **How to Invest in Gold**, a book which reviews precious-metal strategy and can be downloaded from GEnie's IBM PC Software Library.

New York Commodity Exchange circa 1910—from CompuServe's Archive Forum

On the Net

Across the board

clari.biz.market.commodities (ng) Need news on the international coffee market? How about pork bellies? This newsgroup collects Reuters and Associated Press news releases pertaining to world commodities markets. ✓**CLARINET $**

Commodity Reports Searches for commodities by name or type and offers a brief report. ✓**INTERNET**→*gopher* calypso.oit.unc.edu →Internet Dog-Eared Pages (Frequently used resources)→Search Many WAIS Indices→agricultural-market-news.src <?>

Advice

How to Invest in Gold Full text of Adam Starchild's book on investing in gold. ✓**GENIE**→*keyword*

ibm→IBM PC Software Library→Set Software Library →Games & Entertainment→*Download a file:* BUY GOLD2.ZIP

Current quotes

Commodity Quotes Want some numbers for gold puts and gold calls? How about Chicago corn? Commodity quotes are listed by ticker symbol; searches can be made with keywords. ✓**DELPHI**→ *go* bus fin com **$**

Gold Prices Provides morning and afternoon prices for London gold, as well as daily quotes from Englehard Corp.'s industrial gold bullion and Handy and Harman's base price for gold. Look up ticker symbols for gold under the info button and then search by symbol. ✓**EWORLD**→*go* market quotes

News-a-Tron Market Reports News, analytical features, and cash quotes for selected commodities

and currencies (livestock and meats, grains, cash metals), updated daily. ✓**COMPUSERVE**→*go* nat **$** ✓**DELPHI**→ *go* bus fin **$**

World Gold Update All that glitters may not be gold, but some of it certainly is, and Prodigy has prices for it—daily gold quotes from Hong Kong, Zürich, London, and New York. ✓**PRODIGY**→ *jump* world gold

Historical quotes

Historical Commodity Prices Look up any historical commodity price, by day, week, or month. ✓**COMPUSERVE**→*go* cprice

Symbol lookup

Commodity Symbols Tired of using a cumbersome index to find the ticker symbol for your favorite commodity? This service provides instant access to ticker symbols. ✓**COMPUSERVE**→*go* csymbol

Tracking futures

The risky world of futures trading isn't often recommended as an entry point for per-

sonal investors, but if you're the risk-taking kind, there are plenty of Net services that will help you throw your hard-earned cash into this incredibly chancy arena. If you're eager for chat, counsel, and commiseration, read **misc.invest.futures**, the newsgroup of choice for futures traders of online America. Investors in search of good advice should spend some time looking at **Futures Recommendations** and the **Futures Newsletter**. And if you don't want to buy and sell futures but still want to talk about—maybe someday—doing it, check out the **Glossary of Futures-Related Terms**.

Across the board

Glossary of Futures-Related Terms A dictionary of the language of futures and options, produced by the Chicago Mercantile Exchange. Here you'll find terms Webster's never dreamed of: Back months. Round turn. Strike price. Long hedge. ✓**INTERNET**→*www* http://www.interaccess.com/users /wilbirk/glossary.html

misc.invest.futures (ng) Provides a window into the extremely

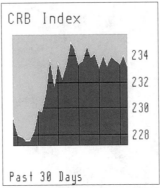

CRB Index

234
232
230
228

Past 30 Days

Screenshot of chart from Closing Futures feature on Prodigy

risky world of futures trading. While much of the conversation is about specific futures, there's also a fair amount of chat about futures investment, and the odd mix of historical analysis and high-risk trading. ✓**USENET**

Quotes & analysis

Closing Futures Charts the Commodity Research Bureau index of 27 leading commodities, and also gives closing prices for various futures in fuel (crude oil, unleaded gas, heating oil, natural gas) and metal (gold, silver, platinum, copper, and palladium). ✓**PRODIGY**→*jump* closing futures

Futures Newsletter Most of the talk about futures is crossed fingers and fervent speculation; still, those investors interested in learning about futures trading should check out this newsletter, which offers analysis of the futures market as well as recommendations. ✓**COMPUSERVE**→*go* aci **$**

Daily Futures Quotes (j) Mailed just after closing every market day, the report includes price and volume information for currency, commodity, and securities futures. ✓**INTERNET**→*email* futures-request@netcom.com ✍ *Type in message body:* join data <your full name>

Futures Quotes Current futures quotes. ✓**DOW JONES NEWS/RETRIEVAL**→*//*futures **$**

Futures Recommendations With so much uncertainty in the futures market, not even Heisenberg would feel qualified to make a recommendation. Still, the financial analysts at News-a-tron put together an impressive list of suggested futures for private investors, and it's available for a modest fee. ✓**DELPHI**→*go* bus fut **$**

Huang's Future Market Report Concise and insightful information about and analysis of U.S. futures markets, delivered electronically once a week. Voice call 416-785-7915 for more information. ✓**INTERNET**→*gopher* wuecon. wustl.edu 671→Huang's Weekly Futures Market Report

Weekly Futures Market (j) This weekly newsletter includes a chart of profit/loss percentages for over 25 commodity and currency futures contracts, as well as brief discussions of current market trends. ✓**INTERNET**→*email* pcyhuang@tpts1.seed.net.tw ✍ *Write a request* <your full name> <your profession> <your interest in the newsletter>

Economics 101

Once upon a time, maybe college, maybe high school, you took an economics course,

and you learned about supply-side theories, and the law of diminishing returns, and stagflation, and John Maynard Keynes. But that was so many years ago, and you haven't been keeping up on the news, and in today's complicated economic climate, you frequently find yourself at a loss. Get back in the game with these basic economic resources, mostly online documents and databases that can help you understand the circulation of money—the give-and-take, the warp-and-weave, the rise-and-fall. Curious what university economists are teaching? Check out the **Collection of Economics Syllabi**. Still upset about the downfall of Eastern Bloc Communism? Compare state socialism with the original theory by perusing the **Collected Works of Marx and Engels**. The numerous economic mailing lists reconfigure the electronic world as a huge classroom, with courses on Ecological Economics, Keynesian Economics, Labor Economics, and Economic Problems in Less Developed Countries. And if you need

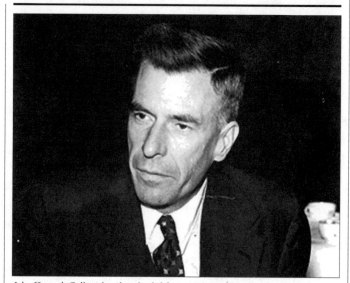

John Kenneth Galbraith—downloaded from GEnie's Archive Forum

to locate any economic resource on the Net, make a beeline for **Resources for Economists** on the Internet, a fully linked hypertext document with active paths to hundreds of services and documents.

On the Net

Across the board

Collection of Economics Syllabi With Sam Houston State's Collection of Economics Syllabi, you can find out the leading titles concerning such topics as comparative economics, economic history, industrial organization, international economics, microeconom-

ics, macroeconomics, and econometrics. ✓**INTERNET**→*gopher* niord. shsu.edu→Economics (SHSU Network Access Initiative Project)→ Course Syllabi for Economics

Economics (echo) Has anyone read the book *Bankrupt 1995*? Does anyone want to explain the basics of Marxist thought? General discussion about economics that, while not especially well-attended, does generate some fine insights. The quality is uneven, however; you're just as likely to receive a paid advertisement for small business solicitation as you are to stumble into a nuanced investigation of the effect of pro sports on the national economy. ✓**ILINK**

Economics Gopher Links to dozens of economic gophers (from the World Bank to the Economics Collection at Texas A&M), Web pages, and mailing list archives. ✓**INTERNET**→*www* gopher:/galaxy. einet.net:80/hGET%20/galaxy/So cial-Sciences/Economics.html

List of the Society for Computational Economics (ml) A vehicle for announcing economics conventions and symposia, and for occasionally raising issues about the use of computers in economics and management. Otherwise not very busy. ✓**INTERNET**→*email* listserv@sara.nl ✍ *Type in message body:* subscribe sce-list <your full name>

sci.econ (ng) Home to debates and discussions about the economy, particularly the political economy. ✓**USENET**

Articles & research

Collected Works of Marx and Engels The communist forefathers' key economic writings are available here for your file transfer and perusal. ✓**INTERNET** ...→*gopher* english-server.hss.cmu.edu→Government, Law and Society→Marx and Engels ...→*ftp* english-server. hss.cmu.edu→anonymous→ <your email address>→/Marx

Economic Democracy Information Network Devoted to delivering information that has impact on economics and business but doesn't often show up in the business pages, EDIN offers myriad documents on human rights, education and training, political organization, labor organization, health care, race, and the environment. EDIN does not link to other sites, but it does describe them in detail, and it is invaluable as a source of "alternative"economics and business information—news about Internet sites in Cuba, for instance. ✓**INTERNET**→*gopher* garnet.berkeley.edu 1250

Karl Marx—downloaded from http:// www.uni-trier.de/trier/marx.gif

sci.econ.research (ng) Discuss economic research in this dense and moderated newsgroup. ✓**USENET**

Working Paper Archive Research articles and abstracts on more than 20 topics, including microeconomics, econometrics, and international finance. ✓**INTERNET**→*gopher* econwpa.wustl.edu

Economists

Directory of Economists For those urgent cases when you need a good doctor of economics. Names are collated from a variety of professional organizations and academic rosters. ✓**INTERNET**→*gopher* niord.shsu.edu→Economics (SHSU Network Access Initiative Project)→Directory of Economists (by name)

List of Nobel Laureates in Economics From Franco Modigliani to James Tobin, they're all here, that elite group of economists whose efforts have been rewarded with the highest honor in the dismal science. ✓**INTERNET**→*gopher* niord.shsu.edu→Economics (SHSU Network Access Initiative Project)→Nobel Laureates in Economics

Environmental

Ecological Economics (ml) Money is green and ecology is green, and yet the two rarely meet on the old conceptual color wheel. But in this mailing list, there's significant interpenetration between the camps.

Subscribers, for instance, wonder about how governments can reconceptualize macroeconomic data in ways that better suit environmental needs.

Or they review the ecological/ economic distinction between "chrematistics" and "oikonomia" (the former relates to "the manipulation of property and wealth so as to maximize short-term monetary exchange value to the owner," the latter to "the management of the household over the long run"). ✓**INTERNET**→ *email* listproc@csf.colorado.edu ✍ *Type in message body:* subscribe ecol-econ <your full name>

> "Money is green and ecology is green, and yet the two rarely meet on the old conceptual color wheel. But in the Ecological Economics mailing list, there's significant interpenetration between the camps."

Feminists

Feminist Economics Discussion List (ml) Discussions about economics and business from a feminist perspective. As you might expect, feminist economics is a heterodox discipline, with many differing ideas about how, when, and why to practice the dismal science. Is capitalism inherently patriarchal? How about property itself? ✓**INTERNET**→*email* listserv@bucknell.edu ✍ *Type in message body:* subscribe femecon-l <your full name>

Net resources

Gophers Devoted to Economics (ml) Notifies list subscribers of new or changing economic and financial sites on the Internet. ✓**INTERNET**→*email* listserv@shsu.edu ✍ *Type in message body:* subscribe egopher <your full name>

Resources for Economists on the Internet A massive hypertext bibliography with links to most of the major economic resources on the Internet. From the Economic Bulletin Board at the University of Michigan's Library Gopher to the Vienna Stock Market, a significant part of the electronic economic information of the planet is at your fingertips—just click and feast. ✓**INTERNET**→*www* http://riskweb.bus.utexas.edu/goffe/FAQ_7_11.html

Political economy

Economic Problems in Less Developed Countries (ml) Can socialism work in Africa? What industries might revive the slumping Nicaraguan economy? This mailing list wonders what will happen to less industrialized and developed countries—both internally and within the context of the world economy. One geography professor suggests "if one takes, for example, the oversupply of skills and technology in the North, the 900 million illiterate people in the South can be read as an example of potential complementarity." Read on. ✓**INTERNET**→*email* listserv@acadvm1.uottawa.ca ✍ *Type in message body:* subscribe econo-my <your full name>

Government Information in Canada/Information Governmental au Canada (j) Many of Canada's economic policy decisions are subjects for discussion in this bilingual electronic journal. ✓**INTERNET**→*www* http://www.usask.ca/library/gic/index.html

Labor Economics (ml) The participants in this mailing list demonstrate a deep conviction that labor lies at the heart of all macroeconomic and microeconomic questions, and their postings range from explanation of the Davis-Bacon Acts to musings about online resources for labor organizers. ✓**INTERNET**→*email* mxserver@shsu.edu ✍ *Type in message body:* subscribe labor <your full name>

Schools of thought

Post-Keynesian Thought (ml) Is unemployment a public policy problem? Paul doesn't think so, but Randy does. So leave the peacemaking to Steve, who steps in to opine that "both Paul and Randy seem to agree that inflation is mismeasured to some degree." This mailing list, devoted to post-Keynesian economic theories and thoughts, is populated mostly by academic economists. ✓**INTERNET**→*email* listproc@csf.colorado.edu ✍ *Type in message body:* subscribe pkt <your full name>

"This term 'chrematistics' was new to me as I read Juan Martinez-Alier's 'Ecological Economics.' Dont miss it if you haven't read it. Roughly defined as the study of the pursuit of wealth for its own sake, rather than as a means of living well, this is an important notion. While we are beating each other about the head with scholastic fine-points, let us not lose sight of the main chance. We simply are asking too much of Nature and we had better slow down.

"And while our greed may be understandable in a world where such extravagance seems inevitable, we ought to know better by now. Let's cut the crap. Are we too simpleminded to stop asking, 'Do we have too many asking too much?' -- a question that has been answered -- and get on with asking 'How can we move to another level?' So far IMHO we ain't cutting it. Hayes' offering was a nice beginning. On the other hand if I'm so smart...."

—from the **Ecological Economics** mailing list

Data from the EBB

When you need economic statistics for the old US of A, there's simply no better place

in Cyberspace than the **Economics Bulletin Board**. Overseen by the U.S. Department of Commerce's Office of Business Analysis, the EBB offers one-stop shopping for all kinds of economic information. Drawing on press releases and statistical information from most major federal agencies, the EBB presents thousands of informational files clearly organized within easy-to-use menus—from **Employment Statistics** to **Energy Statistics**, from **Price and Productivity** to **U.S. Treasury Auction Results**.

On the Net

The Economics Bulletin Board One of the richest economics resources on the Net. ☎→*dial* 202-482-2167/202-482-3870/202-482-2584 ✓INTERNET→*gopher* una.hh.lib.umich.edu

Best Market Reports Full-text reports that analyze domestic and worldwide performance of several industries ✓INTERNET→*gopher* una.hh.lib.umich.edu→ebb→Best Market Reports

Economic Indicators Lists everything from the composite index of leading economic indicators to more specific bellwethers of economic performance such as new-home sales and cold-storage holdings of shrimp. ✓INTERNET→*gopher* una.hh.lib.umich.edu→ebb→Economic Indicators

Employment Statistics Employment statistics for states and major metropolitan areas. ✓INTERNET→*gopher* una.hh.lib.umich.edu→ebb→Employment Statistics

Energy Statistics Crude oil, coal, heating fuels, motor gasoline, natural gas, propane, and more. Each fuel comes complete with its own statistics, stocks, and prices as well as industrial overviews. ✓INTERNET→*gopher* una.hh. lib.umich.edu→ebb→Energy statistics

Foreign Assets Control Program A fascinating meeting of politics and economics that lists embargos and other occurrences of international financial choreography. ✓INTERNET→*gopher* una.hh.lib. umich.edu→ebb→Foreign Assets Control Program

Foreign Trade Lists of key dollar exchange rates, summaries of international transactions, and export and import data. ✓INTERNET→*gopher* una.hh.lib. umich.edu→ebb→Foreign Trade

Industry Statistics Quarterly Commerce Department reports on more than 40 industries ranging from the aerospace industry to truck-trailer manufacturers. ✓INTERNET→*gopher* una.hh.lib.umich.edu→ebb→Industry Statistics

Monetary Statistics Foreign exchange rates are posted at 10 a.m. and noon. Daily and monthly Treasury statements, Federal Reserve data, and historical money information is also posted. ✓INTERNET→ *gopher* una.hh.lib.umich.edu→ebb→Monetary Statistics

Price and Productivity Find consumer price indexes, producer price indexes, and import and export price indexes. ✓INTERNET→*gopher* una.hh.lib.umich.edu→ebb→Price and Productivity Statistics

Regional Economic Statistics A list of disposable, per capita income by state, and projections for personal income in major metropolitan areas. ✓INTERNET→*gopher* una.hh.lib.umich.edu→ebb→Regional Economic Statistics

State-By-State Export Resource Listings Names and phone numbers for agencies and organizations assisting with international trade. ✓INTERNET→*gopher* una.hh.lib.umich.edu→ebb→State By State Export Resource Listings

Summaries of Current Economic Conditions A composite index of 11 leading economic indicators, as well as summaries of other financial and economic factors—including housing starts, personal income, producer prices, and durable-goods orders. ✓INTERNET→*gopher* una.hh.lib.umich.edu→ebb→Summaries of current economic conditions

U.S. Treasury Auction Results Auction results for a variety of Treasury Department issues, including notes and T-bills of various durations. ✓INTERNET→*gopher* una.hh.lib.umich.edu→ebb→U.S. Treasury Auction Results

Watching the economy

How complicated is the United States economy? Well, it's like one gigantic maze that

peels away to show 50 smaller mazes, each with hundreds and hundreds of smaller mazes lurking beneath it. Amazingly complicated and intricate, the push and pull of consumer forces, manufacturing output, and government regulations is hard to follow—and harder still if you don't have the appropriate data. So where is the data? Well, on the Net. Between the New England stats at **NEEEDc**, the Arizona stats at **ASEDD Economic Database**, and the more general national resources (**Budget of the United States**, **Business Statistics and Census Data**, and the **Federal Reserve**), there's a tremendous amount of national economic information available. There's even **U.S. Debt v5.3**, a shareware program that continually calculates the national debt. And that doesn't even scratch the surface of the vast databases devoted to the world economy, such as the mammoth **National Trade Data Bank** and the **World Trade Outlook**. Compared to the world, the U.S. economy looks like a lemonade stand.

Dollar bill—downloaded from GEnie

On the Net

Domestic

ASEDD Economic Database From the Metropolitan Phoenix Consumer Index, all the economics information you could ever want about the great southwestern state of Arizona (and sometimes more: to wit, a document titled "Arizona Employment Shift to Private Sector"). ✓**INTERNET**→*gopher* info.asu.edu→ASU Campus-Wide Information→ASEDD Economic Database (ASU)

Basic Economic News Extremely basic and practical economic information, such as advice on preparing for a recession and safer ways to save. Though it may not help you understand macroeconomic trends, the digest does a good job of explaining how those trends affect daily life, and the prose is clear and concise. ✓**PRODIGY**→*jump* cr money→The Economy

Budget of the United States

What does the government spend on your favorite social programs? Thanks to the Library of Congress, you can use online technology to browse or search the federal budget. ✓**INTERNET** ...→*gopher* marvel.loc.gov→Global Electronic Library (by Subject)→Economics and Business→US Budget Information ...→*gopher* sunny.stat.usa.gov→ Budget of the United States Government, Fiscal Year 1995

Business Statistics and Census Data Information on monthly retail sales, manufacturing and trade inventories and sales, county business patterns, and quarterly financial reports. Some of the information is general, but the stats get pretty specific. Did you know that a 1987 survey of minority- and women-owned businesses revealed that more than 90 percent of women-owned businesses were sole proprietors? ✓**COMPUSERVE**→*go* cendata→Menu Item 10 Business Data

Economic Conversion Information Exchange Supplies U.S. regional statistics for a variety of economic categories, including employment by major industry, personal income and earnings, transfer payments, as well as state-by-state analyses. ✓**INTERNET**→*gopher* cher.eda.doc.gov→Economic Conversion Information Exchange Gopher

---

Economic Estimates and Market Analysis Provided by Money Market Services International, this service includes domestic economic data and projections—free reports on currency market analysis, Treasury market analysis, monthly and quarterly economic forecasts, as well as a weekly economic survey. In case you feel that investment isn't really investment without an outlay, you can also take advantage of the premium features, and pay surcharges for daily reports on currency, equity, and debt. ✓**COMPUSERVE**→*go* mms **$**

Economic Indicators Current statistics and analysis for unemployment, consumer prices, consumer confidence, retail sales, housing starts, home sales, factory orders, purchasing, and the trade deficit, plus summaries of leading economic indicators. ✓**PRODIGY**→*jump* economic indicators

---

Federal Reserve If you're curious about the role of the Federal Reserve in maintaining and defining our national economy, you might want to download some statistical and explanatory documents here—Flow of Funds Tables, Industrial Production and Capacity Utilization, Reserves of Depository Institutions, Assets and Liabilities of Large Commercial Banks, and more. ☎→*dial* 314-621-1824→Federal Reserve Board ✓**INTERNET**→*gopher* town.hall.org→Federal Reserve Board

---

National Archives Center for

Electronic Records Index Search an index (no documents yet) to the archive's thousands of pages of information from such Federal departments as the Bureaus of the Census, Economic Analysis, and Labor Statistics; the Civil Aeronautics Board; the Department of Transportation; the IRS; the SEC; and the Social Security Administration. Instructions on how to order electronic files on tape reels or cartridges are also available. ✓**INTERNET**→*www* ftp:// ftp.cu.nih.gov/NARA_ELECTRONIC

New England Electronic Economic Data Center (NEEEDc) Direct from the Federal Reserve Bank of Boston, NEEEDc specializes in the New England economy, from current economic data from the Bureau of Economic Analysis to the historical statistics published in the Federal Reserve Bank of Boston's New England Economic Indicators (almost 100 variables from 1969 for all states and some metropolitan areas). ✓**INTERNET**→*ftp* neeedc.umesbs.maine.edu→anonymous→<your email address>→/access

---

Savage Archive A collection of public-domain files with an immense amount of material on investments and economics. Worth a visit for investors interested in hard core financial data. ✓**INTERNET**→*ftp* dg-rtp.dg.com→anonymous→<your email address>→/pub/misc.invest

---

U.S. Debt v5.3 Macintosh shareware that displays current U.S. national debt, showing each citizen's share. Also gives U.S. and world populations. ✓**INTERNET**→*ftp* mac.archive.umich.edu→anonymous→<your email address>→/mac/util/organization→usdebt5.3.sit.hqx

International

Bank of Ireland Trinity Branch Foreign Exchange Information Service So, just how much is the dollar worth against the Irish pound? And how does the Spanish peso fare? Revised weekly, the service converts foreign currency amounts into the Irish pound (IEP). ✓**INTERNET**→*www* http://www.webnet.ie/cust/boi/foreign_exchange/fx_service.boi.html

---

CIA World Factbook The fruits of CIA labor are collected in this database of country statistics and profiles. Not at all secretive, it's one of the easiest-to-use—albeit slightly dated—resources on the Net. ✓**INTERNET**→*wais* world.factbook.src

---

Citibank Global Report Updates on a wide variety of international markets, as well as currency exchange rates. ✓**COMPUSERVE**→*go* cointl **$**

> "The fruits of CIA labor are collected in the CIA World Factbook of country statistics and profiles. Not at all secretive, it's one of the easiest-to-use—albeit slightly dated—resources on the Net."

Country Reports on Economic Policy and Trade Practices for 1992 Published by the U.S. Department of State, these reports provide thumbnail sketches of world economies and economic policies, including trade policies that affect relations with the United States. ✓ **INTERNET**→*gopher* umslvma.umsl.edu→The Library→Government Information (US Federal & State Info & Docs)→Country Reports-Economic Policy & Trade Practices NTDB

Currency Converter If you want to find out how much that Mark is worth, or you're thinking of trading in your pounds for pennies, you might want to use the famed Koblas Currency Converter, which uses recent currency rates updated weekly. ✓ **INTERNET**→*www* http://www.ora.com/cgi-bin/ora/currency

Dollar Commentary Calculator Track the performance of the U.S. dollar against the most active foreign currencies. ✓ **DELPHI**→*go* bus fin dol

Foreign Exchange Rates This currency calculator gives two-day tables of foreign exchange rates; the dollar is measured against all traded foreign currencies. ✓ **DELPHI** →*go* bus fin for

Luxembourg Income Study (LIS) This academic research project collates more than 60 economic surveys from 21 countries worldwide to create a superdatabase of international incomes. All in all, more than 180,000,000 households are represented, and the database—which requires registration for use—contains extensive help on search, retrieval, and analysis of the information. *Register:* ✓ **INTERNET**→*email* eplisjr@luxcep11.bitnet ✍ *Write a request*

Manchester Computing Centre - National Dataset Service Registered NDS users earn access not only to the IMF's International Finance Statistics Reports and the Government Finance Statistics Yearbook, but also to household income statistics, trade statistics, labor statistics, and assorted other macroeconomic indicators—both for the UK and for more than 150 countries worldwide. At present, only British netters can use the service, but this may change in the near future. ✓ **INTERNET**→*gopher* cs6400.mcc.uk→MIDAS Datasets Service

National Trade Data Bank One of the most impressive statistical databases online, with hundreds of documents ranging across a broad spectrum of topics pertaining to international trade. From a glossary of commonly used international trade terms to country-by-country commercial guides, from reports on key officers of foreign-service posts to analyses of patterns of foreign terrorism, this data bank contains such a staggering amount of information that it's almost futile to summarize the holdings.

Stock Price Indices for the G-10 countries? Russian Defense Business Directory? If statistics can take your breath away, prepare to be breathless. Access to this marvelous repository of national and international economic information used to be free, but it now carries an $8-per-month subscription fee. ✓ **INTERNET**→*gopher* sunny.stat-usa.gov→STAT-USA a Source of Economic, Social, and Environmental Data Bank→National Trade Data Bank **$**

World Bank Public Information Center (PIC) The World Bank's Public Information Center includes national economic re-

ports, environmental assessments and projections, and explanations of new World Bank projects. ✓ **INTERNET** ...→*www* http://www.worldbank.org/html/pic/PIC.html ...→*gopher* gopher.worldbank.org→Public Information Center

World Dollar Tracks the U.S. dollar against major foreign currencies. ✓ **PRODIGY**→*jump* world dollar

World Trade Outlook A sort of online primer to trade, this document sketches today's international business and investment climate in some of the broadest terms imaginable ("From the U.S. point of view the modern world was divided until recently between good guys and bad guys").

In addition to America's position in the global economic scene, issues such as European unity and trade in the Americas are addressed. ✓ **PRODIGY**→*jump* world trade

> "From a glossary of commonly used international trade terms to analyses of patterns of foreign terrorism, the National Trade Data Bank contains a staggering amount of information."

Being your own broker

What's the difference between a full-service broker and a discount broker? Well, it's

like comparing apples and oranges—or apples and very different apples. Full-service brokers not only handle buys and trades of stocks, bonds, and options, but also ferret out financial strategies traditionally unavailable to the lay investor—obscure foreign investments, for example, or initial public offerings (IPOs). But this special attention comes at a premium. Discount brokerages, on the other hand, limit their active strategizing, preferring instead to confine their services to buying and selling domestic issues and providing basic market information to prospective investors. As the name implies, discount brokers earn much lower commissions: on the other hand, they are likely to charge for services a full-service broker would render free of charge, such as the processing of paper certificates. Most of the online brokers are discount brokers—whether CompuServe's **QuickWay**, Prodigy's **PC Financial Network**, or **Wall Street Investor Service**. And while some of the services are relatively skeletal—buy, sell,

Screenshot from Charles Schwab StreetSmart

limit or stop, change or cancel—others, like **Charles Schwab StreetSmart**, offer more extensive financial management. If the whirl of brokers is dizzying, steady yourself with **Ratings of Brokerage Houses**, a valuable introductory document that analyzes and ranks national brokers.

On the Net

Online brokers

Charles Schwab Brokerage Services Charles Schwab online brokerage service allows you to trade in stocks, bonds, options, and mutual funds. Enter special trade conditions, check trade confirmations online, cancel or change any outstanding orders. Receive real-time quotes along with historical information. ✓**GENIE**→*keyword* schwab $

Charles Schwab StreetSmart

Brokerage Services The main feature of this this well-rounded portfolio management package is the online brokerage—the ability to trade stocks, mutual funds, bonds, and options through Schwab's own linkup. You can issue just about any instruction you would leave with a living, breathing broker—orders to buy or sell, short, switch, limit or stop, day or good-till-canceled, and change or cancel (open orders can be revised until executed)—and there's even a 10% discount on commissions. The service also includes extensive portfolio management features, current and historical stock quotes, and an online library that connects to Dow Jones News/Retrieval, Standard & Poor's MarketScope, and Company Reports. ✓**CHARLES SCHWAB STREETSMART $**

Dreyfus Corp. Like an online shopping mall for mutual funds, complete with basic information about the products. ✓**COMPUSERVE** →*go* dr

E*Trade Securities, Inc. Available at basic-connect rates, this online brokerage service supplements its brokerage duties with basic investment management features (quotes, news, portfolio reports). With commissions of only 1.5 cents per share, it is one of the cheapest brokerage services available anywhere in Cyberspace. ✓**COMPUSERVE**→*go* etrade

Fidelity On-line Xpress (FOX)

"Your direct line to Wall Street." Online trading and real-time quotes for stocks, options, and mutual funds from one of the country's largest discount brokers. MS-DOS software includes Turbo Trade for preparing orders off-line and executing same-day trading and money management features to track your portfolio holdings with a complete history of brokerage and funds balances and transaction history. The Fidelity On-line Xpress package will also access Dow Jones News/Retrieval, Telescan, and Standard & Poor's MarketScope (although you must sign up separately), and it will keep a running record of year-end tax reports like Schedule D information. Voice call 800-544-9375 for more information. **$**

Tickerscreen: Max Ule Discount Brokerage

Much like other online brokers, Max Ule offers trading control, portfolio updates, and basic investment advice. Ule be thrilled to use this service. ✓**COMPUSERVE**→*go* tkr-323

PC Financial Network

Carries the full run of standard brokerage features—online trading control, daily portfolio updates, free market reports, and commissions that, while not rock-bottom, are at least comparable with those of other discount brokers. See Cyberpower!™ for a walk-through ✓**PRODIGY**→*jump* pcfn

QuickWay An online brokerage service provided by the discount brokerage firm of Quick & Reilly which lets you place stock and option orders, change or cancel those orders, and review your history of online transactions. ✓**COMPUSERVE** →*go* qwk **$**

Wall Street Investor Services

Discount broker that features low "institutional" rates and the Traders Express online service for placing orders. Interest is paid on credit balances, customer accounts are SIPC-covered, and there are absolutely no access charges for using Traders Express. Trading software is available for DOS, Windows, and Macintosh. Voice call 800-487-2339 for more information. **$**

Ratings

Ratings of Brokerage Houses

An extensive list of brokerage houses, both electronic and conventional, along with phone numbers and brief summaries of available services. The report also calculates and compares commission rates for a wide range of sample portfolios, and publishes the results of an investor satisfaction survey of misc.invest subscribers. Though it's long and has few search features, this text file is nonetheless an extremely valuable resource for anyone who is interested in selecting a broker, or who wants to find out more about online brokerages. ✓**INTERNET**→*www* http://www.cs.cmu.edu:8001/afs /cs.cmu.edu/user/jdg/www/in vest_brokers.html

---

CYBERNOTES

An approximation of full service broker commissions for $2,000 trades, listed in three different price/volume configurations. Amounts are for stocks only and include miscellaneous fees not necessarily part of the commission.

Firm	400/$5	100/$20	50/$40
Accutrade	48.00	48.00	48.00
Aufhauser	37.49	25.49	25.49
Bidwell	41.25	27.25	25.75
Brown	29.00	29.00	29.00
Fidelity	63.50	54.00	54.00
Kennedy, Cabot	38.00	38.00	23.00
Olde Discount	35.00	40.00	40.00
Pacific	39.00	29.00	29.00
Andrew Peck	100.00	100.00	100.00
Quick&Reilly	50.00	49.00	49.00
Schwab	64.00	55.00	55.00
Seibert	75.00	75.00	75.00
Vanguard	57.00	48.00	40.00
Waterhouse	35.00	35.00	35.00
Jack White	45.00	36.00	34.50
Full Price	88.37	53.70	52.12

—from the **Ratings of Brokerage Houses** Web page

Portfolio management

Buying stocks is only half the battle, of course. The other half is knowing when to sell.

How is your entire portfolio doing? Are there certain issues that are dragging down the package, and would it better serve you if they were converted into another stock, or even into savings? Keeping track of stock holdings isn't impossible, but it is complicated. Prodigy's **Quote Track** helps investors set up two full portfolios, and then retrieves news and quote data each day. **Wealth-Builder** includes links to Reuters News Service and publications such as *Money* magazine. And **Charles Schwab StreetSmart** supplements its online brokerage service with extensive financial management resources. All the services track profit and loss, and print easy-to-read statements. So when someone asks you how your stocks are performing, don't waste time tracking down your broker. Get what you want from the Net.

Screenshot of Quote Track feature on Prodigy

holdings, automatically downloading price information and updating portfolio positions every time you connect.

Issues can be organized by type, market value, yield, or gain and loss. In addition to graphing and formatting portfolio reports, the program can export its data to Excel, Lotus, and Quicken, and reports can be saved in several formats.

If you want to speculate a bit, the program can also track hypothetical holdings and handle multiple accounts. Available for Windows and Macintosh. Voice call 800-334-4455 for more information.

Portfolio Valuation If you're holding a handful of stocks but can't seem to make heads or tails of their gains and losses, don't despair. This service will report the original and current value of each individual security and the portfolio as a whole. ✓**COMPUSERVE**→*go* port

Quicken Online One of the

most popular personal finance management programs in the world, with a full complement of banking, budgeting, and organizing features.

The online version supplements the basic Quicken package with a limited but nevertheless useful investment section that comprises stock quote updates, historical quote information, performance reports and graphs, as well as an investment budget and planning program. Voice call 602-295-3220 to order the software.

Quotes & Portfolio AOL's portfolio tracking tools watch up to 100 investments, listing issues alongside their purchase price and current price and calculating the net gain or loss. ✓**AMERICA ONLINE** →*keyword* quotes

---

Quote Track Allow you to set up two complete portfolios of securities (actual or hypothetical), and then retrieves current market and quote data relevant to those investments, as well as pertinent company news. ✓**PRODIGY**→*jump* quote track

---

WealthBuilder A portfolio management program with access to a variety of news services including *Money* magazine, CNBC, Morningstar, and Reuters' Money Network. Enter your financial information and define your goals, and WealthBuilder will assist you in allocating expenditures and investments, with an eye toward current market conditions. Voice call 610-277-7600 for more information. **$**

On the Net

Charles Schwab StreetSmart
In addition to its online brokerage capabilities, StreetSmart provides excellent portfolio management. The service keeps track of your

CYBERPOWER!™

Playing the Market

I'm not an expert investor, and whenever I've invested in the past I've used a broker. But now I want to try to buy some stocks myself. Can I make a stock purchase with my computer and my modem? I've been eyeing Microsoft, although I don't think I want to spend more than $3,000, commissions notwithstanding.

Buying a stock online may seem like a nightmarish prospect. It's not, at least not for members of Prodigy's PC Financial Network (PCFN). While you'll first have to clear the hurdle of opening an account, the application process is more time-consuming than rigorous, with a series of rudimentary questions regarding your trading needs, personal financial status, and insider affilation. And after you have opened an account, it's simple to travel from the main PCFN screen to the Trading menu, from the Trading menu to the Stock menu, and from the Stock menu to the Buy Stock screen. When you arrive at the Buy Stock screen, you can breathe a brief sigh of relief; in the feast of stock purchasing, this screen is the meat of the meal. First-timers and shaky traders may want to activate Trade Assist, PCFN's equivalent of balloon help, for on-screen explanation and annotation. Braver souls can just forge ahead with this guide, keeping in mind the sage advice of the Jackson 5: "It's as easy as 1-2-3."

1. Select your stock. First, enter the ticker symbol of the stock you want to buy—if you do not know the symbol, enter the first few letters of the company's name, and PCFN will produce a list from which you can select. Microsoft? That's MSFT, traded on the NASDAQ/OTC, and according to PCFN's real-time ticker, the stock is currently priced at $61.50 per share.

2. Define your buy order. Before you can secure your securities, you'll need to make several decisions about the parameters of your purchase. PCFN can handle not only market orders (in which a buy is executed at the best available price at the time the order is issued), but also limit orders (in which the stock will not be purchased unless its price is at or under a designated level) and stop orders (which choose a certain trigger price, and activate the buy as a market order after that price is reached). All right, you don't want to spend more than $3,000 on Microsoft; at current prices, you could purchase just under 49 shares. But rather than deal with odd numbers, why don't you issue a limit order for 50 shares at $60 or less per share? If you decide on a limit order or a stop order, remember to instruct PCFN whether to keep your order active until its conditions are met or you decide to cancel it (that's known as a GTC, or Good-Til-Canceled, order), or whether to cancel the order automatically at the close of the trading day (that's known as a day order). And finally, don't forget to note if you want to buy on margin—in a margin buy, the broker loans you a portion of the purchase price, with the value of your securities serving as collateral.

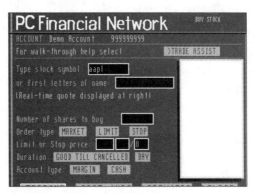

PCFN on Prodigy

3. Verify and send your order. After you have defined your transaction, wait for PCFN to open a Recap Window that displays the terms of your buy order. Review them, correct any errors, and then send the order to PCFN. If the market swings accordingly, you may be the proud owner of 50 shares of Microsoft. Otherwise, keep trying; the stock is bound to be in your reach sometime soon. Unless instructed, PCFN will keep all securities and profits in your online account, which you can review at any time.

Investment simulations

Playing the market is not only exhilarating, but also dangerous. Investments may sky-

rocket (instant millionaire!) or plummet, and unless you become an expert at reading tiny market shifts, you'll approach every stock purchase with great trepidation. The Net can help. Before you risk real money, try one of the many online investment simulations, which let Monday-morning speculators buy up stocks and then watch the performance of their issues. Spend your fake $100,000 on blue chips, or dump the whole load into penny stocks. In most of the online games—**E*Trade Stock Market Game**, **Bulls and Bears**, and others— you'll be competing against other would-be stock kings, and the player with the greatest profit often wins a small cash prize. Bored with being an ordinary investor? Check out **WSRAID: V 3.01** and become a corporate raider.

On the Net

Bulls and Bears Compete against other investors with $100,000 in a world of stock fantasy. Buy and sell virtual shares! Receive virtual dividend checks in your virtual mailbox! Drive yourself into virtual ruin! ✓**AMERICA ONLINE**→*keyword* bulls and bears

Capital An investment simulation game for DOS computers. ✓**EXEC-PC**→File Collection Menu→ Mahoney IBM Compatible DOS→ *Download a file:* CAPITAL.ZIP

Corporate Traders Form companies and then buy and sell stock, trying to amass more wealth than your opponents. Two, three or four people can play in this Windows shareware game. ✓**GENIE**→ *keyword* windows→Windows Software Libraries→Set Software Library→Windows Games→*Download a file:* COTRADER.ZIP

E*Trade Stock Market Game Ever wonder what it would be like to have $100,000 to play the market? Wonder no longer. With E*Trade's market game, you can dabble in stocks and options like the big boys. The E*Trade program uses actual market data and prices to determine your success or failure over four weeks, and keeps track of commission costs for extra realistic profit and loss calculation. Join this month's game to compete against other CompuServe subscribers, and try to win the monthly $50 cash prize. ✓**COMPU-SERVE**→*go* etgame

GEnie Contests There's always some contest on the burner. The "Pick of the Month Club," for instance, invites GEnie users to select a single stock and track its profitability over the course of one month. The winner gets the satisfaction of having won (and perhaps a prize, if the contest is sanctioned by GEnie's higher-ups). ✓**GENIE**→*keyword* invest→Investors' Bulletin Board→set 12

MAMMON Stock-Picking Tournament This stock simulation gives participants $100,000 in imaginary money and one very real objective: make more imaginary money than your opponents. New players join monthly heats, and the player with the greatest profit at the close of each month is declared victor. ✓**INTERNET**→*telnet* mammon.media.mit.ed 10900

Wall Street Simulator v1.0 Realistic simulation shareware of a brokerage account: trade with real market prices, analyze results, and compare to other users. Register and get a manual, upgrades, and a newsletter. ✓**PC OHIO**→d→*Download a file:* WSSW10.ZIP

WSRAID: V 3.01 Become a corporate raider. Play against the computer or other players; simulated financial news, a stock ticker, and a dynamic economy lend an air of authenticity to the game. PC shareware. ✓**AMERICA ONLINE**→*keyword* pc games→Software Library→*Search by file name:* WS RAID30.ZIP

> "Buy and sell virtual shares! Receive virtual dividend checks in your virtual mailbox! Drive yourself into virtual ruin!"

Collectibles

In some ways, the online world seems like a strange

place for collectibles. Not only does the bit stream thwart the physical world, but the constant push for newer, faster, and better leaves little room for old things, especially old things of unstable value. That's where the collectors come in. Uncertain what to do with that Olivia Newton-John LP or that John Anderson campaign pin? What about the *Hawkman* comic book and the Six-Million Dollar Man doll (complete with bionic eye!)? Get in touch with other pack rats, and see what your junk is worth. AOL's **Collector's Corner**, CompuServe's **Collectibles Forum** both host general discussions for those with a knack for the knickknack. And more specific collectors can settle into the forum of their choice, from Delphi's **Animation Gallery** to GEnie's **Stamp Collector's Round-Table**. Everyone knows the value of Grandpa's solid silver pocket watch, or the half-dollar with a missing mint imprint, but the real treasures are the unexpected ones—that complete set of Star Wars glasses, for in-

1901 stamp misprint—from America Online's Smithsonian Forum

stance. Polish them and let the force of collectibles be with you. You may be sitting on a gold mine.

On the Net

Across the board

Collectibles Forum Stamps, comics, coins, sports cards, telecards, books, autographs, dolls, diecast cars, pins, games, and political memorabilia are all lovingly anatomized here. People not yet bitten by the bug may want to check out the autograph library, which includes a GIF of Elvis's signature on his notarized will. ✓COMPUSERVE→*go* collectibles

Collectibles RoundTable Not much here for collectors of coins or stamps; the RoundTable is geared toward the smaller populations of the collectors' universe whose interests run to dolls, records, toys, delftware. With the real-time conference and the software library, you can buy, sell, and price collectibles. But be warned: When archaeologists from the 35th century excavate North

America, they'll spend weeks trying to make sense of the perfectly preserved Ken dolls scattered near your skeleton. The library archives databases for easy electronic pricing of toys, antiques, and baseball cards, along with a specialty newsletter on dollhouses and data management programs to keep track of all your collectibles. ✓GENIE→*keyword* collect

Collector's Archive Huge collection of buying guides, collectible images, and information about stamps, antiques, and coins. ✓INTERNET→*ftp* ftp.netcom.com→anonymous→<your email address>→/pub/collector

The Collector's Corner Trying to find the original LP of the Memphis album? Eager to unload the Tiffany-style lamp your grandmother left you? AOL's exchange offers a switchboard for information and coversation about all types of collectibles—not only coins, stamps, and baseball cards, but airplane models, antiques, books, comic books, toys, railroad cars, records. ✓AMERICA ONLINE→*keyword* exchange→Collector's Corner

rec.collecting (ng) Whether you're obsessing about missing the second character in the Disney crystal figurine series or you desperately need Franklin Roosevelt's autograph or you're interested in attending the next Barbie doll convention, this may be the place for you. Both serious and casual collectors post their requests. ✓USENET

Animation

Animation Gallery Are all your friends two-dimensional? Do you find yourself dreaming about wisecracking wabbits and mutant ninja turtles? The gallery offers a meeting place for animation collectors to discuss their obsession. Deals with cels and other collectibles associated with animation, right down to that Tasmanian Devil massager. ✓**DELPHI**→ *go* cus 316

Antiques

Antique Forum This forum, which addresses questions of antique trading and collecting, requires that online advertisements be identified as such. ✓**DELPHI**→*go* cus 297

rec.antiques (ng) Is that wood stove (substitute stove with coffee pot, egg beater, lamp, chair, dollhouse, painting, cash register, and any other item that might turn up while cleaning the cellar) an antique? Hundreds of people log in trying to determine if they've stumbled on a fortune, but the group is also home to antique buffs who discuss restoration, post about upcoming antique shows, and ask for help finding that elusive piece. ✓**USENET**

Cards

Gum Card Trading Post Baseball cards are big business, and as in business, values go up and down. What's a Gooden rookie card worth now that his image and talent have tarnished? How much will a Frank Thomas card set you back? And there's always O. J.—OK, maybe he never played baseball, but his the skyrocketing value of his memorabilia carries a valuable lesson about the amorality of fame. This forum handles all major sports trading cards, as well as non-sports cards, and includes a "Pit" for trade and auction lists. ✓**DELPHI**→*go* cus 340

rec.collecting.cards (ng)

There's big money (and a hefty dose of collector's pride) involved with sports cards. And, this newsgroup, with its nonstop card auction, is a great way to gauge just how much your collection is worth. ✓**USENET**

Coins

Coin Collecting Buried in the Stamps roundtable, this message board is a little slice of numismatic nirvana, a dizzying whirl of mint dates, errors, varieties. If you've never collected coins, consider it. The change might do you good. ✓**GENIE**→*keyword* stamps→Stamp Collecting Bulletin Board→Set Category→Coin Collecting

rec.collecting.coins (ng) Not as active as the other collecting newsgroups, but includes a fairly savvy membership—fluent in both domestic and international coins. ✓**USENET**

Jewelry

Jewelry Collecting Forum Break out your brooches, baubles, bracelets, rings, necklaces, cufflinks, earrings, and stickpins, and book passage for this forum, which addresses the collection of old jewelry, real and costume. ✓**DELPHI**→*go* cus 330

Pop culture

Data Base In Data Base ("The Eclectic Place!"), the order of the day is pop schlock elevated to collectible status by '60s, '70s, and even '80s nostalgia brokers. The forum is devoted largely to Star Trek material, but it also traffics in Christmas collectibles, Hot Wheels, Hello Kitty, Weebles, Lego, and all the other junk your parents urged you to throw out. Revenge is sweet, no? ✓**DELPHI**→*go* cus 159

Stamps

rec.collecting.stamps (ng) Russian stamps, baseball stamps, stamp catalogs, stamp trader lists, and Christmas seal questions fill the group. If your passion is stamp collecting, you'll find a knowledgeable group of collectors here. ✓**USENET**

Stamp Collectors RoundTable They say that flattery will get you nowhere, but philately is a different matter entirely. Stamp collecting is the most revered of the collecting arts, and stamp collectors have their own RoundTable. In this strange world, where cancellation doesn't refer to a bad sitcom or a magazine subscription, and a misprint is a godsend, stamp vets speak knowingly about foreigns, specialties, and topicals, and speculate on how stamp collecting is changing in the computer age. The libraries feature pricing guides for stamps and inventory managers to help you keep track of your collection. ✓**GENIE**→*keyword* stamps

> "In this strange world where cancellation doesn't refer to a bad sitcom or a subscription, and a misprint is a godsend, stamp vets confer in the Stamp Collectors RT."

Part 5

Careers

Starting the job search

Don't sit around waiting for the help-wanted section of the Sunday newspaper. The Net

has it all: electronic want ads, resume banks, and even career counseling services to help you on your way to job satisfaction (or at least job possession). Start off in one of the megaservices, such as **E-Span** or **Employment Opportunities and Resume Postings. Career Direction** and **Mind Garden**, both on eWorld, probe your psyche and then help you use that new-found self-awareness to land a job (be it in public service or cutthroat high finance).

Depression-era unemployment—downloaded from CompuServe's Archive Forum

Across the board

BBS Job Listings Good Net-Samaritan Harold Lemon has assembled a list of BBSs that proved useful to him in his own job search; he's noted which BBSs charge fees and which are mainly of local interest. ✓**INTERNET**→*www* http://www.review.com/

Career Center Quite a trip. You probably won't use all the resources here, but the center has that do-everything-in-the-comfort-of-your-own-home feeling that takes the edge off the anxiety-filled process of job searching. From job listings to resume advice to one-on-one private counseling, the center is packed with services, each of which is described in greater detail throughout this sec-

tion of the book. First-timers should start their investigation in the Career Guidance section. ✓**AMERICA ONLINE**→*keyword* career

Careers BB Some members are just seeking advice about life in the office; others are eagerly seeking work in every field imaginable (broadcasting, court reporting, farming). There's lots of electronic interviewing going on here, with prospective employees far outnumbering prospective employers (most of whom run computer-related businesses). And finally, there's plenty of professional networking. ✓**PRODIGY**→*jump* careers bb

E-Span One of the most complete and omnipresent job-search services in Cyberspace, E-Span features career advice, resume-building assistance, interviewing suggestions, and job listings. The heart of E-Span is its database of job listings, which can be searched

by occupation or location. Employers range from Sony to the state of Wisconsin; while job postings are voluminous, they favor the computer and financial industries. Listings remain on E-Span for up to four weeks and are updated weekly. Responses should be sent directly to the potential employer, although E-Span is happy to accept resumes for its online file bank. Note to AOL users: at present, the counseling portion of the service is not available. ✓**AMERICA ONLINE**→*keyword* jobs ✓**COMPUSERVE**→*go* espan ✓**GENIE**→*keyword* job ✓**INTERNET**→*www* http://www.espan.com/js/js.html *Register:* ✓**INTERNET**→resumes@ espan3.espan.com ✍ *Email resume for inclusion in database*

Employment Opportunities and Resume Postings This mega-index of job services provides links to several government job centers, the bionet Usenet groups (which are filled with help-wanted postings for the sciences), and personnel listings for many academic institutions. The *Occupations Outlook Handbook*, a very good source for career planning, can also be reached from this site. Overall, a good place to begin a job search. ✓**INTERNET**→*gopher* cwis.usc.edu→Other Gophers and Information Resources→Gopher Jewels→Personal Development and Recreation→Employment Opportunities and Resume Postings→Employment Opportunities and Resume Postings

Online Career Center This well-designed site is a not-for-profit cooperative that provides career counseling and a growing database with about 8,000 jobs and resumes. Job listings range from openings for trading-room support on Wall Street to emergency-room nurses in Ohio to marketing executives in Zurich. In addition to the large number of entry-level positions directed toward the Net-savvy college crowd, the OCC lists opportunities for experienced professionals. Participating employers include giants like AT&T, Bank of America, Eastman Kodak, Kraft, Unisys, and the CIA. Both job and resume files are searchable. The service also lists local employment job fairs. While the OCC charges nothing for resume listings, companies advertising jobs pay a one-time fee of $3,900 and subscription dues of $50 a year. ✓**INTERNET**→*gopher* garnet.msen.com→Online Career Center→Online Career Center

The Princeton Review WWW server Though it's known primarily as a college counseling service, the Princeton Review also offers career advice for recent grads. Called "How to Survive Without Your Parent's Money," this online

document leads former students through the initial motivational process, the inevitable procrastination that ensues, resumes, interviews, and even the alternating exhilaration and disappointment of the first job. Princeton's advice on internships and career changes is well presented. ✓**INTERNET**→*www* http://www.review.com/career/8000.html

Rice University Job Information So, you want to search for a job online, and you don't want to miss anything. Suggestion: don't miss Rice, which links to all the major online career databases, U.S. government job listings, relevant Usenet newsgroups, and many college and university job listings. ✓**INTERNET**→*gopher* riceinfo.rice.edu→Information by Subject Area→Jobs and Employment

Finding yourself

Career Analysis Service Just download the service's questionnaire, complete it, and email it back to the online career counselor, who will consider your answers in the context of 13,500 different jobs. Doctor? Lawyer? Indian chief? Butcher? Baker? Candlestick maker? Dishwasher? Freelance writer? Pharmaceutical representative? There is an additional charge of $39.95 for this service. ✓**AMERICA ONLINE**→*keyword* career →Career Guidance Services→Career Analysis Service **$**

Career Direction Just lost your job and need to regroup? Concerned that your career options aren't what they could be? The Lee Hecht Harrison career-consulting firm has prepared a series of self-awareness tests and a strategy guide to help you find a job by finding yourself. In the Personal Values and Mission survey, you'll

be asked to do a little soul-searching—What are the things you are passionate about? Do you believe that family is more important than work? The Career Options section helps you assess your skills and abilities; if you're in between jobs and financially insecure, the Transition Preparation guide proposes strategies for coping with the psychological and fiscal strain. ✓**EWORLD**→*go* lhh→Career Direction

Career Focus 2000 If you don't know what you want to do, this is the place to zero in on your options. This series of four downloadable workbooks helps you analyze your career leanings by matching your test results to the interests and skill requirements of 1,000 jobs, then helps guide you in your job search. ✓**AMERICA ONLINE**→*keyword* career→Career Guidance Services→Career Focus 2000

Job Hunting Get a job! And get one with this guide, which helps you plan your assault on companies and recruiters. From cover letters to follow-up calls, Lee Hecht Harrison explains it all, demystifying the career search. ✓**EWORLD**→*go* lhh→Job Hunting

Mind Garden: Personal & Career Understanding "Who am I? Why am I? Which am I? How am I?" Heady questions, certainly, but never fear: the answers are growing in the Mind Garden. Through a series of interactive online workbooks, various occupational professionals help you know yourself. Who are you? Well, you're someone of uniquely imbalanced aptitudes, and you need to "learn to change unwanted attitudes and behavior" by embarking on "a journey of self-discovery." Why are you? Clarify your values to steel yourself for tough life decisions. Career or family? More money or better hours? (Those without values of their own will be happy to learn that the Mind Garden furnishes "historical values.") Which are you? Decide by learning about popular personality classification systems such as the Meyers-Briggs type indicator, psychological temperament indicators, the Enneagram, and five factor codes. And finally, how are you? Anxious and fretful, and desperately in need of the Mind Garden's stress-beating strategies. ✓**EWORLD** →*go* mindgarden

Online Counseling Free consultation with a professional career counselor: just leave a message on the Appointment Book board to schedule your meeting. Another message board, Ask the Counselor, creates a public discussion area where both counselors and members offer advice on jobs and job hunting. And who are these counselors? Their profiles are available online. ✓**AMERICA ONLINE**→*keyword* career→Career Counseling Services

Advice columns

Dr. Job This weekly question-and-answer session with *Crain's* business journalist Sandra Pesman addresses everything from succeeding at a second career to keeping a job during the difficult process of sex-reassignment surgery. Past issues, archived online, contain a plethora of useful tips for job hunters. Do you know how to tailor your resume for computer keywords or how to dress for success on an interview? Ask Dr. Job. ✓**GENIE**→*keyword* dr.job

Counselors

JobPlace (ml) They write in from the career guidance offices of Smith, Skidmore, Syracuse, and other colleges and universities asking the list a host of questions: How to advise their students who are job searching, develop better career resources for their school, or get further training as a counselor? Even if you're not a guidance counselor, this list is still an interesting place to lurk and learn about job market do's and don'ts. Listen as one counselor asks if a student with a foreign sounding name should note his citizenship on a resume, as another questions how a full-time student and former homemaker who's been out of the workforce for 12 years should explain her hiatus on her resume, and as yet another wonders if resumes in Germany are handwritten? ✓**INTERNET**→*email* listserv@ukcc.uky.edu ✍ *Type in message body:* subscribe jobplace <your full name>

Employment agencies

The Employment Agency Databases Information on thousands of employment agencies and headhunters, primarily executive-search firms. The Custom Data-banks Database offers descriptions of thousands of search firms, while the Recruiters Plus Database lets the search firms create their own profiles. Search either database by locale, field, or job title. ✓**AMERICA ONLINE**→*keyword* career→Employment Agency Database

State Employment Offices (All States) A list of all 50 state employment offices, complete with mailing addresses and phone numbers. ✓**INTERNET**→*gopher* gopher.uoregon.edu→UO Colleges and Schools→School of Law→Law Career Services→Career Services Notices→State employment offices for all states (Large File!)

Networking contacts

Job Seeking (echo) In this conference, members involved or interested in particular professions post brief notes and queries which can be (and most often are) answered by others in the field. ✓**JOBNET**

Talent Bank You've probably heard it a hundred times: to find a job, you need to network. Believe it or not, that word hasn't always carried online connotations. In the Talent Bank, the fine art of meeting and greeting flourishes—each participant fills out a personal profile which is then filed in a searchable database. Want to find someone else interested in a career in desktop publishing? Curious how electrical engineers slightly older than yourself are faring in the job market? Just tinker with your search terms, make a match, and discuss your occupational hopes and fears. ✓**AMERICA ONLINE**→*keyword* career→Talent Bank

Products

Career Resource Library Tunnel into the stacks of the library for information about job resources not currently available on America Online. Intended to be a clearinghouse of catalogs and product announcements by those in the career-guidance business, the library is dominated by the products and services of JIST Works, Inc. ✓**AMERICA ONLINE**→*keyword* career→Career Resource Library

JobHunt v5 Complete job-search tool. Provides contact info, prints personalized letters, labels, and envelopes. Search companies by different criteria. ✓**PC OHIO**→ d→*Download a file:* JOBHUNT5.ZIP (DOS)

CYBERPOWER!™

Finding A Job

I worked as a radio engineer in northern Illinois until late last winter, when I was fired. At first, I thought I would bounce right back, but I've had a hard time finding work. I feel like my interview skills are rusty, and I have nightmares about rumpled suits and ink-stained resumes. How do I get my confidence back, and how do I get a job? I'll go anywhere.

Most career counseling and placement services recognize that unemployment wreaks psychological havoc in addition to its economic effects, and the best online services take pains to address various aspects of joblessness. Take E-SPAN's Interactive Employment Network, and particularly the Career Manager service (http://www.espan.com/js/js.html), which contains dozens of resources for the occupationally gun-shy.

You mention that you're afraid of ruining your chances by submitting a sloppy resume. Well, don't let that happen. Visit Joyce Lain Kennedy's Electronic Resume Writing Tips, and learn how to write the best resume you possibly can. Then enter E-SPAN's job library and see what might be waiting for you in the world of occupational opportunity. E-SPAN has sorted its jobs by both keyword and region, so if you get an endless list of available positions, you should narrow your search until the results are specific enough to digest. For radio engineers in the Midwest, the forecast is bright—we took the liberty of conducting a search for you, and turned up nearly a dozen jobs, from electronic packaging engineers in Nebraska to cellular telecommunications engineers in Ohio. If you want to develop radio test equipment and optimization techniques, you might want to think about the Ohio job, which includes extensive travel in the domestic United States. But the best bet is right in your backyard—Maxwell-Marcus is looking for a Senior RF systems engineer in the Chicago suburb of Hoffman

Estates, Illinois. "Work in the advanced cellular technology department. Applicants need MSEE and should be very experienced in theoretical modeling of radio systems and radio hardware architecture. Candidates are invited to send a resume." Senior RF systems engineer, Maxwell-Marcus...it has a nice ring to it, no?

If one of your brilliant resumes actually nets you an interview with the company, you'll almost certainly want to use E-SPAN's interview resources to prepare for your meeting. Study the practice questions and answers in the online version of "You're Hired!—The Ultimate Job Search Simulator," or order the entire simulator for $26.95. (This may be $26.95 more than you can afford so long as you are out of work, but it is probably a good investment.) Tell me about yourself. What are your major strengths? What are some of your biases or hangups? What is your idea of success? What have you learned from your failures? And are you continually invigorated by the world of radio engineering?

E-SPAN Home page

Finally, if your job hunt doesn't go as smoothly as you had hoped—say the man at Maxwell-Marcus didn't like your rumpled suit—spend some time with E-SPAN's support group, which addresses the difficulties of financial management, the tricky business of motivation, and even emergency "CPR for a Lifeless Job Search."

The job market

What do almost all workers have in common? A desperate need to understand the

changing job market. A good place to start is the **Department of Labor Occupational Outlook Handbook** which offers detailed profiles of thousands of careers. A wealth of statistics has been compiled and analyzed to project the hottest careers in the handbook's "Tomorrow's Jobs." The **US News College Fair Forum** on CompuServe and **Career Articles** on AOL also provide estimates on everything from salary to future job security. Bulletin boards and newsgroups like **Job Discuss**, **Careers Online**, and **misc.jobs.misc** offer dispatches from the working world: find out how others cope with discrimination, job loss, or an especially nasty boss.

Career Mosaic screen shot—from http://www.careermosaic.com/cm

On the Net

Across the board

Career Articles An archive of articles, with new additions each month, about assorted career topics. "Changing Careers: Why and When," "Jobs of the Future," and "Evaluating a Job Offer" are just a few of the titles on file. ✓**AMERICA ONLINE**→*keyword* career→Career Articles

---

Mercury News Employment Articles Part of AOL's extensive Mercury Center, this substantial database collects articles on occupational and employment-related issues from the *San Jose Mercury News.* ✓**AMERICA ONLINE**→*keyword* mercury→Employment→Browse Mercury News Employment Articles

---

US News College Fair Forum Now that you're finishing school, what are you going to do with your life? No, no—beyond the graduation night parties and summer-after-college romances. Stuck for an answer? Well, *U.S. News* has prepared a series of 1995 Career Guides for selected professions— medicine, law, manufacturing, finance, etc.—which provide education, salary, and employment stats, as well as prospects for growth. These files contain excerpts from the Department of Labor's *Occupational Outlook Handbook* (OOH), which detail the duties, earnings potential, and future of selected professions. Other useful portions of the *OOH*—especially

resume-writing tips and job-search contacts—are also available. CompuServants may also download the Federal Jobs database. ✓**COMPUSERVE**→*go* usncollege→Libraries→ Career

Job profiles

Department of Labor Occupational Outlook Handbook A huge, searchable repository of career information including job descriptions, job projections, and career advice. Do you want to be an economist? Actor? Professional fisherman? The *OOH* details education requirements, job conditions, day-to-day responsibilities, labor organizations, and earning potential for each job, along with employment projections that extend well into the next century.

Each job comes complete with a list of relevant professional organizations, unions, publications, etc., which are themselves often sources of job listings and career advice. A feature entitled "Tomorrow's Jobs" collects the Labor Department's educated guesses about work in the upcoming decades. (Health care? Up. Farming? Down. Big surprise.) In addition, the *OOH* includes a wealth of practical job-search information—tips on how to find job leads, craft a powerful resume, and turn an interview into a victory.

And finally, those seeking help in retraining or going back to school will find information on fellowships and public assistance programs. On AOL, the handbook is divided into a searchable database and a set of informative articles called the Occupational Profiles Database. ✓**INTERNET**→ *gopher* umslvma.umsl.edu→The Library→Government Information (US Federal & State Info & Docs)→ Occupational Outlook Handbooks ✓**AMERICA ONLINE**→*keyword* career →Occupational Profiles Database

Job talk

Careers (echo) Get your views on affirmative action off your chest. Exchange tips on career building. Find out the comparative benefits of an electrical engineering or computer science degree. Discussion swings from passionate to downright pragmatic. Most of the positions announced are computer-industry related. Watch out for get-rich-quick-through-your-PC schemes. ✓**ILINK**

Job Discuss (echo) Discussion is a little frantic, and job seekers and employers can't resist posting their ads, but the people here seem willing to help one another. In fact, they can barely restrain themselves—at the drop of a hat, they'll share tips for job-search strategies, offer advice about references, and plan out strategies for dodging the dreaded salary-requirement question. Just yell. ✓**FIDONET**

> **"As for mandatory drug testing. Domino's Pizza? Tests. Barnes & Noble? Doesn't test."**

misc.jobs.misc (ng) Don't post job offers or resumes here, unless they are well disguised as queries about the working world. This group is all talk and no action: speculating, analyzing, anguishing, along with a little networking. Discussions cover topics such as whether casual clothing is appropriate in the workplace, what personality types are best suited for specific jobs, and how the work ethic is faring inside Generation X. There's also some practical interchange—advice on legally relocating to Canada or finding the best headhunter. ✓**USENET**

Labor statistics

Bureau of Labor Statistics Database The massive public database of the Bureau of Labor Statistics—LABSTAT to cognoscenti—furnishes current and historical data from more than 20 statistical surveys that pertain to consumer health and employment. Employment projections by industry? Geographical profiles? Department store inventory price index? All available. ✓**INTERNET**→*gopher* stats.bls.gov

Lifestyle profiles

Career Mosaic "Who's doing the cool work these days?" asks this site's home page. The answer?

Computer science majors. Sponsored by an advertising agency, the service is geared toward college students and provides information about hot companies and lifestyles around the world. To date, Career Mosaic has only a dozen sponsor companies, and although no jobs are posted here, the service allows searches of the ba.jobs.offered newsgroup and contains a library full of useful information, including a sample interactive resume and information on the top 50 job markets in the U.S. ✓**INTERNET**→ *www* http://www.careermosaic. com/cm

Rights & assistance

Careers On-Line A service for disabled workers. Find out about your rights and your employer's obligations. Job listings are also available here. ✓**INTERNET**→ *www* http://disserv.stu.umn.edu:80 /cl

Catalogue of Federal Domestic Assistance Find out what government assistance you are entitled to for a job search or retraining. This is not a listing of jobs available in the federal government (see FEDJOBS), but it is a listing of federal job programs. Displaced homemakers, senior citizens, victims of industrial migration—you may be eligible! ✓**INTERNET**→*gopher* gopher.rtd.utk.edu→ Federal Government Information→ Catalogue of Federal Domestic Assistance→Jobs

Piss List A list of companies with mandatory drug testing—often referred to by the euphemism "human quality test programs"—as well as those that have policies against testing. Domino's Pizza? Tests. Barnes & Noble. Doesn't test. ✓**INTERNET**→*www* http://raf-ferty.com/~piss/

Jobs by state

Are there really more paid holidays in the state of Washington than anywhere else in

the nation? What about Hawaii's great health plan? Or Wisconsin's day care? Check out the local jobs venues for the answers. Many of these groups are still dominated by the computer industry, but some of the larger markets, especially California, Texas, Washington, D.C., and North Carolina, have evolved into more generalized boards. Wisconsin, New York, and North Carolina have their state government jobs online, and **George Washington University's Computerized Job Listing Service** lists civil service placements in the D.C. area. Take note, some groups are for posting resumes only or posting jobs only! Traffic on these local boards can vary widely.

On the Net

Across the board

Job Fairs (echo) Listings of job fairs from Georgia to Maryland. These are not just the biggies: the fair held at the high school at the end of your street may be listed. ✓ **JOBNET**

Alabama

hsv.jobs (ng) Announcements for employment positions in the

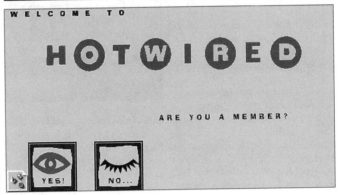

Hotwired—http://www.wired.com/

Huntsville area. ✓ **USENET**

Atlanta

atl.resumes (ng) Resumes of job seekers in the Atlanta area. ✓ **USENET**

California

ba.jobs.contract (ng) Announcements of freelance and temporary work in northern California. ✓ **USENET**

ba.jobs.misc/ba.jobs.offered (ng) Proximity to Silicon Valley makes the Bay Area groups among the largest job posting services online (both averaging 800+ postings). Post resumes and opportunities in ba.jobs.misc and look for work in ba.jobs.offered. While enamored of silicon and microcircuitry, these groups also list banking, advertising, and publishing positions. ✓ **USENET**

la.jobs (ng) Positions announced and sought in the greater Los Angeles area. ✓ **USENET**

Mercury Center Employment Classifieds Pick a job, any job. From accounting to receptionist to writer, a steady stream of job openings flows into the pages of the *San Jose Mercury News* and onto the screens of AOL's Mercury Center. If you're job hunting in the Bay Area, take a look here. Once you've searched the Help Wanted ads electronically, you may never have the patience to wade through them offline again. The bulk of the listings are in the By Job section. ✓ **AMERICA ONLINE** →*keyword* mercury→Employment

sdnet.jobs (ng) Announcements for jobs in San Diego. ✓ **USENET**

WIRED Magazine Help wanted ads for positions at the hot print magazine and its electronic counterpart, *HotWIRED*. The site also lists job announcements from other companies in and out of California. ✓ **INTERNET** → *www* http://www.wired.com→<your user name>→<your password>→Coin icon→Classifieds

Florida

fl.jobs (ng) Tap into the Florida job market with postings from both employers and job seekers. ✓**USENET**

Georgia

atl.jobs (ng) Job annoucements for the Atlanta area. ✓**USENET**

Illinois

chi.jobs (ng) Position announcements and resumes related to the Chicago job market. ✓**USENET**

Chicago Tribune—Help Wanted Probably the most extensive listing of Chicago-area jobs is printed in the *Chicago Tribune*, and you can browse or search a full week of the newspaper's classifieds (including Sunday) on AOL. Career services, job fairs, school guides, and both part- and full-time jobs are advertised here. To place an ad, you must voice call the *Trib* at 312-222-2222. ✓**AMERICA ONLINE**→*keyword* tribune→Help Wanted

Indiana

in.jobs (ng) Job announcements for the Hoosier state. ✓**USENET**

Michigan

Detroit Service Center (bbs) Looking for a job in Detroit? (No, they're not all in the auto industry.) Try the federal government's Detroit Service Center bulletin board, which carries information about living in the greater Detroit area and job posts. ☎→*dial* 312-226-4423

mi.jobs/mi.wanted (ng) Job announcements and resumes from job seekers in Michigan. Very ac-

> **"Everything's bigger in Texas. Hats, cars, boats, and job newsgroups."**

tive. ✓**USENET**

Milwaukee

milw.jobs (ng) Jobs and job seekers in Milwaukee. ✓**USENET**

Missouri

stl.jobs (ng) Jobs in the St. Louis area. ✓**USENET**

New England

ne.jobs (ng) The Route 28 computer boom is still fueling ne.jobs to the tune of 1,500 listings at any time. Job questers post their resumes and potential employers extend offers for both contract and permanent work. ✓**USENET**

New Mexico

nm.jobs (ng) Search for work in Albequerque, Santa Fe, and outlying areas. ✓**USENET**

New York

li.jobs (ng) Positions available in the Long Island area. ✓**USENET**

Michael Wolff & Company, Inc. Manhattan-based print and electronic publisher is always hiring full-time and freelance editors, writers, and techies. Editors and writers should have extensive experience with the Net and knowledge of Net culture as well as a journalism background. Work involves research, writing, and editing of consumer-oriented books,

magazines, and online content. Technical positions include system administrators, programmers experienced in building UNIX-based software systems, technical support staff (experience with UNIX and SLIP/PPP implementation on Mac and Windows platforms), and support personnel for Macintosh DTP network. Long hours, hard work, and sometimes lots of fun. ✓**INTERNET** ...→*email* positions@ypn.com ...→*www* http://www.ypn.com

ny.wanted (ng) Amid the offers of plane tickets and rooms for rent, you'll find scattered job offers across New York state. ✓**USENET**

North Carolina

North Carolina Job Openings Job openings at North Carolina Univesity, Duke Medical Center, the University of North Carolina—Chapel Hill, and the North Carolina Office of State. The universities include both faculty and nonfaculty positions. ✓**INTERNET**→*gopher* tfnet.ils.unc.edu→Business→Job openings

Tech Transfer News - Job Openings The major high-tech companies in the North Carolina Research Triangle place job postings here. Systems managers and programmers are very much at a premium. ✓**INTERNET**→*www* http://iridium.nttc.edu/jobs.html

triangle.jobs (ng) North Carolina's Research Triangle computer industry dominates this newsgroup with a large number of job offerings. ✓**USENET**

Ohio

cmh.jobs (ng) Job announcements for the Columbus area. ✓**USENET**

Oregon

pdaxs.jobs* (ng) An impressive number of separate newsgroups for Oregon job announcements, by career type (e.g., clerical, engineering, domestic, construction, retail). ✓**USENET**

Tennessee

memphis.jobs (ng) If Beale Street could talk, it might say some of the same things as this newsgroup, which combines positions sought and jobs offered in the Memphis metropolitan area. ✓**USENET**

Texas

dfw.jobs (ng) A very active newsgroup with job announcements for the Dallas–Fort Worth area. ✓**USENET**

houston.jobs.offered (ng) Positions available in the Houston area. ✓**USENET**

houston.jobs.wanted (ng) Posts from people interested in working in the Houston area. ✓**USENET**

Job Trac BBS (bbs) Featuring more than just job listings for the Dallas–Fort Worth area, the BBS also has career forums and a resume upload system. ☎→*dial* 214-349-0527

Texas Listings of employment opportunities at Texas A&M and the University of Texas at Austin, two large employers with a broad spectrum of jobs available. ✓**INTERNET**→*www* http://ageninfo.tamu.edu/jobs.html#texas

tx.jobs (ng) Everything's bigger in Texas. Hats, cars, boats, and job newsgroups. Focusing on Dallas, Houston, and Austin, this newsgroup lists a multitude of positions for video game programmers, computer and technical writers, aspiring sales reps, and a wide range of other industry types. Be aware that a number of postings here originate with job-search firms, and not the businesses themselves. ✓**USENET**

Washington

seattle.jobs.offered Job announcements for the Seattle area. ✓**USENET**

seattle.jobs.wanted (ng) Job seekers in Seattle describe skills. ✓**USENET**

Washington, D.C.

Computerized Job Listing Service - George Washington University School of Business The George Washington University School of Business's database provides a comprehensive list of opportunities in everything from conducting dental hygiene research to typing Defense Department memos. It collects federal, National Science Foundation, National Institute of Health, and university jobs in the greater D.C. area. The database can be searched by field. ☎→*dial* 202-785-1523 ✓**INTERNET**→ *gopher* gwis.circ.gwu.edu→Academic Departments→ School of Business and Public Management→Computerized Job Listings

dc.jobs (ng) The bartender who posted his job quest on dc.jobs knew he stood out from the crowd. Why? Well, for one thing, this newsgroup is heavy on computer industry jobs, including related ideas like rent-a-nerd for Net troubleshooting. For more general D.C.-area jobs check out FED-JOBS or the George Washington University School of Business employment service. ✓**USENET**

Wisconsin

University of Wisconsin, Madison (State Civil Service Listings) The great Midwestern state that brought you Summerfest and the Cheese Castle now brings you comprehensive occupational listings. Along with North Carolina and New York, Wisconsin has publicized all its state government job vacancies on the Net. This well-organized gopher has a well-organized FAQ, a weekly bulletin updating job listings, and a database that can be searched by location or job type. ✓**INTERNET**→*gopher* gopher. adp.wisc.edu→Employment, Financial Aid, Scholarships and Grants→Employment→ State of Wisconsin Classified Civil Service Listings

> "The bartender who posted his job quest on dc.jobs knew he stood out from the crowd. Why? Well, for one thing, this newsgroup is heavy on computer industry jobs, including related ideas like rent-a-nerd for Net troubleshooting."

Jobs across the U.S.

Cast a wide Net. Misc.jobs.offered and biz.jobs.offered are heavy on computer industry

listings. Classifieds on AOL and CompuServe tend to be less heavily computer-dominated, but watch out for overtly commercial "make a million bucks at home" come-ons. If you want the buyer to come to you, post your resume on **misc.jobs. resumes** or **Resumes-Misc** on JobNet. **Misc.jobs.entry** and **RSI Resume/Job Information** cut down on wasted time, limiting their listings to entry-level positions. Recent college grads should check here first. Don't want to be tied down to a 9–5 existence? **Misc. jobs.contract** and **Contractor's Exchange** primarily serve the burgeoning computer contract sector, but they also provide very useful information about working for oneself. **Adia** temporary services on eWorld will even let you order a temp online.

Monster Board home page—http: //www.monster.com/b/search

On the Net

Across the board

biz.jobs.offered (ng) The biz here is overwhelmingly computer-related, although execs and publishing professionals have also made a home for themselves. The conference jargon may take some time to pick up, but this is a serious group of people offering positions from Ottawa to Wall Street. ✓ **USENET**

Career Link, Inc. (bbs) A far-ranging selection of jobs in the U.S. and abroad. There is a fee for this BBS. ☎ →*dial* 602-841-2134 **$**

Classified—MultiList (echo) Agencies and companies with multiple job openings post on this conference. Kelly Services, a national temp agency, even advertises its job opportunities here. ✓ **JOB-NET**

D.I.C.E. National Network (bbs) This California-based BBS has a good selection of contract and permanent jobs, mostly within the computer industry. ☎ →*dial* 408-737-9339

Employment Opportunities/Available for Work In addition to the usual spate of computer jobs, Delphi's huge classifieds section features opportunities of surprising variety. Here people are looking for party planners in New York City and staff for cruise ships in the Mediterranean. This eclecticism carries over into the less-populated Available for Work section, where bookkeepers and toolmakers sell their skills next to contract programmers. ✓ **DELPHI**→ go bus for clas→Employment Opportunities *or* Available for Work

Employment/Education Classifieds with more ads in the "positions wanted" category than the "positions offered." This area also has its share of unbelievable "make millions" claims. The exception, as usual, is the computer-related jobs category. ✓ **COMPUSERVE**→go classifieds→Employment/Education

Help Wanted USA Large California hospital seeks transplant specialists. Small Wisconsin company seeks accountants. Brooklyn school department seeks teacher to work with AIDS children. This database claims up to 4,000+ job listings each week, collected by private consultants nationwide, and while there aren't always jobs listed in Arkansas (sorry, Bill), larger states are usually well represented. Broader in appeal than the job newsgroups, this database offers a good selection of computer-related jobs, along with large numbers of medical, social service, and business positions. Search the database by specific terms (obstetrics RN) or by general terms (sales and marketing). Updated every Wednesday. √**AMERICA ONLINE**→ *keyword* help wanted

InfoMat BBS (bbs) Collects employment echoes from JobNet, Laran Communications, RelayNet, and Intelec, providing easy access to national job classified conferences. No fee is required to use the service. ☎→*dial* 714-841-8728

The Job Board Jobs, mainly computer related—and mostly in the odd trio of Canada, Saudi Arabia, and Connecticut—are posted here. Run by a professional recruiter, this service collects resumes and cover letters and then reports back with yeas or nays. √**INTERNET**→*www* http://www.io.org/~jwsmith/jobs.html

Job Finders The creators of the site have done more than organize resume databases and collect a massive number of job-related links; they've annotated them to assist in narrowing your search. Job Finders is also the best gateway to information on colleges and universities here in the U.S. and throughout the world. √**INTERNET**→*www* http://infonext.nrl.navy.mil/job.html

Job Listings from Around the Globe—University of Texas Access to a wide range of jobs, including those listed on hundreds of university computers, in the

federal jobs database, and in other major career databases. There's also a regional component to the database, with government job listings for North Carolina and Wisconsin. √**INTERNET**→*gopher* bongo.cc.utexas.edu→Information About Gopher→World→Jobs

Job Offers (echo) Announcements about opportunities to teach English in Korea or to work as a programmer or analyst almost anywhere else. The group is active and large. √**FIDONET**

Job Opportunities 1 (Academia) Another gateway to the major employment services and large academic and government jobs databases. For instance, link to listings from major employers like Oak Ridge National Laboratory, the Library of Congress, and Integrated Computer Solutions. Lots of avenues here for eager job seekers. √**INTERNET**→*www* http://agen info.tamu.edu/jobs.html

Job Opportunities 2 If you want to work in the government or in higher education, stop by here. This University of California-based job page has access to the federal government jobs database at Dartmouth and the Academic Position Network and Chronicle of Higher Education listings. √**INTERNET**→*gopher* sdacs.ucsd.edu→Reference Shelf→Job Opportunities

JOBBS! (bbs) Send your resume to sysop Bill Griffin and he'll add it to his database of 30,000+ candidates. The system also provides information on employers, companies, applicants, and career lifestyles. ☎→*dial* 404-992-8937 $

JOBS-BBS (bbs) Nationwide jobs for all professional categories. This

is the home of the JOBS-NOW echo, a mammoth job listing conference that is updated three to four times each day. ☎→*dial* 503-281-6808

misc.jobs.offered (ng) Are 5,000 opportunities enough for you? There is frequent discussion on the Net about splitting this unwieldy newsgroup because of its volume. But if you're seeking a job in the computer industry, misc.jobs.offered provides the most bang for the buck, assuming you can make your way through the long listings. Large corporations and start-up firms post their needs here for systems managers, programmers, and analysts. Outside the computer industry, pickings are slimmer—lots of opportunities, of course, to become a millionaire through telemarketing. √**USENET**

Monster Board Two offers here: T-shirts with monsters on them and jobs. If you're more interested in the jobs, check out the searchable database. The majority of the 300+ jobs listed are in high-tech and biotech industries in the Northeast. √**INTERNET**→*www* http://www.monster.com/b/search

Online Classifieds Although there are topics for Help Wanted, Positions Wanted, and Career Services, the listings are mostly for junk jobs. Earn millions stuffing envelopes at home! Explore the wonderful world of exotic dancing! Offbeat career opportunities are common here: a Bay Area man seeks "treasure hunter and psychic" for a rewarding quest. The Career Services topic is filled with people advertising employment-oriented products or services. √**PRODIGY**→*jump* classifieds→Read/Place Ads→Browse Ads→Help Wanted *or* Positions Wanted *or* Career Services

On-Line Job Services From this single Web page you can access job-related web sites, gophers, newsgroups, and lists of BBSs. ✓ **INTERNET**→*www* http://rescomp. stanford.edu/jobs_html

Professional Salaried Jobs Along with the dozens and dozens of computer-related job listings, there are others: actors under 5'8"; flight attendants; bilingual Vietnamese/English victim assistance counselors. To check out the jobs, read the Professional Employment Offered board. If you want to advertise your skills, post on the Professional Employment Sought board. The last of the three boards in the classified section, Professional Job-Hunting Help, is filled with offers of free advice available by email. ✓ **AMERICA ONLINE**→*keyword* classifieds→Business & Jobs Postings→Professional Salaried Jobs

Talk about Jobs Job announcements (called Job Leads on this board) and resumes dominate, although career advice is also sought and offered. Companies frequent the board to look for the likes of CPAs, graphic artists, architects, and (of course) computer professionals. ✓ **EWORLD**→*go* lhh→Talk about Jobs

Job seekers

misc.jobs.resumes (ng) More than 3,000 people have posted their occupational profiles on this newsgroup. The trick to success is undoubtedly making yourself stand out among all the other programmers and engineers. "Willing to relocate," "Japanese bilingual," or "MARKETING" catch the eye. There is a great variety of job skills here—from aquaculturists and actuaries, to wireless tech engineers

> "No Mickey Mouse organization, Disney employs more than just artists and smiling youths in costumes singing 'It's a Small World.' Email your resume and wish upon a star. "

and semiconductor specialists. Potential employers respond privately. ✓ **USENET**

Resumes—Misc (echo) This collection of resumes is truly eclectic. The earnest efforts of a credit manager and hairdresser are followed by a programmer who would like to move to Norway or Sweden "to see what it's like." ✓ **JOBNET**

Corporate giants

Microsoft Corporation Bill Gates needs someplace to put those billions of dollars. How does your pocket sound? This page lists employment opportunities in all areas of the Microsoft Corporation. ✓ **INTERNET**→*www* http:// www.microsoft.com/pages/misc/ jobops/default.html

Walt Disney Productions No Mickey Mouse organization, Disney employs more than just artists and smiling youths in costumes singing "It's a Small World." They also run one of Hollywood's biggest studios. So, email your re-

sume and wish upon a star. ✓ **INTERNET**→*email* resumes@disney.com

Entry level

Chinese Community Information Center On the face of it, the Chinese Community Information Center may seem an unlikely place to job hunt. However, it houses the Academic Exchange Information Center News Release, a weekly collection of jobs in biology, computer science, math, medicine, and even philosophy. A good hunting ground for recent graduates. ✓ **INTERNET**→*gopher* ifcss.org→job→cal pak *or* federal

misc.jobs.entry (ng) Every year the colleges flush out a new crop of eager youngsters to flood the job market. Misc.jobs.entry attempts to introduce inexperienced, yet knowledgeable, people to jobs. There are jobs available and jobs sought, and while most are computer-industry oriented, the newsgroup's name has attracted everything from textile manufacturers to Club Med. ✓ **USENET**

RSI Resume/Job Information This resume and job database serves college seniors and recent graduates interested in jobs in computing, mathematics, and education. History grads from the Naval Academy and PoliSci wonks from Harvard post their skills here along with computer science majors. The resumes are categorized by field of interest and available for investigation by interested employers. Several companies also post job openings: PBS's Math Line, Xerox, and the NASA Classroom of the Future are featured. Sponsored by Admiral Rickover's Center for Excellence in Education. ✓ **INTERNET**→*www* http:// rsi.cee.org/jobs.html

JOBNET

Search BBS 206-253-5213	**ECCO*BBS** 415-331-7227	**Dobbs Enterprises** 707-427-0277
The Career Network 213-629-1472	**The Job Search Board** 416-588-9690	**Chicago Syslink** 708-795-4442
The Digital X-Connect BBS 214-517-8315	**The Realm Infoservices** 502-254-7036	**InfoMat BBS** 714-492-8727
Job Trac BBS 214-349-0527	**JOBS-BBS** 503-281-6808	**AVADS-BBS** 800-368-3321
The Lunatic Fringe BBS 214-235-5288	**Techlink BBS** 503-297-0117	**Planet Reisa BBS** 801-596-7350
Online Opportunities 215-873-7170	**Accurate Services** 508-829-7294	**Condell Online** 803-686-3465
OPM FEDJOBS 215-580-2216	**Careers On-Line** 508-879-4700	**Falcon's Crest BBS** 804-737-1625
Census Personnel Board 301-763-4574	**Bust Out BBS** 510-888-1443	**The Resume File** 805-581-6210
The Control Room 307-789-7121	**hi-TEC BBS** 512-475-4893	**A to Z Classifieds** 813-726-8088
Detroit Service Center 313-226-4423	**Turning Point** 512-219-7848	**The BizBoard** 813-532-4473
The Brainwave System 314-434-9814	**Silicon Garden** 516-736-6662	**J-Connection** 813-791-0101
San Jose Connection 408-956-8819	**Poindexter Online** 609-486-1983	**The Looney Tunes BBS** 814-825-3304
Career Systems 413-592-9208	**The Second Stage** 610-397-1638	**DP Careers** 817-268-2193
National Technical Search 413-549-8136	**Employment Board** 619-689-1348	**Impact Employment BBS** 818-879-7405
Exec-PC BBS 414-789-4210	**J-Connection** 703-379-0553	**Jobbs 'n Stuff** 818-999-0928
Career Connections 415-903-5815	**Society For Tech. Comm.** 703-522-3299	**FJOB BBS** 912-757-3100
DP NETwork 415-788-7101	**Computer Careers** 704-554-1102	**Access America** 918-747-2542

Professional careers

Accountants should rush to JobNet's AcctFin; bosses should try ProfMgmt, and those

that really run the company will find opportunities in **ClerAdm** and **HumResor**. Lawyers can get the public service experience that looks good on a Supreme Court resume through **Attorney Job Listings: U.S. Department of Justice**. The creatives can find opportunities and advice for making wit, words, and a good eye pay in **Journalism Forum**, **Techwr-L**, the **Broadcast Professional's Forum**, and the **Photo Professional's Forum**. Whatever your occupational ambitions, the jobs are here.

On the Net

Accountants

Classified - AcctFin (echo) Sometimes, companies outside of the computer industry look for accounting help online. Recent posts to this JobNet category came from the University of Florida, a bank in Maryland, an insurance firm in California, in addition to hundreds of computer companies. ✓**JOBNET**

Attorneys

Attorney Job Listings: U.S. Department of Justice The Department of Justice posts announcements online about several hundred job openings, organized

Simpson attorneys Cochran & Shapiro—from CompuServe's Reuters News Forum.

by state and territory (Alabama to Puerto Rico) and by specialty (immigration review, criminal division, civil rights, narcotics and drugs, environment and natural resources). If you're one of the many J.D.'s currently hunting a job, this site is certainly worth a visit. ✓**INTERNET**→*gopher* justice2.us-doj.gov →Justice Department Attorney Job Listings

Legal Forum Attorneys wanted to draw up wills, sue the State Department, and process a divorce. Firms across the country are seeking J.D.'s—maritime lawyers in Boston, commercial bankruptcy experts in Arkansas. Whether you're a New York ADA looking for civil rights work or an environmental rights attorney desperate to sell out to a huge Beantown firm, try your luck. ✓**COMPUSERVE**→*go* lawsig→Messages *or* Libraries→ Attorney Wanted

Broadcasters

Broadcast Professionals Fo-

rum It takes a lot of people to put a television or radio show on the air—engineers, producers, salespeople, and even on-air "personalities." If you're a broadcast professional, post your resume in the Resumes/Jobs/Class library and read the Classifieds/Jobs message board. See you on the air. ✓**COMPUSERVE** ...→*go* bpforum→Libraries →Resumes/Jobs/Class. ...→*go* bpforum→Messages→Classifieds/Jobs

Economists

Job Openings for Economists The American Economic Association states that its members have "a professional obligation" to list their job openings here—and they obey. Each month, there are nearly a hundred openings in academia, government (State Dept., Federal Reserve, Veterans Affairs), private research, and the corporate world. Search by area or specialty or just browse. ✓**INTERNET**→*gopher* vuinfo. vanderbilt.edu→Employment Opportunities→Job Openings for Economists (JOE)

Executives

Classified - ProfMgmt (echo) Employers who advertise here are looking for upper management personnel. The Bank of America seeks a managing director, a recruiting firm hopes to find a partner, a satellite operation wants a technical director. Climb that ladder of success. ✓**JOBNET**

Resumes-ProfMmgt (echo) There is really only one way that executives and senior management personnel get new jobs: they network. But most of them aren't doing it on the Net, at least not yet. Those who are, however, have this JobNet conference available to them. ✓ **JOBNET**

Health care

Academic Physician and Scientist The two journals sponsor this voluminous listing, which primarily offers adminstrative, research, and teaching positions in colleges and hospitals. FDA positions are also listed here. ✓ **INTERNET**→*gopher* aps.acad-phy-sci.com

Classified - Medical (echo) More pharmaceutical companies tend to advertise here than hospitals, so expect to find more positions for medical researchers than GPs. ✓ **JOBNET**

Medsearch This large database of job notices is free to employers and prospective employees in the health care industry. In addition to its database of job postings and resumes, Medsearch offers career advice, including tips on interviewing, networking, and evaluating a job offer. The future of the health care industry is also explored in a series of articles archived at the site. ✓ **INTERNET**→*www* http://www.medsearch.com:4001

MEDSIG Forum Physicians talk about consulting partnerships and health-care reform. Medical students gather to exchange war stories. But on the Students/Employment library and message board, the bulk of traffic is related to finding a job. Health policy advisor wanted in Gorno-Badakhshan, Tajikistan. Clinical preventive medicine specialist seeking career opportunities in the western U.S. ✓ **COMPUSERVE**→*go* medsig→Libraries *or* Messages→Students/Employment

> **"Even the C.I.A. advertises for clerical and administrative help on ClerAdm. (You will, however, be required to take a polygraph.)"**

Human resources

Classified - HumResor (echo) Recruiters and personnel experts look here for job opportunities. ✓ **JOBNET**

Marketing & admin

Classified - ClerAdm (echo) Even the C.I.A. advertises for clerical and administrative help here. (You will, however, be required to take a polygraph.) ✓ **JOBNET**

Classified - Marketing (echo) The computer industry is searching for marketing specialists to peddle their products, and one of the places they're looking is on this conference. ✓ **JOBNET**

PR & Marketing Forum Product evangelist? There are firms crying out for your services. Talk to other sales and marketing specialists about strategies, sales figures, and selling in Cyberspace. The PRL: Jobs Online board has postings from employers seeking ad writers, high-tech marketers, and research analysts. In the PRL: Jobs Online library, PR professionals post their resumes. ✓ **COMPUSERVE** →*go* prsig→Libraries *or* Messages→PRL: Jobs Online

Resumes-ClerAdm (echo) Sales and marketing professionals, bookkeepers, and administrative assistants from around the country post their resumes. ✓ **JOBNET**

Photographers

Photo Professionals Forum Career profiles (or resumes) of photographers from around the world, with specialties ranging from digital imagery to Australian wildlife. ✓ **COMPUSERVE**→*go* propho-to→Libraries→Pro Classifieds

Writers

bit.listserv.techwr-l (ml/ng) Members on this no-nonsense list discuss resume writing, new software, word usage, and job hunting. ✓ **USENET** ✓ **INTERNET**→*email* listserv@vm1.ucc.okstate.edu ✍ *Type in message body:* subscribe techwr-l <your full name>

Classified - TechWrit (echo) Are you a medical writer familiar with "Class 3 implantable devices"? Technical writing is an extremely specialized field, but there's no shortage of need. Many of the job listings on this conference are for writers interested in tackling online software help and computer manuals. ✓ **JOBNET**

Journalism Forum Both the libraries and bulletin boards of this forum have a Jobs/Stringers section. Want to be a copyeditor in Hong Kong? How about reading news copy at a Texas TV station? This is a truly international meeting place: French reporters seek German correspondents, and a stringer in Morocco asks for technical assistance from his British friends. ✓ **COMPUSERVE**→*go* jforum→Libraries *or* Messages→Jobs/Stringers

Government jobs

You've complained about it all your life—the unwieldy, overstaffed government bureau-

cracy, but it never goes away. So if you can't beat 'em, join 'em. The really great thing about having government in all aspects of our lives is that the job opportunities are correspondingly diverse. If you drive heavy machinery, program computers, teach French, know a lot about spawning fish or messing up foreign policy, you can find a federal job anywhere in this great nation. **FedJobs**, **OPM Mainstreet**, and **Fed-World** all contain essentially the same thousands of job listings, updated daily. (Public dispersal of job information is mandated by law.) Also available at these sites is help in negotiating the sometimes time-consuming and confusing federal job application process. Specific agencies, the Library of Congress, Department of Agriculture, and Department of Interior maintain their own jobs boards—all opportunities will also be in the general listings. For the generous, and adventurous, souls who would like to give something back, **VISTA-L** and **bit.org.peace-corps** offer information about their work programs.

Postal worker—downloaded from America Online's Smithsonian Forum.

On the Net

Across the board

Federal Employment Service No actual job listings, but lots of information on the types of employment opportunities in government, the relevant educational requirements, and the way to contact your government personnel office. ✓**AMERICA ONLINE**→*keyword* career→Federal Employment Service

FEDJOBS (ml) Keeps you up-to-date with weekly additions to the nationwide federal jobs listings. ✓**INTERNET**→*email* listserv@dart cms1.dartmouth.edu ✍ *Type in message body:* subscribe fedjobs <your full name>

FEDWORLD—the U.S. Government Bulletin Board (bbs) This board is run by the National Technical Information Service and provides information on jobs openings (item J) as well as gateways to other government services and agencies. General outlines and mission statements for each agency are also included. ☎→*dial* 703-321-8020 ✓**INTERNET**→*telnet* fedworld.doc.gov

Job Openings in the Federal Government This is the best place online to look for U.S. government jobs. Organized by agency and by major metropolitan areas (including civilian jobs at

> "'Job Openings in the Federal Government' is the best place to look. Organized by agency and by metropolitan area, the thousands of jobs advertised here are accompanied by descriptions and instructions on how to apply."

military bases in Europe and Asia), the thousands of jobs advertised here are accompanied by brief descriptions and instructions on how to apply. This mammoth site also provides very useful information for the uninitiated on federal pay scales, veteran and disability benefits, and how to fill out the notorious SF-171 federal job application. ☎→*dial* 912-757-3100 ✓**INTERNET** ...→*gopher* dartcms1.dartmouth.edu→Job Openings in the Federal Government→...→*telnet* fjob.mail.opm.gov

OPM Mainstreet (bbs) OPM (Office of Personnel Management) Mainstreet was designed to serve the needs of federal employees, but access is free to all. Helpful information on the government job application process accompanies job listings from the Federal Job Information Centers. ☎→*dial* 202-606-4800

By agency

AVBADS-BBS (DOI) (bbs) Since the Department of the Interior oversees the outdoors—including the National Park Service, the Bureau of Land Management, and the U.S. Fish and Wildlife Service—is there a Department of the Exterior responsible for regulating track lighting and wallpaper? Not yet. But that's neither here nor there, and what is here is the on-line job listings of the DOI, hundreds of positions in archaeology, forestry, and engineering. ☎→*dial* 800-368-3221

CITE Job Bank Archive Your background is in communications, you want to work for the government, and the agricultural department sounds exciting. What are you waiting for? The Job Banks newsletter from the Communication, Information, and Technolo-

gy Staff Extension Services at the U.S. Department of Agricultural is online and archived. ✓**INTERNET**→ *gopher* esusda.gov→USDA and Other Federal Agency Information→Job Openings in the Federal Gov't (from OPM listings)

Library of Congress The Library of Congress does not just hire librarians; it sponsors research programs, runs a publishing company, and is responsible for keeping the nation's library state-of-the-art—which means that it offers professional opportunities in everything from public relations to computer catalog design. Look here for listings. ✓**INTERNET**→*gopher* marvel.loc.gov→Employee Information→Employment Opportunities, Pay and Benefits

Volunteerism

bit.org.peace-corps (ng) "Ask not what your country can do for you, but what you can do for your country." And so it began. Almost three decades later, Peace Corps representatives are on the Net rousing support for one of the most well-known volunteer organizations in the world. Along with the official presence, former and current volunteers share personal anecdotes, and the discussion doesn't whitewash the Corps—there's plenty of criticism. ✓**USENET**

VISTA-L (ml) Do you have a desire to help others instead of earning scads of cash as soon as you graduate? VISTA may help you make your ideals real. Access information about this public service organization through the bimonthly newsletter posted on the gopher site and published on the mailing list, or turn to the newsletter for contact information on nationwide projects. ✓**INTERNET** ...→*email* listserv@american.edu ✍

Type in message body: subscribe vista-l <your full name> ...→*www* gopher://gopher.hanover.edu/11/ Hanover_College_Information/ Career_Planning_and_Placement/ jobs/vista

---

CYBERNOTES

"My perspective on US foreign policy slowly changed during the six years I worked in Zaire. One day at the airport, I saw long, long lines of Angolan refugees waiting to get onto US sponsored planes to fly back to their side of the Civil War--years of bloodshed propped up by US financial and military support.

"But for every negative thing there are dozens of marvelous anecdotes... Floating down the Zaire River atop an old boat, sipping a cold brew with the headmaster from your village, listening to the sultry music drifting up from the bar below, watching the people in the dug-out canoes trying to latch onto the big boat, hearing hunters haggling the price of antelope with the market mamas, getting sleepy under the swollen moon, looking out over the endless forest."

—from **bit.org.peace-corps**

High tech & engineering

The modern working world has been taken over by geeks and nerds. If you are a com-

puter industry professional or high-tech researcher, the problem isn't finding a job on the Net, it's paring down the thousands upon thousands of possibilities! Thank God, most jobs services have sophisticated search engines to narrow the field down. Just graduated? Quite a few high-tech firms are scouting for young, sizzling (and cheap) talent on **HEART**. Dreaming of joining the crumbling empire? IBM puts its openings on **Supernet International**.

On the Net

Across the board

ACM SIGMOD's Database Job Listings Computer science and engineering professionals will find a long list of international jobs in the technology industry and in academic research. ✓**INTERNET**→*www* http://bunny.cs.uiuc. edu/jobs

Autodesk Forum The specialized partnership between technical drafting and computer science is the focus of this forum, and job hunters flock to the Take 5/Want Ads message board and library. Be warned: you may have to wade through general shop talk and equipment classifieds. ✓**COMPUSERVE**→*go* acad→Libraries *or* Messages→Take 5/Want Ads

Hoover Dam—downloaded from CompuServe's Go Graphics Forum.

Classified - DPSoftw (echo) Caters to the computer systems crowd, where supply never seems to oustrip demand. ✓**JOBNET**

Computer Careers (bbs) Free service for nationwide computer industry positions. ☎→*dial* 704-554-1102

HEART About twenty large, high-tech companies post job openings on this site, which can be searched by company, locale, or discipline. Favoring job seekers with computing, science, law, or business backgrounds, the site also has a "new grad" feature where those looking for their first break can post a resume. Job listings remain online until they are filled. HEART describes itself as an "on-line interactive recruitment network" and it's free; all that's required is that you register before beginning a job search.✓**INTERNET**→*telnet* career.com

Jobs Listing at Computing Research Association (CRA) Computer-science job listings from a consortium of U.S. and Canadian universities and govern-

ment agencies. ✓**INTERNET**→*ftp* cra.org→anonymous→<your email address>→/pubs/jobs

National Information on Software Service (NISS) You can search this index of computer science jobs in the United Kingdom and the Commonwealth countries—a hefty number. ✓**INTERNET**→*telnet* niss.ac.uk

Supernet International IBM and the other industry biggies use this service to find qualified technical staff. Job announcements are posted on the site and in HPCWIRE—the magazine which is published as an electronic journal. If you would like more details on the jobs offered, email the three-digit job reference number to the "more" email address. To get a trial subscription to the journal, send your email request to the "trial" address. To subscribe regularly, email your request to the "sub" address. ✓**INTERNET**...→*telnet* supernet.ans.net→HPCWIRE...→ *email* more@ hpcwire.ans.net ✍ *Type in subject line:* <three digit job reference number>...→*email* tri al@hpcwire.ans. net ✍ *Write a request*...→*email* sub@hpcwire. ans.net *Write a request*

Research centers

Classified - CivilEng If it has been your lifelong goal to "decommission radioactive facilities," you have reached the right conference. All sorts of opportunities in civil engineering are posted. ✓**JOBNET**

Integrated Computer Solutions, Cambridge, MA From

High Tech & Engineering Careers

salesmen to system managers, this Boston-area computer company posts its job openings online, updating when positions are filled. ✓**INTERNET**→*www* http://www.ics.com/Jobs.html

IPC Technologies An in-house job listing for this Richmond-based high-tech company, with about 10–20 select professional openings at any given time. ✓**INTERNET**→*www* http://www.ipctech.com/~jobs/joblist.html

Lawrence Berkeley National Laboratory (LBNL) All is not geothermal reservoir engineering at this prominent laboratory focusing on energy sciences. The laboratory updates its administrative, clerical, scientific, engineering, and crafts positions weekly. The Website also offers transit information. ✓**INTERNET** ...→*www* http://www.lbl.gov/LBL-Work/LBL-Workplace.html ...→*gopher* gopher.llnl.gov→Employment Opportunities

Massachusetts Institute of Technology (MIT) Jobs and Volunteer Opportunities In addition to being the premier scientific education institution in the country, MIT also runs a publishing company and hospital system. Include reference number when responding to job advertisements. ✓**INTERNET**→*www* http://www-penninfo.upenn.edu:1962/tiserve.mit.edu/9000/25751.html

National Center for Atmospheric Research Newsletter A weekly newsletter of openings at the National Center for Atmospheric Research in Colorado. ✓**INTERNET** ...→*email* majordomo@ucar.edu ✍ *Type in message body:* subscribe ucarline <your full name> ...→*gopher* info.ucar.edu→NCAR/UCAR News and Information→Employment Information

Oak Ridge National Laboratory The laboratory is always hiring, and qualified personnel in science and computer fields are eagerly sought. The site also provides information about the lab's locale and the continuing-education perks offered by the lab. ✓**INTERNET**→*www* http://www.ornl.gov/employment.html

Optolink Employment Service Job listings organized by educational level required. There is also a separate listings area for consultants seeking employment. ☎→*dial* 206-733-2998→ optolink→guest→ Employment ✓**INTERNET** ...→*www* http://www.spie.org/web/employment/employ_home.html ...→*ftp* spie.org→optolink→guest ...→*telnet* spie.org→optolink→guest→Employment

Society for Technical Communication (bbs) Access to job listings is free to members of the Society for Technical Communication. ☎→*dial* 703-522-3299

United Technologies Research Center Based in Hartford, Connecticut, this high-tech R&D center often has professional position openings, which are detailed at this site. ✓**INTERNET**→*www* http://utrcwww.utc.com/UTRC/Jobs/Jobs.html

Engineering

Biomedical Engineering Vacancies in R&D in the growing biomedical technology industry. ✓**INTERNET**→*www* gopher://niblick.ecn.purdue.edu/11/jobs

Classified - ChemEng (echo) This classified listing of chemical engineering opportunities includes everything from a forensic pathologist in Seattle to a molecular biology specialist for a Colorado phar-

maceutical company. ✓**JOBNET**

Classified - ElecEng (echo) Plug into opportunities in the electrical engineering field—there are plenty of jobs for semiconductor experts and cellular switch engineers at some of the biggest outfits in the nation. ✓**JOBNET**

Classified - MechEng (echo) If Benjamin Braddock were graduating today, he'd still be advised to look into plastics. If you're after jobs involving injection-molding systems, or any other aspect of mechanical engineering, check out these job listings. ✓**JOBNET**

Classified - MiscEng (echo) Companies are looking here for process engineers, refinery engineers, structural engineers, and all other manner of engineers, save those who work the railroads. ✓**JOBNET**

Classified - TechEng (echo) Classified ads announcing technical engineers positions around the country. ✓**JOBNET**

Engineering Automation Forum This is an engineering employment grab bag. "Airbag plastics engineer" looks for work by posting a resume in the Classifieds/Jobs library. Companies seek "embedded programmers" and specialists in yacht and ship design. ✓**COMPUSERVE**→*go* leap

ENGINET Technical professionals share resources and job contacts. Comes complete with an online Technical Resume Database and links to engineering newsgroups. ☎→*dial* 513-858-2688

Resumes-TechEng (echo) Engineers of all stripes post their resumes here. ✓**JOBNET**

Jobs in the sciences

There is a universe of career opportunities for all manner of scientists on the Net.

Sci.research.careers covers job openings from all fields. The **Young Scientists Network** offers pointers for inquiring minds just starting out on the cutting edge, while those who look into worlds beyond can find job postings from the **American Astronomical Society**. The career opportunities carried by the **American Physiological Society** tend toward academic and research positions, and **AIPJOBS** serves those who know how velocity, time, and gravity come together to make the world go round, offering a wide variety of physics-related positions.

On the Net

Across the board

sci.research.careers (ng) Positions in scientific research. The group also carries posts from job seekers. ✓ **USENET**

YSN (ml) The Young Scientists Network runs this list for young scientists to discuss employment and career issues. ✓ **INTERNET**→ *email* ysnadm@crow-t-robot.stanford.edu ✉ *Write a request*

Astronomers

Jobs—Astronomy Related Even the relatively small world of

Boris Karloff, Mad Scientist—from CompuServe's Archive Forum.

stargazing has a significant number of openings to post. Like many research institutions, large observatories also need support and technical staff. ✓ **INTERNET** → *www* http://www-astro.physics.ix.ac.uk/jobs.html

Astronomy

American Astronomical Society The online version of the society's Job Register lists dozens of new astronomy jobs and postdoctoral fellowships each month. ✓ **INTERNET**→ *www* http://blackhole.aas.org/JobRegister/aasjobs.html

Biologists

American Physiological Society The University of Texas hosts the American Physiological Society's job listings. There are academic and research positions for biologists and postdocs. Recent listing: an opportunity to study "space biology" with the Space Shuttle team. ✓ **INTERNET**→ *gopher* oac.hsc.uth.tme.edu:3300→Employment Opportunities

Biology and Ecology Jobs Both private industry and academia post biology-related positions here. Biological planners are wanted by cities, ecologists by foreign governments, and animal behavior specialists by universities. If you are in the life sciences, this is a great place to start looking. ✓ **INTERNET** ...→ *gopher* atlantic.evsc.virginia.edu→Opportunities→ESA_jobs ...→ *email* listserv@umdd.umd.edu ✉ *Type in message body:* get JOBS JOB_LST

bionet.jobs, bionet.jobs.wanted Molecular plant nematology, genetic engineering, or oceanography—these and other science-related jobs are the domain of the bionet groups. Professionals from academia and the growing bio-tech industry meet here to offer or seek positions. For students, the bionet groups also include valuable internship notices and scholarship information. ✓ **BIONET** ✓ **INTERNET**→ *gopher* net.bio.net→employment *or* employment wanted

Physicists

AIPJOBS PINET and the American Institute of Physics Career Planning and Placement Division maintain this resume and job posting service. Updated monthly, private industry and academic institutions use this venue to look for candidates and list their openings. There are positions in practical engineering, computer science, etc. Once you've registered with AIPJOBS, the service is free. ✓ **INTERNET**→ *telnet* pinet.aip.org→aipjobs→aipjobs

Positions in academia

Oh, the ivy-cloaked halls, the musty libraries brimming with knowledge, the free exchange

of ideas, the low salaries... Wait, there are lots of opportunities in that enclave of higher education and not all require years of study, student loans the size of the national debt, or tweed blazers—everything from clerical help to high-tech medical research to copyediting. To accesses this bounty of employment, link up with your local university's job centers through **Colleges and Universities Job Menu**. If, somehow, you actually are an academic, the **Academic Positions Network** and the **Chronicle of Higher Education**'s online listings are indispensable.

On the Net

Across the board

Academic Positions Network The Academic Position Network is organized by location rather than by subject, and includes many listings from non-U.S. universities, especially in Latin America. ✓**INTERNET**→*gopher* cwis.usc.edu→Other Gophers and Information Resources→Gopher Jewels→Personal Development and Recreation→Employment Opportunities and Resume Postings→Academic Positions

Chronicle of higher Education - Academe This Week, also found as **Job Openings in**

Harvard logo—from http://golgi. harvard.edu/harvard.html

Academe Essential for anyone seeking a job in academic teaching, research, or administration. The jobs are listed by field, location, and institution. Also notes opportunities in foundations, museums, and research institutions for both humanists and scientists. ✓**INTERNET**→*www* http://chronicle. merit.edu/.ads/.links.html

College & Universities Job Menu Professors are not the only ones employed by colleges and universities. Opportunities range from food-preparation specialists to high-tech researchers to accountants to administrative assistants. And let's not forget that many universities run major hospital centers and have their own publishing operations. Search for jobs at schools in your area—or wherever you'd like to live. ✓**INTERNET**→*www* http://ageninfo.tamu.edu/jobs.html #universities

By discipline

American Mathematical Society Postings for opportunities in

the math departments at universities—no private industry listings. ✓**INTERNET**→*gopher* e-math.ams. org→Professional Information for Mathematicians→Professional Opportunities for Mathematicians

American Philosophical Association Bulletin Board This bulletin board, sponsored by the Center of American Academic Philosophy, not only includes a professional newsletter and bibliography, but also lists grants, fellowships, and employment opportunities in philosophy. *Reine Vernunft!* ✓**INTERNET**→*telnet* atl.cal-state.edu→apa

College & Research Libraries - job postings by job title Some of the first Net aficionados were librarians, and there are presently hundreds of mailing lists devoted to librarian interests that also serve as informal job grapevines. But, if you're looking for a clearinghouse of opportunities in both public and private institutions for archival management or high-tech research, you should explore these listings. ✓**INTERNET**→*gopher* uicvm. uic.edu→The Library→College & Research Libraries NewsNet→Job postings by job title

History Jobs Historians can enter the computer age with this monthly compendium of job openings around the nation. Most positions are in academia, with the occasional listing for a position at a museum or research institute. ✓**INTERNET**→*gopher* ukanaix.cc. ukans.edu→hnsource→H-Net_ news→Jobs

Working overseas

Are distant shores calling to you? Foreign recruiters, corporations, and entrepreneurs

utilize **ICEN-L**, the **Tri-State University Gopher**, and JobNet's **International Classifieds** to seek scientists, programmers, bankers, and English teachers. Find postings from Saudi Arabia to New Zealand. The **Indiana University Network** and **ICEN-L** also provide valuable information about the legal issues of working abroad. Jobs newsgroups have sprung up to talk about opportunities all over the world, from Russia (**rel-com.commerce.jobs**) to South Africa (**za.ads.jobs**) to Canada (**can.jobs, tor.jobs**). Some postings are made only in the country's native language (a sure gauge as to whether you are qualified for the postion is if you can read the job description). Most groups, like the popular UK Professionals Forum, also provide discussion of the state of the British job market. We hear there's an opening for Princess of Wales.

Saudi Arabia Oil Well—from http://snake2.cr.usgs.gov/overview.html

On the Net

Across the board

Classified - Int'l (echo) Want to get out of town? A telecommunications company needs an expert for its China base. And if you are an agronomist under 30—and who isn't?—there may be a job waiting for you in Japan. International jobs, not all of which require foreign languages. ✓**JOBNET**

ICEN-L (ml) Sponsored by Indiana's International Career Employment Network, the list is for those interested in working abroad. Up-to-the-minute job postings and information about headhunters and recruitment fairs specializing in international placement are announced regularly. Professionals with experience working overseas are usually available to answer questions and share tips. ✓**INTERNET**→*email* listserv@iubvm.ucs.indiana.edu ✍ *Type in message body:* subscribe icen-l <your full name>

Tri-State University Gopher This gopher provides several services for finding a job or investment opportunities outside the United States. A bulletin periodically posts job offerings for the adventurous (banking in South Korea, accounting in Indonesia, data analysis in Budapest). Advice in gaining jobs in foreign climates is provided by employers and headhunters, and entrepreneurs use this service to seek U.S. partners and suppliers for such diverse projects as open-heart surgery in Japan and frozen food in Mexico. ✓**INTERNET**→*gopher* gumby.tristate.edu→Job Searches

Australia

aus.ads.jobs (ng) Job announcements or resumes for positions in the Australian market. ✓**USENET**

Canada

ab.jobs (ng) Job announcements or resumes for the Alberta area. ✓**USENET**

can.jobs (ng) Can.jobs has several types of postings—job opportunities in Canada, notices from Canadians seeking employment, and general questions and answers. Recruiters and job seekers actively discuss interview etiquette: is it wrong to wear per-

> "If you are an agronomist under 30—and who isn't?—there may be a job waiting for you in Japan."

fume or cologne to an interview? Many Canadian companies use this group to recruit fellow citizens for job opportunities abroad. ✓**USENET**

kw.jobs (ng) Job postings for Kitchener-Waterloo, Canada. ✓**USENET**

ont.jobs (ng) Announcements for jobs in Quebec. ✓**USENET**

tor.jobs (ng) Positions announced for the Toronto area. ✓**USENET**

Chile

chile.trabajos (ng) Job announcements for positions in Chile. ✓**USENET**

Denmark

dk.jobs (ng) Employment opportunities in Denmark. ✓**USENET**

Germany

bln.jobs (ng) Ads for jobs in Berlin or surrounding areas. ✓**USENET**

de.markt.jobs (ng) Job announcements for positions in Germany or for German speakers. ✓**USENET**

de.markt.jobs.d (ng) Discuss the job announcements in de.market.jobs or introduce yourself as a job seeker. ✓**USENET**

Israel

il.jobs.misc An Israeli newsgroup established for discussing careers. ✓**USENET**

il.jobs.offered (ng) Job announcements for positions in Israel. Also, for job announcements

with various American Jewish organizations. ✓**USENET**

il.jobs.resumes (ng) Resumes of those interested in working in Israel or advertising their skills to the U.S. Jewish community. ✓**USENET**

New Zealand

Jobs Online New Zealand No jokes about sheep farmers, please: this service offers online position and resume listings for New Zealand. ✓**INTERNET**→*www* gopher://central.co.nz/11/Jobs%20 Online%20New%20Zealand

Russia

relcom.commerce.jobs (ng) Look for employment opportunities in Russian-speaking communities in Canada and U.S., and the former Soviet republics. Most postings are in Russian, with the exception of the Russian-English translator seeking work. ✓**USENET**

South Africa

za.ads.jobs (ng) Resumes and job announcements for the South African market. ✓**USENET**

Sweden

swnet.jobs (ng) Announcements for positions available in Sweden and those seeking positions in Sweden. ✓**USENET**

United Kingdom

uk.jobs.d, uk.jobs.offered, uk.jobs.wanted (ng) Read uk.jobs.offered for computer-related and biotech opportunities, or sell yourself (professionally speaking) on uk.jobs.wanted. The newsgroup uk.jobs.d provides interesting discussion of the E.C.

and its effect on the European job market. ✓**USENET**

UK Professionals Forum Health care, police, and law are the most popular professional categories in this very busy forum. Here bobbies give each other moral support, barristers exchange research, and other professionals chat about their work. In the United Kingdom, resumes are called CVs (curricula vitae—it's Latin), and there are quite a number of them in the Job Opportunities library. ✓**COMPUSERVE**→*go* ukprof→Libraries *or* Messages →Job Opportunities

---

CYBERNOTES

"I have a PhD, but am about to start applying for jobs in a field where not only a PhD is not required, but will undoubtedly be a handicap. There is little doubt in my mind that any perspective employers seeing 'PhD' on my CV will undoubtedly write me off as a boffin, hopelessly over-qualified for the job, out of touch with the real world, etc. My point is: what are the ethics and legalities involved if I simply leave this information off my applications and CV? Why should anyone ever know about it? Does it matter?"

—from **CompuServe's UK Professionals Forum**

Writing a resume

If all they're going to see of you is a single sheet of bond paper or a few hundred lines

of ASCII, your resume had better shine. JobNet's **Resume Writing**, AOL's **Resume Templates** and eWorld's **Write a Better Resume** help job seekers prepare a standout, action verb-packed document. After the resume hurdle is overcome the dreaded interview looms. eWorld's **Interviewing and Negotiating** has loads of helpful tips on making a great impression. Before even sending a resume or attempting an interview, savvy job seekers know to carefully research their target company, a task made easier by **Hoover's Handbook.** AOL's **Employment Contacts** lets you know who the movers and shakers are, and how to reach them.

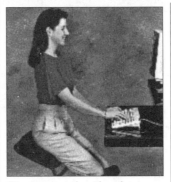

Woman typing—http://branch.com: 1080/jdi/jdi.html

On the Net

Across the board

Career and Job Hunting Software Using software packages to help you through the job hunt isn't cheating. It's showing that you're resourceful and open to new technology. And there are plenty of technological resources in this software library. *Resume 1.0* is available to help customize cover letters and resumes; and *Job Hunter 1.0* keeps an electronic log

of job contacts made. Then there are programs that simulate interviews, test your job skills, and schedule your interviews. There are also those files that are just as helpful as software: a list of action verbs to punch up a lackluster resume effort, sample cover letters, and even thank-you notes. ✓**AMERICA ONLINE**→*keyword* pfsoftware→ Free Software Libraries→Career and Job Hunting

Cover letters

Cover Letter Library You're finally ready to sell yourself. Inquiry letters, application letters, follow-up letters, interview confirmation letters, job acceptance (and rejection) letters, and thank-you letters are all part of the process. If you need help deciding the right format or what to say, browse these sample missives. ✓**AMERICA ONLINE**→*keyword* career→Cover Letter Library

Resumes

Career Resumes Guaranteed to

get you an interview in 30 days or they will rewrite it for free. Priced from $150 to $350, depending on length and complexity. ✓**INTERNET**→*www* http://branch.com: 1080/cr/cr.html

OnePage Easy-to-use resume creator. ✓**PC OHIO**→d→*Download a file:* ONEPAGE.ZIP DOS

PC Personal Resume Kit v1.2 Allows you to build an electronic resume, complete with digitized image of yourself. ✓**PC OHIO**→ d→*Download a file:* RESKIT 12.ZIP

> **"So you have the suit, three copies of your resume, and recently brushed teeth— what more do you need? 'Traps to Avoid' makes sure you don't come off as too ignorant or too obnoxious, and 'Interview Skills' touts the values of active listening."**

Resume Templates Will you use the functional, chronological, or targeted resume? Samples of each are available in separate folders along with explanations of resume-writing services and a large library of resumes. And the library is not just for resume ideas: it's one more place to advertise your own job search. ✓ **AMERICA ONLINE**→*keyword* career→Resume Templates

Resume Writing (echo) Resumes are not posted here to get jobs, but to get feedback. Several samples are included, and people are very willing to critique your effort or to share the approach that has worked for them. ✓ **JOBNET**

Write a Better Resume The Resume Quiz tests your assumptions about what employers want to learn from that sheet of paper. You may be surprised. In addition to instructions on writing a resume, sample resumes and a collection of action words are available. The "Ten Common Myths and Mistakes" section puts to rest common misconceptions that undermine an otherwise good resume. For example—the one-page rule is out, and get rid of ellipses and bullets. ✓ **EWORLD**→*go* lhh→ Write a Better Resume

Research

Employer Contacts Database It's resume time and you need addresses and fax numbers. This database lists the ticker tags, CEOs, CFOs, phone and fax numbers, and addresses of the 6,000 companies on the New York and American Stock Exchanges and NASDAQ. ✓ **AMERICA ON- LINE**→*keyword* career→Employer Contacts Database

Hoover's Handbook Profiles So you've sent out cover letters

and patiently waited. Now Company X wants to see you on Thursday, and the Y Corporation has Friday morning free. How are you going to keep all these prospective employers straight? Try these profiles, which are an excellent source of basic company information from histories to profits to personnel. Hoover's Handbook can be searched by name, industry, and geographical location. ✓ **AMERICA ONLINE**→*keyword* company ✓ **COMPUSERVE**→*go* hoover ✓ **EWORLD**→*go* hoovers

Interviewing

Interviewing (echo) Those who do the hiring are willing to answer the questions of nervous job seekers in this forum. Recent threads have asserted that while bringing crib notes is fine, taking notes is even better. And conference members never tire of discussing (and debating) what personal information employers can legally ask interviewees. ✓ **JOBNET**

Interviewing and Negotiating So you have the suit, three copies of your resume, and recently brushed teeth—what more do you need? A lot. You can never be too prepared for an interview, and the Lee Hecht Harrison's career-consulting firm provides several guides and checklists to help job seekers land the job. "How to Interview the Interviewer" offers advice on getting the most information about a position during the interview. "Traps to Avoid" makes sure you don't come off as too ignorant or too obnoxious, and "Interview Skills" touts the values of active listening. The sections on negotiating a job offer help successful candidates get what they need and want out of the new position. ✓ **EWORLD**→*go* lhh→Interviewing and Negotiating

You're Hired! v1.32 Job interview simulator gives professional advice on job hunting. Can add, change, or print questions and advice. Shareware. ✓ **PC OHIO**→d→ *Download a file:* YH132.ZIP DOS

CYBERNOTES

Common Resume Myths

Myth: Personal information will make me appear more 'well rounded.'
Reality: Personal data such as age, marital status, number of children, and health is not appropriate for the resume. Use it only if there is some good reason to add it to your resume, i.e. a hobby that contains skills relevant to the job.

Myth: Resumes should detail every job equally.
Reality: Devote more space to recent jobs than you do earlier ones because employers are generally interested in most recent experience."

Myth: Resumes should tell the exact truth -- good or bad.
Reality: Only information that will benefit you as a job candidate should be on the resume.

—from **eWorld's Job Search With Lee Hecht Harrison**

The workplace

Work takes up so much of our lives, we need to talk about it. The Net offers multiple

opportunities to analyze, complain, and, well, unite. AOL's **Careers Board**, GEnie's **Workplace RoundTable,** and AOL's **Professional Organizations** are prime sites for networking and information gathering whatever your calling. **Careers and Workplace** holds the answers to many pressing employment questions in its large library. Separate forums provide a place to compare notes and pass on trade secrets. Architects convene in **Architronic**, aviators discuss safety and downsizing in the **Aviation Special Interest Group**, cops and firemen trade true war stories on **Safetynet,** and writers exchange survival strategies in GEnie's **Writer's Ink RoundTable**. The **Medical** and **Law** bulletin boards on GEnie offer the newest thinking in everything from thoracic surgery to Cyberspace and the law.

On the Net

Across the board

Careers and Workplace How do you train for the foreign service? What are your career options at the zoo? What laws govern child labor? And, can an employer re-

Downtown Los Angeles—from AOL's Pictures of the World Forum

quire you to take a lie detector test? If there's a publication with the answers, the Information USA database has the address or contact information for it. Covering career and job training, employee benefits and rights, federal employment opportunities, occupational health and safety, and research grants, with addresses for almost any career-related question or opportunity. ✓**COMPUSERVE**→*go* lesko→Careers and Workplace

Careers Board Informal and chatty jobs message board. ✓**AMERICA ONLINE**→*keyword* exchange→ Home/Health/Careers→ Careers Board

EmployFair (echo) Advice on fairness in employment issues is freely proffered here, along with warnings about the many employment scams in Cyberspace: "make thousands at home," "guaranteed green card." ✓**JOBNET**

Professional Organizations Whether you are a nurse practitioner, a family therapist, or a hair

stylist, you're faced with a specific set of occupational concerns, and who better to understand them than others in your field. This message board sets up folders so that you can speak with others in your chosen profession. ✓**AMERICA ONLINE**→*keyword* exchange→ Home /Health/Careers→Professional Organizations

Workplace RoundTable The broad coverage of work-related topics on this bulletin board distinguishes it from the majority of job-related discussion groups on the Net. Most members are already employed or are employers. Subjects are wide-ranging: the changing workplace, where the jobs are and how to get them, peer-to-peer network, and having fun in the workplace. Most preoccupying topic is how to keep jobs threatened by downsizing or restructuring. Board members give a lot of weight to personal experi-

> "In the Workplace RoundTable, employers freely give advice on what they like to see in a resume and how to make a good impression on interviewers."

ence: there are more than one hundred messages describing personal tales of success and failure. Employers freely give advice on what they like to see in a resume and how to make a good impression on interviewers. Employers frequently debate management issues. The other career-related RoundTables on GEnie (law, medical, writers, law enforcement, aviation) also offer personal job-seeking advice and a few job postings. ✓ **GENIE**→ *keyword* workplace→ Workplace Bulletin Board

Architects

Architronic An electronic newsletter for architects who are interested in the effects of technology on the profession. Includes articles on new advances in the discipline, why buildings fall down, roadside treasures, and the widening rift between civil engineers and architects. ✓ **INTERNET**→ *www* gopher://dewey.lib.ncsu.edu/11 /library/stacks/arch

Aviators

Aviation Special Interest Group Forum Real pilots appear to find jokes about being asleep at the controls funny; at least those who meet on this busy forum do. In the Training & Careers topic, pilots look for old friends, trade anecdotes, and network. Although there are no jobs posted here, pilots do point their cohorts toward job listings and suggest companies who might be hiring. ✓ **COM-PUSERVE**→ *go* avsig→Libraries *or* Messages→Training & Careers

Consultants

Classified - Contract (echo) The contract classified section of JobNet is very busy—offering $50/hour opportunities to com-

"How do you train for the foreign service? What are your career options at the zoo? What laws govern child labor? And, can an employer require you to take a lie detector test? If there's a publication with the answers, the Information USA database has the address or contact information for it."

puter consultants nationwide, as well as other contract opportunities. ✓ **JOBNET**

Computer Consultant's Forum An incredible resource for computer consultants, this forum has message boards filled with advice and libraries stuffed with software and sample documents related to proposal writing, client issues, contracts, fair compensation, and liability. And, beyond the business issues, there are discussions about the work itself: computer connectivity, minicomputers and mainframes, and software. ✓ **COM-PUSERVE**→ *go* consult

Consultant's Corner Computer consultancy is a burgeoning business and a complicated one at that. How do you set a price schedule? What are your competitors offering? When do you advertise, and do you do it online? Consultants share advice with each other about both the business and tech aspects of the work. ✓ **GE-NIE**→ *keyword* hosb→HOSB Round-Table Bulletin Board→13 The Consultant's Corner

Contractors Exchange (bbs) Serving the ever growing needs of computer companies for contractors, this BBS has a large number of listings from the Silicon Valley area. ☎→ *dial* 415-334-7393

misc.jobs.contract (ng) The volume of postings to misc. jobs.contract (often around 3,000 posts every few weeks) shows that at least in the computer industry, contract employment is rapidly expanding. In addition to posting job opportunities, this newsgroup provides a forum for discussion of how to get the most out of a contract, finding good benefits packages, and general issues related to contract employees. ✓ **USENET**

Copy editors

Copyediting-L (ml) Professional copy editors discuss the trade, career opportunities, and the nuances of copyediting. (What do you think about a comma preceding the "and" before the final entry of a series?) ✓ **INTERNET**→ *email* listserv@cornell.edu ✍ *Type in message body:* subscribe copyediting-l <your full name>

Freelance & temp

Adia Temporary World at Work This online temporary employment agency not only offers advice to potential temps and employers, it also hires people and fulfills company personnel needs. For those interested in being a temp, there is information on skill requirements and pay scales nationwide. For managers, there are suggestions on hiring and dealing with agencies. Adia has offices in states across the country. Search their directory. If there's an office near you, then you can order a temp online or sign up for work. Simply fill out a brief application. ✓**EWORLD**→*go* adia

Health care

Medical Center Some people never get tired of talking about their work. Physicians, psychiatrists, psychologists, nurses, and paraprofessionals meet here to exchange ideas, discuss research and technological advances, and just talk about the business of health care. Nurses unite in category 10, Nurse Werks, to discuss patient care and doctors' attitudes. The private Doctor's Forum (category 4) allows physicians to network without nettling questions from the general public about nasty rashes. Paraprofessionals discuss career training and advancement in category 14. ✓**GENIE**→*keyword* medical →Medical Bulletin Board

Law

Law RoundTable If you're entranced by the glamour of *L.A. Law*, the majesty of the Supreme Court, or America's never abating supply of celebrity lawsuits, you may want to drop into the Becoming a Lawyer category to receive advice about the rigors and rewards of law school. In need of a new career? Explore the paralegal field in category 4. The real networking hub of this bulletin board, the Professional's Category

(category 20), is private, but once admitted, lawyers can aid each other in job searches, career advancement, or with specific cases. ✓**GENIE**→*keyword* law→Law Bulletin Board→Professional's

Law enforcement

A Law Enforcement Round-Table (ALERT) Cops, firemen, EMTs, correctional officers, and detectives are not just the stars of prime-time "true story" television. They're also online talking about the challenges of their chosen careers. If you're a law enforcement professional, stop by to find out how others deal with department politics and public opinion, swap critiques of new protective gear, and debate gun control. Women breaking into these formerly male-dominated fields will find strategies for survival and advancement; union representatives are online to answer questions about benefits and rights. ✓**GENIE**→*keyword* alert→ A.L.E.R.T. Bulletin Board

---

Safetynet Safetynet is a gathering spot for enforcement, security, fire, and rescue professionals. There are weekly deconstructions of *Rescue 911* and *Cops*, but more time is spent discussing the newest safety products, most effective training courses, and office politics. (Official requirements for the FBI Academy are also available.) ✓**COMPUSERVE**→*go* safetynet

Museum workers

bit.listserv.museum-l (ml/ng) Carries museum exhibition notices, education suggestions from professionals, and internship and job announcements for museum positions. ✓**USENET** ✓**INTERNET**→ *email* listserv@unmvma.edu ✐ *Type in message body:* subscribe museum-l <your full name>

Writers

Writers' Ink RoundTable What if Edgar Allan Poe had been able to sell his work during his lifetime? Maybe he would have succeeded with the help of the writing community on GEnie. Profit from the stories of writers who've moved from starving artists to published, well-fed professionals. In Speaking of Fiction (category 2), the services of professional editors are bought and sold. The American Society of Journalists and Authors has a category for research-assistance want ads (category 24). Writer's Information Exchange (category 4) provides tips on getting the best agent and carries tons of help wanted postings. The Working Writers section (category 28) is private, but once you're admitted, there are detailed discussions of taxes, the writing market, and selling your work. Even poets discuss making a living with their versification in category 3, topic 4—Market Discussion. ✓**GENIE**→ *keyword* writers→Writer's Bulletin Board

> **"The private Doctor's Forum on GEnie's Medical Center allows physicians to network without nettling questions from the general public about nasty rashes."**

Women & minorities

Everybody works. Women gather to exchange strategies for dealing with sexual harass-

ment or starting a business in the **US News Women's Forum** and **Women and Business**. **AfriNET**, **Mela-Net**, GEnie's **African-American and Minority Business** bulletin board and AOL's **African American Board** offer business discussion and job exchange for African Americans. Amid the community news and cultural exchange on **LANIC** and the **Hispanic Board**, job seekers can find career advice and frank discussion of economic opportunity. The **National Indian Policy Center** carries employment offerings along with its political and social information. Don't feel left out.

Rosie the riveter—downloaded from CompuServe's Bettmann Archive Forum

On the Net

African American

African American Board African American businessmen and entrepreneurs talk survival and strategy in the workplace. Job seekers, employers with openings, and businesses hoping to make relationships with other minority-owned businesses advertise here as well. ✓**AMERICA ONLINE**→*keyword* communities→African American Board

African-American and Minority Businesses Do a higher percentage of Jews than blacks suc-

ceed in business? How about Koreans? And what is the role of the neighborhood barbershop in the ghetto economy? You'll find highly charged discussion in this message board, which revolves around the hottest of Af-Am business debates—how can African American entrepreneurs gesture toward the larger market without compromising their role as community leaders? There's also a special service here that provides African American and minority business people with help online. ✓**GENIE**→*keyword*

hosb→HOSB RoundTable Bulletin Board→14 African-American and Minority Business

AfriNET A comprehensive information and communication network for African Americans. Includes a clipping service for news articles and speeches of interest to African Americans, as well as an employment office that lists jobs and resumes and gives basic advice on minority strategies for obtaining and retaining employment. AfriNET offers subscription accounts for individuals, groups, and organizations. ✓**INTERNET**→*www* http://www.afrinet.net/ **$**

Culture of Trade Whether you're looking for businesses in Zimbabwe or an African-American insurance agent in New Jersey, this board can introduce you to a broad range of African- and African-American-oriented opportunities. ✓**COMPUSERVE**→*go* afro→Messages→Culture of Trade

MelaNet Offers a central location for black businesspeople to discuss their role within the larger business community along with issues relevant to black empowerment worldwide. Includes the MelaPages (an worldwide listing of black-owned businesses), Mela-Link (connections to other Internet resources), and the Melanin Library, which is not just a catchy name but an actual collection of research articles and books about melanin. ✓**INTERNET**→*www* http://www.melanet.com/melanet/

Chicano & Latino

Chicano-Latinonet Includes cultural and statistical information on Chicano and Latino communities throughout the United States, as well as an employment center that includes job postings and employment listing services. ✓**INTERNET**→*gopher* latino.sscnet.ucla.edu

Hispanic Board In between chat about cuisine and movies, and political and social talk by gay Latinos and Latina feminists, there's the occasional discussion about employment and economic opportunity. Translators and interpreters advertise their services. ✓**AMERICA ONLINE**→*keyword* exchange→Communities Center→Hispanic Board

LANIC Links Latin American Net

users to academic and news services around the world, many of which touch on occupational issues. ✓**INTERNET**→*www* http://info.lanic.utexas.edu

Native American

National Indian Policy Center Documents and data on the cultural, political, and economic realities of Native American life at the end of 20th century. Includes Native American job listings. ✓**INTERNET**→*www* gopher://gwis.circ.gwu.edu/11/Academic%20Departments/National%20Indian%20Policy%20Center/

Women

US News Women's Forum Women exchange strategies for dealing with sexual harassment, job discrimination, and the old boy network. For instance: What to do at a medical conference when a presentation begins with a slide of a naked woman and a slightly off-color joke? Learn about your rights. The forum's library contains articles on women in the corporate world and how women's salaries compare with those of men. ✓**COMPUSERVE**→*go* women→Messages→Working Women

Women and Business The goals: success and sanity. After a day of striving to meet them, a group of professional women gather here to discuss the benefits and drawbacks of self-employment, health concerns in the workplace, and the problems that sometimes arise between a working woman and her spouse—among other things. The online chapter of the American Business Women's Association (ABWA) has a presence here and the category itself is a conduit for career net-

working among its members. Not quite kicking back and relaxing, but necessary information for women on the move. ✓**GENIE**→*keyword* hosb→HOSB RoundTable Bulletin Board→Category 29 ## Women's Business ##

Women's Center The discussion can be rather intense around here, and if you're a woman starting up or running a business, it's a great place to blow off steam and meet other entrepreneurs. Not solely dedicated to issues of work, but it's always a hot topic. ✓**AMERICA ONLINE**→*keyword* communities→Women's Board

---

CYBERNOTES

"I was hired by a big car dealership even though I had no experience (getting the picture?). It was the most disgusting work experience I've ever had. I was advised not to wear underwear when climbing in and out of the Jeeps. I was called outside by the son of the owner (my sales manager) and told that if a customer thought I'd sleep with him if he bought the car, I should let him think that. My reply was, 'OK, so if he's gay should I turn him over to you?' I only worked there for 6 weeks but I have enough material to write a book!"

—from **AOL's Women's Center**

Part 6

Business

Business basics

Businesspeople like to do two things: conduct business and talk about it. Whether

they're grumbling about federal regulations or recommending motivational videotapes, these birds of a feather stick together, and much of today's sticking occurs online—from the WELL's **Business Conference** to Delphi's **Business Forum**. But maybe you're not interested in talking to others in the business world. Maybe you just want a set of introductory documents to read at your leisure. Well, step right up to **Business Strategies** or the **Information Please Business Almanac.**

On the Net

alt.business.misc (ng) Mostly a place for advertisements (some hard sell, some veiled), this newsgroup also includes discussion of products and strategies: Want to know what makes for the most effective calling cards? How to go about importing exotic fruit juices? Many questions and almost as many answers. ✓**USENET**

Business Book Bestsellers The month's best-selling business titles, compiled by Harry W. Schwartz Booksellers of Milwaukee, Wisconsin. ✓**EWORLD**→*go* ref-press→Business Book Bestsellers

Business Forum The forum gives access to Reuters Business

Welcome to the electronic ver *Stanford Business School Mag*

Stanford Business School—http://gsb-www.stanford.edu/sbsm/sbsm.html

News and an extensive shopping service, plus text files and software on automation, real estate, consulting, management, insurance, human resources, import/export, investments, direct marketing, public relations, sales and marketing, taxation and accounting, venture capital, and home business. ✓**DELPHI**→*go* gro bus

Business Strategies Find articles on venture capital for start-ups, microloans and veteran loans from the Small Business Administration, leases and joint ventures, and FCC telemarketing regulations. The Strategies Library contains case studies and newsletters, and there's also a message board where you can discuss plans with other AOLers. ✓**AMERICA ONLINE**→*keyword* business strategies

Chicago Online Business Guide You'll find a complete list of Chicago-area businesses, as well as an archive of the business columns from the *Chicago Tribune*. The Business Calendar lists conventions, meetings, and

public relations events in Chitown. Profiles of the city's largest corporations are found in Top 100 Companies. ✓**COMPUSERVE**→*go* col business

Information Please Business Almanac The online version of this well-known compendium of thousands of business-related facts includes corporate rankings, contracts, articles, tables, and GIFs of charts. The database can be searched by keyword or read topic by topic (Business Law & Government, Communications, Corporate Administration, Finance, Human Resources, International, Manufacturing, Marketing, Office Management, Personal Computers, and Reference/Index). ✓**COMPUSERVE**→*go* alm

LEADERSWeb — Financial Economic Studies at Clemson Started by students in Clemson University's economics program, the Website links to business-related sites and makes available resumes for participating students. ✓**INTERNET**→*www* http://www.clemson.edu/~marrm/leader.html

Stanford Business School Magazine Articles by leading economists and business gurus. ✓**COMPUSERVE**→*go* http://gsb-www.stanford.edu/sbsm/sbsm.html

U.S. Government Publications A wide variety of government publications that analyze the world of business may be ordered here, including the *U.S. Industrial Outlook, Commerce Business Daily*, and reports from the energy industry. ✓**COMPUSERVE**→*go* gpo

Starting a business

Maybe you're thinking of getting into business yourself. Well, start online, with intro-

ductory resources such as **Small Business Resources**, which collects basic articles on important business topics. If you'd rather talk to other small businesspeople, both newcomers and veterans, visit the **Microsoft Small Business Center**. Businesses in need of a little software boost should check out AOL's **Small Business Software Library**. And if you're opening a new luau-catering company, give a little Hawaiian punch to your plan with the help of the **Maui Small Business Development Center**.

Mom-and-Pop grocery—downloaded from CompuServe's Bettmann Archive

Across the board

Business (echo) The conference is a no-nonsense information exchange for the small business owner, with advice on such topics as how to travel with children during business trips, tips on software, and recommendations for office products. √**FIDONET**

Business_Ad (echo) Small business owners—ranging from a 15-year-old in Indiana with a limited liability company to a Saudi Arabian advertising executive who is tired of paying long-distance fees to access the professional resources on CompuServe—discuss the ins and outs of setting up and run-

ning a business. Traffic is low, but the discussion stays focused. √**SMARTNET**

Business Conference In-depth discussions of business strategies. √**WELL**→*g*business

The Business Resource Directory A database of small businesses, job seekers, service providers, wholesalers, agencies, and others hoping to make business contacts. The first time you visit, you can add your company or resume to the database for no charge. √**GENIE** →*keyword* directory

Entrepreneur Magazine Small Business Forum An online catalog of business start-up guides, books, software, and other small business tools to help you succeed in building and running your own small business. Also in-

cludes a list of the ten hottest companies. √**COMPUSERVE**→*go* ent-32

Microsoft Small Business Center Whether you already own a small business or are thinking about starting one, you'll find ample assistance here: A message board examines small businesses, home businesses, and consulting opportunities; and a real-time conference room enables you to converse with others about legal issues, marketing and advertising, sales, and women in business. Members of the Service Corps of Retired Executives visit the conference room every Wednesday night from 7p.m. to 11p.m. (EST) to give wise counsel. √**AMERICA ONLINE**→*keyword* small business

Small Business Resources Short articles on the various organizations that assist in starting and operating a small business, including the Service Corps of Retired Executives, the Small Business Administration, Nolo Press, and the U.S. Chamber of Commerce. Some of the entries contain publication and shareware catalogs. ✓**AMERICA ONLINE**→*keyword* small business→Small Business Resources

White House Conference on Small Business

Direct from 1600 Pennsylvania Avenue, a small business conference that covers such topics as capital formation, community development, environmental policy, human capital, international trade, procurement, regulation and paperwork, taxation, and the technology revolution. ✓**AMERICA ONLINE**→*keyword* whcsb

Hawaii

Maui Small Business Development Center Go West, young man. Way West. This Website, cosponsored by the University of Hawaii at Hilo and the Small Business Administration, encourages the development of small businesses on our only island state. The page links to short essays about the center's workshops, libraries, and counseling services. ✓**INTERNET**→*www* http://www. maui.com/~sbdc/

Software & support

Classifieds Software Library If you've just placed an ad on a classifieds board and expect a flood of responses, you may want to pick up some software to manage the influx. Packed with shipping and tracking software, the library has an assortment of postal calculators, Zip Code databases, invoice generators, and address managers for Mac and PC owners. ✓**AMERI-**

CA ONLINE→*keyword* classifieds→ Classifieds Software Library

Office Automation Vendor Forum Cardiff Software, Prentice Hall, Synex Systems, and other software publishers who specialize in office-automation support (accounting, communication, organization) have message boards and libraries in this forum dedicated to the efficient office of tomorrow. ✓**COMPUSERVE**→*go* oaforum

Small Business Software Library Part of Microsoft's Small Business Center, this software library contains dozens of Macin-

tosh and IBM programs designed to help small-business owners start and operate their companies. ✓**AMERICA ONLINE**→*keyword* small business→Software Library

Survey

Entrepreneur Magazine Small Business Survey CompuServe users have a standing invitation to participate in this survey, which poses a series of questions about owning and operating a small business and then charts the reponses. ✓**COMPUSERVE**→*go* entmagazine

---

CYBERNOTES

"Current tax policies and regulations do little to encourage initial investment and reinvestment in small businesses. Some good recommendations have been made to remedy this situation. Participants have suggested that government encourage lending institutions to relax regulations on collateral, and make provisions for public and private pension funds to invest in or extend credit to small businesses without suffering increased tax liability. Small business would also like to see the tax code revised to lower tax rates and ensure that the code is simple and fair. In addition, participants have suggested adopting a flat income tax.

"As we noted in our last update, there is a great deal of frustration among small-business people over the volume, complexity, and redundancy of regulations. Participants believe that agencies such as OSHA and the EPA, whose regulations they single out as being the most burdensome on small business, should begin the practice of seeking input from the affected business groupings before regulations are published. This practice would encourage regulations that help rather than hinder small business, while preserving protections for the workplace and the environment."

-- from America Online's White House Conference on Small Business

Small business shareware

A Project/Event Planner 2.2 Program for planning and organizing projects and events. Assign costs, schedule events, allocate tasks. ✓**INTERNET**→*ftp* ftp.cica. indiana.edu→anonymous→<your email address>→/pub/pc/win3 /util→ aplanr22.zip (Windows)

AB31 Pop-up alarms, weekly and monthly overviews, task tracking, and a contact database. ✓**COM-PUSERVE**→*go* pearl→Browse Libraries→Office/Finance→ AB31-X.EXE (Windows)

Accounting Helper v2.4 Comprehensive accounting help guide: nearly 300 "how to" examples from basic to advanced accounting. Can be used with any text-based accounting package. ✓**EXEC-PC**→File Collection Menu→Mahoney IBM Compatible DOS→ ACCTH.ZIP (DOS)

Advertising Primer Stack Gives inside tips on how to advertise effectively; discusses frequency, reach, gross rating points, etc. Needs Hypercard 2.1 or later. Shareware. ✓**AMERICA ONLINE**→ *keyword* mbs→Software Libraries→ *Search by file name:* AD CONSUL TANT.SEA (Macintosh)

Bill Maker Needs Hypercard. Automatically calculates billing for hourly charges. Prints professional-looking forms. ✓**AMERICA ON-LINE**→ *keyword* pfsoftware→Accounting→ Bill Maker (Macintosh)

Billing Manager An accounts receivable and billing program for self-employed persons and small businesses. ✓**AMERICA ONLINE**→ *keyword* win→*Search by file name:* FFBMGR.ZIP (Windows)

BPlan Developer v3.5 Helps you create "market-driven" business plans to get your project funded. ✓**EXEC-PC**→File Collection Menu→Mahoney IBM Compatible DOS→BPLAN35.ZIP (DOS)

Business Calculator v2.20 Performs business functions such as calculating Net Present Value, Internal Rate of Return, Present and Future Value, Interest dividends, and more. Extensive help file. ✓**EXEC-PC**→File Collection Menu→MS Windows→BCALC22. ZIP (Windows)

Business Plan Master v1.0 Acclaimed business plan program with powerful text and spreadsheet templates. Generate reports and anaylsis to track business growth. ✓**EXEC-PC**→File Collection Menu→MS Windows→BPMWIN 1A.ZIP (Windows)

Business Plan Master v2.0 Includes template files to create financial plans for businesses. ✓**IN-TERNET**→*ftp* sumex-aim.stanford. edu→anonymous→<your email address>→/info-mac/app→business-plan-master-20.hqx (Macintosh)

Business Planner Template files for producing business plans and financial reports. Files in Word-Perfect 5.1, Word for Windows, Works 3.0, 1-2-3, and Excel formats. Shareware. ✓**COMPUSERVE**→ *go* smallb→Browse Libraries→Software/Hardware→BUSPLA.ZIP (Windows)

BusinessCards for Windows v.2.00 Track ideas and address information. Store articles. Document collectibles. Index-card-like. ✓**INTERNET**→*ftp* ftp.cica.indiana.edu →anonymous→<your email ad-

dress>→/pub/pc/ win3/util→ bcards20.zip (Windows)

CheckMate Plus v1.50 Double entry accounting program. Prints checks; has flexible reports, search and filter functions. ✓**EXEC-PC**→File Collection Menu→Mahoney IBM Compatible DOS→ CMP 150A.ZIP *and* CMP 150B.ZIP (DOS)

CJPOS Complete point-of-sale system for small businesses. Writes invoices or estimates, tracks inventory and salespersons, performs sales analysis, and more. Extremely easy to use. Shareware. ✓**EXEC-PC**→File Collection Menu→Mahoney IBM Compatible DOS→ CJPOS210.ZIP (DOS)

Client Biller v1.2 Create, edit and print client invoices (for small businesses or consultants). Shareware. ✓**PC OHIO**→d→*Download a file:* CBILL 12.ZIP (Windows)

Easy Agent v1.46 Sales/purchase real estate program calculates costs for sellers, buyers, FHA down payments, etc. Shareware. ✓**PC OHIO**→d→ *Download a file:* EASY_A.ZIP (DOS)

Easy Inventory v1.0 Inventory program. ✓**PC OHIO**→d→*Download a file:* EASINV 10. ZIP (DOS)

Employee Evaluator v1.21 Evaluate and keep track of your workers' progress. Shareware. ✓**PC OHIO**→d→ *Download a file:* EVAL 121.ZIP (DOS)

EZ Cash v1.0 Cash register program for small businesses. User-friendly and easy to customize. ✓**PC OHIO**→d→*Download a file:* EZ-CASHV 1.ZIP (DOS)

Small business shareware (continued)

EZ-Biller v2.1 Invoicing program keeps track of customers, inventory, sales staff, taxes, back orders, etc. ✓**PC OHIO**→d→*Download a file:* EZBILL21.ZIP (DOS)

F.Y.I.2 v2.3 Complete business office manager. Resume writer, cardex, mailing labels, projects database, and more. Shareware. ✓**PC OHIO**→d→*Download a file:* YI2V23.ZIP (DOS)

Fastmail v2.30 Mailing list management program; supports laser printers; export utility and more. ✓**PC OHIO**→d→ *Download a file:* FSTML230.ZIP (DOS)

FedEZ Print out Federal Express airbills on a dot matrix printer. ✓**INTERNET**→*ftp* ftp.cica.indiana. edu→anonymous→<your email address>→/pub/pc/win3/util→ fedez13.zip ✓**AMERICA ONLINE**→ *keyword* win→*Search by file name:* FEDZ13.ZIP (Windows)

FileMaker Store v2.1 FileMaker Pro v2.0 templates to keep track of store's sales, inventory, expenses, payroll, etc. ✓**INTERNET**→*ftp* mac.archive.umich.edu→anonymous→<your email address>→ /mac/util/organization→filemaker store2.1. cpt.hqx (Macintosh)

Financial Manager v1.01e Evaluates company performance; makes corporate valuations and assists with the preparation of short-term cash flow plans. Shareware. ✓**PC OHIO**→d→*Download a file:* FINMN10E.ZIP (Windows)

For Accountants Only v1.9 Single-entry bookkeeping system for keeping clients' accounts. ✓**PC OHIO**→d→*Download a file:* FOA19. ZIP (DOS)

Freight Program figures UPS shipping charges. ✓**PC OHIO**→d→ *Download a file:* FRB11.ZIP (DOS)

Instant Office v3.91 Database keeps track of client/customer list; can create instant memos, faxes, mailing labels, letters, etc. ✓**EXEC-PC**→File Collection Menu→Mahoney IBM Compatible DOS→ INOF391.ZIP (DOS)

The Invoice Store v3.1 Invoicing, P.O.S. and customer tracking system. Easy but powerful. Writes reports, schedules appointments, prints mailing labels. Built-in help. Invoicing program keeps track of customers, inventory, sales staff, taxes, back orders, etc. ✓**PC OHIO**→d→*Download a file:* INV31.ZIP (DOS)

INVOICE-IT Use .dbf format to make sales invoices and print them. ✓**INTERNET**→*ftp* ftp.cica.indiana.edu→anonymous→<your email address>→/pub/pc/win3/util→ invit200.zip (Windows)

Lost Wages 1.1b Comprehensive accounting program for home or small business. Manual included. ✓**EXEC-PC**→File Collection Menu→Mahoney IBM Compatible DOS→LW11B.ZIP (DOS)

MDS OBRA Assessment Tool v3.3 Quality control program featuring MDS data assessment, resident quality review, RAP summary, and more. ✓**PC OHIO**→ d→*Download a file:* MDS.ZIP (DOS, Windows)

More Forms v1.0 Create forms with boxes, lines, text, special characters, and shading. Uses any fonts your printer can. Can enter info or fill out by hand. ✓**PC**

OHIO→d→*Download a file:* MOR FORM1.ZIP *and* MORFORM2.ZIP (DOS)

Motelmax 2.0 Management program for hotels, motels, Bed & Breakfasts, and resorts. Shareware. ✓**PC OHIO**→d→*Download a file:* MOTEL210.ZIP

Newbiz v1.0 Brainstorming program for entrepreneurs. Holds 200 personal assets and 200 business ideas; context-sensitive help included. ✓**PC OHIO**→d→*Download a file:* NEWBIZ10.ZIP (DOS)

Office Supplies Tracker v1.42 Tracking system for supplies; maintains inventory/locations, generates purchase orders and requisitions and sets notification levels for stock depletion. ✓**PC OHIO**→d→*Download a file:* OST142.ZIP (DOS)

Organize! Your Business (Industrial Version) v5.65 Database designed specifically for cataloging business-related info: tool inventory, motor inventory, vehicles, maintenance records, and more. Menu operated; prints reports. Shareware. ✓**EXEC-PC**→File Collection Menu→Mahoney IBM Compatible DOS→OYI565.ZIP (DOS)

PayWindow Full-featured payroll program for hourly, salaried, commissioned, and 1099 workers. Prints checks and reports. ✓**AMERICA ONLINE**→*keyword* mbs→Software Libraries→*Search by file name:* PAYWINDOW INSTALLER (Macintosh)

PayWindow Payroll for Windows Full-featured payroll system for hourly, salaried, commis-

Small business shareware (continued)

sioned and even 1099 workers. Prints checks, W2s, 1099-MISC, 941 form worksheet and more. Calculates federal, local and all 50 state taxes plus D.C. and Puerto Rico. ✓**INTERNET**→*ftp* ftp.cica. indiana.edu→anonymous→<your email address>→/pub/pc/win3 /util→paywin10.zip ✓**AMERICA ON-LINE**→*keyword* pfsoftware→Accounting→Paywindow Payroll Program ✓**PC OHIO**→d→*Download a file:* PAYWIN10.ZIP (Windows)

Pinky 3.0 Telephone message system. Helps you keep track of incoming phone messages. Shareware. ✓**PC OHIO**→d→*Download a file:* PINKY3.ZIP (DOS)

ProBill s1.0 A billing and accounts-receivable program. ✓**COMPUSERVE**→ibmapp→Libraries→ *Search for a file:* PROBIL.ZIP (DOS)

QuickBill v1.20 Very simple invoicing, bidding, and accounts receivable program. ✓**INTERNET**→*ftp* mac.archive.umich.edu→anonymous→<your email address>→ mac/util/organization→ quickbill1.20.cpt.hqx (Macintosh)

QwikBILL (v1.22) Invoicing Shareware, point-and-click program for invoices, bidding, and accounts receivable. Use with QwikBILLTIME and QwikMAIL (in same library) for client time billing and mail list managing. ✓**AMERICA ONLINE**→*keyword* mbs→ Software Libraries→*Search by file name:* QWIKBILL (V1.22)SW.SEA ...→*keyword* mbs→Software Libraries→*Search by file name:* QWIKBILLTIME (v1.22)SW.SEA ...→*keyword* mbs→Software Libraries→*Search by file name:* QWIKMAIL SW.SEA (Macintosh)

The Retailer v4.05 Inventory control for small to medium-sized retail stores. Handles up to 5 locations. Tracks back orders and more. ✓**PC OHIO**→d→*Download a file:* RET405.ZIP (DOS)

Ridematch v1.0 Matches employees for carpools. Unlimited records, supports all printers. Shareware. ✓**PC OHIO**→d→*Download a file:* RIDE.ZIP (DOS)

Rockford v3.5 Business card maker: has fonts, clip art, and line drawing tools. New version with more features. Shareware. Requires VBRUN300.DLL. ✓**EXEC-PC**→File Collection Menu→MS Windows→ROCKFORD.ZIP (Windows)

SalesTax&IncomeReports Stack Generates reports based on income and collected sales tax to help figure quarterly income and quarterly sales tax figures. Needs Hypercard. ✓**AMERICA ONLINE**→ *keyword* mbs→Software Libraries→ Applications→SALESTAX&INCOME REPORTS 1.2.1.SIT (Macintosh)

The Small Business Advisor Perfect for small businesses or entrepreneurs. Deals with federal regulations, taxes, and more. Commercial program: register for updates. ✓**EXEC-PC**→File Collection Menu→Mahoney IBM Compatible DOS→SBAPRO1.EXE (DOS)

Small Business Payroll Microsoft Excel template for payroll functions for small businesses. ✓**AMERICA ONLINE**→*keyword* pfsoftware→Accounting→Small Bus Payroll XL (Macintosh)

SOB v6.0 Signout board to track employees' comings and goings. Network compatible, instant data

updates. ✓**PC OHIO**→d→*Download a file:* SOB60.ZIP (DOS)

Strategic Business Simulator v1.0 Management decision-making game: a mathematical model of a business economy, with several firms competing for market share. You're the executive in charge. Shareware. ✓**EXEC-PC**→File Collection Menu→MS Windows→SBS.ZIP (Windows)

TimeBook 2.3.1 Easy-to-use client billing program with pop-up menus. Needs Hypercard 2.1 or later. Tutorial included. ✓**AMERICA ONLINE**→*keyword* mbs→Software Libraries→*Search by file name:* TIMEBOOK 2.3.1.SEA (Macintosh)

TimeFacts A billing program that assists in tracking projects, conferences, and time logs. Staff can merge time logs when invoicing clients, and information can be exported. ✓**AMERICA ONLINE**→*keyword* win→*Search by file name:* TF223.ZIP (Windows)

Visual Accounting System v1.0 Uses linked spreadsheets and databases. Generates reports, ledgers, or compound transactions for any given date. ✓**EXEC-PC**→File Collection Menu→MS Windows→VAS10. ZIP (Windows)

Wild Cardz Create business cards, post cards, or greeting cards. ✓**AMERICA ONLINE**→*keyword* mbs→Software Libraries→Applications→WILD CARDS (Macintosh)

Xpens v1.2 Program allows you to enter expense account information and print expense reports. ✓**PC OHIO**→d→*Download a file:* XPENS12.ZIP (DOS)

SBA Online

True to its name, the Small Business Administration of- fers detailed assistance to small businesses, helping entrepreneurs develop their business ideas, finance them, and bring them to the marketplace. What the name doesn't communicate is how successful the SBA has been at bringing its resources to the electronic era. From the huge **Small Business Administration Online** bulletin board to individual services for the **Small Business Advancement Center** and **Small Business Innovation Research Program**—SBIR, the SBA offers a incredible wealth of financial, legal, and regulatory resources to the small-business owner.

SBA Online home page—http://www.sbaonline.sba.gov/

world.gov→D→40 *or* 41

On the Net

Small Business Administration Online With resources that are deeper than the Marianas Trench and easier to use than a mirror, the Small Business Administration Online is the Mecca of aspiring tycoons. The massive database treats such topics as business development, company financing, government contracting, legislation and regulation, and minority assistance. Local Small Business Administration resources—business information centers, preferred lenders, small business counselors—are listed. ✓**INTERNET** ...→*telnet* sbaonline. sba.gov ...→*www* http://www.fed

Small Business Administration Web Server The home page for the online component of the Small Business Administration, this site introduces the organization, lists current events, and gives basic advice on starting, financing, and expanding a small business. It also links to the vast network of Small Business Administration services and databases. ✓**INTERNET**→*www* http://www. sbaonline.sba.gov/

Small Business Advancement Center This national and international research, training, consulting, and information center is funded primarily by the U.S. Congress and administered by the SBA. The highlight is the Small Business Advancement Network, the largest electronic library in the world pertaining to small business and entrepreneurship. The extensive list of documents and publications—bulletins, case histories, journals, proceedings, and statistical databases—are available for browsing or searching. ✓**INTER-NET**→*www* http://161.31.2.174/

Small Business Development Center The hundreds of Small Business Development Centers across the country are devoted to encouraging prudent expansion in business ventures. With the interactive map at this Website, small business owners can find the closest development center and also check their local weather forecast. ✓**INTERNET**→*www* http://www. sbaonline.sba.gov/regions/region-map.html

Small Business Innovation Research Program—SBIR A huge federal program designed to encourage innovative research and product development, SBIR uses its Website to announce upcoming offline conferences, explain the needs of participating federal agencies, and provide basic advice on preparing proposals. New services are added regularly, so don't forget to sign up for the program's mailing list (postal not email). ✓**INTERNET**→ *www* http://www. sbaonline.sba. gov/sbir/sbir.html

Small Business Institute Program Operating at the intersection of commerce and academics, the program offers small-business owners management counseling from graduate and undergraduate business students, guided by faculty members. With more than 500 business schools participating, this is one of the largest programs of its kind, and although the online features are limited to background information and a database that helps small-business owners locate participating institutions in their area, this is nonetheless a valuable resource. ✓**INTERNET**→*www* http:// www.sbaonline.sba.gov/busi ness_management/sbi.html

Entrepreneurs

If you're trying to take the highroad to business success rather than climbing the cor-

porate ladder, you'll find tremendous support on the Net. From the Canadian publication **Big Dreams** to the **Entrepreneur's Network**, the online world is full of men and women who have pledged to chase their dream no matter what the obstacles. Still trying to find someone to help you market your new and improved Fishing Magician? Determined to make your home graphic-design business work? Drop in to eWorld's **Working Solo** or GEnie's **Home Office/Small Business RoundTable**. And if you just can't wait another minute to realize your dreams of becoming a multi millionaire, strap on your rocket boots and hightail it on over to **alt.make.money. fast**, where greed and speed are more than just rhyming words.

Apple Computer founder Stephen Wozniak—from ftp.funet.fi

On the Net

Entrepreneurs

Big Dreams Though this Canadian publication tends to slip into motivational business babble ("Change must come from within"), the waters of rhetoric do part occasionally to reveal some solid practical advice—for instance, es-

timate the start-up capital you'll need and then multiply by a factor of two or three. ✓ **INTERNET**→*www* http://www.wimsey.com/~dun cans/

Entrepreneur (echo) David sends Jerry a list of his suppliers, Thom advises Joel on how to automate a dial-out telephone message, and Carol tells Steve how to register a new business. You can't blatantly advertise your business here, but you can brainstorm with other members about money-making ideas, ask advice about business costs, and make business contacts. ✓ **FIDONET**

The Entrepreneur's Forum Entrepreneurs of all shapes and sizes populate this forum, browsing a menu that offers advice on start-up strategies, contacts, market research, franchising, and more. Take a break at a message board that attempts to duplicate the atmosphere of the office watercooler. ✓ **COMPUSERVE**→*go* usen

---

Entrepreneur's Network Part

of FEDnet (Foundation for Enterprise Development), this network includes a variety of documents designed to answer the most common questions an inexperienced entrepreneur might have. How easy is it to start a business? How soon should you expect to turn a profit? Is expansion generally a wise decision or a foolish one? ✓ **INTERNET**→*www* http://www. itl.saic.com/fed/

Ernst & Young Business Series The Ernst & Young Entrepreneurial Services Group, a worldwide professional services firm, publishes a series of articles and brochures for entrepreneurs. Covering topics such as hiring, marketing, and ways to obtain

> "The waters of rhetoric do part occasionally in Big Dreams to reveal some solid practical advice—for instance, estimate the start-up capital you'll need and then multiply by a factor of two or three."

loans and to structure an executive board, these reports are a valuable primer for new businessmen and businesswomen, and a good reminder of the fundamentals for hardened veterans. ✓**AMERICA ON-LINE**→*keyword* news→Ernst & Young

misc.entrepreneurs (ng) This newsgroup is really a two-for-the-price-of-one deal—as both a site for entrepreneurs to discuss their marketing and expansion strategies and a place for them to practice those strategies—"Have I got a deal for you." ✓**USENET**

Franchises

Franchise and Business Opportunities Ever thought about owning a McDonald's franchise, but never quite knew how to go about getting one? Or maybe your tastes run toward Kenny Rogers Roasters or Blockbuster Video. Published by *Entrepreneur Magazine*, the annual Guide to Franchise and Business Opportunities explores the ins and outs of buying into existing businesses. In addition to introductory articles on franchising and business opportunities, the guide contains addresses, phone numbers, and contact names for hundreds of companies, and descriptions of what they're offering. ✓**COMPUSERVE**→*go* ebs-4

Home office

Home Office/Small Business RoundTable For those working at home, the same questions crop up again and again, and they're considered in this discussion space. What percentage of your rent can you deduct at tax time? Which computer equipment best serves your needs? Is it legal to lock your husband in the hall closet every evening so that you can get some work done? There's also a

> **"What percentage of your rent can you deduct at tax time? Is it legal to lock your husband in the hall closet every evening so that you can get some work done?"**

software downloading area with hundreds of helpful programs. ✓**GENIE**→*keyword* hosb

Home & Small Business Answer Book Excerpts Written by RoundTable sysop Janet Attard, this book contains answers to more than 900 of the most frequently asked questions about starting and running home-based and other small businesses. ✓**GENIE**→*keyword* hosb→Home & Small Business Answer Book Excerpt

Working-From-Home-Forum When you work from home, there are hundreds of bumps on the road to profitabilty. This forum tries to pave over some of them, with extensive message boards and libraries that target topics ranging from office hardware to working at home with the kids and the pets. Check in and learn what to do when Fluffers munches on that important proposal (the new take on the old saw, "My dog ate my work at home," won't do). ✓**COMPUSERVE**→*go* work

Quick fix

alt.business.multi-level (ng)

What's a multilevel business? Sometimes it's a marketing innovation, sometimes it's a pyramid scheme, sometimes it's a nightmarish tangle of recriminations and shady profits. Enter the fray of this newsgroup, which combines discussion and online advertising. ✓**USENET**

alt.make.money.fast (ng) If you've ever concocted a get-rich-quick scheme or thought seriously about making one work, this may be the place for you. From telemarketing to Herbalife to O. J. Simpson T-shirts to NuSkin, this newsgroup preaches the gospel of lining your pockets without lifting a finger. Half consumer-warning forum, half celebration of the easy strike, it's a schizophrenic place where the hum of fast money is always in the air. ✓**USENET**

Self-employment

Self-Employment Forum Founded by self-proclaimed self-employment specialist Bill Benitez, this forum teaches the basics of bossing yourself. Make your computer pay for itself by freelancing graphic design from the home. Keep the cats from climbing up on the keyboard. And, when the prospect of facing another day is overwhelming, answer the following question over and over again: Would you be happy working for someone else? ✓**DELPHI**→*go* cus 276

Working Solo Produced by Terri Lonier, author of the award-winning book *Working Solo*, this forum includes important news for the self-employed businessperson, a resource library, and the Solo Connections message board, where solitary businesspeople can post stories, questions, and advice. ✓**EWORLD**→*go* solo

Inventors' corner

When Thomas Edison invented the incandescent light, did he have the vast invention

resources of the Net at his fingertips? Of course not. But you're no Edison, and late-twentieth-century inventors, whether hobbyists or professionals, would be well-advised to make use of Cyberspace. First, bone up on invention law and regulation with documents such as **The Patent Process One Step at a Time**, **Patent FAQ**, and the **US Patent Act of 1994**. Then check out the competition by perusing online invention databases—the **Research Ideas Home Page** features a robotic cat. Next, chew the fat with other would-be Edisons in CompuServe's **Ideas & Inventions Forum**. And when you've finally started to get a feel for the process, treat yourself to a full-blown **Patent Search** courtesy of the U.S. Patent and Trademark Office. Maybe you'll discover that someone's already invented your invention.

Tesla publicity shot—downloaded from CompuServe's Bettmann Archive.

Security envelopes that destroy their contents if tampered with. Spray-on hair. Next time an innovation tickles your mind, bring it over to this forum, which includes creativity workshops, scheduled seminars on marketing novelty items, and conferences on new technology. ✓**COMPUSERVE**→*go* ideas

Patent FAQ One of the best basic guides to the patent process available online, with chapters on career opportunities for the inventor, the history of the patent process, the necessity of a patent, the cost of a patent, and "defensive driving" for the inventor. ✓**INTER-NET**→*www* http://www.sccsi.com /DaVinci/patentfaq.html

The Patent Process One Step at a Time If you're getting tired of hearing Grandpa's cautionary stories about how he invented the VCR and forgot to patent it, you might want to peruse this docu-

ment, which leads would-be inventors through the process of applying for, drafting, and filing a United States patent. ✓**INTER-NET**→*www* http://www.ora.com /gnn/bus/nolo/patent.html

Patents and Trademarks The

On the Net

Across the board

Ideas & Inventions Forum Suddenly an idea hits you. A clip to hold socks together in the dryer.

> **"Suddenly an idea hits you. A clip to hold socks together in the dryer. Security envelopes that destroy their contents if tampered with. Spray-on hair."**

electronic version of information guru Matthew Lesko's book, *Information USA*, tells you where you file and research patent applications, get transcripts of the *Copyright Royalty Tribunal*, view a collection of patent drawings from 1835-1871, file patent rights on vegetable seeds, join programs that encourage inventors, and tap into a host of other patent and trademark resources. ✓**COMPUSERVE**→*go* ius-12423

Research Ideas Home Page A clearinghouse of ideas, inventions, and innovations that tend toward high-tech research, including speech-recognition systems, sample compression algorithms, and "The Cat" ("an incarnation of a real cat but oddly enough in robotic form"). ✓**INTERNET**→*www* http://ugsun1a.ph.bham.ac.uk:300 6/research/concepts.html

Patent advice

NASA Patent Counsel Team Though of use primarily to inventors who are also NASA employees, this Website illustrates some of the issues at stake in any invention, namely the complex legal and bureaucratic processes that accompany any new idea. ✓**INTERNET**→*www* http://tag-fileserver. larc.nasa.gov/TAG.Files/patent. html

Patent law

U.S. Patent Act (1994) This Website permits a full-text search of the most recent invention and patent Act, along with online excerpts and highlights. Did you know, for instance, that "except when authorized by a license obtained from the Commissioner a person shall not file or cause to be filed in any foreign country prior to six months after filing in the

United States an application for patent or for the registration of a utility model, industrial design, or model in respect of an invention made in this country"? No? Well, now you do. And be careful about it, too. ✓**INTERNET**→*www* http:// www.law.cornell.edu/usc/35/i_iv/ overview.html

Patent searches

Best North American Inventions Check out the competition with this searchable database, which collects the best North American inventions in medical and technical fields. Though it requires a Web client with form support and employs an extremely complicated search engine—inventions are listed by accession number, name of inventor(s), title of invention, abstract, keywords, and patent status—the retrieval powers are magnificent. And where else are you likely to learn about a recombinant DNA vector for the molecular cloning of very large eukaryotic DNA segments in *E. coli*? ✓**INTERNET**→*www* http:// medoc.gdb.org/work/inv-fields/ yale.html

Patent Research Center Contains the full texts of U.S. patents since 1974, abstracts for claims and patents since 1950, and summaries of various world patent databases since 1960. Search specialists will help narrow your search. ✓**COMPUSERVE**→*go* pat **$**

Patent Search The next time you have a bright idea, spend a few minutes to make sure it's not a reflection of someone else's brilliance. This service, provided by the U.S. Patent Bureau, conducts comprehensive keyword searches through the nation's patent and trademark database, and returns reports that include the patent number along

with a brief description of the item or process patented. It does everything but pour your morning coffee. (Hmm...an online patent-searching service that also brews coffee....) ✓**INTERNET** ...→*gopher* town.hall.org→US Patent and Trademark Office ...→*www* http://town. hall.org/cgi-bin/srch-patent

Financing a business

If you need cash for your company, turn to the Net's extensive corporate finance services,

including **SBA Financing Assistance** and the **Federal Grant Database**, both of which direct small businesses toward government resources for start-up and expansion funds. Newcomers should also visit the **Guide to Business Credit**, which answers basic questions about companies and credit.

On the Net

Across the board

Entrepreneurial and Business Funding How do you get federal grants? Why is venture capital simpler than it seems? What are sources of state money? The Information USA databank, based on the book of the same title, gives you the names and addresses of the sources of information. ✓**COMPUSERVE**→*go* ius-8679

SBA Financing Assistance James Brown thought that "money won't change you." The Small Business Administration hopes it will. This service details funding options available to small-business owners, including regular business loans, security bonds, the LowDoc lending program, and disaster assistance. ✓**INTERNET**→*telnet* sbaonline.sba.gov→[2] Services Available→[3] Financing Services

Corporate giants

Catalogue of Federal Domestic Assistance This is a clearing-house of information on grants, scholarships, and jobs programs administered by the federal government, with background information on grant regulations and legislation as well as elaborate listings for federal-assistance programs. Search by keyword. ✓**INTERNET**→ *gopher* gopher.rtd.utk.edu →Federal Government Information →Catalogue of Federal Domestic Assistance

Federal Grant Database Grant listings from the Catalog of Federal Domestic Assistance, which comprises more than 1,300 assistance programs administered by 52 federal agencies. The full-text searchable database is divided into 20 major categories, including agriculture, cultural affairs, education, energy, housing, and transportation. ✓**GENIE**→*keyword* directory→Federal Grant Database

FEDIX/MOLIS - Federal Information Exchange, Inc. Information on corporate assistance programs and grants offered by federal departments and agencies: the Department of Energy, Housing and Urban Development, Commerce, U.S. Agency for International Development, Office of Naval Research, National Aeronautics and Space Administration, Air Force Office of Scientific Research, National Science Foundation, and Federal Aviation Administration. In addition, this service is useful for obtaining second-hand office equipment and other products at a low cost. ✓**INTERNET** →*www* http://web.fie.com

Foundation and Corporate

Grants Alert A monthly publication that not only offers advance listings of foundation and corporate grant opportunities, but also covers such issues as trends in corporate funding and the ins and outs of grant writing. ✓**INTERNET**→*gopher* gopher.enews.com→ Magazines, Periodicals, and Journals→Foundation and Corporate Grants Alert

The Grant Getters Guide to the Internet This guide delineates strategies for obtaining federal funding for large and small businesses. ✓**INTERNET**→*gopher* uidaho. edu→Science, Research, & Grant Information→Grant Information

Credit

Guide to Business Credit Contains basic information about business credit, including types of loans, standard procedure if credit is refused, alternate sources of capital, and federal regulations. ✓**AMERICA ONLINE**→*keyword* business strategies→Guide to Business Credit

Internet Credit Bureau Worried that your customers (or investors) won't come through with the cash? Turn to this online credit bureau. They will create a full credit profile for any individual or business. The bureau tracks down missing persons and retrieves basic information about any Social Security number. Fill out an online customer request form or email them. ✓**INTERNET** ...→*www* http:// www.satelnet.org/credit/ ...→ *email* icb@satelnet.org ✍ *Email with a customer request*

Accounting & bankruptcy

When the creditors come to repossess your mannequins, what are you going to do?

Are you going to kick and scream? No. Weep and wail? Certainly not. Are you going to turn to the Net to learn more about responsible accounting, bankruptcy, and auditing? Now you're talking. From **ANet/The International Accounting Network**—which outlines the accounting profession and contains links to many other accounting-related sites—to a worldwide list of accounting organizations, the Net has dozens of resources to help you manage your business in times of fiscal crisis. And if you could be running a tighter ship, check out **Dartmouth Hitchcock Medical Center Internal Auditing**, which helps companies learn the art of the internal audit.

On the Net

Accounting

AAA/IEEE Information Home to the American Accounting Association, this gopher contains working papers on accounting as well as publications on the role of artificial intelligence in finance. ✓**INTERNET**→*gopher* cwis.usc.edu→University Information→Academic Departments→School of Business Administration→Research, Journal and Meeting (AAA/IEEE) Information

Leona Helmsley—downloaded from CompuServe's Bettman Archives Forum

Accounting Organizations Trapped in Azerbaijan with a ledger full of figures and an audit on the way? This Website allows for keyword searches of all worldwide accounting organizations. It also lists them by country. ✓**INTERNET**→*www* http://elli.scu.edu.au/11/anet/assns

ANet/The International Accounting Network Exchange ideas, strategies, and insights into the accounting and auditing professions. Includes a list of international accounting organizations. ✓**INTERNET**→*www* http://www.scu.edu.au/ANetHomePage.html

CTI-AFM CTI-AFM stands for the Computers in Teaching Initiative Center for Accounting, Finance, and Management. A Web page based at the University of East Anglia in England, with links to conference proceedings and the academic journal *Account*. ✓**INTERNET**→*www* http://www.sys.uea.ac.uk/cti/cti-afm.html

Rutgers Accounting Web Someday, the Rutgers Accounting Web, which is still being developed, may be the United States' central Website for accountants, with links to the world's accounting and auditing resources. ✓**INTERNET**→*www* http://www.rutgers.edu/Accounting/raw.html

The SUMMA Project/ICAEW From the Institute of Chartered Accountants of England and Wales, a list of worldwide educational programs in accounting, professional organizations, accountancy firms, conferences, and employment opportunities. ✓**INTERNET** →*www* http://cen.ex.ac.uk/economics/ICAEW/summa/ICAEWTEST.html

Bankruptcy

BankrLaw (ml) Handles common and less common topics regarding the legal dimensions of bankruptcy. ✓**INTERNET**→*email* listproc@polecat.law.indiana.edu ✍ *Type in message body:* subscribe bankrlaw <your full name>

Internal auditing

Dartmouth Hitchcock Medical Center Internal Auditing Links to the home page of the Internal Auditing World Wide Web—frequently asked questions about the audit, listings of conferences and professional societies, and a database of articles and white papers on auditing. ✓**INTERNET**→*www* http://mmm.dartmouth.edu/pages/dhmc/iawww-folder-v1.0/darthome-iawww-exec.html

Human resources

No doubt your company has some problematic employees, like the woman who always

answers questions even when they're not directed at her, and the twice-divorced executive who likes to knock back a six-pack during lunch. And don't forget about that mid-level manager who has been slapped with three sexual-harassment complaints. What's the best way to deal with these headaches, other than scrapping the whole operation and spending the balance of your days in Bora Bora? Well, for one thing, use the Net's personal-management resources. From general databases like **The Management Archive** to specialty publications such as **Drugs in the Workplace**, from discussions in industrial and organizational psychology (**IOOB-L**) to management case studies (**Case On-Line Information Systems**), the Net contains dozens of ways to improve management-employee relations. And if you're in the mood for a lighter treatment of these issues, try **GEnie's WorkPlace Round-Table**, which includes a real-time area for complaining about a deadline or lamenting the way your annoying new boyfriend keeps calling you at the office.

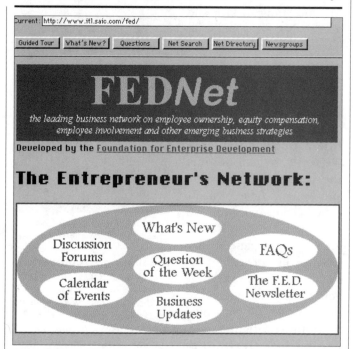

FEDnet Web page—http://www.itl.saic.com/fed/

On the Net

Across the board

Books on Human Resources and Personnel Managing people can be tough. Just ask Buddy Rich or Tommy Lasorda. It's difficult to allocate human resources without wasting time, bruising egos, and incurring unnecessary expenses. This site contains summaries and brief excerpts of books on personnel management. All books can be ordered online. ✓**INTERNET**→*www* gopher://usa.net/00/News%20and%20Information/books/Human%20Resources-Personnel%20Management

Business Resource Directory at FEDnet The Foundation for Enterprise Development has more than 150 documents on such topics as employee empowerment, employee ownership of companies, equity compensation methods, and employee motivation. ✓**INTERNET**→*www* http://www.itl.saic.com/fed/

Journal of Economics and Management Strategy Edited by economists and management-strategy scholars, this quarterly journal investigates such business principles as competition and organization, with both theoretical and empirical consideration of industrial superstructure, applied game theory, and management strategy. Heady stuff, but important considerations for managers. ✓**INTERNET**→*gopher* gopher.enews.com→Business Publications→Journal of Economics and Management Strategy

---

The Management Archive A forum for management ideas and information, the archive provides easy access to working papers and papers-in-progress in the management and organizational sciences, recent paper calls, course syllabi and teaching materials, conference announcements, archives of management-related discussion lists, and easy connections to relevant Net resources. ✓**INTERNET**→*gopher* ursus.jun.alaska.edu

---

Management Policies and Personnel Law This biweekly publication helps corporate managers address human resource needs and avoid legal problems. Each issue describes creative personnel policies and provides coverage of important legal decisions and arbitration rulings that pertain to the workplace. ✓**INTERNET**→ *gopher* gopher.enews.com→Business Publications→Management Policies and Personnel Law

Drugs

Drugs in the Workplace This monthly publication provides news and analysis of drug use in the workplace—one of the nation's leading problems—with special focus on treatments, employee assistance programs, and actual workplace cases. ✓**INTERNET**→*gopher* gopher.enews.com→Magazines, Periodicals, and Journals→ Drugs in the Workplace

Employee relations

Case On-Line Information

Systems (mgmt case studies) What should a company do when a woman joins its all-male sales force? Assume that nothing is different? Counsel her on the difficulties she might encounter? Speak to the men in an attempt to forestall any problems? These three collections of case histories, assembled by Harvard Business School, University of Western Ontario, and the European Case Clearing House, include technical notes, industry notes, case software, and course materials. ✓**INTERNET**→*telnet* vaxvmsx.babson.edu→colis

---

Employee Relations in Action Drawing on arbitration rulings on such issues as hiring and firing, employee benefits, privacy, sexual harassment, and workplace violence, this publication grapples with sensitive workplace issues in clear prose. ✓**INTERNET**→*gopher* gopher.enews.com→Business Publications→Employee Relations in Action

---

HRD-L (ml) An intelligent and focused forum for discussing human resources in the workplace. ✓**INTERNET**→*email* listserv@mizzou1.missouri.edu ✍ *Type in message body:* subscribe hrd-l <your full name>

Human Resources Development Canada Includes updates on Social Security reform and detailed fact sheets on various employment and family issues, including poverty, youth, women and Social Security, work, and families. ✓**INTERNET**→*gopher* gopher.worldlinx.com

---

TrDev-L (ml) Extensive discussions about human resources by academics and professionals. ✓**INTERNET**→*email* listserv@psuvm.psu.edu ✍ *Type in message body:* subscribe trdev-l <your full name>

Org. behavior

EAWOP-L (ml) A publication on organizational psychology in Europe that attempts to promote cooperation between scientists and professionals. ✓**INTERNET**→*email* listserv@hearn.nic.surfnet.nl ✍ *Type in message body:* subscribe eawop-l <your full name>

Flexwork (ml) Do sliding hours and frequent changes in environment increase productivity or decrease confidence? Gain some insight into flexible employment conditions and their effects. ✓**INTERNET**→ *email* listserv@psuhmc.hmc.psu.edu ✍ *Type in message body:* subscribe flexwork <your full name>

IOOB-L (ml) Just how does the office environment influence employee productivity? Well-lit workspaces are obvious musts, but do you have to get rid of that orange furniture and the old Jethro Tull posters? This mailing list entertains a range of discussions in industrial and organizational psychology. ✓**INTERNET**→*email* listserv@uga.cc.uga.edu ✍ *Type in message body:* subscribe ioob-l <your full name>

The workplace

WorkPlace RoundTable The message boards cover a broad spectrum of workplace issues, ranging from evergreens (how to deal with a boorish boss) to this season's crop of curios (how to defuse postelection tension). Politically charged issues of the day—sexual harassment, AIDS in the workplace, and age discrimination—are met head-on. There's also a real-time chat area and a business software library. ✓**GENIE**→ *keyword* workplace

PR & advertising

You have an office. You have a product. But the phones aren't ringing. You need to

move into the market, but how? Learn the tricks of hawking wares with the broad spectrum of marketing resources available online. From advertising (**Ad Age/Creativity Online**) to public relations (**Public Relations and Marketing Forum** and **PR Newswires**), electronic databases and forums offer assistance for the small business looking to expand. Whether you're reviewing the FTC's advertising regulations in **Advertising Law** or reading about the intersection of marketing and technology in the **MARTECH** mailing list, the Net will meet your needs. It's new! It's improved! It's easy to use!

Greencard spam lawyers Canter & Siegel—ftp:lld.armory.com/pub/user/leavitt/gif/ch5

Across the board

Ad Age/Creativity Online News, features, detailed analysis of marketing and creativity issues, and real-time conversations with the leading names in marketing. ✓ **EWORLD**→*go* ad-age

Marketing/Management Research Center Provides access to a broad spectrum of business and marketing publications, as well as marketing research reports, market studies, statistical reports, and company newsletters. Most articles can be retrieved in full-text form. ✓ **COMPUSERVE**→*go* mrk **$**

Real-Time Marketing Strategies and anecdotes from real-world marketing campaigns, plus a forum where amateurs and professionals exchange ideas. ✓ **EWORLD**→ *go* realtime

Advertising

Advertising Law Information from the FTC's Advertising Guidelines, plus discussions of topics ranging from acceptable business names to deceptive pricing strategies. ✓ **INTERNET**→*www* http://www.webcom.com/~lewrose/home.html

Marketing

MARTECH—Marketing with Technology Tools (ml) Swap your thoughts with other marketing professionals about faxes, videophones, and all the other accoutrements of the modern office. ✓ **INTERNET**→*email* listserv@cscns.com ✉ *Type in message body:* subscribe martech <your full name>

Public relations

PR Newswires Press releases from hundreds of companies, all collected, and tagged by date and time. A useful place for learning how companies promote themselves. ✓ **DELPHI**→*go* bus pr

Public Relations and Marketing Forum Talk here revolves around how best to spin a product, the pros and cons of electronic seminars, the costs and benefits of traditional advertising, and the growing popularity of online marketing techniques. ✓ **COMPUSERVE** →*go* prsig

Trademark research

Can you think of adhesive strips without thinking of Band-Aids? Can you imagine gelatin

dessert without imagining Jell-O? A good trademark or trade name is often the difference between corporate mediocrity and superstardom, and if you're starting a new business, you'll certainly want to spend some time researching these issues of nomenclature. The Net offers a wide variety of search services, including **Trademarkscan**, **The Trademark Group**, and **British Trademarks**—while prices vary, all the services permit search-and-retrieve operations through huge databases of trademarks and trade names. And if you simply can't think of a name for your wonderful new product, pay a visit to Master-McNeil, Inc, a trade-name consultation firm that will help you select a name that conveys trust and desirability all across the The Business World.™

Ubiquitous Windows logo—downloaded from http://www.microsoft.com

ing to pay anything to wrest it from its current owners? Need to create a product name that will not carry unfortunate connotations in foreign tongues (remember the Chevy Nova disaster—the car that "doesn't go" in Spanish)? Well, just bring your business to Master-McNeil, Inc. Their clients include Apple Computer, Sprint, VISA USA, and Sega. ✓**INTERNET**→*www* http://www.naming.com/naming/company.html

Trade Names Database Band-Aid, Xerox, and Scotch tape are only a few of almost 300,000 trade names indexed here, along with brief product descriptions and distributor information. ✓**GENIE**→*keyword* tradenames **$**

Trademarks

British Trademarks Find regis-

tered U.K. trademarks and pending applications, as well as lapsed trademarks and applications since 1976. ✓**COMPUSERVE**→*go* uktrademarks **$**

Trade Marks Groups Retrieve information on hundreds of thousands of U.S. trademarks from the database of the U.S. Patent and Trademark Office. ✓**GENIE**→*keyword* trademarks **$**

The Trademark Group This service will see if your chosen business name is in use anywhere else, and will note first usage date, filing date, and recording date. Although the rates are not cheap ($99 for the first two names searched and $25 for each additional name), they're cheaper than lawyers' fees. ✓**INTERNET**→ *email* 6950774@mcimail.com ✍ *Write for help & support* **$**

Trademarkscan Combining two databases, one federal and the other state by state, Trademarkscan indexes well over a million registered trademarks. Enter the keyword in question, and the service will return five trademark names containing the word for $10. The retrieval is a bit slow, but it is comprehensive, and full reports include international and U.S. product classifications, serial numbers, filing dates, orginal applicants, and filing correspondents. Be warned: Even if a trademark is not listed in this database, it may still be a common-law trademark currently controlled by a business or an individual. ✓**COMPUSERVE**→*go* trd **$**

On the Net

Trade names

Master-McNeil, Inc. This Berkeley-based company is entirely devoted to the resolution of corporate naming issues. Think you might be using a trademark that's already taken? So desperate for an existing trademark that you're will-

Demographic research

Business is all about informed decisions, and sometimes it's important to know a little

bit about the community where you plan to locate your operation. For example, you wouldn't want to open a skateboard shop in a retirement community, or cut the ribbon on a huge McDonald's in a devout Hindu enclave. The Net is a good place to start looking for demographic insights. If it's hard data you want, head for CompuServe, where **Business Demographics**, **Neighborhood Demographics**, **State-County Demographics**, and **Supersite Demographics** provide a vast array of informative reports. You'll have to pay a bundle, but if it means the difference between a busy drive-through window and Chapter 11, you'll consider it money well spent.

On the Net

Across the board

Census Bureau Data While it contains some hard data, the Census Bureau's online service is useful primarily as a set of footnotes, offering methodological and regulatory information regarding the nation's statistics. Whether the data concern agriculture, business, construction and housing, foreign trade, government, international trade, manufacturing, population,

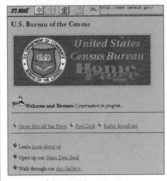

Bureau of Census Home page—http://www.census.gov

or genealogical distribution, there are rules for polling, verification, and disclosure, and Cendata reviews all those standards in detail. ✓ **COMPUSERVE**→*go* cendata

Demographics Lists state government bureaus responsible for providing statistical reports and abstracts, including statistics on crime, labor, health, and highway safety. Not much in the way of actual data, but a good starting point for the statistically minded. ✓ **COMPUSERVE**→*go* ius-10388

Definitions

Geographic Definitions An easy-to-use glossary of census terminology. ✓ **COMPUSERVE**→*go* dem-435

Demographic data

Business Demographics If you're thinking of opening a supermarket in northern Wyoming or selling office equipment in Maine, you'll probably want to know all about the business condi-

tions—not only how many competing businesses there are, but how many people they employ, and how they compare with other industries and services. This service offers reports by Zip Code, county, state, Metropolitan Statistical Area, Arbitron TV Market, or Nielsen TV Market, and furnishes basic statistical information on utilities, retail, wholesale, and financial businesses. ✓ **COMPUSERVE**→ *go* busdem **$**

Neighborhood Demographics What do you want to know about a neighborhood before you open a business there? Population breakdowns by age, race, family status, occupation, and income? The age of the buildings? Reports, which can be broken down by Zip Code, are $10 each. ✓ **COMPU-SERVE**→*go* neighbor **$**

State-County Demographics Basic census information by state, county, or neighborhood (Zip Code), as well as special neighborhood reports on civic and leisure activity. Reports sell for a flat fee of $10 each. ✓ **COMPUSERVE**→*go* usstcn **$**

Supersite Demographics You can select any combination of Zip Codes, counties, and states for up to 50 geographic areas, and retrieve detailed demographic data consolidated into a single report. Reports cost about $45 per category; more extensive reports, with data on socioeconomic status, racial background, and age breakdown, can run more than $100. ✓ **COMPUSERVE**→*go* supersite **$**

The corporate lawyer

Everybody needs a lawyer. You may not think you do, but you do. There's wrongful ter-

mination. There's the customer who claims that your urinal tried to kill him. From **Legal Research FAQ**, which offers a good introduction to the American justice system, to GEnie's **Law Center**, the online world offers a plethora of legal references and resources. Some, like eWorld's **Nolo Press**, are designed specifically as self-help law institutes. If you want to limit your interests to business law, check out the **Center for Corporate Law** and the online version of the **Uniform Commercial Code**. And if you want to prepare your business for future growth, don't forget to visit the variety of services that offer online incorporation, including **The Company Corporation** and **Corporate Agents, Inc.**

On the Net

Across the board

The Legal Forum Business-minded visitors can direct financial and corporate questions to the host of lawyers online. ✓**COMPUSERVE**→*go* legal

Legal Research FAQ Confused about the difference between a statutory citation and a regulatory citation? Curious about the struc-

The Corporate Agent— from http://www.corporate.com/

ture of federal district courts? This FAQ gives an introductory tour through the American justice system. ✓**INTERNET**→*ftp* rtfm.mit.edu→anonymous→<your email address>→/pub/usenet/news.answers/law/research

misc.legal.moderated (ng) The premier newsgroup for legal questions and answers. You'll be rewarded with legal conundrums, anecdotes from litigious readers, and occasional postings from legal experts. ✓**USENET**

Nolo Press As self-help law centers go, there are few as friendly as Nolo Press, which includes articles on recent legal developments, a large archive of briefs, and a catalog that lists related books, videotapes, and software. There's also plenty of interaction with eWorld's other legal hobbyists—real-time conferences on important issues and message boards where curious citizens can post queries to experts. Best of all, the atmosphere is one of friendly self-deprecation: The service includes

an archive of lawyer jokes ("Did you hear about the new sushi bar that caters exclusively to lawyers? It's called Sosumi."), and legal materials are referred to as "shark paraphernalia." ✓**EWORLD**→*go* nolo

Business & corporate

BizLaw-L (ml) Deals with the academic side of business law, presenting not only straightforward regulations but also fascinating hypotheticals. For example: What are the precedents for forcing the new owner of a company to assume responsibility for environmental misdeeds that occurred prior to the purchase of the business? Read on. ✓**INTERNET**→*email* listserv@umab.umd.edu ✍ *Type in message body:*

> **"Misc.legal.moderated is the premier newsgroup for legal questions and answers. You'll be rewarded with legal conundrums, anecdotes from litigious readers, and occasional postings from legal experts."**

subscribe bizlaw-l<your full name>

Center for Corporate Law Located at the University of Cincinnati, the recently established Center for Corporate Law includes the full text of the most important corporate acts of the post-Depression era: the Securities Acts of 1933 and 1934; the Public Utilities Holding Company Act of 1935; the Trust Indenture Act of 1939; the Securities Investor Protection Act of 1970; and more. ✓**INTERNET**→*www* http://www.law.uc.edu/CCL/

Databases

Law Center Know your rights. Know your corporate rights. Know your commercial rights. The center includes articles, decisions, and opinions on virtually every legal question imaginable. ✓**GENIE**→*keyword* lawcenter **$**

Legal Research Center How many companies have been shut down for refusing to comply with environmental regulations? Who exactly is liable for corporate misconduct? Here, you'll find quick and easy access to almost 1,000 legal publications, newsletters, and journals, with a special emphasis on business and finance law. ✓**COMPUSERVE**→*go* las **$**

Federal regulation

Federal Register The main source for all federal business, the *Federal Register* is one of the most important publications for small businessmen, furnishing lists of all new regulations effecting federal agencies. The register is archived online, and can be browsed or searched by agency or keyword. ✓**DELPHI**→*go* ref fed **$**

fedreg.commerce (ng) Though certainly not the busiest place in Cyberspace, it remains a useful site for questions or insights about the government's regulation of private business. ✓**USENET**

Legislation and Regulations What federal laws govern the creation of a new business? To what extent is an employer liable for occupational safety? How about environmental responsibility? And what are the requirements of the groundbreaking (and alliterative) Lead-Based Paint Poisoning Prevention Act? All these questions and more are answered on the Small Business Administration's online service. ✓**INTERNET**→*telnet* sbaonline.sba.gov→<your first name>→<your last name>→[2] Services Available

Incorporation

Business Incorporation Guide This guide includes basic articles on various legal and financial aspects of the incorporation process, including how to form a corporation, what resources are available for small businesses, and what free brochures are published by the government. ✓**GENIE**→*keyword* incorporate

The Company Corporation If you don't know the four types of corporations, or the 16 reasons to incorporate in Delaware, you'll want to visit this site. Answers are given in clear, concise language. In addition, you will have the opportunity to incorporate online for a reasonable fee. ✓**COMPUSERVE**→*go* co-31

Corporate Agents, Inc. Besides answering the usual incorporation questions—Why incorporate? what are the fees?—Corporate Agents, Inc. can incorporate your business in all 50 states or any-where in the world. ✓**INTERNET**→ *www* http://www.corporate.com/

UCC

Uniform Commercial Code Whether you're selling furs or leasing Fords, you must obey the provisions of the Uniform Commercial Code. Articles 1 to 9 of this imposing document are on display in a hypertext document at Cornell University Law School. Learn about bills of lading, bulk transfers, and chattel paper. ✓**INTERNET**→ *www* http://www.law.cornell.edu/ucc/ucc.table.html

---

CYBERNOTES

"U.S. Patent No. 5,163,447--'Force-Sensitive, Sound-Playing Condom.' This invention was the best of the bunch.

"Unfortunately, I did not feel comfortable passing this one out to high school students. As far as I know, this is the only patent to cite the Frederick's of Hollywood catalog as prior art. (p. 68: 'Wedding Surprise.' The mind boggles.) The object of this invention is to provide an invention that plays sounds, including songs or pre-recorded voice messages, so that users will like to use it."

—from **misc.legal. moderated**

Government contracts

Federal and state governments are among our nation's most energetic consumers,

buying billions of dollars annually in products and services from private companies. **Selling to the Government** offers a good introduction to offline resources, including extensive information on how to locate procurements and contracts. Then there are the extensive government resources online—whether you're interested in manufacturing wrenches for the Pentagon or building A-frames for HUD, the Net will help you realize your dream. And **FedWorld** links to a network of bulletin boards that represents the entire U.S. government.

On the Net

Air Force Small Business Bulletin Board RoundTable Want to do business with the Department of Defense or the U.S. Air Force? Meet business contacts and discuss the government's bidding process here. Bulletin-board categories and libraries carry Commerce Business Daily (CBD) announcements and acquisition estimates. ✓**GENIE**→*keyword* afsb3

Commerce Business Daily Interested in researching federal government product and service procurements? Use the Commerce Business Daily, a listing service which posts government an-

Ross Perot—downloaded from Compu-Serve's Archive Forum

nouncements online in advance of their printed appearance. CBD users can browse, or search by product, service, agency, and location. You can either subscribe ($499) at the Internet site and get full access, or perform free searches without the capability of storing any information. A portion of the daily CBD is also available for free on GEnie, in the library of the Air Force Small Business Bulletin Board RoundTable (keyword: afsb3). ✓**AMERICA ONLINE**→*keyword* cbd ✓**COMPUSERVE**→*go* cbd **$** ✓**GE-NIE**→ *keyword* cbd **$** ✓**INTERNET**→*telnet* usic.savvy.com→guest *Info:* ✓**IN-TERNET**→*email* cbd@savvy.com ✍ *Email for instructions*

Federal Register The main source for all federal regulations. Includes contract opportunities. Search by agency, keyword, or browse. (The register is archived online.) ✓**DELPHI**→*go* ref fed **$**

FEDIX/MOLIS A complete listing

of contracts and products available from major federal agencies. ✓**IN-TERNET**→*www* http://web.fie.com

FedWorld FedWorld serves as a gateway to hundreds of U.S. Government bulletin boards. Visit the FDA. Enjoy the friendly confines of the SBA. With agency-specific information on contracts, procurements, and purchasing needs, this is an essential starting point. ✓**IN-TERNET**→*telnet* fedworld.com

Government Giveaways Forum Discuss free government services and products in the areas of travel, health, education, and more. Owners of small businesses will probably be most interested in the Small/Home Business section (Category 13), which includes a library filled with government publications and related documents on microenterprise programs and contract strategies. ✓**COMPUSERVE**→*go* infousa→Government Giveaways Forum

Selling to the Government A complete guide to selling products and services to the government. Includes the protocol for bidding on jobs, and the addresses and phone numbers of major federal agencies. For whistle-blowers, there's the fraud hot line to report companies who are defrauding Uncle Sam. ✓**COMPUSERVE**→*go* ius-9847

U.S. Federal Center Full texts of the *Federal Register*, the *Federal News Service, Federal Research in Progress, Tax Notes Today*, and the *Washington Post* to inform you on the government's business practices. ✓**GENIE**→*go* federalctr **$**

Going international

These days, national identity is on the wane, at least as far as business is concerned.

Multinational corporations and electronic networks thwart national borders, and commerce spans countries and cultures. As a result, any business hoping to survive into the next century should at least consider the possibility of international expansion. On the Net, international business takes a number of forms, from politically oriented activist groups (**Consumers for World Trade**) to general discussions about other economies (**Europe Round-Table**, **Japan Forum**). In addition, there's a vast store of government material pertaining to international trade, from the General Agreement on Trades and Tariffs (**GATT 1994**) to the North American Free Trade Agreement (**NAFTA**). But the real highlight here is the **National Trade Data Bank**, one of the most extensive collection of statistical data anywhere in Cyberspace.

GATT press conference—from CompuServe's Reuters News Pictures Forum.

On the Net

Across the board

alt.business.import-export (ng) This newsgroup collects post-ings on important import and export concerns, and includes discussions about international business. ✓**USENET**

Consumers for World Trade Articles criticizing the United States' protectionist stance, written by a group of people who imagine the world as a global village. ✓**INTERNET**→*www* ftp://ftp.digex.net/pub/access/web/cwt.html

International Trade The business of buying and selling overseas is complicated not only by physical distance, but also by conceptual distance between nations' approaches to investment, insurance, and taxation issues. This document, one of the many helpful resources in the Information USA database, lists federal-assistance programs for businessmen who want to cross national boundaries. ✓**COMPUSERVE**→*go* ius-9962

International Trade BB While much of this bulletin board is concerned with the larger rhythms of international business, there is also a great deal of information about the nuts and bolts of foreign trade. How do you manage insurance

> "Everything is here in the National Trade Databank —from Russian Defense Department manifests to country-by-country, import-and-export profiles to a guide of international trade terms."

costs in distant lands? Where are the cheapest labor pools? √**PRODI-GY**→*jump* international trade bb

International chat

Eastern Europe Business Network (ml) Discuss the ins and outs, pros and cons, risks and rewards of moving venture capital into the space once defined by the Iron Curtain. √**INTERNET**→*email* listserv@pucc.princeton.edu ✍ *Type in message body:* subscribe e-europe <your full name>

Econom-L (ml) The Brazilian economy mailing list probes the economic future of South America's largest but still financially troubled nation. √**INTERNET**→ *email* listserv@ibm.ufsc.br ✍ *Type in message body:* subscribe econom-l <your full name>

Ekonomika (ml) If you can get past the stupid puns—bounced Czechs and so on—you might enjoy this mailing list, which evaluates the economy of Prague and outlying areas. √**INTERNET**→*email* listserver@pub.vse.cz ✍ *Type in message body:* subscribe ekonomika <your full name>

Europe RoundTable Discussion and debate about financial and cultural issues on the Continent. √**COMPUSERVE**→*go* europe

Japan Forum Treats all aspects of Japan: cultural and political trends, as well as those in the worlds of finance and business. √**COMPUSERVE**→*go* japan

Stats and reports

National Trade Data Bank A huge warehouse of statistics and reports pertaining to national and international trade, staggering in its coverage and complexity.

Everything is here, from Russian Defense Department manifests to country-by-country, import-and-export profiles to a guide of international trade terms. The Web server features Historical Trade Leads not on the gopher, and the gopher features Merchandise Trade Import and Export information not on the Web. √**INTERNET** ...→*gopher* sunny.stat-usa. gov→ STAT-USA: A Source of Economic, Business, Social, and Environmental Data Bank→National Trade Data Bank ...→*www* http://www.stat-usa.gov/ben.html $ ...→*ftp* sunny.stat-usa.gov→anonymous→<your email address>→/STAT-USA/NTDB

Trade agreements

GATT 1994 The full text of the General Agreement on Tariffs and Trade, along with analysis of the various planks. √**INTERNET**→*www* http://ananse.irv.uit.no/trade_law/gatt/nav/toc.html

Multilateral Trade Negotiations: The Uruguay Round Another version of the landmark trade document signed in Marraskesh in April 1994. √**INTERNET**→*www* http://heiwww.unige.ch/gatt/final_act/

NAFTA Simple and unadorned, this is the text of the North American Free Trade Agreement. The gopher site includes NAFTA documents, along with daily notes dispatched from the White House and a collection of White House press releases dealing with the agreement. √**INTERNET** ...→*www* http://the-tech.mit.edu/Bulletins/nafta.html ...→*gopher* niord.shsu. edu→Economics (SHSU Network Access Initiative Project)→NAFTA (North American Free Trade Agreement)

Selling in Cyberspace

If there's more fun in the new world, there's also more commerce—the Net has opened

up a wide variety of business opportunities. From online shopping to electronic advertisement, companies are finding their way in the community of computer users—and even flourishing. Fortunately, this rocket to the future comes with its own record; Net companies are scrupulous about documenting the particulars of their emergence into electronics. Check out **Net Commercial Use Strategies** or the **Net Business Journal** for an overview of the process, or dip into the well of advertising and marketing resources (**Net-Advertising FAQ**, **Dos and Don'ts of Online Marketing**, and the provocative **Electronic Billboads on the Digital Superhighway**). And if you already have a Net business but want to know who you're reaching online, you might want to consult **Internet Statistics and Demographics**.

On the Net

Across the board

alt.business.misc (ng) Much of the business here begins and ends online, with advertisements for

Welcome to the Allen Marketing Group Home Page

Allen Marketing Group home page— http://trinet.com/allen.html

temp services, import and export companies, and other providers of goods and services. Keep an eye out for discussions of business protocol and strategy for the online market. ✓**USENET**

Cyber Business Message Board What about Cyberbusiness? Is it the wave of the future or just a passing fad? Contributors tackle the most important marketing and advertising issues of our computer age. ✓**COMPUSERVE**→*go* usen→Messages→Cyber Business [15]

Internet Business Book This is an abbreviated online version of Jill Ellsworth's *Internet Business Book*, which covers the assorted risks and rewards of operating a business on the Internet. It includes a full table of contents, chapter excerpts, and an index. ✓**INTERNET**→*ftp* ftp.std.com→anonymous→<your email address>→ /pub/ibb

Internet Business Center Articles about doing business on the

Internet, along with comprehensive lists of current sites and services and links to other organizations and publications dealing with Cyberbusiness. ✓**INTERNET**→ *www* http://www.tig.com/IBC/in dex.html

Internet Business Journal One of the main publications devoted to online business, the *Internet Business Journal* has an advertising FAQ, as well as other short features and news stories intended to grease the skids for enterpreneurs and similarly minded cybernauts. ✓**INTERNET**→*gopher* gopher. cic.net→ Electronic Serials→Alphabetic List→I→Internet Business Journal

Internet Commercial Use Strategies One of the best starting points for anyone wishing to run a business on the Net, this

> "What about Cyberbusiness? Is it the wave of the future or just a passing fad? Contributors tackle the most important marketing and advertising issues of our computer age."

home page links to dozens of sites focusing on such topics as online marketing, electronic advertising, and corporate strategy. ✓INTERNET→*www* http://pass.wayne.edu/business.html

www-buyinfo Led by researchers at AT&T, the discussions cover topics relating to buying services over the Net: privacy issues, potential payment schemes (from DigiCash to anonymous credit cards). There's also speculation about the range of consumer products that will be available to netters in the future. ✓INTERNET→*email* www-buyinfo-request@allegra.att.com ✍ *Type in message body:* subscribe www-buyinfo <your full name>

Cybermarketing

Allen Marketing Group Home Page Marketing communications firm that provides a full range of interactive marketing services. ✓INTERNET→*www* http://www.trinet.com/allen.html

Discussions of On-Line Marketing From Internet marketing facts to debates over the future of credit cards, this site serves as a locus for discussions of marketing and commerce issues in the era of Cyberbusiness. Will money eventually be supplanted by digital currency? Perhaps. Come here and find out. ✓INTERNET→*www* http://ibd.ar.com/lists/FREE-MARKETS

The Dos and Don'ts of Online Marketing Do set up a registered email address. Don't send unsolicited email to potential customers. Do train your company personnel to understand the nature of the Net. Don't announce a Website before it is built. And do read this document, which furnishes basic tips for the online marketer. ✓INTERNET→*www* http://pass.wayne.edu/dosdonts.html

Electronic Billboards on the Digital Superhighway Written by the working group on Internet advertising, this report takes the pulse of the nation's newest marketing craze and makes some predictions about Madison Avenue's future. ✓INTERNET …→*ftp* ftp.cni.org→anonymous→<your email address>→/CNI/projects/advertising …→*gopher* gopher.cni.org→Coalition FTP Archives→Coalition Working Group Documents (/CNI/wg.docs)→Modernization of Scholarly Publication WG→Advertising on the Internet Project

Electrons vs. Paper An article comparing print and electronic advertising rates, and speculating on the effectiveness of the two media. ✓INTERNET→*www* http://ibd.ar.com/Info/About.Electrons.vs.Paper.html

Interactive Marketing Alert (j) Rosalind Resnick, the co-author of *The Internet Business Guide: Riding the Information Superhighway to Profit*, also publishes *Interactive Marketing Alert*, a free monthly newsletter that discusses how to own and operate a small business in Cyberspace. Features include success stories of "Cyberspace companies," tips on how to get free online publicity, and advice on designing online business cards. ✓INTERNET→*email* majordomo@marketplace.com ✍ *Type in message body:* subscribe cyberbiz-l <your full name>

Internet-Advertising FAQ What are the risks and rewards of placing an advertisement online? Why do some commercial services jump at the chance to hawk products while others watch like hawks for the slightest hint of commercial behavior? Answers to these questions and more. ✓INTERNET→*gopher* gopher.fonorola.net→Internet Business Journal→Internet Advertising FAQ

Cyberservices

Alex Hartley and Associates This group specializes in public affairs consulting services, including grant and proposal writing as well as campaign management. Runs seminars in team-building, leadership training, multicultural awareness, and communications skills. ✓INTERNET→*www* http://www.iquest.net/alex/alex.html

Executive Secretarial Services Full-service support center specializing in information processing, transcription, and database management. ✓INTERNET→*www* http://www.awa.com/ess/ess.html

Net demographics

Internet Statistics and Demographics Here, you'll find maps of the Net, World Wide Web usage statistics, and measurements of online populations calculated by the Global Network Navigator. ✓INTERNET→*www* http://akebono.stanford.edu/yahoo/Computers/Internet/Statistics_and_Demographics

> "Interactive Marketing Alert features success stories of 'Cyberspace companies.'"

CYBERPOWER!™

Setting Up Shop

My grandfather was part Seminole, or said he was, and he taught me how to carve crocodiles and Florida panthers from pieces of driftwood and deadwood. I decided to cut them with hard edges and use them as bookends. Though I am a teacher by trade, I have carved regularly since I was 15 and I have received compliments on my work. About ten years ago, I started selling the bookends at shops in Micanopy, a small town near Gainesville, Florida, and they are selling quite well. My teenage son says that I should sell them online. He's already got a name for the company—Woodn't It Be Nice—and he's designed something he calls a Web page. I would love to set up a little electronic business to sell the bookends, but I must confess that I don't understand a whole lot about the Internet. Am I just kidding myself, or can I really do this?

Sure you can. In fact, you should. Marry the craftsmanship of your grandfather to a cutting-edge electronic medium. Carve out a new market for yourself on the Net. And do so with the help of Global Commerce Link (http://www.commerce.com).

With offices in Boulder, Colorado, and Los Angeles, Global Commerce Link is only one of the dozens of young companies helping other businesses establish a commercial presence on the Net. GCL co-owner Jeff Jordan calls his firm a "designer of electronic storefronts," and in some ways it is exactly that. Businesses, both large and small, work with GCL to create online environments that accurately reflect the goods and services they offer. And then they handle customer traffic within the context of that environment.

This may sound vague. It's not. Say that you wanted to create a brochure to teach potential customers about the history of Seminole crafts, the importance of the crocodile and the panther to the tribe, and the art of whittling. Say that you wanted to connect that brochure to a small catalog of your bookends that featured pictures of completed carvings. And say that you wanted to set up a system that would allow interested consumers in Montana or Moscow to buy your work without trekking out to Micanopy. No problem. GCL can create online advertisements and catalog services, or it can take the ones your son has already created and connect them to the Internet. With the company's help, you can learn to create an electronic mailing list, or respond to questions and complaints online. And if your business diversifies and you start to carve doorstops and walking sticks in addi-

Global Commerce Link Home page

tion to bookends, changing your online ads is as simple as editing a document in a word processor.

GCL doesn't only work with small companies—in fact, they've done work for corporations as huge as AT&T. But do you have hundreds of thousands of dollars to pay for fancy graphics and sophisticated network management? Probably not. So you'll be happy to learn that this basic service—limited online presence that includes introductory marketing materials—costs no more than a few hundred dollars a month. If you sell even a single pair of your bookends every few weeks, you'll be breaking even.

Appendices

Appendices

A selection of the
smartest, richest, and riskiest sites in Cyberspace

Absolutely Do Not Miss

CheckFree ✓**AMERICA ONLINE**→ *keyword* checkfree ✓**COMPUSERVE**→ *go* checkfree ✓**GENIE**→*keyword* checkfree

Dow Jones News/Retrieval ✓**INTERNET**→*telnet* djnr.dowjones. com

Eaasy Sabre ✓**AMERICA ONLINE**→ *keyword* sabre ✓**COMPUSERVE**→*go* sabre ✓**EWORLD**→*go* sabre ✓**DELPHI** →*go* trav→air→sabre ✓**GENIE**→*key-word* sabre ✓**PRODIGY**→ *jump* eaasy sabre

Electronic Tax Filing Informa-tion (1040 BBS) (bbs) ☎→*dial* 202-927-4180→<your login>→ <your password>→/go gateway →D→33 ✓**INTERNET**→*telnet* fed world.gov→<your login>→<your password>→/go gateway→D→33

Supersite Demographics ✓**COMPUSERVE**→*go* supersite **$**

Most Impressive Statistical Databases

The Economics Bulletin Board ☎→*dial* 202-482-2167/202-482-3870/202-482-2584 ✓**INTERNET**→ *gopher* una.hh.lib.umich.edu

Federal Reserve ☎→*dial* 314-621-1824→Federal Reserve Board ✓**INTERNET**→*gopher* town.hall.org→ Federal Reserve Board

National Trade Data Bank ✓**INTERNET**→*gopher* sunny.stat-usa.gov→STAT-USA a Source of Economic, Social, and Environmen-tal Data Bank→National Trade Data Bank ✓**INTERNET**→*ftp* sunny. stat-usa.gov→anonymous→<your email address>→/STAT-USA/NTDB

Best Use of Tax Dollars

ASKERIC ✓**INTERNET**→*www* http:// eryx.syr.edu

Consumer Products Safety Commission ✓**INTERNET** ...→*go-pher* cpsc.gov ...→*email* cpsc/ g=Arthur/i=K./s=McDonald/o=cpsc /ou1=cpsc-hq2@mhs.attmail.com ✍ *File a product complaint*

Patent Search ✓**INTERNET** ...→ *gopher* town.hall.org→US Patent and Trademark Office ...→*www* http://town.hall.org/cgi-bin/srch-patent

Small Business Administra-tion Online ✓**INTERNET** ...→*telnet* sbaonline.sba.gov ...→*www* http:// www.fedworld.gov→D→40 *or* 41

Most Glamorous

GNN Travel Center Region/ Country/City/State Guides ✓**INTERNET**→*www* http://nearnet. gnn.com/gnn/meta/travel/res/ countries.html

Paris ✓**INTERNET**→*www* http://me teora.ucsd.edu/~norman/paris/

Begin Your Investment Day with...

Finance (echo) ✓**RELAYNET**

Investors' RoundTable ✓**GENIE** →*keyword* invest

QuoteCom Data Service ✓**IN-TERNET**→*www* http://www.quote. com/help.html ✍ *Email for auto-mated info*

Finnish Your Investment Day with...

clari.biz.market.report.eu-rope ✓**CLARINET**

Coolest Real-Time Stock Ticker

Signal ☎→*dial* 415-571-1800 (vox) **$**

Netted

Most Foolish

The Motley Fool Investment Forum ✓AMERICA ONLINE→*keyword* fool

Most Amazing Thing Peter Has Ever Done on a Computer

TaxCut Software ✓COMPUSERVE →*go* meca

Raciest

Condom Country ✓INTERNET→*www* http://www.ag.com/Condom/Country

Spaciest

Investors in Space ✓INTERNET→*email* server@lunacity.com ✍ *Type in message body:* join space-in vestors

Spiciest

Chile Today Hot Tamale ✓INTERNET→*www* http://eMail.com/Chile/Chile1.html

Hot Hot Hot ✓INTERNET→*www* http://www.presence.com/hot

Sleaziest

alt.make.money.fast (ng) ✓USENET

Ben's Favorite Official Airline Guide

Official Airline Guide ✓COMPUSERVE→*go* oag $ ✓DELPHI→*go* trav air→oag $ ✓GENIE→*keyword* oag

Ben's Least Favorite Official Airline Guide

Official Airline Guide ✓COMPUSERVE→*go* oag $ ✓DELPHI→*go* trav air→oag $ ✓GENIE→*keyword* oag

Most Crowded

alt.business.misc (ng) ✓USENET

misc.invest (ng) ✓USENET

misc.jobs.resumes (ng) ✓USENET

Most Comforting

The ABCs of Financial Aid ✓EWORLD→*go* rsp→The ABCs of Financial Aid

Retirement Planning ✓AMERICA ONLINE→*keyword* yourmoney→Retirement Planning

Stress Managment ✓AMERICA ONLINE→*keyword* health→Lifestyles & Wellness→Stress Management

Best Theme Park Disguised as a Goverment BBS

FEDWORLD—The U.S. Government Bulletin Board (bbs) ☎→*dial* 703-321-8020→<your login>→<your password>→/go JOBS ✓INTERNET →*telnet* fedworld.gov→<your login>→<your password>→/go JOBS

In Case You're Looking for Blueprints of a Robotic Cat

Research Ideas Home Page ✓INTERNET→*www* http://ugsun1a.ph.bham.ac.uk:3006/research/concepts.html

Most Intricate

Stern School EDGAR ✓INTERNET →*www* http://edgar.stern.nyu.edu/

Town Hall EDGAR ✓INTERNET→*www* http://town.hall.org/edgar/edgar.html

Most Condescending

Big Dreams ✓INTERNET→*www* http://www.wimsey.com/~duncans/

Mind Garden: Personal & Career Understanding ✓EWORLD →*go* mindgarden

Best Self-Help Law Center

Nolo Press ✓EWORLD→*go* nolo

Calling these Sites Boring is an Insult to Boring People

List of the Society for Computational Economics (ml) ✓INTERNET→*email* listserv@sara.nl ✍ *Type in message body:* subscribe sce-list <your full name>

Risk and Insurance Working Papers Archives ✓INTERNET→*www* http://riskweb.bus.utexas.edu/rmi/workingpaper.html

Easiest-to-Use News Service

Industry Decisionlines ✓EWORLD→*go* usa today

Best Online Private Investigator

InPhoto Surveillance ✓INTERNET→*www* http://www.interaccess.com/users/rjones/

Rub Elbows with the Rich and Famous

The Last Will and Testament of Jacqueline Kennedy Onassis ✓COMPUSERVE→*go* legal→Browse Libraries→General→ *Download a file:* JACKIO.ZIP

Michael's Favorite Reference

Hoover's Handbook Profiles
✓**AMERICA ONLINE**→*keyword* com pany ✓**COMPUSERVE**→*go* hoover ✓**EWORLD**→*go* hoovers

Most Futuristic

Ecash ✓**INTERNET**→*www* http:// www.digicash.com

Global Commerce Link ✓**IN- TERNET**→*www* http://www. commerce.com

NeuroQuant Profiles ✓**INTER- NET**→*www* http://www.quote. com/newsletters/neuroquant/ **$**

Most Useful if You Happen to Live in Arizona

ASEDD Economic Database ✓**INTERNET**→*gopher* info.asu.edu→ ASU Campus-Wide Information→ ASEDD Economic Database (ASU)

Best Place to Learn to Cash a Check

Online Banking FAQ ✓**PRODIGY** →*jump* banking faq

Best Place to Learn to Cash a Czech

Ekonomika (ml) ✓**INTERNET**→ *email* listserver@pub.vse.cz ✍ *Type in message body:* subscribe ekonom ika <your full name>

Best Place to Learn to Check a CASHE

CASHE Scholarship Informa- tion ✓**GENIE**→*keyword* cashe **$**

Best Investment Newsletter that also Sounds Like a Palm Reader

Predicto ✓**INTERNET**→*www* http:// www.quote.com/newsletters /predicto/ **$**

Kelly's Favorite Gunsmith

Scott, McDougall, and Asso- ciates ✓**INTERNET**→*ftp* ftp.crl. com→anonymous→<your email ad- dress>→/users/ro/macscott/ firearms

Kristin's Favorite Career Site

E-SPAN ✓**AMERICA ONLINE**→*key- word* jobs ✓**COMPUSERVE**→*go* espan ✓**GENIE**→*keyword* job ✓**INTER- NET**→*www* http://www.espan. com/js/js.html *Register:* ✓**INTER- NET**→ resumes@espan3.espan.com ✍ *Email resume for inclusion in database*

Most Final

Sample Will ✓**AMERICA ONLINE** →*keyword* mbs→Software Libraries →*Search by file name:* WILL_ 93.TXT

Business Boards

by area code

Business Network Source
201-836-1844

Evergreen BBS
201-398-2373

The Market BBS
201-467-3269

Commerce Department Economic BBS
202-482-3870

The CPA's BBS
202-882-9067

BookBBS
203-787-5460

Fun Investing BBS
203-834-0490

The Executive BBS
203-442-3510

DFG Financial BBS
205-745-0579

Investors Online Data
206-285-5359

World Class Software BBS
210-656-7939

Free Financial Network
212-752-8660

Business World BBS
215-643-4025

Greenhill Comp/Line
215-441-8812

The Main Frame I
215-547-9241

PC-Ohio
216-381-3320

ProfitMaker BBS
217-224-3203

Business Online
301-587-8777

CRC Systems Ltd. BBS
303-438-0936

Stoic Financial BBS
303-238-0588

The Board of Directors
303-693-4798

Bob & Vicky's
305-749-8271

Data Highway
305-797-9841

Shareware Online
305-232-8000

CyberKorea
310-926-1899

ECN
310-204-6007

The Bizopps Connection
310-677-7034

Jbs-BBS
312-583-1674

Union Station
316-945-2430

The Stock Exchange BBS
319-236-0834

Synectics BBS
403-484-3954

Business Resource Network
404-564-3556

Steppin Wolf
404-498-8684

Universal Trade Network
404-294-6668

The Cutting Edge BBS
405-793-9728

Mealey's USA Direct
407-881-0358

Micro Key! BBS
407-870-0386

Magnus Online
410-893-4786

Town Center Info Exchange
410-995-1809

Global Trade Net
415-668-0422

ComputerLink Online Inc.
416-233-54101

The U.S.A. BBS
501-753-8575

Space Station Freedom BBS
502-969-0407

Custom Built Systems
503-399-9232

Information Odyssey
503-650-2992

Comm-Net BBS
512-244-9753

Quantum Thump
512-795-9175

Sunriver Corporation
512-835-8082

Tinker Board
512-926-1703

Wallingford Electronic
512-452-0955

Leisure & Business BBS
516-293-7540

Med Link
601-626-7033

Sunwise
602-584-7395

Evening Star BBS
608-752-8935

Strictly Business!
614-538-9250

Masters Place
618-234-4043

BIZynet BBS
619-283-1721

Mexico Online
619-698-5753

Online Resource
619-793-8360

Our House BBS
619-460-8507

The Business Connection
619-576-0049

The Comm Port
619-589-8571

The House That Jack Built
619-484-1998

The Market Hotline
703-633-2178

The Small Business Board
703-941-1831

Black Hole
708-263-7221

Cyber Information Services
708-697-9572

Pitstar BBS
708-687-4413

Cash Cow BBS
714-962-1857

Cyberia
717-840-1444

Pennsylvania Online
717-657-8699

TANSTAAFL BBS
717-432-0764

The Board Room BBS
717-393-2640

Moneyline Express
718-816-5502

The Glendale Tower BBS
718-417-8601

SBA Online
800-697-4636

GAMMA On-line
804-565-3503

Biz-Net 2000 On-Line
810-559-8604

Investment Analysis BBS
810-751-3706

Execuserve-RBBS
813-378-0273

Gemini Dreams
813-942-9602

World Data
815-886-3829

IntelNET
818-358-6538

Sleuth BBS
818-727-7639

Terrapin Station BBS
904-939-8027

Random Walk Investment BBS
905-274-2381

The Wishing Well
908-651-1823

The Library BBS
909-780-6365

BIZtrac BBS
912-786-6249

Go Diamond BBS
914-665-1725

The Trading Post BBS
915-821-8071

Software Support

by manufacturer

Aatrix Software ✓ **AMERICA ONLINE**→ *keyword* aatrix

Abacus ✓ **COMPUSERVE**→ *go* abacus

Acius ✓ **COMPUSERVE**→ *go* acius ✓ **INTERNET**→ *email* D4444@applelink.apple.com

---

Advanced Software, Inc. ✓ **AMERICA ONLINE**→ *keyword* advanced ✓ **COMPUSERVE**→ *go* macdven

---

Affinity Microsystems, Ltd. ✓ **AMERICA ONLINE**→ *keyword* affinity

---

After Hours Software ✓ **AMERICA ONLINE**→ *keyword* industry connection→Business→After Hours Software

---

Ambrosia Software, Inc. ✓ **AMERICA ONLINE**→ *keyword* ambrosia ✓ **GENIE**→ *keyword* macsupport→Macintosh Product Support Bulletin Board→Ambrosia Software, Inc. ...→ *keyword* macsupport →Macintosh Software Libraries→ Set Software Library→Ambrosia Software, Inc.

American Cybernetics ✓ **COMPUSERVE**→ *go* cybernet

Avocat Systems ✓ **AMERICA ONLINE**→ *keyword* avocat ✓ **EWORLD**→ *go* avocatsys ✓ **INTERNET**→ *email* avocat@usit.net

---

Baseline Publishing, Inc. ✓ **AMERICA ONLINE**→ *keyword* baseline ✓ **COMPUSERVE**→ *go* maccven or winapd

---

Best!Ware ✓ **AMERICA ONLINE**→ *keyword* myob ✓ **COMPUSERVE**→ *go* accounting→Browse Messages or Browse Libraries→MYOB

Borland dBASE Forum ✓ **COMPUSERVE**→ *go* dbase

Bottom Line Software, Inc. (bbs) ☎→ *dial* 214-394-4170

Business Sense, Inc. ✓ **AMERICA ONLINE**→ *keyword* business sense

---

CASE-DCI Forum ✓ **COMPUSERVE** → *go* caseforum

CE Software ✓ **AMERICA ONLINE**→ *keyword* ce software ✓ **COMPUSERVE** → *go* macaven ✓ **INTERNET**→ *email* cesoftware@applelink.apple.com

---

Claris ✓ **AMERICA ONLINE**→ *keyword* claris ✓ **COMPUSERVE**→ *go* macclaris *or* winclaris *or* clatech

---

CogniTech ✓ **COMPUSERVE**→ *go* winapf

CoStar Corporation (bbs) ☎→ *dial* 203-661-6292 ✓ **AMERICA ONLINE**→ *keyword* costar

---

Delrina (bbs) ☎→ *dial* 416-441- 2752 ✓ **COMPUSERVE**→ *go* delrina

---

ELAN Software (bbs) ☎→ *dial* 310-459-3443 ✓ **COMPUSERVE**→ *go* elan

---

Equis International Software Forum ✓ **AMERICA ONLINE**→ *keyword* equis

---

Expert Choice Software, Inc. ✓ **AMERICA ONLINE**→ *keyword* expert ✓ **COMPUSERVE**→ *go* pcveni

---

Franklin Quest Company

(bbs) ☎→ *dial* 801-977-1991 ✓ **AMERICA ONLINE**→ *keyword* franklin

---

Hazard Soft (bbs) ☎→ *dial* 405- 243-3200

HDC Computer (bbs) ☎→ *dial* 206-869-2418

Hooper International ✓ **COMPUSERVE**→ *go* pcvenc

Intuit Software ✓ **COMPUSERVE**→ *go* intuit ✓ **GENIE**→ *keyword* chipsoft ✓ **PRODIGY**→ *jump* intuit

---

ISIS International ✓ **AMERICA ONLINE**→ *keyword* aol ✓ **INTERNET**→ *www* ftp://ftp.netcom.com/pub /isis/home.html ...→ *email* isis@ netcom.com

---

Linn Software Forum ✓ **AMERICA ONLINE**→ *keyword* linnsoft

Lotus (bbs) ☎→ *dial* 617-693-7001 ✓ **COMPUSERVE**→ *go* lotusa

---

M-USA Business Systems ✓ **COMPUSERVE**→ *go* pcvenc

Mainstay ✓ **AMERICA ONLINE**→ *keyword* mainstay ✓ **COMPUSERVE**→ *go* macaven

---

Market Master Market Master ✓ **AMERICA ONLINE**→ *keyword* market master

---

Masterclip Graphics (bbs) ☎→ *dial* 305-967-9453

MECA ✓ **COMPUSERVE**→ *go* meca

Micro J Systems ✓ **AMERICA ONLINE**→ *keyword* microj

Microsoft ✓**COMPUSERVE**→*go* microsoft ✓**GENIE**→*keyword* microsoft ✓**INTERNET**→*www* http://www.microsoft.com ...→*gopher* 198.105.232.4 ...→*ftp* ftp.microsoft.com→anonymous→<your email address>→/MSLFILES

MIP Fund Accounting ✓**COMPUSERVE**→*go* pcvenf

New Era Computing ✓**AMERICA ONLINE**→*keyword* new era

Nine to Five Software ✓**AMERICA ONLINE**→*keyword* industry→Companies by Category→Business→Nine to Five

Now Software ✓**AMERICA ONLINE**→*keyword* now ✓**EWORLD**→*go* nowsoft ✓**GENIE**→*keyword* macsupport→Macintosh Product Support Bulletin Board→Now Software ...→*keyword* macsupport→Macintosh Software Libraries→Set Software Library→Now Software ✓**INTERNET**→*email* support@nowsoft.com

Odyssey Computing ✓**COMPUSERVE**→*go* odyssey

Okna Corporation ✓**COMPUSERVE**→*go* okna

Omega Research Forum ✓**AMERICA ONLINE**→*keyword* omega

ON Technology ✓**AMERICA ONLINE**→*keyword* on

Packer Software, Inc. ✓**AMERICA ONLINE**→*keyword* packer

Patton & Patton Software (bbs) ☎→*dial* 408-778-9697

Peachtree Software ✓**COMPUSERVE**→*go* pcvenf *and* winpeach

Polaris Software ☎→*dial* 619-592-2674 ✓**COMPUSERVE**→*go* polaris

Portfolio Software, Inc. ✓**AMERICA ONLINE**→*keyword* dyno ✓**COMPUSERVE**→*go* macaven

Powercore ☎→*dial* 815-468-2633 ✓**COMPUSERVE**→*go* powercore

Raindrop Software ✓**COMPUSERVE**→*go* raindrop

Reality Technologies ✓**COMPUSERVE**→*go* pcvenh

Sharp Electronic Corp. ✓**COMPUSERVE**→*go* sharp

Softek Design, Inc. ✓**AMERICA ONLINE**→*keyword* industry→Companies by Category→Business→Softek Design

Softsync ✓**COMPUSERVE**→*go* macvenc

Spinnaker ✓**COMPUSERVE**→*go* spinnaker

Sundial Systems ✓**COMPUSERVE**→*go* relish→Browse Messages *or* Browse Libraries→Sundial Systems

Symantec Corporation ✓**AMERICA ONLINE**→*keyword* symantec ✓**COMPUSERVE**→*go* symantec ✓**INTERNET**→*www* http://www.symantec.com/

Synex ✓**AMERICA ONLINE**→*keyword* synex ✓**COMPUSERVE**→*go* synex→Browse Messages *or* Browse Libraries→Synex Systems

TeleScan Users Forum ✓**AMERICA ONLINE**→*keyword* telescan

Timeline Software (bbs) ☎→*dial* 415-892-0408

Timeslips Corporation ☎→*dial* 508-768-7581 ✓**AMERICA ONLINE**→*keyword* timeslips ✓**COMPUSERVE**→*go* timeslips

TouchStone Software (bbs) ☎→*dial* 714-969-0688

Trendsetter ✓**AMERICA ONLINE**→*keyword* trendsetter

Visionary Software ✓**AMERICA ONLINE**→*keyword* visionary

WordPerfect Corporation ☎→*dial* 801-225-4444 ✓**AMERICA ONLINE**→*keyword* wordperfect ✓**COMPUSERVE**→*go* wordperfect ✓**INTERNET**→*www* http://www.wordperfect.com/ ...→*ftp* ftp.wordperfect.com→anonymous→<your email address>

Internet Providers

National

AlterNet/UUNet Technologies ☎→*dial* 800-488-6384 (vox) ✓**INTERNET**→*email* info@uunet.uu.net

BIX ☎→*dial* 800-695-4775 (vox) ✓**INTERNET**→*email* info@bix.com ✉ *Email for info*

CERFNet ☎→*dial* 800-876-2373 (vox) ✓**INTERNET** ...→*ftp* ftp.cerf.net →anonymous→<your email address>→/cerfnet/cerfnet_sales ...→*email* info@cerf.net ✉ *Email for automated info*

CR Laboratories ☎→*dial* 415-837-5300 (vox)/415-705-6060→guest ✓**INTERNET** ...→*telnet* crl.com→guest ...→*email* info@crl.com ✉ *Email for automated info*

Delphi ☎→*dial* 800-695-4005 (vox)/800-695-4002→JOINDELPHI→FREE ✓**INTERNET** ...→*telnet* delphi.com→joindelphi→free ...→*email* info@delphi.com ✉ *Email for automated info*

Express Access ☎→*dial* 800-969-9090 (vox)/301-220-0258/410-605-2700/703-281-7997→new ✓**INTERNET** ...→*telnet* access.digex.com→new→new ...→*ftp* ftp.digex.net→anonymous→<your email address>→/pub ...→*email* info@digex.net ✉ *Email for automated info*

Global Enterprise Services ☎→*dial* 800-358-4437 (vox) ✓**INTERNET** ...→*ftp* ftp.jvnc.net→anonymous→<your email address> →/pub/jvncnet-info ...→*email* info@jvnc.net ✉ *Email for auto-*

mated info

Internet Express ☎→*dial* 800-748-1200 (vox)/719-520-1700/303-758-2656/212-843-2102/800-748-3900→new →newuser ✓**INTERNET** ...→*telnet* usa.net→new→newuser ...→*email* service@usa.net ✉ *Email for info*

Netcom Online Communication Services ☎→*dial* 800-353-6600 (vox) ✓**INTERNET** ...→*telnet* netcom.com →guest→guest ...→*ftp* ftp.netcom. com→anonymous→<your email address>→/pub/netcom ...→*email* info@netcom.com ✉ *Email for automated info*

NovaLink ☎→*dial* 800-274-2814 (vox)/508-754-4009/800-937-7644→new ✓**INTERNET** ...→*ftp* ftp.novalink.com→anonymous→<your email address>→/info/novalink-info ...→*email* info@novalink.com ✉ *Email for automated info*

PSILink ☎→*dial* 800-827-7482 (vox) ✓**INTERNET** ...→*ftp* ftp.psi.com→anonymous→<your email address>→/info ...→*email* interramp-info@psi.com ✉ *Email for automated info*

YPN—Your Personal Network ☎→*dial* 800-NET-1133 (vox)/212-376-6276/ ✓**INTERNET** ...→*telnet* ypn.com→ guest...→*www* www.ypn.com ...→*email* info@ypn.com ✉ *Email for automated info*

Alabama

Nuance Network Services ☎→*dial* 205-533-4296 (vox) ✓**INTERNET** ...→*ftp* ftp.nuance.com

→anonymous→<your email address>→/pub/NNS-INFO ...→*email* jkl@nuance.com ✉ *Email for info*

Arizona

Data Basix ☎→*dial* 602-721-1988 (vox)/602-721-5887→guest ✓**INTERNET** ...→*telnet* Data.Basix.com→guest ...→*email* info@data-basix.com ✉ *Email for automated info*

Evergreen Communications ☎→*dial* 602-230-9330 (vox) ✓**INTERNET**→*email* evergreen@enet.net ✉ *Email for info*

Internet Direct, Inc. ☎→*dial* 602-274-0100 (vox)/602-274-9600/602-321-9600→guest ✓**INTERNET** ...→*telnet* indirect.com→guest→guest ...→*email* info@direct.com ✉ *Email for automated info*

California

a2i communications ☎→*dial* 408-293-8078 (vox)/415-364-5652/408-293-9020 ✓**INTERNET** ...→*telnet* a2i.rahul. net→guest→<none> ...→*ftp* ftp.rahul.net→anonymous→<your email address>→/pub/BLURB ...→*email* info@rahul.net ✉ *Email for automated info*

CTS Network Services (bbs) ☎→*dial* 619-637-3637 (vox)/619-637-3640/619-637-3660→help ✓**INTERNET** ...→*telnet* crash.cts.com→help ...→*ftp* ftp.cts.com →anonymous→<your email address>→/ctsnet.info ...→*email* info@cts.com ✉ *Email for auto-*

mated info

DPC Systems ☎→*dial* 818-305-5733 (vox) ✓**INTERNET**→*email* connect@dpcsys.com ✍ *Email for info*

E & S Systems Public Access ☎→*dial* 619-278-8124/619-278-9127/619-278-8267/619-278-9837→bbs ✓**INTERNET**→*email* steve@cg57.esnet.com ✍ *Email for info*

HoloNet ☎→*dial* 510-704-0160 (vox)/510-704-1058→guest ✓**INTERNET** ...→*telnet* holonet.net →guest ...→*ftp* holonet.net→anonymous→<your email address>→/info ...→*email* info@holonet.net ✍ *Email for automated info*

Institute for Global Communications ☎→*dial* 415-442-0220 (vox)/415-322-0284→new ✓**INTERNET** ...→*ftp* igc.apc.org→anonymous→<your email address>→/pub ...→*email* info@igc.apc.org ✍ *Email for automated info*

KAIWAN Internet Services ☎→*dial* 714-638-2139 (vox)/310-527-4279/818-579-6701/818-756-0180/714-539-5726/714-741-2920→guest ✓**INTERNET** ...→*ftp* kaiwan. com→anonymous→<your email address>→/pub/KAIWAN ...→*email* info@kaiwan.com ✍ *Email for automated info*

The Portal System ☎→*dial* 800-433-6444 (vox)/408-725-0560/408-973-1931/415-344-9665/415-366-8089/510-659-0669→help ✓**INTERNET** ...→*telnet* portal.com→online→info ...→*email* info@portal.com ✍ *Email for automated info*

The Well ☎→*dial* 415-332-4335 (vox)/415-332-8410/415-332-6106→newuser ✓**INTERNET** ...→*telnet* well.com→guest ...→*email* info@well.com ✍ *Email for auto-*

mated info

Colorado

Colorado SuperNet, Inc. ☎→*dial* 303-273-3471 (vox) ✓**INTERNET** ...→*ftp* csn.org→anonymous→ <your email address>→/CSN/reports/DialinIno.txt ...→*email* info@csn.org ✍ *Email for automated info*

Old Colorado City Communications ☎→*dial* 719-632-4848 (vox)/719-632-4111→newuser ✓**INTERNET** ...→*telnet* oldcolo.com→newuser ...→*email* thefox@oldcolo.com ✍ *Email for info*

Connecticut

NEARnet ☎→*dial* 617-873-8730 (vox) ✓**INTERNET** ...→*ftp* ftp.near.net→anonymous→<your email address>→/what_is_nearnet.txt ...→*email* nearnet-join@near.net ✍ *Email for info*

DC, MD, VA

CAPCON Library Network ☎→*dial* 202-331-5771 (vox) ✓**INTERNET**→*email* capcon@capcon.net ✍ *Email for automated info*

Clark Internet Services, Inc. ☎→*dial* 800-735-2258ext.410-730-9764 (vox)/410-730-9786/410-995-0271/301-596-1626/301-854-0446→guest ✓**INTERNET** ...→*telnet* clark.net→guest ...→*ftp* ftp.clark.net→anonymous→<your email address>→/pub/clarknet. ...→*email* info@clark.net ✍ *Email for automated info*

Global Connect ☎→*dial* 804-229-4484 (vox) ✓**INTERNET**→*email* info@gc.net ✍ *Email for info*

IMS Intercom ☎→*dial* 301-856-2706(vox)/301-856-0817→

newuser→newuser ✓**INTERNET**→*email* led@imssys.com ✍ *Email for info*

InfiNet ☎→*dial* 800-849-7214 (vox) ✓**INTERNET**→*email* support@infi.net ✍ *Email for info* ✍ *Email for info*

Merit Network, Inc / MichNet ☎→*dial* 313-764-9430 (vox) ✓**INTERNET** ...→*telnet* hermes.merit.edu→help ...→*ftp* nic.merit.edu→anonymous→<your email address>→/michnet ...→*email* info@merit.edu ✍ *Email for automated info*

Delaware

SSNet ☎→*dial* 302-378-1386 (vox) ✓**INTERNET**→*email* info@marlin.ssnet.com ✍ *Email for automated info*

VoiceNet/DSC ☎→*dial* 215-674-9290 (vox)/215-443-7390 ✓**INTERNET**→*email* info@voicenet.com ✍ *Email for automated info*

Florida

CyberGate, Inc. ☎→*dial* 305-428-4283 (vox) ✓**INTERNET**→*email* info@gate.net ✍ *Email for automated info*

The IDS World Network ☎ 401-884-7856 (vox)/305-534-0321/305-428-2663/914-637-6100/401-884-9002/401-294-5779→ids→guest ✓**INTERNET** ...→*telnet* ids.net→guest ...→*email* info@ids.net ✍ *Email for automated info*

Illinois

InterAccess ☎→*dial* 800-967-1580 (vox)/708-671-0237/708-260-8539/312-705-6633→guest ✓**INTERNET** ...→*ftp* interaccess.com→anonymous→<your email ad-

dress> →/pub/interaccess.info ...→*email* info@interaccess.com ✍ *Email for automated info*

MCSNet ☎→*dial* 312-248-8649 (vox)/708-637-0900/708-262-0900/312-248-0900/312-248-5687→bbs→new ✓**INTERNET** ...→*telnet* gateway.mcs.com→mcs→help ...→*ftp* ftp.mcs.com→anonymous→<your email address>→/mcsnet. info ...→*email* info@mcs.com ✍ *Email for automated info*

Prairienet ☎→*dial* 217-244-1962 (vox)/217-255-9000→visitor ✓**INTERNET** ...→*telnet* prairienet.org→visitor ...→*email* info@prairienet. org ✍ *Email for info*

XNet Information Systems ☎→*dial* 708-983-6064 (vox) /708-983-6435/708-882-1101→guest→new ✓**INTERNET** ...→*telnet* net.xnet.com→guest ...→*email* info@xnet.com ✍ *Email for automated info*

Iowa

Iowa Network Services ☎→*dial* 800-546-6587 (vox) ✓**INTERNET**→*email* info@ins.infonet.net ✍ *Email for automated info*

Maine

NEARnet ☎→*dial* 617-873-8730 (vox) ✓**INTERNET** ...→*email* nearnet-join@near.net ✍ *Email for info*

Massachusetts

MV Communications, Inc. ☎→*dial* 603-429-2223 (vox)/603-424-7428/603-645-6387→info ✓**INTERNET** ...→*telnet* mv.mv. com→info ...→*email* info@mv.com ✍ *Email for automated info*

NEARnet ☎→*dial* 617-873-8730 (vox) ✓**INTERNET**→*email* nearnet-

join@near.net ✍ *Email for info*

North Shore Access ☎→*dial* 617-593-3110 (vox)/617-593-4557→new ✓**INTERNET** ...→*telnet* shore.shore.net→new ...→*email* info@shore.net ✍ *Email for automated info*

The World ☎→*dial* 617-739-0202 (vox)/508-366-4422/508-934-9753/617-739-9753/617-826-0290→new ✓**INTERNET** ...→*telnet* world.std.com→new ...→*ftp* std. com→anonymous→<your email address>→/world-info ...→*email* info@world.std.com ✍ *Email for automated info*

Michigan

DialMIDWEST ☎→*dial* 800-947-4754 (vox) ✓**INTERNET**→*email* annp@cic.net ✍ *Email for info*

Merit Network, Inc / Mich-Net ☎→*dial* 313-764-9430 (vox) ✓**INTERNET** ...→*telnet* hermes.mer it.edu→help...→*ftp* nic.merit.edu→anonymous→<your email address>→/michnet ...→ *email* info@merit. edu ✍ *Email for automated info*

MSen ☎→*dial* 313-998-4562 (vox) ✓**INTERNET** ...→*telnet* msen. com→newuser ...→*ftp* ftp.msen. com→anonymous→<your email address>→/pub/vendor/msen ...→*email* info@msen.com ✍ *Email for automated info*

Minnesota

MRNet ☎→*dial* 612-342-2570 (vox) ✓**INTERNET**→*email* info@mr.net ✍ *Email for info*

Nebraska

MIDnet ☎→*dial* 800-682-5550 (vox) ✓**INTERNET**→*email* nic@mid. net ✍ *Email for info*

New Hampshire

MV Communications, Inc. ☎→*dial* 603-429-2223 (vox)/603-424-7428/603-645-6387→info ✓**INTERNET** ...→*telnet* mv.mv. com→info ...→*email* info@mv.com ✍ *Email for automated info*

NEARnet ☎→*dial* 617-873-8730 (vox) ✓**INTERNET** ...→*ftp* ftp.near. net→anonymous→<your email address>→/what_is_nearnet.txt ...→*email* nearnet-join@near.net ✍ *Email for info*

New Jersey

INTAC Access Corporation ☎→*dial* 201-944-1417 (vox)/201-944-3990→newuser ✓**INTERNET** →*email* info@intac.com ✍ *Email for automated info*

Mordor Public Access ☎→*dial* 212-843-3451/201-433-7343→guest ✓**INTERNET** ...→*telnet* ritz.mordor.com→guest ...→*email* ritz@mordor.com ✍ *Email for info*

New Jersey Computer Connection ☎→*dial* 609-896-2799 (vox)/609-896-3191→guest ✓**INTERNET**→*email* info@pluto.njcc.com ✍ *Email for automated info*

VoiceNet/DSC ☎→*dial* 215-674-9290 (vox)/215-443-7390 ✓**INTERNET**→*email* info@voicenet.com ✍ *Email for automated info*

New Mexico

New Mexico Technet ☎→*dial* 505-345-6555 (vox)

New York

The Dorsai Embassy ☎→*dial* 718-392-3667 (vox)/718-392-4060 ✓**INTERNET** ...→*telnet* dorsai.dorsai.com→new ...→*email* info@dorsai.com ✍ *Email for info*

Echo Communications ☎→*dial* 212-255-3839 (vox)/212-989-8411→newuser ✓**INTERNET** ...→*telnet* echonyc.com→newuser ...→*email* info@echonyc.com ✍ *Email for info*

Escape ☎→*dial* 212-888-8780 (vox)/212-888-8212→guest ✓**INTERNET** ...→*telnet* escape.com→guest ...→*email* info@escape.com ✍ *Email for automated info*

The IDS World Network ☎→*dial* 401-884-7856 (vox)/305-534-0321/305-428-2663/914-637-6100/401-884-9002/401-294-5779→ids→guest ✓**INTERNET** ...→*telnet* ids.net→guest ...→*email* info@ids.net ✍ *Email for automated info*

Interport ☎→*dial* 212-989-1128 (vox)/212-989-1258→newuser ✓**INTERNET** ...→*telnet* interport.net→newuser ...→*email* info@interport.net ✍ *Email for automated info*

Maestro Technologies ☎→*dial* 212-240-9600 (vox)/212-240-9700→newuser→newuser ✓**INTERNET**→*email* staff@maestro.com ✍ *Email for info*

MindVox ☎→*dial* 212-989-2418 (vox)/212-989-1550→guest ✓**INTERNET** ...→*telnet* phantom.com→guest ...→*email* info@phantom.com ✍ *Email for automated info*

Mordor Public Access ☎→*dial* 212-843-3451/201-433-7343→guest ✓**INTERNET** ...→*telnet* ritz.mordor.com→guest ...→*email* ritz@mordor.com ✍ *Email for info*

PANIX ☎→*dial* 212-741-4400 (vox)/516-626-7863/212-741-4444/212-741-4545→newuser ✓**INTERNET** ...→*telnet* panix.com→newuser ...→*email* info@panix.

com ✍ *Email for automated info*

The Pipeline ☎→*dial* 212-267-3636 (vox)/212-267-8606/212-267-7341→guest ✓**INTERNET** ...→*telnet* pipeline.com→guest ...→*email* info@pipeline.com ✍ *Email for automated info*

YPN—Your Personal Network ☎→*dial* 800-NET-1133 (vox)/212-376-6276/ ✓**INTERNET** ...→*telnet* ypn.com→guest...→*www* www.ypn.com ...→*email* info@ypn.com ✍ *Email for automated info*

Zone One Network Exchange ☎→*dial* 718-884-5800 (vox)/718-884-5403→guest ✓**INTERNET** ...→*telnet* zone.net→guest ✍ *Email for info* ...→*email* info@zone.net ✍ *Email for automated info*

North Carolina

InfiNet ☎→*dial* 800-849-7214 (vox) ✓**INTERNET**→*email* support@infi.net ✍ *Email for info* ✍ *Email for info*

Vnet Internet Access, Inc. ☎→*dial* 800-377-3282 (vox)/919-406-1544/919-851-1526/704-347-8839/704-825-3442→new ✓**INTERNET** ...→*telnet* vnet.net→new ...→*ftp* vnet.net→anonymous→<your email address>→/vnet-info ...→*email* info@vnet.net ✍ *Email for automated info*

Ohio

APK Public Access ☎→*dial* /216-481-9436/216-481-1960→bbs ✓**INTERNET** ...→*telnet* wariat.org→bbs ...→*ftp* ftp.wariat.org→anonymous→<your email address>→/pub/user.new ...→*email* info@wariat.org ✍ *Email for automated info*

Oregon

Rain Drop Laboratories ☎→*dial* 503-452-0960 (vox)/503-293-1772/503-293-2059→apply ✓**INTERNET** ...→*telnet* agora.rdrop.com→apply ...→*ftp* agora.rdrop.com→anonymous→<your email address>→/pub ...→*email* info@agora.rdrop.com ✍ *Email for info*

Teleport ☎→*dial* 503-223-0076 (vox)/503-220-1016/503-220-0636→new ✓**INTERNET** ...→*telnet* teleport.com→new ...→*email* info@teleport.com ✍ *Email for automated info*

Pennsylvania

Telerama Public Access Internet ☎→*dial* 412-481-3505 (vox)/412-481-5302/412-481-4644→new ✓**INTERNET** ...→*telnet* telerama.lm.com→new ...→*ftp* telerama.lm.com→anonymous→<your email address>→/info ...→*email* info@lm.com ✍ *Email for automated info*

VoiceNet/DSC ☎→*dial* 215-674-9290 (vox)/215-443-7390 ✓**INTERNET**→*email* info@voicenet.com ✍ *Email for automated info*

Rhode Island

The IDS World Network ☎→*dial* 401-884-7856 (vox)/305-534-0321/305-428-2663/914-637-6100/401-884-9002/401-294-5779→ids→guest ✓**INTERNET** ...→*telnet* ids.net→guest ...→*email* info@ids.net ✍ *Email for automated info*

NEARnet ☎→*dial* 617-873-8730 (vox) ✓**INTERNET** ...→*ftp* ftp.near.net→anonymous→<your email address>→/what_is_nearnet.txt ...→*email* nearnet-join@near.net ✍ *Email for info*

Internet Providers

Tennessee

InfiNet ☎→*dial* 800-849-7214 (vox) ✓**INTERNET**→*email* support@infi.net ✎ *Email for info* ✎ *Email for info*

Magibox ☎→*dial* 901-757-7835 (vox)/901-757-2081→new ✓**INTER-NET**→*email* lmarcus@magibox.net ✎ *Email for info*

Texas

The Black Box ☎→*dial* 713-480-2684 (vox)/713-480-2686→guest ✓**INTERNET**→*email* info@blk-box.com ✎ *Email for automated info*

DFW Net ☎→*dial* 817-332-5116 (vox)/214-988-6206/817-332-6642/817-429-3520→info ✓**INTER-NET** ...→*telnet* dfw.net→info ...→*email* jwb@dfw.net ✎ *Email for automated info*

Illuminati Online ☎→*dial* 512-462-0999 (vox)/512-448-8950→new ✓**INTERNET** ...→*telnet* io.com→new...→*ftp* io.com→ anonymous→<your email address> →/newuser-info ...→*email* info@ io.com ✎ *Email for automated info*

NeoSoft ☎→*dial* 713-684-5969 (vox) ✓**INTERNET**→*email* info@neosoft.com ✎ *Email for automated info*

On-Ramp Technologies,Inc. ☎→*dial* 214-746-4710 (vox)/713-964-0500→guest ✓**INTERNET** → *email* info@onramp.com ✎ *Email for automated info*

Real/Time Communications ☎→*dial* 512-451-0046 (vox)/512-459-0604→new ✓**INTERNET** ...→ *telnet* vern.bga.com→new ...→*ftp* ftp.bga.com→anonymous→<your email address>→/pub/realtime ...→*email* hosts@bga.com ✎ *Email for info*

South Coast Computing Services, Inc. ☎→*dial* 713-917-5000 (vox)/713-917-5050→newuser ✓**IN-TERNET**→*email* acs@sccsi.com ✎ *Email for info*

Texas Metronet ☎→*dial* 214-705-2900 (vox)/817-261-1127/214-705-2901→info→info ✓**INTERNET** ...→*telnet* fohnix.metronet.com→info→info ...→*ftp* ftp.metronet.com→anonymous→<your email address>→/pub/info ...→*email* info@metronet.com ✎ *Email for automated info*

Vermont

NEARnet ☎→*dial* 617-873-8730 (vox) ✓**INTERNET** ...→*ftp* ftp.near.net→anonymous→<your email address>→/what_is_nearnet.txt ...→*email* nearnet-join@near.net ✎ *Email for info*

Washington

Eskimo North ☎→*dial* 206-367-7457 (vox)/206-742-1150/206-838-9513/206-367-3837/206-362-6731 ✓**INTERNET** ...→*telnet* eskimo.com→new→<your name> ...→*email* nanook@eskimo.com ✎ *Email for info*

Halcyon ☎→*dial* 206-455-3505 (vox)/206-382-6245→new ✓**IN-TERNET** ...→*ftp* ftp.halcyon.com→ anonymous→<your email address> →/pub ...→*email* info@halcyon.com ✎ *Email for automated info*

Olympus Net ☎→*dial* 206-385-0464 (vox) ✓**INTERNET**→*email* info@olym pus.net ✎ *Email for automated info*

Canada

Communications Accessibles Montreal ☎→*dial* 514-288-2581 (vox) ✓**INTERNET** ...→*ftp* ftp.CAM.ORG→anonymous→<your email address>→/CAM.ORG-info ...→ *email* info@cam.org ✎ *Email for automated info*

HookUp Communication Corporation ☎→*dial* 519-747-4110 (vox) ✓**INTERNET**→*email* info@hookup.net ✎ *Email for automated info*

IslandNet ☎→*dial* 604-479-7861 (vox)/604-477-5163→guest ✓**IN-TERNET** ...→*telnet* islandnet.com→guest ...→*email* mark@islandnet.com ✎ *Email for info*

UUNET Canada, Inc. ☎→*dial* 416-368-6621 (vox) ✓**INTERNET** ...→*ftp* ftp.uunet.ca→anonymous→ <your email address>→/pub/uunet.ca-info ...→*email* info@uunet.ca ✎ *Email for automated info*

UUnorth ☎→*dial* 416-225-8649 (vox)/416-221-0200→new ✓**INTER-NET** ...→*telnet* uunorth.north.net→new ...→*email* info@uunorth.north.net ✎ *Email for automated info*

@	Separates the **userid** and **domain name** of an Internet address. Pronounced "at."
anonymous FTP	Method of logging in to public file archives over the **Internet**. Enter "anonymous" when prompted for a **userid**. See **FTP**.
anonymous remailer	Service that encodes the return address in **email** and then forwards it. Good remailers allow replies to be sent back without revealing the original identity. Anon.penet.fi is the most popular remailer on the **Internet** (see pages 18-20).
Archie	A program that lets you search **Internet FTP** archives worldwide by file name. One variant is called **Veronica**.
ASCII	A basic text format readable by most computers. The acronym stands for American Standard Code for Information Interchange.
backbones	The high-speed networks at the core of the **Internet**. The most prominent is the NSFNet, funded by the National Science Foundation.
bandwidth	The data transmission capacity of a network. Used colloquially to refer to the "size" of the Net; some information transmittals (e.g. multitudes of graphic files) are considered to be a "waste of bandwidth."
baud	The speed at which signals are sent by a **modem**, measured by the number of changes per second in the signals during transmission. A baud rate of 1,200, for example, would indicate 1,200 signal changes in one second. Baud rate is often confused with **bits per second (bps)**.
BBS	"Bulletin-board system." Once referred to stand-alone desktop computers with a single modem that answered the phone, but can now be as complicated and interconnected as a commercial service.
binary	A file format in which data is represented by binary numbers (based on 1s and 0s); generally used to store software and pictures. One binary integer is called a bit (see **bits per second**).
binary transfer	A file transfer between two computers that preserves **binary** data.

Net Speak

bits per second (bps) The data-transfer rate between two **modems**. The higher the bps, the higher the speed of the transfer.

bot A computer program with humanlike behavior (short for "robot"). In live-chat areas like **IRC** channels or **MUD**s, bots are often programmed to represent their creators, to moderate games, or to perform such tasks as delivering local **email** messages.

bounced message An **email** message "returned to sender," usually because of an address error.

bye A log-off command, like "quit" and "exit."

carrier signal The squeaking noise that modems use to maintain a connection. See also **handshake**.

cd "Change directory." A command used, for example, at an **FTP** site to move from a directory to a subdirectory.

cdup "Change directory up." Can be used at an **FTP** site to move from a sub-directory to its parent directory. Also **chdirup**.

channel operator User with special powers in an **IRC** channel, most notably the ability to kick other users off the channel.

chdirup See **cdup**.

client A computer that connects to a more powerful computer (see **server**) for complex tasks.

commercial service General term for large online services (e.g., America Online, CompuServe, Prodigy, GEnie).

compression Shrinkage of computer files to conserve storage space and reduce transfer times. Special utility programs, available for most platforms (including DOS, Mac, and Amiga), perform the compression and decompression.

cracker A person who maliciously breaks into a computer system in order to steal files or disrupt system activities.

dial-up access Computer connection made over standard telephone lines.

dir "Directory." A command used to display the contents of the current directory.

domain name The worded address of an **IP number** on the **Internet**, in the form of domain subsets separated by periods. For example, cunix.columbia.edu would be the address of a **server** named cunix located at Columbia University, which is in the .edu hierarchy (refers to educational institutions). Other domain hierarchies include ".com" (for companies, such as ypn.com), ".org" for organizations (such as eff.org), ".net" for network provider (such as sura.net), ".gov" for government addresses (such as whitehouse.gov), and ".mil" for military facilities (such as nic.dnn.mil). Sites in foreign countries have a two-letter country abbreviation as the last subset of their domain name. The full address of an **Internet** user is **userid@domain name**.

email	"Electronic mail."
emoticon	See **smiley**.
Ethernet	A fast and widely used type of **LAN**.
FAQ	"Frequently asked questions." A file of questions and answers compiled for **Usenet newsgroups**, **mailing lists**, and games to reduce repeated posts about commonplace subjects.
file transfer	Transfer of a file from one computer to another over a network.
finger	A program that provides information about a user who is logged into your local system or on a remote computer on the Internet. Generally invoked by typing "finger" and the person's **userid**.
flame	A violent and usually ad hominem attack against another person in a **newsgroup** or message area.
flame war	A back-and-forth series of **flames**.
fluxer	As in "influx." Alternate for **newbie**.
Free-Net	A community-based network that provides free access to the **Internet**, usually to local residents, and often includes its own forums and news.
freeware	Free software. Not to be confused with **shareware**.
front end	A program used in conjunction with another program to alter the appearance—for visual appeal and ease of use—of the screen. The front end is often run locally on a user's machine.
FTP	"File transfer protocol." The standard used to transfer files between computers.
get	An **FTP** command that transfers single files from the **FTP** site to your local directory. The command is followed by a file name; typing "get file.name" would transfer only that file. Also see **mget**.
GIF	Common file format for pictures first popularized by CompuServe, standing for "graphics interchange format." Pronounced with a hard *g*.
gopher	A menu-based guide to directories on the **Internet**, usually organized by subject.
GUI	"Graphical user interface" with windows and point-and-click capability, as opposed to a command-line interface with typed-out instructions.

Net Speak

hacker	A computer enthusiast who enjoys exploring computer systems and programs, sometimes to the point of obsession. Not to be confused with **cracker**.
handle	The name a user wishes to be known by; a user's handle may differ significantly from his or her real name or **userid**.
handshake	The squawking noise at the beginning of a computer connection when two modems settle on a protocol for exchanging information.
Home Page	The main **World Wide Web** site for a particular group or organization.
hqx	File suffix for a BinHex file, a common format for transmitting Macintosh binary files over the **Internet**.
hypertext	An easy method of retrieving information by choosing highlighted words in a text on the screen. The words link to documents with related subject matter.
IC	"In character." A game player who is IC is acting as his or her **character**'s persona.
Internet	The largest network of computer networks in the world, easily recognizable by the format of Internet **email** addresses: **userid**@host.
Internet Adapter, The (TIA)	A new commercial UNIX program that emulates a **SLIP** connection over a standard **dial-up** connection.
Internet provider	Wholesale or retail reseller of access to the **Internet**. YPN is one example.
IP connection	Full-fledged link to the **Internet**. See **SLIP**, **PPP**, and **TCP/IP**.
IP number	The unique number that determines the ultimate **Internet** identity of an **IP connection**.
IRC	"**Internet** relay chat." A service that allows **real-time** conversations between multiple users on a variety of subject-oriented channels.
jpeg	Common compressed format for picture files. Pronounced "jay-peg."
knowbot	An experimental computer program designed to retrieve information anywhere on the **Net** in response to a user's request.
LAN	"Local area network." A network of computers limited to a particular physical site, as opposed to the massive cyber-sprawl of the **Internet**, which encompasses networks all around the world.
ls	"List." A command that provides simplified directory information at **FTP** sites and other directories. It lists only file names for the directory, not file sizes or dates.
lurkers	Regular readers of messages online who never post.

lynx	A popular text-based **Web browser**.
mailing list	Group discussion distributed through **email**. Many mailing lists are administered through listserv.
mget	An **FTP** command that transfers multiple files from the **FTP** site to your local directory. The command is followed by a list of file names separated by spaces, sometimes in combination with an asterisk used as a wild card. Typing "mget b*" would transfer all files in the directory beginning with the letter *b*. Also see **get**.
modem	Device for establishing a connection between two computers, usually over standard phone lines. Most modem **bandwidths** range between 2,400 and 28,800 **baud**. From the technical name "MOdulator-DEModulator."
multi-tasking	The capability of a computer to perform more than one job simultaneously.
Net, the	A colloquial term that is often used to refer to the entirety of Cyberspace: the **Internet**, the **commercial services**, **BBSs**, etc.
Net guru	A person with unimpeachable **Net** expertise who can answer any question.
netiquette	The rules of Cyberspace civility. Usually applied to the **Internet**, where manners are enforced exclusively by fellow users.
newbie	A newcomer to the **Net**, to a game, or to a discussion. Also called **fluxer**.
newsgroups	The **Usenet** message areas, organized by subject.
newsreader	Software program for reading **Usenet newsgroups** on the **Internet**. (See page 17.)
NIC, the	Short for the InterNIC ("Network Information Center"), the Virginia-based authority that, among other things, registers **Internet domain names** on a famous first-come, first-serve basis. Pronounced "nik."
nick	Short for the nickname you set for yourself in **IRC**.
port number	A number that follows a **telnet** address. The number connects a user to a particular application on the telnet site. LambdaMOO, for example, is at port 8888 of lambda.parc.xerox.com (lambda.parc.xerox.com 8888).
post	See **posting**.
posting	The sending of a message to a **newsgroup**, bulletin board, or other public message area. The message itself is called a **post**.
pwd	A command used at an **FTP** site to display the name of the current directory on your screen.
real-time	The **Net** term for "live," as in "live broadcast." Real-time connections

Net Speak

	include **IRC** and **MUDs**.
remote machine	Any computer on the **Internet** reached with a program such as **FTP** or **telnet**. The machine making the connection is called the home, or local, machine.
RL	"Real life."
server	A software program, or the computer running the program, that allows other computers, called **clients**, to share its resources.
shareware	Free software, distributed over the **Net** with a request from the programmer for voluntary payment.
sig	Short for **signature**.
signature	A file added to the end of **email** messages or **Usenet** posts that contains personal information—usually your name, email address, postal address, and telephone number. **Netiquette** dictates that signatures, or **sigs**, should be no longer than four or five lines.
SLIP and PPP	"Serial line **Internet** protocol" and "point-to-point protocol." Connecting by SLIP or PPP actually puts a computer on the Internet, which offers a number of advantages over regular **dial-up**. A SLIP or PPP connection can support a graphical **Web browser** (such as Mosaic), and allows for multiple connections at the same time. Requires special software and a SLIP or PPP service provider.
smiley	Text used to indicate emotion, humor, or irony in electronic messages—best understood if viewed sideways. Also called an **emoticon**. The most common smileys are :-) and :-(
snail mail	The paper mail the U.S. Postal Service delivers. The forerunner of **email**.
spam	The posting of the same article to multiple **newsgroups** (usually every possible one) regardless of the appropriateness of the topic (e.g., "Make Money Fast"). Virtual hangings of spammers take place in the newsgroup news.admin.misc. Thought to come from the mind-numbing repetition of Monty Python's "Spam Song."
sysop	"System operator." The person who owns and/or manages a **BBS** or other **Net** site.
TCP/IP	The "transmission control protocol" and the "**Internet** protocol." The basis of a full-fledged Internet connection. See **IP Connection**, **PPP**, and **SLIP**. Pronounced "T-C-P-I-P."
telnet	An **Internet** program that allows you to log into other Internet-connected computers.
terminal emulator	A program or utility that allows a computer to communicate in a foreign

or nonstandard **terminal mode**.

terminal mode	The software standard a computer uses for text communication—for example, ANSI for PCs and **VT-100** for UNIX.
thread	Posted **newsgroup** message with a series of replies. Threaded **newsreaders** organize replies under the original subject.
timeout	The break in communication that occurs when two computers are talking and one takes so long to respond that the other gives up.
tty	A plain-vanilla terminal protocol for transmitting text over computer connections. Comes from "teletypewriter," the original electromechanic typewriter that could transmit and receive messages by electrical signals carried over telephone wires.
URL	"Uniform resource locator." The **World Wide Web** address of a resource on the **Internet**.
Usenet	A collection of networks and computer systems that exchange messages, organized by subject in **newsgroups**.
userid	The unique name (often eight characters or less) given to a user on a system for his or her account. The complete address, which can be used for **email** or **finger**ing, is a userid followed by the @ sign and the **domain name** (e.g., Bill Clinton's address is president@whitehouse.gov).
Veronica	See **Archie**.
VT-100 emulation	Widely used terminal protocol for formatting full screens of text over computer connections.
WAIS	"Wide area information server." A system that searches through database indexes around the **Internet**, using keywords.
Web browser	A **client** program designed to interact with **World Wide Web servers** on the **Internet** for the purpose of viewing **Web pages**.
Web page	A **hypertext** document that is part of the **World Wide Web** and that can incorporate graphics, sounds, and links to other **Web pages**, **FTP** sites, **gophers**, and a variety of other **Internet** resources.
World Wide Web	A **hypertext**-based navigation system that lets you browse through a variety of linked **Net** resources, including **Usenet newsgroups** and **FTP**, **telnet**, and **gopher** sites, without typing commands. Also known as WWW and the Web.
zip	File-compression standard in the DOS and Windows worlds.

Index

Index

Index

Index

Index

F

Fannie Mae Online, 64
fantasy
    books, 108
    Dancing Dragon Designs, 115
FAQ, 1-19
Farcast, 142, 155
Fast EDGAR's Mutual Funds Reporting, 162
FCR Software, Inc., 113
FDA Info and Policies, 45
Federal Center, 143
Federal Employment Service, 199
Federal Filings Notification, 148
federal government
    employment, 199-200
    regulations, 236
    See also U.S. Government
Federal Grant Database, 228
Federal National Mortgage Association (FANNIE MAE), 64
Federal Register, 236, 237
Federal Reserve, 171
Federal Securities Acts of 1933 and 1934, 133
FEDIX/MOLIS - Federal Information Exchange, Inc., 80 228, 237
FEDJOBS, 199
fedreg.commerce, 236
FedWorld, 237
FEDWORLD - The U.S. Government Bulletin Board, 199
Fellowships/Scholarships for Women (Albany), 82
Feminist Economics Discussion, 168
Fidelity On-line Express (FOX), 139
Fidelity On-Line Investment Center, 99
Fidelity On-Line Investor Center: Saving for College, 78
Figi's, 115
Files for Quicken on the Macintosh, 32
Final Markets End-Of-Day Price Service, 152
finance, 131

employment, 197
    online, 1-19
    See also business, investment
financial aid, 78-82
    graduate school, 80
    minority, 80
Financial Aid Library, 81
Financial Aid News, 79
Financial Aid Offices, 79
Financial Executive Journal, 133
Financial Information on Insurance Companies, 43
financial planning,
    budgeting, 48
    children, 47
    college, 69-71, 78-82
    credit, 38-39
    estate, 101
    insurance, 40-43
    mortgages, 64, 66-67
    real estate, 63-67
    retirement, 98-100
    software, 30-31
    taxes, 50-55
    trusts, 101
    wills, 101
Financial Software, 29
Find a Gift, 116
Finding the Best Mortgage, 66
Firebirds, 62
First Federal Savings Bank of Indiana, 67
fl.jobs, 191
Flexwork, 231
Florida
    employment, 191
    travel, 97
Florida Atlantic University, 73
Florida Fruit Shippers, 115
Florida International University, 73
Florida State University, 73
Flower Stop, The, 115
flowers, 115
Flowers, Gennifer, 108
Fodor's World View, 95
food, 115-116
    consumer information, 45
Food and Drug Administration, 45
For Sale By Owner Magazine, 64
Ford cars, 60, 62
Ford Simulator 5.0, 61

Foreign Affairs, 139
Foreign Assets Control Program, 169
foreign exchange (currency), 171-172
Foreign Exchange Rates, 172
Foreign Trade, 169
foreign trade, 169, 238-239
Forest Hill Vineyard, 122
ForSale, 123
Fortune Magazine, 137
Foundation and Corporate Grants Alert, 228
Foundation Center, The, 81
Four Circles Realty, 65
4-Sale, 123
France
    travel, 96
    See also Europe
Franchise and Business Opportunities, 225
franchises, 225
Franklin & Marshall College, 73
fraternities, 83
Free College Money, 81
Frequently Asked Questions, 50
Frequently Asked Questions About Credit, 38
Fringeware, Inc. Online Catalog, 121
fruit, 115
Fruit Baskets - from Pemberton Orchards, 116
FTD Online, 115
FTP, 16
FTP Directory of public financial and market information, 132
Fulbright Scholar Program, 81
Fundamental Issue Analysis, 159
Funding Graduate School, 80
FundWatch Online, 162
furniture, 117
Future Fantasy Bookstore, 108
futures, 165
    See also stock market, investing
Futures Newsletter, 165
Futures Quotes, 165
Futures Recommendations, 165

G

H

Index

J

Index

Index

Index

Index

Index

Index

Notes

Notes

Notes

Michael Wolff & Company, Inc.

Michael Wolff & Company, Inc., digital publisher and packager, specializing in information presentation and graphic design, is one of the leading providers of information about the Net. The company's book *Net Guide*, published with Random House, has spent almost a year on bestseller lists, and is now a monthly magazine published by CMP Publications.

MW& Co., and its team of Net surfers, is embarked upon a project to map all corners of the Net. This means that the growing community of Net adventurers can expect a steady flow of new Net baedekers. *Net Guide* has now been joined by *Net Games, Net Chat,* and *Net Money,* and will shortly be followed by *Net Trek, Net Sports,* and *Net Tech.* MW&Co.'s Internet service, YPN—Your Personal Network, features a hypertext version of the entire series. It is the most comprehensive Net source available anywhere.

Among the company's other recent projects are *Where We Stand—Can America Make It in the Global Race for Wealth, Health, and Happiness?* (Bantam Books), one of the most graphically complex information books ever to be wholly created and produced by means of desktop-publishing technology, and *Made in America?,* a four-part PBS series on global competitiveness, hosted by Labor Secretary Robert B. Reich.

Kelly Maloni, who directed the *Net Money* project, is the managing editor of MW&Co. and, at 26, one of the most experienced travelers in Cyberspace. Senior editor Ben Greenman has written pop-culture criticism for many publications, including *Miami New Times,* the *Chicago Reader,* the *Village Voice,* and *Rolling Stone.* Senior Editor Kristin Miller has taught in the history department at Columbia University, and contributed to many books, among them *Where We Stand, Net Chat,* and *Net Games.*

The credit card finally caught up with the information age.
CompuServe Visa.®

The card for an instant world.

CompuServe members, **GO CARD** for your CompuServe Visa® Gold Card with CONDUCTOR Card Review. Now members can access their updated CompuServe Visa files online 24 hours a day, 7 days a week.

A breakthrough in money management.

CONDUCTOR Card Review's conversion software lets you load statement information into most any personal finance program. Plus it has a low introductory 12.9% APR, and no annual fee if you use the card just six times a year.

Take it for a spin.

CompuServe members, **GO CARD** to see for yourself how it all works. Don't forget to enter **Offer #CSV500** when you apply for your card.

Nonmembers can call 1-800-487-5391 for a CompuServe Visa Card application.

Get free time online, too.

When you're accepted, you'll also get a $27.50 usage credit toward CompuServe extended services.

Experience the future of credit cards today.

GO CARD now.

Get The Most Comprehensive Online Service Ever Offered To Private Investors.

Call Now And Get One Month Free.

The most successful investors have always been the ones with the best information. Which is exactly what you'll get when you go online with Dow Jones Market Monitor℠—the most comprehensive online service ever offered to the private investor.

Retrieve Quotes On Stocks, Bonds And Mutual Funds. Starting at 7:01 p.m., Dow Jones Market Monitor lets you retrieve quotes on stocks,

Online Service Features	Dow Jones Market Monitor	Reuters Money Network	Compu-Serve	Prodigy	DialData
The Wall Street Journal & Barron's - full text articles	✓				
Hundreds of Industry Publications	✓		✓		
Dow Jones News Service	✓	✓		✓	
All Dow Jones News Wires	✓				
Stocks, Options, Indexes, Bonds, Futures	✓		✓	✓	✓
Corporate Earnings Reports - 4 sources	✓				
Over 4,500 Mutual Funds	✓	✓			
Download 20 Years of Pricing Data	✓*				✓
Insider Trading Activity	✓				

*With Dow Jones Market Monitor Plus.

bonds, mutual funds, indexes, options and futures. Access articles from *The Wall Street Journal, Barron's* and hundreds of other business and financial publications.

Check Insider Buying/Selling. Track corporate earnings and P/E ratios, compare mutual fund performance reports, check insider buying/selling, analyze stock movements and download data into your favorite spreadsheet or technical analysis program.

Even receive exclusive market moving news from five Dow Jones news wires. No other online service offers as much.

Need More In-depth Pricing Data? For an additional charge, Dow Jones Market Monitor Plus includes Tradeline, the largest source of historical pricing and performance information available. It has over 20 years of daily prices, dividends, splits, interest

payments, exchange rates and beta analysis reports, plus built-in screening capabilities.

Subscribe Now And Save. Try our three-month introductory offer for Dow Jones Market Monitor and we'll waive the $29.95 start-up fee and give you a fourth month free. A $149.75 value for just $89.85. It's a small price to pay to become one of the best-informed investors on Wall Street.

> **Call 800-815-5100, Dept. 213**
> **And Get One Month Of**
> **Dow Jones Market Monitor Free.**

DOW JONES
MARKET MONITOR

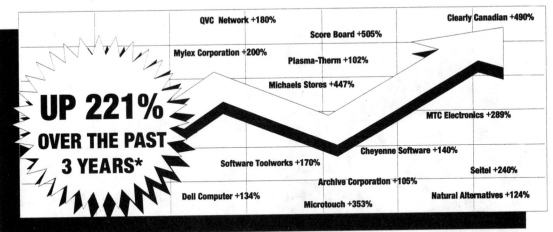

* As tracked by the Hulbert Financial Digest. The gains shown are based on date of recommended sale or closing prices as of 11/10/94. Past performance is not a guarantee of future results.

One in five of our stock recommendations has increased more than 100%

INDIVIDUAL INVESTOR'S
SPECIAL SITUATIONS REPORT

Every month you'll receive an in-depth, confidential report on the single most promising stock SSR identifies as positioned for extraordinary growth– *our unqualified #1 buy recommendation.*

Every month, in addition to the Report's new buy recommendation, you'll receive valuable updates on all of the stocks featured to date. When action is required, you'll be on top of the situation, knowing precisely what your next moves should be.

Stay on top of your investments with our followup buy-sell-hold recommendations.

SUBSCRIBE NOW AND SAVE!

SPECIAL SITUATIONS REPORT

WHY HOLD ON LINE WHEN YOU CAN SHOP ON-LINE.

The Internet Shopping Network. The place where you can shop and not have to listen to elevator music while waiting for your questions to be answered. ISN connects you directly to over 22,000 of the best software and hardware bargains anywhere on the planet. It's the best place in cyberspace to get reviews on software and hardware and to download full demos before you buy. We'll give you more information than a little paragraph in any catalog ever could. So call for your free internet access software at 1-800-677-SHOP or stop by and check us out the next time you're net surfing at http://shop.internet.net. If using the phone scares you, e-mail for more information at info@internet.net.

It's the best way to shop and the one place you'll never hear someone say "Dude, let me put you on hold while I check with my supervisor."

The Internet Shopping Network gives you more access to product info than any catalog ever could.

Internet Shopping Network

The largest shopping mall in the world.™

THE PROFIT*LINK*

Investment Advisories

PERSONAL FINANCE

PERSONAL FINANCE is an award-winning biweekly financial newsletter that has provided investors a total approach to investing and money matters for over 20 years.

Its wealth-building philosophy is simple: To identify new investment trends yielding value-priced investments that can be bought for above average returns and below market risk.

ONE-YEAR (24 ISSUES) $59 TWO-YEARS (48 ISSUES) JUST $118. 12 PAGES/EDITOR, STEPHEN LEEB. ITEM# S00272.

WALL STREET BARGAINS

The only investment advisory devoted exclusively to top-quality small stocks and mutual funds priced between $5 and $25. Easy to understand explanations and reasoning makes WALL STREET BARGAINS the perfect advisory for any investor just starting out. And those without a lot of extra cash can purchase a fully diversified portfolio of small stocks and mutual funds for $2,500.

ONE-YEAR (12 ISSUES) $39 TWO-YEARS (24 ISSUES) JUST $78. 8 PAGES/EDITOR, GREGORY DORSEY. ITEM# S00280.

THE BIG PICTURE

THE BIG PICTURE provides traders average profits of 20% to 30% by disclosing the top moneymaking investment trends for the next one to twelve months, before others spot them.

Editor Stephen Leeb feeds his proprietary computer model, the Master Key, a vast collection of economic data and indicators to uncover the best aggressive growth stocks and funds, S&P futures, S&P Depositary Receipts, short sales, and options. A weekly telephone hotline keeps you abreast of late-breaking market changes.

ONE-YEAR (12 ISSUES) $127 TWO-YEARS (24 ISSUES) JUST $199. 8 PAGES/EDITOR,STEPHEN LEEB. ITEM #S00297.

GROWTH STOCK WINNERS

Growth Stock Winners provides investors the TOP 1% of all growth stocks through their greatest growth period.

Take advantage of Editor Jim Collins' 5 year total profit return of 432.1%. Build your own portfolio from the Top 50 stock table, or follow his model portfolios.

ONE-YEAR (12 ISSUES) $59 TWO-YEARS (24 ISSUES) JUST $118. 8 PAGES/EDITOR, JIM COLLINS. ITEM #S00305.

High Stakes FAX Services

SPECIAL ALERT BULLETIN

The Special Alert Bulletin provides sophisticated investors with short-term special situation investments yielding spectacular returns.

Each "buy" recommendation is sent to you via fax on the day it is uncovered. A monthly update keeps you posted on any changes that take place and a "sell" bulletin is faxed when it is time to get out. For the past 3 years, the Bulletin has racked up annualized gains of 54% for its small circle of members.

ONE-YEAR (10 BULLETINS) $1450. ITEM #S00313.

WINNING WITH OPTIONS

Profit in both up and down markets with this weekly fax service. WINNING WITH OPTIONS recommends EXACTLY what options to buy, how much to spend, how to execute the trades, how long to hold them and when to sell...taking all the confusion out of options trading.

You'll receive each 8-page FAX over the weekend for Monday morning trading in the 10-Day speculative portfolio, or the more conservative 90-Day portfolio.

ONE-YEAR (52 ISSUES) $3000 8 PAGES/EDITOR, JIM YATES ITEM #S00321.

ORDER A FREE SAMPLE

For a FREE sample please fax your name, address, phone number and the item number to: 703-683-6974, attention: Investors Service Center.

KCI Communications, Inc. • 1101 King Street, Suite 400 • Alexandria, VA 22314

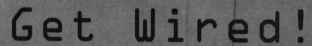

No postage
necessary if
mailed in the
United States

BUSINESS REPLY MAIL
FIRST CLASS MAIL PERMIT NO. 25363 SAN FRANCISCO, CA

Postage will be paid by addressee

PO Box 191826
San Francisco CA 94119-9866

GET WIRED!

GET WIRED!
AND STAY WIRED
BY READING NET SURF,
EXCLUSIVELY
IN WIRED.

If you want to keep up with the Digital Revolution, and the dozens of new sites that are appearing on the Net monthly, you need *Wired* and its Net Surf column – *Wired*'s guide to the best of the Net.

From its online presence (gopher, WWW, Info-rama@wired.com, WELL, and AOL) to its focus on convergence and the communications revolution, *Wired* is one of the most Net-savvy publications in America today.

That's because *Wired* is the only place where the Digital Revolution is covered by and for the people who are making it happen – you.

Since its launch in January 1993, *Wired* has become required reading for the digerati from Silicon Valley to Madison Avenue, from Hollywood to Wall Street, from Pennsylvania Avenue to Main Street.

But *Wired* may be hard to find on newsstands (we're printing almost 250,000 copies and still can't satisfy demand).

So if you want to get *Wired* regularly and reliably, subscribe now – and save up to 40 percent. If for any reason you don't like *Wired*, you can cancel at any time, and get your full subscription price back – that's how sure we are that you will like *Wired*.

If you want to connect to the soul of the Digital Revolution, our advice to you is simple.

PLEASE FOLD ALONG THIS LINE AND TAPE CLOSED. (NO STAPLES)

I want to get Wired – reliably and regularly. Begin my subscription immediately, if not sooner, saving me up to 40% off the newsstand price. If for any reason, I don't like Wired, I can cancel at any time, and get my full subscription back. I would like (check one below):

		Can/Mex	Other
Individual subscription			
1 Year (12 issues)	☐ $39.95 (33% off single copy of $59.40)	☐ US $64	☐ $79
2 Years (24 issues)	☐ $71 (40% off single copy of $118.80)	☐ US $119	☐ $149
Corporate/Institutional subscription*		Can/Mex	Other
1 Year (12 issues)	☐ $80	☐ US $103	☐ $110
2 Years (24 issues)	☐ $143	☐ US $191	☐ $210

Foreign subscriptions payable by credit card, postal money order in US dollars or check drawn on US bank only.
* We have a separate rate for corporate/institutional subscribers because pass-along readership is higher. We felt it would be unfair for individual readers to, in effect, subsidize corporate/institutional purchasers.

Name _____

Job title _____

Company _____

Street _____

CityStateZipCountry _____

Phone _____ This is your ☐ home ☐ office ☐ both

E-mail address _____
Very important! This is by far the most efficient way to communicate with you about your subscription and periodic special offers, and to poll your opinion on *WIRED* subjects.

Payment method   ☐ Check enclosed   ☐ Bill me (for corporate/institutional rates only)
                        ☐ American Express   ☐ Mastercard   ☐ Visa

Account number _____ Expiration date _____ Signature _____

Please Note: The "Bill Me" box above is only for corporations and institutions needing an invoice – which will be for the higher corporate/institutional rates. There is no "Bill Me" option for individuals.

WIRED rents its subscriber list only to mailers that we feel are relevant to our readers' interests. To remove your name from the rental list, please check this box ☐.

AGL